Indigenous Peoples and the Geographies of Power

Tracing key trends of the global–regional–local interface of power, Inés Durán Matute through the case of the indigenous community of Mezcala, Mexico demonstrates how global political economic processes shape the lives, spaces, projects and identities of the most remote communities. Throughout the book, in-depth interviews, participant observations and text collection offer the reader an insight into the functioning of neoliberal governance, how it is sustained in the networks of power and rhetorics deployed and how it is experienced. People, as passive and active participants in its courses of action, are being enmeshed in these geographies of power seeking out survival strategies, but also constructing autonomous projects that challenge such forms of governance.

This book, by bringing together the experience of a geopolitical locality and the literature from the Latin American Global South into the discussions within the Global Northern academia, offers an original and timely transdisciplinary approach that challenges the interpretations of power and development while also prioritising and respecting the local production of knowledge.

Inés Durán Matute, a doctoral graduate of the University of Sydney, Australia, is currently a postdoctoral fellow at the Centro de Investigaciones y Estudios Superiores en Antropología Social (CIESAS), Mexico.

Routledge Studies in Latin American Politics

16 **The Politics of Capitalist Transformation**
Brazilian Informatics Policy, Regime Change, and State Autonomy
Jeff Seward

17 **Negotiating Trade Liberalisation in Argentina and Chile**
When Policy creates Politics
Andrea C. Bianculli

18 **Understanding Cuba as a Nation**
From European Settlement to Global Revolutionary Mission
Rafael E. Tarragó

19 **Challenging the U.S.-Led War on Drugs**
Argentina in Comparative Perspective
Sebastián Antonino Cutrona

20 **Manipulating Courts in New Democracies**
Forcing Judges off the Bench in Argentina
Andrea Castagnola

21 **Crime, Violence and Security in the Caribbean**
M. Raymond Izarali

22 **Young People and Everyday Peace**
Exclusion, Insecurity, and Peacebuilding in Colombia
Helen Berents

23 **Indigenous Peoples and the Geographies of Power**
Mezcala's Narratives of Neoliberal Governance
Inés Durán Matute

www.routledge.com/Routledge-Studies-in-Latin-American-Politics/book-series/
RSLAP

Indigenous Peoples and the Geographies of Power

Mezcala's Narratives of Neoliberal Governance

Inés Durán Matute

LONDON AND NEW YORK

First published 2018
by Routledge

2 Park Square, Milton Park, Abingdon, Oxfordshire OX14 4RN
52 Vanderbilt Avenue, New York, NY 10017

Routledge is an imprint of the Taylor & Francis Group, an informa business

First issued in paperback 2019

Copyright © 2018 Taylor & Francis

The right of Inés Durán Matute to be identified as author of this work has
been asserted by her in accordance with sections 77 and 78 of the
Copyright, Designs and Patents Act 1988.

All rights reserved. No part of this book may be reprinted or reproduced or
utilised in any form or by any electronic, mechanical, or other means, now
known or hereafter invented, including photocopying and recording, or in
any information storage or retrieval system, without permission in writing
from the publishers.

Notice:
Product or corporate names may be trademarks or registered trademarks,
and are used only for identification and explanation without intent to
infringe.

Library of Congress Cataloging-in-Publication Data
A catalog record for this title has been requested

ISBN: 978-0-8153-6315-6 (hbk)
ISBN: 978-0-367-46371-7 (pbk)

Typeset in Times New Roman
by Wearset Ltd, Boldon, Tyne and Wear

Contents

List of Figures		vi
Preamble		vii
ROCÍO MORENO		
Preface		ix
JORGE ALONSO		
Acknowledgements		xii
	Introduction	1
	INÉS DURÁN MATUTE	
1	The Local Impact of Political Culture	26
2	The Local Workings of a Global Political Economy	58
3	The Transnationalisation of Informal Power: Setting the Path to 'Progress'	93
4	Tourism: A Fight to Define Progress	128
5	Identities Across Borders: Legitimising or Challenging Stratifications?	166
	Conclusions	202
	Postface	210
	JOHN HOLLOWAY	
	Index	212

Figures

0.1	*Centro de Mezcala*	2
0.2	Children playing in the streets	2
0.3	Elder resting	3
0.4	Women selling crops in their *tiendita*	3
0.5	View of Mezcala from the *malecón*	4
0.6	The church	8
0.7	*Danza de los Tlahualiles*	9
1.1	*Comunero*	39
1.2	Regular assembly	43
2.1	*Chayotes*	70
2.2	Fishing boats	73
2.3	The border of opportunities	81
3.1	Streets in the *Centro* of Mezcala	95
3.2	Distributing *Oportunidades*	98
3.3	The library	120
4.1	*Comuneros* shocked by the reconstruction	147
4.2	The militarisation of the Island	149
4.3	*Paraje Insurgente*	155
5.1	Mezcala: a treasured place	173
5.2	Children exploring the Island	188

Preamble

Rocío Moreno

I met Inés some years ago when she was completing her Bachelor of Sociology. Accompanied by Dr Jorge Alonso, they arrived at an assembly of *comuneros* of Mezcala. There, she spoke, and with the approval of the *Asamblea*, she started a research work on politics, the autonomy of our traditional government. Inés has been a friend who for at least the last decade has been accompanying our community in those organisational processes that have been promoted to conserve the territory and the self-government of our people. Her work made me wonder: why study Mezcala? What can make the case of Mezcala visible regarding the Mexican society?

I consider that the Coca community of Mezcala, Jalisco, reflects aspects, characteristics of the native communities of this racist Mexico we inhabit today. An example of this is the discussion that exists concerning the origin of Mezcala. This community belongs to the Coca people of the *Señorío de Coinan*. It has been a community deprived of its origin since the arrival of the conquerors, in approximately 1533. The territorial extension that it possessed at that time was immense (from the town of La Barca to the limits with Tonalá); however, currently only two communities self-inscribe to this people: Mezcala and San Pedro Itxicán. Mezcala lost its language, the Coca. According to the linguist Dávila Garibi the loss was caused by the conquerors due to the linguistic diversity that existed in this region; thus, they chose to impose the Náhuatl and Spanish as official languages, and in a few years the native language was displaced. At present, Coca is no longer spoken; it is a language that was completely lost as a result of the Conquest since there is no speaker, nor any document that allows the reconstructing of the language. There are only a little more than 100 words that are still used, as they are names of hills, animals or characters of the community.

For the indigenous community of Mezcala, the loss of their language has been a blow to their culture; however, the community has taken refuge and strengthened from what it did preserve, such as the territory, the *fiestas*, the historical memory and the self-government. That is, it conserves 3,600 hectares of communal land and the possession of two islands located in Lake Chapala; performs around 28 celebrations a year organised with community *cargos*, dances, offerings and rituals that strengthen the bonds among different members of the community (children, the youth, women, elderly, authorities); remembers and transmits the history of the community with poems, parades, writings, workshops, plays, exhibitions of

viii *Rocío Moreno*

historic ornaments; walks around the territory with the youngest and newest members of the village; preserves and strengthens its traditional government that is governed by its *usos y costumbres*, and is represented by the *Asamblea General de Comuneros*, the highest communal authority.

Mezcala, like many of the native communities of this country, has been deprived of a fundamental part of its culture but has managed to preserve itself against the adversities it has confronted over time. The native peoples of this racist Mexico, which through its actions discriminates against them for being a distinct culture, have had to adapt in the best way, so as to remain as people even when their laws, their lands, their language, their dress, their customs are repressed and criminalised by the different governments that have existed for the last 500 years. Mezcala is, therefore, one of those communities that have resisted and have fought to preserve the little that still remains in the middle of this war.

It should also be said that the Coca village of Mezcala is a very unique one. It is far from the traditional standards with which the Mexican state measures the recognition of an indigenous people, as Mezcala is a community connected to large urban centres such as Guadalajara, Chapala and Ocotlán. Its inhabitants, mostly young people, daily go out to work in these urban centres, and a large number of families have had to migrate to the metropolitan areas of Guadalajara, Tijuana and the United States. This mobility has brought changes in the daily life of this indigenous community, but what is interesting is that it continues to reproduce its culture and traditions, undoubtedly with changes like some objects, but the essence continues to prevail, which is the strengthening of the community ties that are weaved there. Therefore, in the United States and Tijuana, traditional celebrations are organised, while those that are closer participate with their cooperation and specific tasks that can be done from there.

The work that Inés has done shows how this community has had to build strategies that, in the midst of this apparent disarticulation, have produced organisation inside and outside the territory of Mezcala. This village is a mirror of hundreds of communities that day after day struggle against the oblivion and extermination that the state produces by reason of its way of life.

The current situation of native peoples of Mexico is precarious since everything points to their disintegration and extermination. One may wonder if therefore the original peoples of Mexico will disappear. And our answer is 'No'. But we must accept that they are forgotten, denied and, day by day they are being displaced by this neoliberal capitalist system that seeks to govern the world, as if it was one, one language, one belief, one culture. Speaking and researching about the original peoples of the world, reminds the academy that there is still a historical debt with those men and women who have remained the last 500 years resisting and living with dignity even at the cost of their disdain.

Here is where the work of Inés is located, a woman, intellectual, friend of mine, who has shown her sensitivity and commitment to the problems that our people are facing. These investigations are needed and above all the commitment of those who research and write about determining issues for the construction of the future of a community, of a country.

Preface

Jorge Alonso

The author of this book has been studying the indigenous community of Mezcala, Jalisco for ten years. The book is about an indigenous people who believe and argue that they have had their territory since time immemorial. And there is plenty of evidence to prove this argument. Mezcala has cave paintings and plenty of petroglyphs. But most telling is that the native people have embarked on many struggles to defend their land. In addition, the people from Mezcala have an extraordinary historical identity based precisely on their struggles. The people are most proud of their participation in the struggle for Independence (1810–21). They joined the insurgent troops to shake off the Spanish colonial yoke. Mezcala's geography with a mountain, a riverbank and the lakeside dotted with two islands was used to the people's advantage; this knowledge of the land made them impregnable in their fight against the better-armed viceregal armed forces, who knew not how to decipher the multiple abilities of the inhabitants of this place. Mezcala's current inhabitants claim that their ancestors whisper in their ears for them to continue defending the territory from the attacks of those who intend to plunder them. Recently, local groups participate in the *Concejo Indígena de Gobierno* (Indigenous Council of Government) that, at the national level, has undertaken a fierce defence of indigenous territories against the multiple plunders of neoliberal capitalist modernity.

Inés Durán Matute's study did not fall into the temptation of an, unfortunately, widespread practice called *academic extractivism*; she not only delivered the results of her research to the community, but made them comprehensible to the people during discussions. In her postdoctoral stay at the *Centro de Investigaciones y Estudios Superiores en Antropología Social*, she has continued with long-term research that includes the perspective of international migration. Inés Durán thanked the people of Mezcala and expressed her gratitude to the *comuneros*, the members of Colectivo Mezcala, Club Mezcala and the migrants in California. She shared with these people how they helped her come to understand how the community is part of unequal, unjust and disproportionate networks and connections between different actors that trigger economic, political, cultural and social changes. Her work has unravelled and identified the connections between the local and the global. Her book envisions what she called neoliberal governance by monitoring institutional networks, networks of power, keeping

x *Jorge Alonso*

track of how state and mercantile logics enter the life of the most isolated populations. She learned about how national and global processes have shaped a community. But she has also witnessed how there are collectives trying to create alternative and autonomous ways of living. Her extended fieldwork led her to interact with community members and to learn about the community dynamics by combining the use of archives and publications with an active participation in assemblies and demonstrations, in addition to doing numerous interviews and, in general, accompanying the daily lives of several of the settlers. In this most interesting book, she complements synchronic analysis with a broad diachronic contextualisation. Despite the predominance of forms of domination through patronage, corporatism, division, fraud and corruption by power, she also discovered and documents a struggle from below for the defence of communal land. By studying the labour dynamics of the Mezcalenses, she broadened her gaze to understand the neoliberal world dynamics. She shows how local–global complexities have renewed colonial relations, stratifications and differentiations within and between countries. She delves into the community's living conditions on key health, housing and education issues. She found that some migrants were able to improve their living conditions, even in the midst of dynamics of oppression, discrimination and exclusion on North American soil. Migration has not necessarily involved uprooting; economic and social remittances connect them with their place of origin, and they also make periodic visits specially to mark major local festivities.

The central point of Durán's study is the description and analysis of what corresponds to the specific territory that encompasses Mezcala, in which the past, present and future are contested in a struggle to maintain people's roots, and defend meanings and identities. These people have been told that to benefit from progress, they need to abandon their land as settlers in order to welcome investors, but they know that would mean becoming servants to real estate interests and capitalist tourism. Instead, Mezcalenses have devised alternative community tourism projects without giving up their attachment to the land. Inés Durán shows how the villagers negotiate and re-appropriate their identities, as they have sought to end the colonial legacy of discrimination by strengthening the ethnic identity and consequently the community identity. The author discerned that, if the migrants articulate their claims with those of the local community members and with young people who struggle to retain their territory and empower their identity, a transnational opposition movement could emerge and become strengthened. However, she is aware that betting on this process requires taking risks and facing uncertainties: will the transnational subversive identity become consolidated or will it be absorbed by neoliberal governance?

In sum, Durán's entire study deconstructs the complexity, contradictions, problems and possibilities that open up in the midst of capitalist and state economic and political controls. The researcher is very careful to present different perspectives among the inhabitants, their problems, as well as the tensions in their desire to improve their living conditions. To her credit, she argues that the vitality and strength of the organisation from below, with its drive for autonomy confronting neoliberal capitalist dominance, enables it to resist, defend and even construct alternatives to exploitation and domination. This is an overpowering study that makes a great contribution by showcasing how locality and international migration interact within the domain of a planetary power, but even then we are shown how it becomes possible to build viable alternatives.

Acknowledgements

Hopefully this work repays part of all that my friends in Mezcala have given me. You welcomed me into your homes, you opened up your lives to me and gave me your friendship and trust; I expect that over the years I have done the same thing, and this work expresses my affection and commitment to you. I want to especially thank those who decided to share their experiences and showed me what it means to be Mezcalense; those who accompanied me and helped in this long journey; the comuneros, members of Colectivo Mezcala and Club Mezcala (also its partner in Tijuana), and migrants in Ceres.

I also want to thank two people I found pivotal in delineating this research: Vek, who is not only one of the kindest people I have ever met but also a great guide and an intellectual, professional and personal support; and Jorge, who has been a wonderful mentor and friend, sharing with me his skills and passions. Both of you are in fact persons to admire for your dedication and commitment to making this world a better place.

Along the road, the perspectives, dialogues and support from many people around the world also enriched this project. In Australia, I would like to especially thank Fernanda for her guidance and motivation; also, David, for believing in this project and me, Luis for the lessons and insights, Anne for her care and Adam for the dialogues we established. I'm really thankful for all your help. In Mexico, I would like to thank Santiago who was a great field companion but also is a close adviser in some 'anthropology tasks'. As well, I thank John for the inspiration and comments that nurtured this manuscript, my friends Kike, Adra, Nata, Pau and Chistri, who in different ways accompanied and assisted me with this research, and all those who participated in a collaborative network around Mezcala. I am grateful too to the researchers from Colegio de la Frontera Norte (COLEF) who guided me towards my stay in Los Angeles. In the United States, I wish to thank the Institute for Research on Labor and Employment (IRLE) at University of California Los Angeles (UCLA), and especially Chris who opened doors for me and became a close colleague, and Gaspar who advised me on fieldwork on that side of the border and on issues concerning immigration. In the UK, John provided encouraging feedback on a previous version of this manuscript; I really appreciate your words as they guided me to pursue the materialisation of this book. In France, I thank Pierre who took the time to send his advice, remarks and encouragement to the other side of the world.

This project would not have been possible without the support of the University of Sydney and the University of Guadalajara, which allowed me to take advantage of multiple areas of study and knowledge in different parts of the world, and put bread on my table. Of course, it was the sweetness of my foster and real families, especially Beatriz, Jorge, Ulises, Miguel, Viry, Maca, Caro, Lupita, Claudita and my uncles Vicky and Raul, that transformed these places into homes for me. Besides, in these trips I got to meet and walk with people who nurtured this book with their comments and recommendations and also provided spaces of relaxation and fun with friends here and there. To all of them thanks a million.

Finally, behind the scenes: Adi, Calito, Fer, Pia, Seme and Juanchito, this book was written with your affection. Every day, from near and far, you expressed your concerns, warnings and advice to me, as well as your encouragement, congratulations and love. I simply adore you.

Rod, without you this book would simply not exist, since you assumed different roles: as a dictionary, a translator, legal adviser, audience, travel companion, commentator, reviewer and counsellor, among others. You accompanied me all these years, living through the different emotions that engaging in this kind of project produces, but always taking care of me and making sure that I do not forget to eat, to dream and to laugh. My heart and this book are yours.

Introduction

Inés Durán Matute

Mezcala: A Local Setting of Global Forces

On July 19, 2008, Dr Jorge Alonso introduced me to the community of Mezcala de la Asunción in order to familiarise me with the life, knowledges and struggles of indigenous people in contemporary times. Since then, I have been amazed by this hidden gem on the shores of Lake Chapala, in the *municipio* of Poncitlán, Jalisco, approximately 55 kilometres south-east of Guadalajara, the second biggest city in Mexico. As one approaches it, one takes in the different and contrasting scenarios of contemporary Mexico. First, through a highway one faces the polluted and transited industrial zone (*El Salto)*; then, driving via a narrow and shoddy road the visitor comes upon a valley sheltered by hills, followed by a reconstructed straight road alongside the lake with housing developments for the national and international upper middle class, which have magnificent views in contrast to some small and poor towns at the side of the road; finally, a narrower road leads to a lookout which allows one to appreciate the marvellous exuberant green vegetation growing in the hills that surround the small village and its two islands (Pechilinque and Tlaltequepeque) in the middle of the endless and shiny lake.

In general, life in Mezcala seems to be peaceful; one can observe children in their school uniforms playing on the pavement, the elderly resting at the entrance of their houses after a long day in the crops of chayotes, and ladies selling and buying things in small and diverse *tienditas* (small shops) while taking care of their families. The village is divided between nine *barrios, Ojo de Agua, Zalatita, Azaleas, San Pedro, La Cuesta, El Cerrito, La Cantería, La Cruz* and *El Centro;* and like most of the villages of rural Mexico, in the centre it has its *plaza* with a kiosk and a church, where the population go to either play, chat, meet or just to *dar la vuelta*. In addition, life revolves around the lake, and thus, in the shore there is a *malecón* (boardwalk) with few fish, seafood and beer stalls and several boats for fishing or for tourist trips to the main Island (*the heart of the community*). In fact, although they have a growing tourist industry, their main economic activities are agriculture and fishing. But as these economic activities are becoming devalued, migration has become positioned as an important source of income too. Not only do Mezcalenses cross the border

Figure 0.1 Centro de Mezcala.

Figure 0.2 Children playing in the streets.

Figure 0.3 Elder resting.

Figure 0.4 Women selling crops in their *tiendita*.

4 *Inés Durán Matute*

Figure 0.5 View of Mezcala from the *malecón*.

looking for better opportunities, but they also draw on employment in nearby maquiladoras as buses continually pick up workers in the community. Actually, the region has adhered to the vanguard of 'modernisation', 'development' and 'progress', where industrial employment opportunities are promoted and where the privileged and desirable location of Mezcala is touted as the ideal grounds for the development of residential tourism.

What this description evidences are the relationships, the networks and the connections of different actors that are expressed in an asymmetrical form, that is to say, unequal, unfair and disproportionate, and which have activated rapid economic, political, cultural and social changes. These 'glocal' processes are exactly what this book seeks to unravel; that is, it brings together processes of neoliberal globalisation with local realities, showing the impact but also the active participation by those people found locally in sculpting cultural, social, economic and political processes. In order to achieve this, I rely on the voices, knowledges and experiences of Mezcalenses recorded through phases of extensive fieldwork in Mezcala which spans from my first visit in July 2008 to August 2014 and in Los Angeles, one of the migrants' main destinations, from July 2013 to January 2014.[1] Thus, while I recover the lived experiences, motivations, mechanisms and adaptations of Mezcalenses, the information gathered is put into dialogue with the analysis of the impacts of the neoliberal globalisation model of urban-industrial development.

Dealing with the Legacy of Colonialism

To begin with, we must consider how realities construct and organise social space and how they are outlined by society to serve specific purposes (Massey 1995, 68–9). A brief historical account of the community can serve as a point of departure in revealing the complexities and inconsistencies of Mezcala's social space, and more specifically, in understanding how societies are constructed and structured through power relations, practices and rhetorics that constantly move across spaces and times.

Few studies about the history of Mezcala have been written, and thus, many questions remain unanswered about their past and origin. Nevertheless, Rosa María Castillero's (2005) historical reconstruction reveals that, before the Post-classical period, Cocas occupied this territory in the North of Lake Chapala, and established themselves in dispersed little villages governed by *señores* or *caciques*. For Mezcala, in the same way as for other indigenous communities in Mexico, the Spanish Conquest represents a major menace to territory, and a political, social and cultural threat due to seizure of power and control, as well as the imposition of a language, religion and set of alien practices. Rosa Yañez (1998), for instance, explains that since the sixteenth-century Náhuatl began to replace the Coca language, as it was largely spoken and used by conquerors and evangelisers. Castillero (2005) and Yañez (1998) conclude that by the eighteenth century, most likely the Coca language had disappeared, leaving no literature behind. In parallel, the standardisation of ethnic groups of the region took place, whereby they were all labelled as simply 'indigenous' (Yañez 1998, 21). In this way, the separation strengthened a hierarchical social structure while it fostered in Mezcalenses a detached consciousness from the rest of society.

Furthermore, although the inaccessibility of the village protected them against colonial measures (Castillero 2005) and prevented *mestizaje* (Hernández García 2006, 107–8), menaces over their lands and their sociocultural identity and organisation were present. Indeed, we should understand the history of Mezcala as a continuous narrative of rebellion and struggle for land and its management, as it is frequently framed by Mezcalenses themselves. To begin with, Castillero (2005) discovered that although colonial measures (for example, *tributos*) could not be enforced in the village, not only were Mezcalenses employed in *haciendas*, but they also revolted against them and even managed to compose the *Título Virreinal*[2] to obstruct further invasions and threats. In turn, Álvaro Ochoa Serrano (1985, 2006) narrates how during the Independence movement of 1810, Mezcalenses, led by Encarnación Rosas, José Santana and Father Marcos Castellanos, fortified themselves on the major Island (Tlaltequepeque) to fight against the royal troops of General José de la Cruz, from 1812 until the capitulation on November 25, 1816.

This political transformation, however, did not mean better conditions since in the period of modernity past hierarchies were reinforced, partially restructuring social differentiation. Ruling liberals saw communal property tenure, communal practices and traditions and languages of indigenous peoples as 'the

6   *Inés Durán Matute*

enemies of progress' (Gall 2002, 51), directing their efforts to 'integrate' this population and 'whiten' the Mexican society (Alonso 2004). In this manner, Mezcalenses suffering discrimination and oppression were driven to hide some of their cultural practices, leading to their subsequent transformation. Even later in the context of the Mexican Revolution, authorities fostered 'positive discrimination' in constructing the nation (Knight 1990, 84), and thus reorganised social structures and hierarchies through the creation of a unique superior culture and identity that entailed the mixture of indigenous and Spanish: the Mexican mestizo. *Mestizaje*, for the objectives of this study, can be synthetised as a national project and ideology that obscured the colonial forms of oppression, where indigenous people were excluded and denied but also romanticised and idealised, pushing them towards their commodification, segregation in policies and programmes, the denial of rights and the continuation of racism. In effect, the Mexican state used *mestizaje* to support a national consciousness based on a fantasy that unified an unequal society and to create a modern, distinctive and amalgamated country; while it used *indigenismo* to acculturate and integrate indigenous people by eliminating some features but allowing others to be preserved or even glorified (Alonso 2004; Dietz 1999; Knight 1990).

The state took advantage of the rich pre-Columbian past and culture, emphasising folkloric and exoticised features of the indigenous population; at the same time, it equated 'Indians' with the past (Alonso 2004; Findji 1992, 133), thus making them responsible for the failures of the state and the lack of 'progress'. The national identity discourse thereby allowed a partial and biased incorporation, accentuating and perpetuating differences and stratifications that have been lived out and experienced daily. Furthermore, with the advent of neoliberal globalisation, the Mexican government integrated the ideas of pluriculturality/ multiculturality and democracy into policy and within the national panorama, while leaving untouched said hierarchies, and prolonging discrimination and abuse towards indigenous people. In effect, the reform of Article 2 of the Mexican Constitution and the enactment of the *Ley sobre Derechos y Cultura Indígena*, can be framed in the multicultural policies increasingly instituted in Latin American countries, policies that have been widely criticised and identified as mere formalities alongside tolerable rights towards the *indio permitido* (Hale 2004; Rivera Cusicanqui 2008; Sieder 2002). This reform urged state constitutions to use 'narrow criteria to define indigenous identity' (Blackwell *et al.* 2009, 20), and, as a result, the State of Jalisco enacted the *Ley sobre los Derechos y el Desarrollo de los Pueblos y las Comunidades Indígenas del Estado de Jalisco* (2006) where indigenous peoples in the shores of Lake Chapala stopped being recognised as such. This was the case with Mezcala that 'lost' this recognition on the pretext that they had 'lost' their 'authentic' language and dress; consequently, it created a legal gap and paradox that could allow the state to pursue its tourist plans.

For Mezcalenses, however, their ethnic identity is largely based on the possession of their territory that is made up of 3,602.2 acres of forest, natural resources and a small village, in addition to the two islands. They consider their land invaluable, encompassing archaeological remains in the main Island, and petroglyphs and cave paintings in the hills. 'Territory' for them comprises the place, resources, history, practices and their relationships and identity. Hence, it is their most precious possession. For this reason, to the present day many defend it unceasingly and fiercely, just like *comuneros* who are dedicated to the preservation of territory, and a group of young fighters that have revitalised this struggle while opposing more directly state actions. In this regard, Rocío Martínez Moreno (2008, 2012), a young history student of the community, offers historical studies of the participation of Mezcala in national events, concluding that the claim for land and its management, as perceived by *comuneros*, has been a fight of over 500 years. This has been made possible thanks to a solid cultural, historical and political base that allows the transfer of a physical space where culture and history can be recreated (Martínez Moreno 2012, 2008). So, regardless that nowadays Mezcala can appear at first sight like any other Mexican *pueblo*, the possession of their territory and the history of resistance together with the differentiated treatment and discrimination historically experienced as *indígenas* has impelled many to construct their identity and position accordingly.

At present, Mezcala has a diverse population of 5,871 inhabitants[3] who display a form of syncretism of their own legends and myths with the commitment to Catholic dogmas and saints. In fact, most of them are devoted to the miraculous *patrona la Virgen de la Asunción*, who protects them and is a symbol of their identity. In this respect, one can observe that the community has a busy celebration calendar combining national events, local traditions and Catholic celebrations, imbuing the place with local distinctiveness, organisation and a sense of community. Moreover, there are also a high number of migrants mainly in the Metropolitan Area of Guadalajara, Tijuana and the United States, predominantly in California. This sector is commonly known as the *Hijos Ausentes* (Absent Sons), who in general maintain ties with the community and facilitate other Mezcalenses' way to the North, helping in the consolidation of Mezcala as a transnational community. Thus, despite the diversity of profiles and the multiple locations of Mezcalenses,[4] they are organised in *cargos* (duties) and *cumplidos* (compliments/gifts) that denote their generosity, reciprocity and respect.[5] Furthermore, being indigenous in Mezcala, in agreement with Santiago Bastos (2012, 225–9), is lived out through social organisation, as well as in the celebrations, dances and traditions.[6]

However, as this book reveals, the 'incorporation' of indigenous people has been through all aspects of culture, migration, economic processes and privatisation of communal land, while the 'mestizo' category has encouraged some to find channels to climb up the social structure. In effect, the whole situation experienced in Mezcala made me think of how historical processes are intertwined. In this regard, theorists of the decolonial turn have contended that modernity and coloniality cannot be perceived as two different processes, but are 'two sides of the same coin' (Escobar 2005; Mignolo 2000; Quijano 1992; Quintero 2010). It is evident that in Mexico forms of 'colonisation' and 'subalternisation'

Figure 0.6 The church.

Figure 0.7 Danza de los Tlahualiles.

have been renewed, since ethnic/racial classifications and hierarchies, along with the efforts to 'incorporate' indigenous peoples, have continued to mark economic, political and social relationships and legitimise the supremacy of one culture over the others. Multiculturalism displayed continuity with *mestizaje* as a national project, although with its different traits, participants and relationships (Hale 2002; Wade 2009) while, as observed by Genner de Jesús Llanes Ortiz (2008, 52), it is via the renovation and continuation of the official discourse, the practice of *neoindigenismo*, that racism and domination against indigenous people have been secured.

Nonetheless, as disclosed in this book, we should also grasp, following the critiques of Maurício Domingues (2009) of the post/decolonial project, the escalating complexity of modernity; that is, in order to perceive both its oppressive and emancipatory characteristics. In this context, what Mezcala conceals is a population that, with their own problems and contradictions, claim their indigenous past and identity. In fact, a group of inhabitants, mainly members of Colectivo Mezcala, a movement of opposition to state actions in the community, have forged an historical connection, and as a consequence, are hindering the materialisation of Cocas' disappearance. This situation matches how scholars have been pointing out the strengthening and re-emergence of indigenous groups (Alonso 2004; Benavides Vanegas 2010; De La Cadena and Starn 2009; Kearney 2004; Kradolfer 2010; Ramos 2006; Speed 2002), and the creation of new identities (Hernández Navarro 2009, 43) to challenge state categorisations and identifications.

10 *Inés Durán Matute*

On this matter Bastos (2011a, 2011b, 2012) offers an account of how the ethnic identity is recreated in Mezcala, revitalising the rights and the meanings of being indigenous, while analysing how the community introduces itself into globalisation. In this vein, the present book—by deepening the data and relying on the concrete experiences of a variety of Mezcalenses—offers new insights that connect the transnational sphere and the production of a multiplicity of identities and projects that emerge across times and spaces. In this way, issues around recognition are discussed throughout this book, principally via a consideration of how social actors respond to this setting by challenging how meanings, identities and social relations are being created. Clearly, with this background, Mezcala provides a distinctive and fascinating case worth exploring to broaden our understanding of indigenous communities nowadays.

Enmeshed in Neoliberal Governance

This research, accordingly, is informed by the legacy and discussions of post-colonial, decolonial and subaltern; in so doing it seeks to scrutinise the persistence of relations of power based on the colonial experience. Nonetheless, although I follow theorists of this school's interpretations on culture, economy and colonialism, my intention is to employ critically some of their ideas as well as those of other schools of thought in order to make use of the prior knowledge in the field regardless of disciplinary disputes. My point of departure derives from how internal colonialism has established the continuation of the colonial structure within the nations after decolonisation, by drawing a link between inter, intra and transnational spheres to understand neoliberal globalisation and the prevalence of world power centres with their corporate networks and the support of internal dominant groups as their allies, as proposed by Pablo González Casanova (2006, 425–30).[7] Therefore, central to this book is the concept of neoliberal governance; it is deployed in these pages in order to outline and conceptualise the institutional arrangements at play in the relations and processes examined.

Pivotal to this concept is that neoliberalism in view of this should not only be considered a set of economic policies compiled by the Washington Consensus (Williamson 2003, 2004) but a social and political regime (de Sousa Santos 2009) that establishes an ideological power (Babb 2001, 197; Harvey 2007, 68–9; Rapoport 2002, 360). Neoliberalism is characterised by a reconfiguration of class struggle for the management of wealth and of economic, financial and cultural institutions (Gandásegui Hijo 2011, 287) and for 'the control and restoration of the class power of the elite' (Harvey 2007, 208). The concept of governance, as developed by Massimo De Angelis (2005, 233–4), is key here as it allows us to identify how its neoliberal form is based on an institutional structure and upon networks among different sectors of society, from International Financial Institutions (IFIs), transnational corporations, governments, businessmen, technocrats and politicians to their clienteles and different allies at the local level who are exposed to manoeuvres of imposition and persuasion, and to negotiations to regulate life, spaces and minds.

Introduction 11

Global governance is linked not only to a discourse that manages societies, but also to the accumulation and management of social conflict that includes 'techniques of classification and knowledge production' (De Angelis 2005, 229–43). Along these lines, Boaventura de Sousa Santos argues that governance is 'a matrix that combines horizontality and verticality in a new way' where 'the demand for participation and inclusion' and 'for autonomy and self-regulation' aim to be combined in a time when the failures of the market become evident (2009, 2–4). In line with this tendency, Hale (2002) argues that a new conception of citizenship began to be framed in the strategy of neoliberal governance that allows concessions and opens new political spaces in an era where militancy increases together with democracy claims. As a key concept employed in this book, and contributing to this debate, neoliberal governance should be understood as an operational logic that deceptively infringes upon peoples' lives by enmeshing them deeply into capitalist and colonialist structures of power and discourses. Neoliberal governance reinserts relationships marked by difference and power, where also the forms of recognition and the vindications from below can be embedded into colonialist perspectives and the logic of the market.

In this sense, this book argues that Mezcala, in all probability, provides an instance of the lived experience of how colonialism prevails as a system of classifications that influences national imaginaries, not only based on race, but also on ethnicity, class and gender, among others.[8] My proposal goes beyond this by also considering how power and space are imbricated through policies, practices, subjects and rhetorics that shape neoliberal processes that perpetuate structures and hierarchies. Hence, in this book I pursue the question of how neoliberal governance permeates minds and enmeshes lives even in the most isolated communities via state and market logics while at the same time I investigate how positions are managed and negotiated through transnational dynamics showing the mutations, complexities, multiplicities and deregulations in identities and classifications. Here, it is important to reflect on how, as illustrated in these pages, the Mexican state relies on informal power to govern and maintain social structures and distinctions, often accompanying this with violence and criminalisation. In this fashion, this research explores the socio-political dynamics in the national sphere, and illuminates the pattern of peculiarities engendered through the practice and transnationalisation of the inherited political culture, and the reconstitution of colonial forms of oppression. That is, by having a transnational approach to analyse local politics and economic processes, this research connects the uneven relationships between and within countries through relations of power and the hegemonic rhetorics deployed.

In doing so, this book discloses how subjects are connected simultaneously across multiple locations and communities, while being embedded in networks of power and the manifold discourses, techniques and practices that are traversed by different eras. To this effect, also crucial for the development of my argument is how the discourses of 'development', 'progress' and 'modernisation' are master narratives that have acted as catalysts in the minds of Mezcalenses to mould their lives and projects, and establish the position into which they are

12   *Inés Durán Matute*

located accordingly. As a background, Alejandro Portes and John Walton (1981, 129–35) argue that throughout history the social structure has been legitimised by dominant sectors in power through ideologies; 'developmentalism' being the latest one that justifies their privileges while the burden is placed on the 'masses'. What is more, in the mid-twentieth century a new conception of 'development' arose at the service of the U.S. hegemony (Esteva 1992) and by the 1980s, 'development' was perceived as a solution for 'Third World' problems and to reach growth, serving to justify the adoption of neoliberal policies (Escobar 2007).

Moreover, within neoliberal governance this discourse has included not only the economic but also the social sphere (Esteva 1992), while ranking spaces according to different stages of development (Massey 2005, 86–7). In this sense, the United States has been portrayed and mystified as the land of dreams and identified as a bearer of 'progress', 'civilisation' and 'development', having a great effect throughout Mexican society. 'Development' is attached to both institutional networks and peoples' subjectivities in a transnational fluidity. Therefore, the perspective offered in this book would be incomplete without the tenets of post-development theory who conceive it as an economic and political project, a discourse to manage society that has even been adopted by local elites (Escobar 1992); it is a way of thinking about the world and eliminating other possibilities and it arises as a form of power (Storey 2000, 40).

In this sense I consider that different actors have come together to mediate and manage their claims while they persist in drawing the lines between inclusion and exclusion of participants in the neoliberal project. This implies that, within the era of neoliberal governance, Mezcalenses are rendered 'subcitizens' as they are integrated into institutions in a subordinated (Chauvin and Garcés-Mascareñas 2012) and stigmatised position through the use of categories from which they must negotiate. This study, like so, adds complexity to previous studies, by observing the continuity of the colonial past, and putting together the different and paradoxical interpretations, projects, and experiences of Mezcalenses around 'progress' within the era of neoliberal governance. In view of that, this research challenges the rhetorics associated with the narratives of modernity and transcends the problems of the post-development theory, especially in reference to its own 'rhetoric' and 'posturing' (Nederveen Pieterse 1998, 2000) and its assumptions about and romanticised formulations of social change (Nederveen Pieterse 1998; Storey 2000).

Mapping Key Trends of the Global–Regional–Local Interface of Power

In order to map these key trends of the global–regional–local interface of power in the context of neoliberal governance, first I should describe how the community is organised by different political figures. These are: *jueces de barrio,*[9] whose task is to be representative and consult and organise people in their *barrio* to meet their needs, the *Asamblea General de Comuneros*, installed in the 1970s

Introduction 13

but known as the traditional authority that is responsible for protecting the territory and *usos y costumbres*, and the *Delegado Municipal*, who is the representative of the *Municipio*,[10] in charge of managing the community. In addition, we can identify two new political figures: Colectivo Mezcala, which involves mainly young inhabitants and has engaged in the revitalisation of their identity and traditional authority and allied with other indigenous communities, the Zapatista movement and other social movements, and several academics;[11] and Club Mezcala, a Hometown Association (HTA) based in Los Angeles that has been providing better conditions for the migrant population while influencing community life from abroad.

For this study, I chose 32 participants (26 men and six women)[12] who were *comuneros*, young supporters and/or migrants, as I identified their different approaches to improving life conditions in the community. This book therefore explores the experiences of the *comuneros* and a group of young supporters of the indigenous community of Mezcala who have been raising concerns about the plans of the Mexican state over their territory, and about Mezcala's migrants to the U.S.[13] and some cities in Mexico, who are forced to leave due to economic, political and social conditions but retain a commitment to the ones left behind.[14] The criteria that guided the selection were flexible and decided upon over the course of the project, as I interviewed those with whom I had established a prior relationship of trust or who had agreed to participate as a result of a snowball effect.[15] Questions asked were in reference to their own experiences and issues related to their local authorities, the social, economic and political transformations of the community, migration, projects and needs, as well as history and identity.

Although I tried in broad terms to interview the same number of *comuneros*, young fighters and migrants, the categories were difficult to determine since in many cases they overlap and show inconsistencies. Participants are complex subjects who inhabit different positions; they are part of a dense network of relationships and move constantly. Thus, throughout this book one can find a brief explanation of who is speaking, that was considered the best fit in that context of the discourse presented. Additionally, to respect the decision of participants, the names used are sometimes real and other times pseudonyms, but I opted not to distinguish between them due to the insecurity and violence experienced by many of them. Here I would stress that it is of lesser importance whether the narration of events achieves the status of the truth claim or might be called objective; what is more important is to hear how the views are expressed and to map social relations (Smith 2005, 138) of different local, regional, national and transnational subjects with all their paradoxes, conflicts, challenges, ambiguities, strategies and negotiations.

Throughout this book, then, the reader will find Mezcalenses' narratives embedded within the text in order to expand their knowledge about the functioning of neoliberal governance, how it is sustained in networks of power and rhetorics, and how it is experienced. As I aimed to establish a research 'in' and 'with'—following the Zapatista logic—and to give voice to the subjugated

14 *Inés Durán Matute*

actors, I opted to develop my methodology following Institutional Ethnography. This 'alternative sociology' uses narratives to recuperate the voice, experience, perceptions, actions and knowledge of subjugated actors with the intention to map the social organisation of local realities and provide an understanding of the everyday world by linking the local and the global, the micro and macro levels in order to find solutions to problems and transform social relations (Campbell and Gregor 2004; Kinsman 2006; Smith 2005). In view of this, I do not position myself as an 'academic', 'expert' or 'translator', but as a companion in the efforts of the participants in my study in order to transform reality, with the belief that 'theory is practice' (Holloway 2010; Kinsman 2006). In fact, since my first visit and after presenting myself in an assembly of the *Asamblea General de Comuneros*, I have become committed to the community, to help and accompany them in their conflicts and actions. I attended assemblies, cultural events, workshops, legal appointments, etc. while supporting their struggles, thus, becoming a researcher–activist.

Working with an indigenous community brings challenges in terms of how to address research procedures appropriately, as the culture, subjectivity, relationships and mechanisms of interaction are different, but as my research acquired a 'pre-phase' (2008–11), I was able to adapt to their conditions and methods and gain their trust. Furthermore, I designed and developed this project according to their experiences, demands and practices, even though it was not formulated in a dialogue with them. For instance, I was not able to discuss with them the lines to be researched and the topics of interviews due to problematics experienced by the community and its members, and the poor methodological flexibility and strict timeframes often particular to postgraduate studies. These limitations were partially overcome thanks to this long-term commitment and involvement with the community and its members, and open interviews that allowed participants to talk about the issues they were more concerned with and were willing to share.[16]

So, as I share knowledges and experiences throughout this book, I want to eradicate the fallacy that the researcher somehow is the holder and purveyor of 'theory' and indigenous people 'practice' (Blackwell *et al.* 2009). How can theoretical abstractions created apart from the empirical contribute to the study of indigenous communities? Accordingly, this research seeks another way of learning that is based on how putative 'others' express, understand and experience their realities. Although there are several possible readings, the discussions and analysis found here are an attempt to construct other forms of research in order to engage—in tandem with the ideas of Xochitl Leyva Solano (2014)—in an epistemic struggle that challenges how and for whom we produce knowledge; thus, to stop reproducing 'validated' knowledges and distancing ourselves from people and reality.

Given this, my personal and institutional place of enunciation should be made evident in order to give the reader the elements to distance her or himself and engage in critical reading. I believe, as the feminist Chicana thinker Gloria Anzaldúa argued, that our knowledge is always located and we

Introduction   15

always speak from a position in the world. My position, then, is as a Mexican middle-class young female who moved to Australia to pursue her postgraduate studies, but has been engaged with and supported the claims of subjugated actors and is committed to the search for an alternative to the current world order. I identify with Peter Wade when he asserts that one 'can never escape one's positioning', but 'one can recognise one's positioning and adopt some strategies that work against its grain' (2009, 250). So, as I engage in a continuous self-reflexive task, I regard other knowledges while acknowledging the implication of power within and appreciate the awareness and agency of the participants. Inspired by Latin American discussions regarding critical thinking, I propose to change how we do research and recuperate the validity of local knowledges emerging from the people, knowledges that are in movement and allow us to stand up to neoliberal processes, while accounting for internal contradictions, conflicts and ambiguities.

By sharing the voices, knowledges and experiences, and analysing the actions, feelings and perspectives of these different groups, this book thus reveals the diversity and complexity of local experiences while disclosing how relationships, connections and networks are engrained within them, shaping lives, territories, projects and identities. I work from a multiple-modal theory[17] of local–national–global political, economic, cultural, social processes that demonstrates internal–external concurrent and interdependent cycles, and highlights the actors, networks, relationships, and institutions that perpetuate, in the era of neoliberal governance, a dynamic established by a capitalist world system cast in the image of modernity/coloniality.[18] The objective is to enter a multi-level analysis that connects global institutions, nation-states, transnational actors and local elites, but also social movements and people. Mezcala can be used as a striking example since it is a community that is at a juncture of economic, political, social and cultural changes linked to neoliberal governance, and demonstrates the possibility of being simultaneously captivated by or challenging such forms of governance.

Indigenous People and the Geographies of Power

Adelo is a parent of three boys and a girl, but he is also a peasant, a son of *comunero*, a migrant and a Zapatista militant. When I formally met him on March 7, 2009, he used to spend seven months in the U.S., the rest of the year he was living with his family in Mezcala. Besides cultivating chayotes in his orchard by the lake, he was committed to *comuneros'* struggle and was close to Colectivo Mezcala. Adelo was one of most reluctant and active members, participating with the Zapatistas and voicing their discontent. He lived between both countries for more than 20 years, but was tired and in November 2009 decided no longer to return to the U.S. due to the discrimination and the economic crisis. However, soon he managed to obtain papers for his family, and I met him again in Ceres, California in November 2013 when I attended a *kermesse* to collect funds for the construction of a library in Mezcala. Now he was living there with

16   *Inés Durán Matute*

his whole family trying to secure better opportunities for his children while working in the fields or warehouses. Nonetheless, he expressed to me that life was harsh and 'the idea, I think everyone, everyone always has in mind is to return'.

This scenario evidences the inconsistencies, interests and opposing agendas of Mezcalenses as they deal with power relations and social structures, proving their diversity in the face of the working of neoliberal governance. Many Mezcalenses like Adelo are caught up in ambiguities and contradictions, trying to find survival strategies or even to construct autonomous projects. Therefore, the purpose of this study is not only to advance the understanding of the functioning of institutional networks, as well as relationships and structures of power, revealing how people might reproduce hegemonic models, but also to trace how some of them, despite that, are trying to go beyond institutionalised forms of reality construction in order to reshape their circumstances. I follow Gary Kinsman's (2006) proposal of mapping the organisation of 'social forces of opposition, resistance and transformation' and their relation, since on his terms, while capitalists aim to decompose and fragment people, struggles and groups provide new conditions that might allow us to re-compose them. In this sense, rather than engage with the body of knowledge known as 'social movement theory', I address the transformative potential of everyday collective social organisation, bearing in mind, as suggested by Raúl Zibechi (2006, 130–1), those 'mobile', 'changeable', 'fragmented' and 'dispersed' movements.

In summary, this study creates a space for the voices of local knowledges to be channelled, showing the simultaneity, contradiction and multiplicity of experiences. Furthermore, it reveals how the political and economic processes shape the community—together with their projects and identity—providing insights into how development is understood and what are the different path designs that reproduce, challenge and transform the neoliberal model. So I grasp the inconsistencies, revealing Mezcalenses' agency, how they negotiate and participate within and beyond the networks of power that sustain this global system. Accordingly, I propose that the following three key questions should be borne in mind throughout this book: how does 'progress' operate to sustain the colonial and capitalist dynamics of neoliberal governance? Why and how are people coerced and seduced, as De Angelis (2005) argues, into this operational logic? What is the role of individuals and collectivities in accepting or defying the hegemonic structures and rhetorics? In this sense, as suggested by these questions, this research is not only a critique of modernisation theory, but more importantly, it scrutinises how these kinds of theories have been shaping mentalities and generating new aspirations to achieve a 'modern' life.

Organisation of This Book

As I have endeavoured to outline in this Introduction, in this book the local and the global meet. In the course of the chapters that follow, I explore, through Mezcalenses' experiences and narratives, how neoliberal governance displays

Introduction 17

itself in the community; that is, how power is organised, and influences local realities. I hence highlight the mechanisms, connections, dynamics and institutions that sustain but also challenge the current world order. Moreover, I offer new insights that connect the transnational sphere showing new understandings of times and spaces to comprehend how societies are constructed and structured. For this, I employ a transdisciplinary approach that brings together the experience of a geopolitical locality and the literature from the Latin American 'Global South' into the discussions within the 'Global Northern' academia. In this way the book ponders the prior knowledge of the field and perceive the gaps where a contribution is needed while voicing experiences and displaying the theoretical potential of other knowledges.

In order to take the most from this book, I recommend readers to read it conventionally. This will help them to grasp all the complexities, antagonisms and conflicts within the community and appreciate the multiple voices included here. Furthermore, it promises to facilitate setting up a comprehensive understanding of how, under the working of neoliberal governance, global political economic processes—enacted through policies, but mainly via the rhetoric of actors and institutions—shape the lives, projects and identity of most remote communities, like Mezcala, that passively and actively participate in these courses of action. Indeed, although the first three chapters focus on politics, economics and social problems respectively to contextualise the community, they trace important connections between these spheres, their processes, rhetorics, subjects and practices.

First, Chapter 1 examines Mezcala within the Mexican political culture in order to understand the inheritance of practices, the impacts on the *usos y costumbres* and the particularities of its inhabitants, and more broadly, the political structures, practices, disputes and discourses that nourish neoliberal governance. Accordingly, I draw a picture of the national historical processes and political changes in the community. I undergird this panorama by explaining the characteristics of two political figures in the village, *delegados* and *comuneros*, their current role, practices and representativeness. In this way, the chapter analyses how clientelism, corruption, corporatism and *caciquismo* have manifested themselves in the village while reflecting on a continuation of populism and challenging the idea of such a 'democratic advance'. More precisely, this chapter offers a detailed explanation of the political structure and organisation of the village evidencing how it perpetuates economic, social and cultural differences. This element of the study is key to providing a picture of politics, its discourses and subjects involved, but also of how strategies, resistance and transformations are being shaped. The chapter thus helps to delineate the workings of global–national–local networks and begins to advance our understanding of the lives of Mezcalenses.

Chapter 2 is dedicated to the economic sphere, aiming to disclose the contemporary transformations, mainly in relation to labour dynamics under the neoliberal model. Here I engage with the well-known position that migration processes are connected to regional changes and economic developments happening at a transnational juncture. In view of that, the aim of this chapter is to

18 *Inés Durán Matute*

expand our understanding of the functioning of a global system that exacerbates differences and perpetuates unequal structures and stratifications that are experienced locally and lived out daily. In this chapter I hence show the impact of neoliberalism on the lives, spaces, practices, relationships and organisation of Mezcalenses across the Mexican–U.S. border. In this vein, Mezcalenses narrate the dynamics of their labour experiences helping us to identify how and why they are migrating and participating in *maquiladora* employment, and why their main survival and economic activities, agriculture and fishing, are being abandoned and devalued. The intention is to contour our understanding of the specific reality in Mezcala from above, bringing together the micro and the macro, the local and the global, and thus, further outline the functioning of networks of power, the practices and rhetorics deployed, and their diverse and opposing outcomes.

Chapter 3 examines the community socially, bringing together the political and economic spheres explored in the foregoing chapters. Here I break down the rhetoric of 'development' together with state policies, programmes and actions framed within the rationale of neoliberal governance. In light of this, the chapter seeks to analyse how inhabitants are driven into using informal channels, creating networks where corruption and clientelism are reproduced even at a transnational level that helps sustain social structures and hierarchies. In this sense, while the chapter reveals the persistent marginalisation and use of informal power in the village, it also explores how the discourse of 'progress' is shaping the minds, actions and relationships of Mezcalenses to improve the living conditions in the village. Accordingly, it scrutinises the myth of the 'American Dream' and the emergence of a new transnational subject, Club Mezcala, its institutionalisation and actions to illustrate how elites and a sector of migrants use the rhetoric of 'development' to shape aspirations, lives and projects. Furthermore, the chapter complicates the expression of citizenship to discern the manifold actions that sustain and challenge the neoliberal paradigm.

In the subsequent chapters, I present further and more profound analyses that place together the different processes already outlined with reference to Mezcalenses' territory and identity. In this way, Chapter 4 continues the investigation of the discourse of progress, but most specifically in reference to cultural and residential tourism. The focus in this chapter is on the relationship between tourism and development in its transnational mode, tracing how different subjects come into conflict in the management of lives and territories in a context of the ruling of the global design of developmentalism. On the one hand, this chapter analyses how political and economic elites have allied and positioned themselves subjectively, materially, symbolically and rhetorically under the flag of 'progress'. In this way, they not only legitimise their actions and shape the life and visions of Mezcalenses, but they also sustain the workings of neoliberal governance together with a way of life that perpetuates structures and hierarchies—capturing the continuity in a rhetoric framed within the colonial past. On the other hand, the chapter explores the emergence of opposition and alternative plans arising from within the community, especially via Colectivo Mezcala and its design of

Introduction 19

autonomous projects. In this sense, this chapter delves into the struggle over meanings and representations of territories, showing how local knowledges are engaged in a redefinition of progress, proposing other ways of being, thinking and living.

The final chapter adds force to the arguments presented in Chapter 4, by linking the construction of identities to the meanings of place, thus allowing multiple manipulations that stress their relationship with power. As such, it explores the notions of indigeneity nowadays and seeks to understand the different forms of identity construction and how they interplay and are reshaped and constructed in a transnational setting where discourses and structures expand across spaces. I argue that Mezcalenses are engaged in a process of 'identity politics' that influences how societies are constructed transnationally. Thus, even if identities might be constructed to favour the functioning of the networks of power and the prevalence of racist practices, Mezcalenses demonstrate how they can also be constructed to support their own position and challenge capitalist and colonialist social constructions. In this sense, this chapter, while identifying the contradictions and paradoxes within Mezcalenses, ends with an encouraging picture of how identity is a resource, and visualises how indigenousness can be revived and dignified in a sort of ethnogenesis to incite the defence of territory, a sense of community and even autonomy—and possibly as an outlet away from a capitalist world system cast in the image of modernity/coloniality.

Finally, this book draws to a close by giving some thought to the outcomes of this research in regard to the local implications of global designs, rhetorics and structures. This breakdown of the global–regional–local interface, scrutinised in detail in previous chapters, provides some insights to reflect on concerning the possible future scenarios for Mezcalenses, but more generally for societies immersed in the workings of neoliberal governance. At this point transnationalism surfaces as a force that can either fragment or unite the community, to uphold or disassemble the global structures of power and institutions, their discourses and stratifications that traverse geographic, collective and personal frontiers. In addition, this section presents the lessons learned and discusses theoretical and methodological contributions considering future scholarly engagement and issues that need to be further explored.

I am aware that this research perhaps will not disband the hegemonic machinery that prevails in the relationships of power explored in this book but, as a contribution arising from critical sociology, it can at least enrich several fields of inquiry and assist in delineating local solutions to global problems and in the transformation of our realities through the construction of alternative, autonomous projects locally. The significance of this research, therefore, is that it provides an interconnected vision that shows how everyday practices and realities interplay with the different political, economic, social and cultural processes happening in the local–national–global interface. In parallel, the methodology used supports the community while showing the theoretical potential of narratives. This may help to raise awareness, to ponder and to motivate the reader in

20 *Inés Durán Matute*

order to open more spaces of dialogue and action, helping to construct a different world while deconstructing 'hegemonic knowledge'.

Supported by local knowledges, what the reader will engage with in this book challenges the epistemic forms of how we produce and validate knowledge, offering an approach that might help to disband the network of power, its practices, structures and discourses. I do believe the perceptions, constructions, representations, practices, negotiations and relationships contained here could prove useful to a broad range of communities experiencing the workings of neoliberal governance. My purpose is to provoke readers to think how, not only Mezcalenses but, all of us find ourselves entangled on these geographies of power challenging and reproducing at the same time the neoliberal model. So these insights might actually help raise consciousness around how we are embedded in the dynamic of neoliberal governance and the paths we can use or create to change our position, and ways of being and thinking.

Notes

1 Although data from 2015 and 2016 is sometimes provided, the intention is only to update some of the information. The ethnographic phases of this research span from 2008 to 2014 where I collected data through participant observation and interviews, but also through news, pamphlets and declarations of the community.
2 This vice-regal document granted by the Spanish Crown (1534) proclaims that Mezcalenses are the eternally legitimate owners of the land and natural resources in their territory from time immemorial. However, it is believed that Mezcalenses wrote the *Título* between the middle of the seventeenth century and the beginnings of the eighteenth century. Yet, as pointed out by Castillero (2005, 258–9), although *Títulos Primordiales* might be inauthentic and out-dated, these documents are key instruments in safeguarding the origins and lands of indigenous communities.
3 According to the *Censo de Población y Vivienda* (INEGI 2010), displaying a growth rate of around 20 per cent every ten years.
4 The word 'Mezcalense' refers to people from Mezcala, including inhabitants—those who live there—and migrants—those who most or at all times live away.
5 *Fiestas* and *cargos* in the community are so important that families make many sacrifices and invest huge amounts. In some cases, these celebrations have even been identified as a reason to migrate.
6 The patron-saint *fiestas* are the most important festivities in the community, eagerly anticipated throughout the year, celebrated in August for 12 days, including a *novenario*, and with a day devoted to fishermen, peasants and *Hijos Ausentes*. In order to organise the *fiestas*, Mezcalenses contribute through *cooperaciones* for the *banda* (music), *compostura* (flowers and ornaments) and *castillo* (fireworks), demonstrating the strong bond between the different sectors and the organisational capacity of the community.
7 Due to the complexity and variety of each area and the different degrees and manners of how oppression is experienced, I prefer to avoid dichotomous differentiations such as core/periphery, First World/Third World, hegemonic/non-hegemonic countries, North/South, etc. I believe that such perceptions perpetuate social and economic stratifications, so I try as much as possible to be specific in the actors involved and portray the complexity of reality. However, sometimes this has not been possible due to the long and extensive use of such differentiations in academia, or because I want to emphasise a kind of irony; in these cases I use quotation marks.

Introduction   21

8 It is not the purpose of this research to explore gender differences, but clearly, this is an avenue that cannot be ignored. Thus, the reader should endeavour to read this dimension between the lines at all times.

9 *Jueces de Barrio* precede the actual figures of *comuneros* and *delegados*, being very influential and respected, having a moral power beyond the political one. However, although their role has diminished, as exposed in Chapter 1, nowadays they might bring inhabitants' voices to the *Asamblea de Comuneros*.

10 I distinguish between *municipio*, the territorial entity, and *Municipio*, the Municipal government, which might include formal and informal authorities.

11 The work and reflections of these academics (Alonso 2010a, 2010b, 2012; Bastos 2011a, 2011b, 2012, 2013; Sandoval 2009), and some of the community adherents (Martínez Moreno 2008, 2009, 2012, 2014; Moreno 2010, 2011; Moreno, Jacobo and Godoy 2006; Paredes 2010, 2012) and supporters (Hipólito Hernández 2012) are valuable and undergird this research.

12 Although the number of women engaged in the different fronts and fights is increasing, men still predominate as *comuneros*, young fighters and leading migrants.

13 I use 'United States' or 'U.S'. to abbreviate United States of America due to practical reasons since I support the claim that it should not be called 'America' or its citizens 'Americans'. When it is used, as in the case of the 'American Dream', it is to emphasise the fantasy, while implying a kind of irony.

14 The interviews with migrants were performed mainly in south-east Los Angeles and its surrounding areas; but I also interviewed a migrant in Tijuana and two in Ceres, California, as during my fieldwork I was invited to events with migrants in these cities.

15 I also carried out an interview with a liaison member of Club Mezcala in Mezcala that does not fit any of these categories, but his insights were key to getting to know this organisation better, its standpoint and ways of working.

16 I am aware of how my presence might have influenced these narratives, but this is the reason why I invite the reader to keep in mind that people, in line with the ideas of Anna De Fina (2003), might present themselves in a diversity of ways and assume different roles, being part of a constant negotiation of their identities.

17 A preliminary version of this theory and brief application can be found in: Durán Matute (2015).

18 In order to avoid repetition, the reader should keep in mind that throughout this book I refer to this setting when using the words 'system', 'world system', 'global system' and so on.

References

Alonso, Ana María. 2004. "Confronting Disconformity: Mestizaje, Hybridity, and the Aesthetics of Mexican Nationalism". *Cultural Anthropology* 19 (4): 459–90.

Alonso, Jorge. 2010a. "La lucha contra el neoliberalismo por medio de la autonomía comunal, el caso de Mezcala, Jalisco". *Autonomia y Emancipación.* http://autono miayemancipacion.org/la-lucha-contra-el-neoliberalismo-por-medio-de-la-autonomia-comunal-el-caso-de-mezcala-jalisco-jorge-alonso/ [accessed September 2011].

Alonso, Jorge. 2010b. "La persistente defensa de la autonomía del pueblo de Mezcala como una creación de espacio público no estatal". In *¿Qué tan público es el espacio público en México?*, edited by Mauricio Merino, 311–46. Mexico City: FCE; CONACULTA; Universidad Veracruzana.

Alonso, Jorge. 2012. "El bicentenario vivido desde Mezcala". In *Mezcala: la memoria y el futuro. La defensa de la isla en el Bicentenario*, edited by Santiago Bastos, 155–67. Guadalajara, Mexico: Centro de Investigaciones y Estudios Superiores en Antropología Social.

22   Inés Durán Matute

Babb, Sarah. 2001. *Managing Mexico: Economists from Nationalism to Neoliberalism*. Princeton, NJ: Princeton University Press.

Bastos, Santiago. 2011a. "La comunidad de Mezcala y la recreación étnica ante la globalización neoliberal". *Revista CUHSO* 21 (1): 87–103.

Bastos, Santiago. 2011b. "La nueva defensa de Mezcala: un proceso de recomunalización a través de la renovación étnica". *Relaciones* 32 (125): 86–122.

Bastos, Santiago. 2012. "Mezcala: despojo territorial y rearticulación indígena en la Ribera de Chapala". In *Jalisco hoy: miradas antropológicas*, edited by Renée De la Torre and Santiago Bastos, 223–56. Guadalajara, Mexico: Centro de Investigaciones y Estudios Superiores en Antropología Social—Unidad Occidente.

Bastos, Santiago. 2013. "La micropolítica del despojo: Mezcala de la Asunción en la globalización neoliberal". *Revista de Estudios e Pesquisas sobre as Américas* 7 (2): 105–34.

Benavides Vanegas, Farid Samir. 2010. "Movimientos indígenas y estado plurinacional en América Latina". *Pensamiento Jurídico* 27 (January–April): 239–64.

Blackwell, Maylei, Rosalva Aída Hernández Castillo, Juan Herrera, Morna Macleod, Renya Ramírez, Rachel Sieder, María Teresa Sierra, and Shannon Speed. 2009. "Cruces de fronteras, identidades indígenas, género y justicia en las Américas". *Desacatos* (31): 13–34.

Campbell, Marie, and Frances Gregor. 2004. *Mapping Social Relations: A Primer in Doing Institutional Ethnography*. Walnut Creek, CA: AltaMira Press.

Castillero, Rosa María. 2005. *Mezcala: expresión de un pueblo indígena en el período colonial. Vicisitudes y fortalezas*. Guadalajara, Mexico: Universidad de Guadalajara.

Chauvin, Sébastien, and Blanca Garcés-Mascareñas. 2012. "Beyond Informal Citizenship: The New Moral Economy of Migrant Illegality". *International Political Sociology* 6 (3): 241–59.

De Angelis, Massimo. 2005. "The Political Economy of Global Neoliberal Governance". *Review (Fernand Braudel Center)* 28 (3): 229–57.

De Fina, Anna. 2003. *Identity in Narrative. A Study of Immigrant Discourse*. Amsterdam: John Benjamins Publishing Company.

De La Cadena, Marisol, and Orin Starn. 2009. "Introducción". In *Indigeneidades contemporáneas: cultura, política y globalización*, edited by Marisol De La Cadena and Orin Starn, 9–42. Lima: IEP; IFEA.

de Sousa Santos, Boaventura. 2009. "Governance: Between Myth and Reality". *RCCS Annual Review* 0: 1–14.

Dietz, Gunther. 1999. *La comunidad purhépecha es nuestra fuerza. Etnicidad, cultura y región en un movimiento indígena en Michoacán, México*. Quito: Ediciones Abya-Yala.

Domingues, José Maurício. 2009. "Global Modernization, 'Coloniality' and a Critical Sociology for Contemporary Latin America". *Theory, Culture & Society* 26 (1): 112–33.

Durán Matute, Inés. 2015. "Los comuneros de Mezcala en confrontación con las redes institucionales de poder". *Espiral, Estudios sobre Estado y Sociedad* 22 (62): 205–32.

Escobar, Arturo. 1992. "Culture, Economics, and Politics in Latin American Social Movemet Theory and Research". In *The Making of Social Movements in Latin America. Identity, Strategy and Democracy*, edited by Arturo Escobar and Sonia E. Alvarez, 62–85. Boulder, CO: Westview Press.

Escobar, Arturo. 2005. *Más allá del Tercer Mundo. Globalización y diferencia*. Bogota: Instituto Colombiano de Antropología e Historia.

Introduction   23

Escobar, Arturo. 2007. *La invención del Tercer Mundo. Construcción y deconstrucción del desarrollo*. Caracas: Fundación Editorial el Perro y la Rana.

Esteva, Gustavo. 1992. "Development". In *The Development Dictionary. A Guide to Knowledge as Power*, edited by Wolfgang Sachs, 6–25. London: Zed Books Ltd.

Findji, María Teresa. 1992. "From Resistance to Social Movement: The Indigenous Authorities Movement in Colombia". In *The Making of Social Movements in Latin America. Identity, Strategy and Democracy*, edited by Arturo Escobar and Sonia E. Alvarez, 112–33. Boulder, CO: Westview Press.

Gall, Olivia. 2002. "Estado federal y grupos de poder regionales frente al indigenismo, al mestizaje y al discurso multiculturalista. Pasado y presente del racismo en México". In *Etnopolíticas y racismo. Conflictividad y desafíos interculturales en América Latina*, edited by Carlos Vladimir Zambrano, 47–72. Bogota: Universidad Nacional de Colombia.

Gandásegui Hijo, Marco A. 2011. "La crisis del imperialismo. América Latina y Panamá enfrentan cambios épicos en sus relaciones con los Estados Unidos". In *América Latina y el Caribe: escenarios posibles y políticas sociales*, edited by Theotonio Dos Santos, 183–311. Montevideo: FLACSO; UNESCO.

González Casanova, Pablo. 2006. "Colonialismo interno (una redefinición)". In *La teoría marxista hoy. Problemas y perspectivas*, edited by Atilio A. Borón, Javier Amadeo and Sabrina González, 209–434. Buenos Aires: CLACSO.

Hale, Charles R. 2002. "Does Multiculturalism Menace? Governance, Cultural Rights and the Politics of Identity in Guatemala". *Journal of Latin American Studies* 34 (3): 485–524.

Hale, Charles R. 2004. "Re-pensando la política indígena en la época del 'indio permitido'". Construyendo la paz: Guatemala desde un enfoque comparado, Guatemala City, Guatemala, October 26–27, 2004.

Harvey, David. 2007. *Breve historia del neoliberalismo*. Madrid: Akal.

Hernández García, Adriana. 2006. "Mezcala: encuentros y desencuentros de una comunidad". *Espiral, Estudios sobre Estado y Sociedad* 12 (36): 97–128.

Hernández Navarro, Luis. 2009. "Movimiento indígena: autonomía y representación política". In *Otras geografías. Experiencias de autonomías indígenas en México*, edited by Giovanna Gasparello and Jaime Quintana Guerrero, 33–61. Mexico City: Redez tejiendo la utopía.

Hipólito Hernández, Adrián Guillermo. 2012. "Mezcala: La lucha por la defensa del Cerro del Pandillo. Historia reciente de una resistencia contra el despojo". B.A. diss., Departamento de Historia, Universidad de Guadalajara.

Holloway, John. 2010. *Cambiar el mundo sin tomar el poder*. Mexico City: Sísifo Ediciones; Bajo Tierra Ediciones; Benemérita Universidad Autónoma de Puebla.

INEGI. 2010. Censo de Población y Vivienda. Mexico City.

Kearney, Michael. 2004. *Changing Fields of Anthropology: From Local to Global*. Lanham, MD: Rowman & Littlefield Publishers, Inc.

Kinsman, Gary. 2006. "Mapping Social Relations of Struggle: Activism, Ethnography, Social Organization". In *Sociology for Changing the World: Social Movements/Social Research*, edited by Caelie Frampton, Gary Kinsman, A. K. Thompson and Kate Tilleczek, 133–56. Halifax, Canada: Fernwood Publishing.

Knight, Alan. 1990. "Racism, Revolution, and Indigenismo: Mexico, 1910–1940". In *The Idea of Race in Latin America, 1870–1940*, edited by Richard Graham, 71–113. Austin, TX: University of Texas Press.

Kradolfer, Sabine. 2010. "Categorización y culturalización de lo indígena en Argentina durante las últimas décadas". *Quaderns-e* 15 (2): 60–7.

24 *Inés Durán Matute*

Leyva Solano, Xochitl. 2014. "Luchas autonómicas y epístemicas en tiempos de crisis y guerras múltiples". In *Movimiento indígena en América Latina: resistencia y proyecto alternativo*, edited by Fabiola Escárzaga and Raquel Gutiérrez Aguilar, 209–25. Mexico City: Universidad Autónoma Metropolitana – Unidad Xochimilco; Centro de Investigaciones y Estudios Superiores en Antropología Social; Benemérita Universidad Autónoma de Puebla; Centro de Estudios Andinos y MesoAmericanos.

Llanes Ortiz, Genner de Jesús. 2008. "Interculturalización fallida: desarrollismo, neoindigenismo y universidad intercultural en Yucatán, México". *TRACE* 6 (53): 49–63.

Martínez Moreno, Rocío. 2008. "La comunidad indígena coca de Mezcala, el sujeto de la historia en la defensa de la tierra". B.A. diss., Departamento de Historia, Universidad de Guadalajara.

Martínez Moreno, Rocío. 2009. "Mezcala, un pueblo coca en defensa de su memoria". In *Mezcala: una larga historia de resistencia*, edited by Rocío Martínez Moreno and Jorge Alonso, 11–23. Guadalajara, Mexico: Taller Editorial La Casa del Mago.

Martínez Moreno, Rocío. 2012. "Tierra, historia y pueblo. Memoria y acción política en la comunidad indígena de Mezcala, Jalisco". Master diss., División de Estudios Históricos y Humanos, Universidad de Guadalajara.

Martínez Moreno, Rocío. 2014. "La lucha actual de la comunidad indígena coca de Mezcala, Jalisco". In *Movimiento indígena en América Latina: resistencia y proyecto alternativo*, edited by Fabiola Escárzaga and Raquel Gutiérrez Aguilar, 40–6. Mexico City: Universidad Autónoma Metrópolitana – Unidad Xochimilco; Centro de Investigaciones y Estudios Superiores en Antropología Social; Benemérita Universidad Autónoma de Puebla; Centro de Estudios Andinos y MesoAmericanos.

Massey, Doreen. 1995. "The Conceptualization of Place". In *A Place in the World?: Places, Cultures, and Globalization*, edited by Doreen Massey and Pat Jess, 45–85. Oxford: Oxford University Press.

Massey, Doreen. 2005. *For Space*. London: SAGE Publications.

Mignolo, Walter. 2000. *Local Histories/Global Designs*. Princeton, NJ: Princeton University Press.

Moreno, Rocío. 2010. "Mezcala: la isla indómita. Las luchas por la tierra y la isla de Mezcala hoy". *Desacatos* 34: 170–4.

Moreno, Rocío. 2011. "La experiencia de Mezcala. Jóvenes e historia, una fatal combinación para el sistema capitalista". *Desinformémonos. Periodismo de abajo*, November. http://desinformemonos.org/2011/11/jovenes-e-historia-una-fatal-combinacion-para-el-sistema-capitalista/ [accessed November 4, 2011].

Moreno, Rocío. Manuel Jacobo, and José Godoy. 2006. "Los coca de Mezcala siguen vivos". *Ojarasca*.

Nederveen Pieterse, Jan. 1998. "My Paradigm or Yours? Alternative Development, Post-Development, Reflexive Development". *Development and Change* 29 (2): 343–73.

Nederveen Pieterse, Jan. 2000. "After Post-Development". *Third World Quarterly* 21 (2): 175–91.

Ochoa Serrano, Álvaro. 1985. *Los insurgentes de Mezcala. Estudio preliminar, selección documental y notas de Álvaro Ochoa S.* Zamora, Mexico: El Colegio de Michoacán; Gobierno del Estado de Michoacán.

Ochoa Serrano, Álvaro. 2006. *Los insurrectos de Mezcala y Marcos. Relación crónica de una resistencia en Chapala.* Zamora, Mexico: El Colegio de Michoacán.

Paredes, Vicente. 2010. "Mezcala: la isla indómita. Las luchas de los insurgentes en Mezcala". *Desacatos* 34: 167–70.

Paredes, Vicente. 2012. "Historia y comunidad indígena de Mezcala de la Asunción, Jalisco, invadida y humillada por autoridades de los tres niveles de gobierno". In *Mezcala: la memoria y el futuro. La defensa de la isla en el Bicentenario*, edited by Santiago Bastos, 89–92. Guadalajara, Mexico: Centro de Investigaciones y Estudios Superiores en Antropología Social.

Portes, Alejandro, and John Walton. 1981. *Labor, Class, and the International System*. New York: Academic Press.

Quijano, Aníbal. 1992. "Colonialidad y modernidad/racionalidad". *Perú Indígena* 13 (29): 11–20.

Quintero, Pablo. 2010. "Notas sobre la teoría de la colonialidad del poder y la estructuración de la sociedad en América Latina". *Papeles de Trabajo* (19): 1–15.

Ramos, Alcida Rita. 2006. "Political Construction and Cultural Instrumentalities of Indigenism in Brazil". In *Cultural Agency in the Americas*, edited by Doris Sommer, 229–47. Durham, NC: Duke University Press.

Rapoport, Mario. 2002. "Orígenes y actualidad del 'pensamiento único'". In *La globalización económico financiera. Su impacto en América Latina*, edited by Julio Gambina, 357–63. Buenos Aires: CLACSO.

Rivera Cusicanqui, Silvia. 2008. *Pueblos originarios y Estado*. La Paz: Servicio Nacional de Administración de Personal.

Sandoval, Rafael. 2009. "La lucha por la defensa del patrimonio cultural implica hoy la lucha contra el despojo, la explotación y la opresión capitalista". Foro de Defensa del Patrimonio Cultural de los Trabajadores del INAH, Mexico City.

Sieder, Rachel. 2002. *Multiculturalism in Latin America. Indigenous Rights, Diversity and Democracy*. London: Palgrave Macmillan.

Smith, Dorothy E. . 2005. *Institutional Ethnography. A Sociology for People*. Walnut Creek, CA: AltaMira Press.

Speed, Shannon. 2002. "Global Discourses on the Local Terrain: Human Rights and Indigenous Identity in Chiapas". *Cultural Dynamics* 14 (2): 205–28.

Storey, Andy. 2000. "Post-Development Theory: Romanticism and Pontius Pilate Politics". *Development* 43 (4): 40–6.

Wade, Peter. 2009. *Race and Sex in Latin America*. London: Pluto Press.

Williamson, John. 2003. "No hay consenso. Reseña sobre el Consenso de Washington y sugerencias sobre los pasos a dar". *Finanzas & Desarrollo* 40 (3): 10–13.

Williamson, John. 2004. "A Short History of the Washington Consensus". Conference "From the Washington Consensus towards a new global governance", Barcelona, September 24–5.

Yañez, Rosa. 1998. "Modificaciones lingüísticas en la margen norte de la rivera del lago de Chapala, en los siglos XVI-XVII". *Memoria del ciclo de conferencias sobre la historia de la región, Ciénega de Jalisco* 11–29.

Zibechi, Raúl. 2006. *Dispersar el poder. Los movimientos como poderes antiestatales*. Guadalajara, Mexico: Taller Editorial La Casa del Mago; Cuadernos de la Resistencia.

1 The Local Impact of Political Culture

I spent one morning talking with, but mainly listing to Don Salvador who helped me understand the complexities of being a *comunero* in Mezcala. He was appointed *delegado* twice and belonged to the *Confederación Nacional de Organizaciones Populares*, which represented the popular sector of the *Partido Revolucionario Institucional (PRI)*; but he is also a *comunero* and a fervent defender of the community, of its territory and people. On another occasion, I witnessed a meeting of the *Partido Verde* held in the *plaza*, where many attendees listened to the speeches of some representatives. What gained my attention was another committed *comunero* who was wearing a t-shirt in support of this political party. In fact, later Rocío explained to me that:

> Political parties have never been discussed in the assemblies, but that doesn't mean that some of them do belong to political parties. And here a long time was, the PRI, just like everywhere doing, gathering people. The only thing I think is different from Mezcala regarding political parties is that when it comes to something of the community they take away their banner.

However, *comuneros* are not exempt from internal contradictions; they are an authority on conflicts, divergences and fragmentations that might be elucidated through the exploration on how they are traversed by the national political culture. In this sense, by political culture I mean—borrowing the definition of Guillermo Núñez Noriega (2006, 377)—the social practices and purports through which social classes interact and give meaning to the 'processes of state formation', that shows a public and personal nature. In this regard, the aim of this chapter is to break down the local political structures and identify the consequences of the inherited political culture in the community so as to grasp the functioning of neoliberal governance. For this purpose, I mainly consider the *usos y costumbres* of its inhabitants,[1] specifically regarding the election of local government following customary law. Thus, in the first part, I develop a brief national and regional historical and political framework, taking the creation of the PRI as a starting point, and I relate it to the arrival of the *delegado municipal* in Mezcala. After this historical background, I introduce an analysis of democracy in Mexico in the era of neoliberal governance, as well as complicate assertions about the 'democratic advance', in relation to the political culture and the formal and informal routes of power within the community.

Then, I describe relationships and patterns of community and state alignment and loyalties where the focus is trained on those holding power to begin delineating the role of marginalisation, discrimination and racism in politics. Accordingly, in the fourth part, the aim is to comprehend the rise and location of the 'traditional' authority, and how the inherited political culture is implicated in this. Thus, I describe how this traditional authority was born, and indicate who it comprises and what its function is, moving then to examine its current situation, role and representativeness. This analysis is the first step in understanding the organisation of *comuneros* that somehow has been crossed by the geographies of power, and thus, reproduced or even sharpened the economic, social and cultural differences that undergird neoliberal governance. Nonetheless, this chapter traces the institutional networks at the local, regional and national levels regarding politics that also bring about the growing participation of new sectors into political communal matters for the purpose of changing their situation.

PNR/PRM/PRI: The Expansion of Clienteles, *Caciques* and Corruption

To begin to outline the political panorama lived in the community I must briefly mention some of the impacts and transformations in the organisation of the native population since Spanish colonisation. This will remind us to keep a long-term perspective. As is well known, during this time a political system was established in Mexico in accordance with the social structure, in which not all the population was represented and a powerful group was privileged above the interests of the rest of society. As analysed by Roderic Ai Camp (2000), the inherited Spanish culture imprinted experiences and features over our political system. Specifically, the establishment of communal property aimed to group together and confine native people, while giving Spaniards more extensive control over indigenous communities (Warman 2003, 122–3). This procured in indigenous communities such as Mezcala, the manipulation of their resources and people, and the damage to their political and social organisation.

Notwithstanding, as political culture is historically produced in the interface between state and society (Lewis 2012, 48); over time different historical moments made their influence apparent. Mezcalenses, as noted in the Introduction, have not been oblivious to history, moulding and displaying this in practices, values, processes, positions and relations of specific groups. To this effect, in the context of post-Revolutionary social instability and political crisis, President Plutarco Elías Calles (1924–8) created the *Partido Nacional Revolucionario (PNR)*—nowadays known as PRI—in 1929 to make a move towards a more 'representative' system; still succession was bargained over (González 2008, 12) and only a 'series of puppets' were positioned (Haber *et al.* 2008). The creation of this party, nonetheless, brought about political and organisational transformations, which in Mezcala meant the implementation of new political figures: *delegados* and *comuneros*.

28 *The Local Impact of Political Culture*

Mezcala, by not being a *municipio*, presents a singular case of the functioning of *usos y costumbres* whereby *delegados* are the party formally integrated into 'official politics', and *comuneros*, although they maintain a degree of autonomy and are recognised more as a 'traditional' authority, in fact obey similar processes.

What is more, this party developed a political culture based on client-patron relationships[2] and a corporatist system (Purcell 1981). In fact, authoritarianism persisted, with the difference that since the creation of the PNR many and diverse power-holders linked to an institution, to the official political party, concentrated power in order to maintain the stability of the state (Purcell 1981; Selee 2011). Corporatist relationships in Mexico based on previous authoritarian and paternalist relationships were adapted having a double function as tools of control and subordination of popular classes and as a means of political participation that, nonetheless, helped to reproduce this kind of political culture (Mackinlay and Otero 2006). In this sense, over time the party renovated the corporatist system in order to bring together and control peasants, workers, militaries and the middle class, allowing them to be partially independent of local *caciques* but highly dependent on their national equivalents (Purcell 1981). These sectors were 'integrated into the state by means of state-controlled social corporations' employing clientelism and division (Olvera 2010, 82). And, actually, these corporations allowed the party to maintain control inside and outside different sectors, and those not willing to become part of them were repressed or excluded (Mackinlay and Otero 2006).

But, since the discontent of popular sectors did not disappear and in fact increased, President Lázaro Cárdenas (1934–40) changed tactics and his first action was the transformation of the political party into the *Partido de la Revolución Mexicana (PRM)* in 1938, this time supported especially by peasants and workers. As a matter of fact, with Cárdenas two clientele systems began to operate; on the one hand, national clientelism used the local structures to wash its hands of the growing social discontent, exclusion and repression, in order to institutionalise clients as party members through *Confederaciones*, to display a false image of supremacy and obtain broader social support and control of localities. On the other hand, local *caciques* were rewarded with their power and autonomy (Purcell 1981). Andrew Selee (2011) identified this phenomenon as a 'two-way relationship', where intermediaries gain power from those below and give benefits to those above, constraining local leaders to comply and remain loyal to upper and party decisions. In this sense, power is constantly negotiated and is seen as a win-win relationship, since it entails complicity and dependence, despite disadvantages and the unequal distribution of power. Moreover, this asymmetrical and vertical hierarchy of patron-client relationships occurs at all levels and it is reproduced from the local through to the national.

In this regard, despite the alleged centralisation of Mexico for much of the twentieth century, localities at that time were important in setting up national politics, transforming the first aspiring political position into *Municipios*—as they were also the gateway to move upward and to renegotiate the relations of power (Selee 2011). Therefore, as the case of Mezcala reveals, *Municipios*

The Local Impact of Political Culture   29

sought to control localities through the figure of the *delegado municipal*.[3] In fact, even if this political figure was implemented approximately in the 1920s, since the 1950s it began to be elected by the *Municipio* rather than by the inhabitants, at the same time *jueces de barrio* declined in importance (Bastos 2011). Furthermore, the *delegado municipal* did not represent a mighty power; as Rocío explains 'at the beginning they didn't even have this strong power like authority, because here we had our own authorities'.

In 1946 a new political change took place replacing the PRM with the PRI to emphasise the institutionalisation of the Revolution, but it remained a 'mass party' that continued with a patronage system and followed the same up-down structure of power. The PRI endured as the hegemonic and sole political party and guaranteed its dominance as a result of noncompetition, the corporatisation of society, populist practices, violence, electoral fraud and control over the media. As signalled by Horacio Mackinlay and Gerardo Otero (2006), Mexico is a clear example of state corporatism, that is, with a high level of subordination of different groups to the state, which allows scarce concessions, and is characterised by authoritarianism, patrimonialism and clientelism. Mezcala did not escape this scenario, as some inhabitants joined its clientelist, corporatist and corrupted practices. As Santiago Bastos indicates, their political participation depended on their belonging to 'the official party' (2011: 106).

Concurrently, informal power was strengthened in the region; that is, as defined by Selee (2011), 'a system of hierarchical power relations based on patronage and informal intermediation that serves as an organisational structure linking citizens and groups in society'. Accordingly, in Poncitlán, *la familia Montes*, labelled with the PRI tag and owners of *Montes*, a candy company created in 1938, have been the rulers. The founder of the company, Miguel Montes Castellanos (1917–93), was mayor from 1959 to 1961, but even afterwards he did not lose power. In fact, *caciques*[4] seem to follow a hereditary process, and show a strong familial support, as analysed below. Besides, in the village this patronage system reinforced the dominance of the PRI via local leaders, as Don Chava, a *comunero* and past candidate in the elections for *delegado municipal* (*suplente*), remembers in reference to the words of the party 'if you work, convince people and we win, we are going to make you a new *delegación* [building]'.

The PRI persisted with their corporatist approach to foster industrialisation and modernisation, further incorporate peasants and workers into the structure of power and continue to mediate between the citizens and the state, creating or adapting institutions. In this vein, the hegemony of the PRI and the undemocratic and unequal relations were guaranteed by a system that promoted the sharing of benefits among political leaders and a limited impact of society in politics through clientelism (Selee 2011, 44). Clientelism, thereby, broadly speaking, should be understood as the unequal exchange of private or public goods, favours, patronage, status or power for party loyalty or political support. But, as Tina Hilgers notes, it also 'involves longevity, diffuseness, face-to-face contact and inequality' (2011, 568). As later evidenced, these relationships, these

30   The Local Impact of Political Culture

ways of interacting, are a result of economic and political inequality and needs that are exploited by a sector to build their social support.

Jalisco was no exception in this national panorama; although for the national elections of 1979, the political support diversified towards the *Partido Acción Nacional (PAN)*, at the local level it was more limited (Tamayo and Vizcarra 2000, 66). During these years the PRI 'officially' established itself as the hegemonic party in Mezcala since it had dominion over the population and no real political options existed; just as a Don Chava remembers about the 1970s 'we were all from the PRI ... All the people were from the PRI because no other party worked, just PRI'. Besides, before the 1980s in Mexico, the PRI centralised formal power but maintained highly decentralised informal power, as a 'form of institutionalisation' (Selee, 2011: 11). In Poncitlán, this was manifest in the excessive power of Miguel Montes, as Don Salvador remembers having to deal with him over issues of the community, expressing that 'the president told me, not the president, Mr Montes was the one who *tajaba el queso* [split and distributed benefits] there' and as also Don Chava shared 'the mere cacique, he was the one who had money'; '[he] was the one that was in charge, he was the one that put and removed [people] in the *municipio*'.

In effect, in Mezcala elites from Poncitlán have managed the *municipio* and, therefore, have tried to do the same in the community. So, in Mezcala *delegados* were usually *comuneros* affiliated to the PRI, who most times showed a willingness to work for the community, but usually were abused, unpaid and blocked by the *Municipio*. As noted by Pieter de Vries, 'what makes state power strong is the opportunity to engage in all sorts of opaque, illegal, activities in liminal spaces' that support the existing political system and its rule in the face of the weakness and breaking of public law (2007, 153–4). In this perspective, the figure of the *delegado municipal* appointed by the Municipal President responded to this informality. As experienced by Don Salvador while being elected *delegado* in 1974:

> When the [municipal] president came inside, he says, 'I'm back, let's see tell me whom did you choose?' and they said, 'No ... I suppose Silvino Santos',—'Let's see who Silvino Santos is?', he sees him and says 'It's all right', he says, 'I'm just going to tell you one thing',—'Let's see',—I think that as president I can give one vote, what do you think? '—Oh, we agree'. He walked around and said 'Look', he said, 'I give the vote so this person is the *delegado*', and I was like that on the desk like there, 'Oh' I said, 'no doctor I don't know any of that, I've never been into that', he said 'neither do I and I'm here. It's just the way it is'.

This recollection shows not only the utilisation of informal practices to designate authorities such as the *dedazo*,[5] but also the lack of experience of these public servants to carry out their role and the familial connection, since a close member of his family was previously *delegado*. Accordingly, informality that is usually unwritten and unofficial might be institutionalised through formal channels, helping later in the setting up of neoliberal governance.

The Local Impact of Political Culture 31

Assessing Democracy, the New Face of Informal Power

In 1981 due to internal problems the PRI split up into two different ideological tendencies: Neoliberals and Nationalists. International relationships, especially among the U.S. government and IFIs, helped to define the path the country would take. President Miguel de la Madrid (1982–8) embraced the neoliberal ideology with the help of nascent technocrats, while democratic claims increased. However, as the PRI failed to regain the support of the business elite and social discontent expanded, in order to secure the neoliberal continuance, through the *camarilla*[6] de la Madrid elected Carlos Salinas de Gortari—his pupil and *apadrinado*[7]—as his successor. After a tense, agitated, chaotic and irregular electoral process, Salinas de Gortari (1988–94) was appointed as the new Mexican president. He enforced three electoral reforms, aiming to establish confidence in the election process and to decentralise power. But, they were pointless as the PRI kept managing campaigns, elections and results (Olvera, 2010), while patronage endured. This demonstrated the tendency of neoliberal governance to deceive people in order to co-opt and depoliticise their struggles.

The PRI, in spite of internal disagreements and increased opposition, still managed to retain power, seeing that there was—as pointed out by Stephen Haber *et al.* (2008)—a context of media control, social programmes, the overvaluation of the peso and the menace of instability and violence. Ernesto Zedillo (1994–2000) was elected by Salinas, ensuring the continuous enforcement of neoliberal policies. He promoted a judiciary and electoral reform via fear of social upheaval (Starr 2010, 849), while he decentralised public spending, giving more power to state governors (Olvera, 2010) and *Municipios*. These reforms, nonetheless, did not transform the way in which politics was managed through informal power but reflected the co-optation driven. In this context, governors and *caciques* still functioned as 'carriers and beneficiaries of a dense web of agreements with the de facto powers' (Olvera 2010, 87), just as in the case of Poncitlán, where no real change occurred. Inhabitants affirm that Rodolfo García Becerra (2004–6), affiliated to PRI, had a close relationship with Montes, who later appointed him as Municipal President. Francisco, a migrant who used to work in the candy company, remembers:

> When I was there, Rodolfo was, what was the name? Regional *manager* of all *Montes....* Later Rodolfo came here, he was already president.

Whereas it should be noted that before the reforms, in Jalisco the PAN had already strengthened its political force, alternation was brief and only a ruse, and democracy was far from being achieved. Nonetheless, as the PRI was fragmented and weakened and social discontent increased, the PAN's candidate, Vicente Fox, was able to win the presidential election (2000–6). Despite the fact that in the minds of most Mexicans this revealed that alternation in power was possible, the corporatist relationships were maintained as well as power over society and the economy, but this time were used by the new political party in

32 *The Local Impact of Political Culture*

power (Mackinlay and Otero 2006). As expressed by Arturo Anguiano, although the respect of votes was a novelty in the election of 2000, it did not translate into real political change, rather, clientelism, oppression, injustice, authoritarianism and exclusion persisted, coming to be described as a 'grotesque caricature of PRI government' (2008, 62). Certainly, this transition was democratically deficient as it excluded most subjects while the PRI kept veto power and major control in local governments, the peasant and popular corporations and bureaucracy.

In actual fact, neither the PAN nor the *Partido de la Revolución Democrática (PRD)*, the main 'leftist' political party, have a democratic proposal, reproducing the same political culture and developing their own clientele networks—advised by PRI members—while other small political parties are family businesses and/or opportunistic (Olvera 2010). In this manner, party ideologies can be unimportant, in the face of relations of power and traditional power-holders. Political parties do not offer an alternative and typically do not constitute channels to manage our dissatisfactions; they have no clear direction or ideology, and usually seek alliances either nationally or locally, in order to increase their possibilities and obtain at least a bit of power and control, as was demonstrated in the national elections of 2006. In effect, when the PRI was created, power was distributed in a coalition that entwined subjects of different ideologies; it was a 'party of parties', as Purcell (1981, 203) and Selee (2011, 36) argue. Nowadays, with the 'democratic advance' and political pluralism, this structure continues, but displays itself in diversified images and labels. Moreover, although new pacts have been created, there is a continuation with the past, amalgamating opposing ideologies and procedures, and preserving authoritarian methods (e.g. corporatism and clientelism). Political parties use formal and informal channels of intermediation that go from the local to the national level and vice versa.

In this regard, in spite of the election of Emilio González Márquez (2007–13), from the PAN, as Governor of Jalisco, and the election of Ramón Romo González (2006–9) and Carlos Maldonado Guerrero (2010–12) from the PRD as Municipal President of Poncitlán, politics in the entity did not change. Decentralisation nationalised informal power (Knight 2005), ensuring the continuation of the inherited political culture. In this sense, neither decentralisation nor 'autonomous' electoral bodies, alternation, the growing participation of citizens, the plurality of political parties or regular 'free and fair' elections transformed the undemocratic situation. In effect, political parties entail a complex structure of interests and do not present different proposals or a move away from traditional politics. Rather, they profit to fragment civil society, maintain their dominion and increase their power and wealth. Don Fernando, a *comunero* who since childhood has lived between Mezcala and Guadalajara to study and practice as a teacher, notes:

> One and the other place the foot on the one that is more backward and to achieve his objectives he uses the most oppressed group, and once he reaches power they forget [about them].

The Local Impact of Political Culture 33

Political intermediaries have been offered a new disguise from which to manage institutions to their interests while maintaining order and structure within Mexican politics (Zárate Hernández 2005). Clienteles have founded a sort of parallel state, with their own rules, hierarchies, locus and channels by which they subsist and reproduce (Nieto 2011). Institutionally and culturally, *priísta* values, practices, methods and structure are maintained; and therefore, politics and its processes are not exclusive of the electoral realm but are impressed in daily life. In this context, a democratic change should have included not only the takeover of different subjects, but also a transformation of electoral practices, and more importantly, of the relationships between state and society. In Mexico, we have been living in a *democracia dirigida*—a governmental strategy to maintain power as defined by Don Fernando—or as seen by Walden Bello (2008), an 'elite democracy' or 'polyarchy', where society can only choose between a restricted group that does not really represent different alternatives. At the same time, clientelism, fraud, corruption and corporatism are used as tools to impose the will of the political elite. This fact proved that it does not matter who the intermediaries are, or their names, as the practices and structure remain deep-rooted: institutions are hard to break.

In this sense, democracy in Mexico should be understood as a legacy of the authoritarian and repressive past that was reinvented in the era of neoliberal governance. It is a rhetoric used by elites to maintain and reproduce forms of dominion and stratification, making believe the possibility of change and regaining the support of society. Moreover, Adam David Morton (2012) explains that a limited standard of democracy has been constructed since the 1980s in Mexico and Latin America, when concerns about 'development' began to be replaced by ones of 'democratisation'. This action supported by funds granted by USAID, separated politics from economics, serving national elites and U.S. interests, while perpetuating class structures and disconnecting democracy and capitalist development (Morton 2012). Considering that, as proposed by Guillermo O'Donnell (1994), not all democracies have the same characteristics and we should create a typology based on the historical processes and inherited socioeconomic problems, I propose the concept of 'simulated democracy' (Durán Matute 2015). In this way, I want to emphasise its Eurocentric background, and its current paradox, as representative systems preserve the governance arrangements and perpetuate the domination forms at a transnational level through the rhetoric of democracy that makes people feel closer to equality. Democracy follows a pact between elite members who are part of a network of power that sustains the precepts of neoliberal governance, where they alternate power via fraud, corruption and/or clienteles, where the interests of society are not represented and institutions are not truly transformed.

Like this, the same dynamics, practices and relations of power are maintained while they simulate their renovation and their 'democratic' functioning. At the same time, exclusion, repression, co-option and obstacles are produced to prevent opposition, the transformation of this setting and even to legitimise the form of government. In this fashion, the constitutional design and institutional

34   *The Local Impact of Political Culture*

structure work together to maintain not only an undisturbed dominion of the elite in politics, but also socially, culturally and discursively on a daily basis, in a form of neoliberal governance. And, thus, in the event that this system no longer provides the best opportunity for the elites to preserve and reproduce themselves, they will not hesitate to transform or adjust their discourses, institutions and/or practices. Therefore, this concept should just be used as a guide and not as a strict and defined framework. To break down the political game is not enough to dismantle the structures of domination, but to dare to think beyond them, especially beyond 'democracy' might be.

Managing Contemporary Local Politics Through Informality: *Caciques, Presidentes Municipales* and *Delegados*

In Mezcala political parties made their 'destructive entry', as José Luis, a young inhabitant who has been working with *comuneros* and supporting projects with Colectivo Mezcala argues, dividing inhabitants between different political forces and using the same old practices. He adds, 'Even sometimes there were strong quarrels between families and deaths due to political parties'. During the last 20 years, inhabitants have affiliated to different political forces aiming to access at least some benefits, conceding periods of governance to the PAN (1995, 2001) and to the PRD (2006, 2010); while clienteles and corruption became reinforced and exclusion persisted. The lack of official documentation and the isolation of the village are some of the obstacles blocking full participation, but a large number of inhabitants have also realised that there is a lack of support from the *Municipio* and are adding their voices to manifest their segregation and express their dissatisfaction. So, in the context of the alleged 'democratic advance', Don Fernando comments on the last elections (2012):

> Look, according to the organic law, municipal presidents have the power to appoint the *delegado* of each community or the municipal agents. Lately, municipal presidents seem to want to open themselves a little to democracy, simply with the latter one who is [in office], [he] says 'there will be an election in the village', and that one was elected by the people. But the PRI people, and the PAN people didn't participate. And they have opened themselves a little but I tell you in this election the PRD people, the PAN people … doesn't participate. No, the PRI people were the one that elected the *delegado*.

People get entangled in politics if they see a benefit, not to exert their right to choose: for example, the *sub-delegado* of *La Cuesta* that is supposedly elected, in fact, is 'well, whoever let them' (Rocío 2012). In this manner, democracy allowed local *cacicazgos* to adjust themselves to party pluralism (Pansters 2005, 374), while a 'relational culture'—a political culture based on personal relationships— predominates among political practices and institutions (Zárate Hernández 2005,

The Local Impact of Political Culture   35

274–5). In effect, as a result of a historical process, corruption leads the mobilisation and organisation of the elite through relationships such as *parentesco, amiguismo, padrinazgo, compadrazgo*, clientelism and nepotism, while it also provides them with schemes, references, values and practices (Nieto 2011). Accordingly, *delegados* are just intermediaries, subordinates and supporters of the *Municipio*. In this context, it is not surprising that Chuy, a young deportee in 2008, narrates how the Municipal authorities appointed the *delegado* despite electoral results:

> In the case of Mezcala not, because the *delegado*, is also there not because of the people but because of the president of Poncitlán that removed the *delegado* that people voted and put him, to his *delegado* of Mezcala but that nobody voted for. That now the *delegado* that is [in office], that man eighty per cent of the people don't want him; but it's there due to the municipal president.

The appointment of authorities is still used; the Municipal President, as noted by the sceptical comunero Don Miguel:

> has availed himself to appoint the *delegado* through *dedazo*, how do you do that? He knows that from there he's going to get a lot of profit because it's not for the people, it's for him, he puts and removes him, and the people don't.

In view of that, Don Julián, the husband of Doña Vicenta, a migrant who now lives between LA and Mezcala, notes 'Poncitlán puts, whoever he wants'; thus, 'it's enough to have a relationship with the municipal president' (Don Fernando 2012) or with political parties. In brief, *delegados* are a puppet lacking presence and power within the community, and as remarked by Rocío 'the problem of most *delegados* is that they put themselves at the service of the *Municipio* and not of the community' clashing with *comuneros* and the people. So the Municipal President and the elite that back him are careful in selecting the person to hold this position. As expressed by Francisco:

> They never let a student [to be in office], why? 'X we're going to put you there, but look you don't have to do this, this neither ... when you have to make a decision come and ask us, okay?' Because if not, if he decides by himself because he is *delegado* 'you know what? Here you have to give me, here you have to do this', after a while they show up, 'what happened? We're going to remove you'.

Increasingly, as Adelo, the migrant, observes, 'the *Municipio* began to give much importance to what is the *delegado*, through the *delegado* they [the municipal power-holders] were getting in and holding the power and control of the village'. Moreover, while recently people with 'formal' education have been

36 *The Local Impact of Political Culture*

appointed, inhabitants still know, as Doña Vicenta expresses, that usually 'the *delegado* is always on the side of the president and everything that is for there [Poncitlán]', because, as noted by Don Luis, another migrant, unlike before, 'the salary is given by Poncitlán'. So, as *delegados* seek special privileges and to enhance their profile they are responding to the inherited political culture. However, they not only have no voice and are paid miserably—approximately 2,500 pesos[8] per month to perform all these abuses—additionally, their position is always at risk. As expressed by Pedro, an inhabitant who has been involved with *comuneros, delegados*, Colectivo Mezcala and Club Mezcala, their term lasts 'according to their behaviour'. In this way, inhabitants of the community might be aware that politics are managed through clientelism and corporatism, as the young Carlos detects:

> There are matters where programs come directly here; or that they do arrive to Mezcala but they remain with certain political leaders of the parties here in Mezcala. The city council has dealt with them because they help them to manipulate people, that simple.

In effect, the same dynamics are reproduced; in communities like Mezcala, patron-client relationships and the entire informal power web continues to function, as described by Don Fernando:

> Look here in the community is a 'mini city', the same vices that you have in the high levels happen here, why? Because for example the *delegado* who is now [in office] because he's the brother of one who was previously *delegado* and are hand in glove with those of the PRI of Poncitlán.

In this sense, informality together with marginalisation, discrimination and racism prevail, showing a perverse ramification of neoliberal governance. For instance, *caciques* have actually adapted to new political and social conditions and represent an inherited cultural practice (Knight 2005). Neoliberal governance redefined *cacicazgo* by generating new pacts with local *caciques* and creating tensions in past agreements, while maintaining the political dominion of national *caciques* (Pansters 2005, 372–3). The elite created an illusion among inhabitants of disconnection among political leaders, but, as the case of Mezcala demonstrates, their links have been renewed and the same cacique family is still managing local politics. As noted by Don Rogelio and Don Santos, two Mezcalenses that migrated in the 1970s and are members of Club Mezcala:

DON SANTOS: Now they do want to be living from the people, and to make matters worse, all the presidents who have been from Poncitlán are only family members. Don Rogelio. – Ujum, everyone.
DON SANTOS: Nephew, uncle, cousin....
DON ROGELIO: Years.

The Local Impact of Political Culture   37

DON SANTOS: All the de la Torre [family], and those since it started everything there ... it's only family, all the de la Torre, all the Becerras, all those who are there.

DON ROGELIO: Maldonado.

DON SANTOS: Maldonados, all.

These relations and networks determine who participates not only in political but also in economic, social and cultural processes, prolonging the exclusion of some sectors and thus, social hierarchies. Knight (2005) identifies education and the technocratisation of the offspring of elite families as one factor damaging the 'hereditary principle' among these groups; nonetheless, the case of Poncitlán shows how, within the workings of neoliberal governance, a person's political and economic position can also be simultaneously reinforced by these elements. This is seen in how the new owner of Montes, Juan Carlos Montes Johnston, son of Miguel Montes, has extended links, on the one hand, in politics with the PRI through, for instance, his election as Municipal President in 2015. At the same time in the realm of the economy, the company is continually enlarging its market to the United States, Latin America, South Africa, etc.,[9] and even now has a subsidiary industry in Texas. The economic and political position of the family is boosted while the Montes Company has grown considerably, expanding and diversifying into other industries.

In this respect, inspired by the ideas of Pansters (2005), *caciques* must be seen as complex and changeable subjects who nowadays mix different features: representative and authoritarian power, economic influence and the ability to mediate, institutionalised and non-institutionalised procedures, and territorial and extra-territorial connections. Thus, the persistence of *caciquismo* over time, as noted by José Eduardo Zárate Hernández (2005) might be explained if we see it as a practice and a 'structuring power'—the construction of networks that organise society. *Caciques* are 'active forces' who shape local and regional experiences and actions as well as national politics (Pansters 2005, 364) according to the rationale of neoliberal governance. So, through the example of Mezcala, we can see that intermediaries persist because their role has been renewed and continues to be the most effective channel to securing the pursued benefits, to control and appease society and to maintain undisturbed interests and hierarchies. The local dynamic still follows a system based on informal power, authoritarianism and excluded citizen participation.

Accordingly, even though there is increased active citizen participation and claims, the dynamic and identities of the rulers are unchanged and represent the intent to not lose control. The government discriminates by contending that people of the region lack formal education and training, but as noted by two *comuneros*, 'they don't want someone else to steal' (Don Gabriel 2012), 'they want to see that we still are ignorant, following them and doing what ever they want' (Don Fausto 2012). Therefore, though some people might argue that nationally there has been a 'democratic advance' with the rise of reinforced *Municipios*, as long as locally things remain the same, simulated democracy will

38   *The Local Impact of Political Culture*

persist nationally excluding the majority in the process and representation. In this fashion, the discourse of 'democratic nationalism' proposed by the 'new' PRI (2012), has allowed them to regain power, making use of the same old practices (corruption, clientelism, repression and media control), but now with the support of a distorted image. Nationally, Enrique Peña Nieto (2012–18) has become the new president, as Salinas and the old guard of the PRI backed him up;[10] meanwhile in most state and Municipal elections the same state of affairs developed, as in Jalisco and Poncitlán where PRI returned to rule.

The Mexican political system is embedded with inherited relations of power, institutions, policies, corporations, class configurations and structure; and is based on corrupt and clientelist practices, allowing the *'banalización de la corrupción'*.[11] However, rather than pointing out the practice, which most Mexicans can signal as the obstacle to getting things done, we must reveal the subjects, the local, regional and national intermediaries who function under this logic to understand and confront structures and networks of power, while also being aware that 'even well-meaning individuals can become entangled' in corruption, since it is institutionalised and embedded in a structural perspective, in a network of power that sometimes allows little room for manoeuvre (Anders and Nuijten 2007). Corruption, like other practices of our inherited political culture, is a crucial characteristic of the workings of neoliberal governance; following the ideas of John Holloway (2010), it is the way such power functions, not an abnormality.

The 'Traditional' Authority Traversed by an Inherited Political Culture

The Birth of Comuneros

Although these days the 'official authority' of the community is the *delegado municipal* who is tightly linked to the *Municipio*, for the community, in general, *comuneros* embody the 'authentic' and 'traditional' authority. In the words of Rocío: 'the old figure with the new one was delegated to *comuneros* and not to the *delegado*'. In order to understand the emergence of this political figure and the impact the Mexican political culture has had on it, we must go back to the end of the Mexican Revolution, when the promises on land matters were consolidated with the enactment of Article 27 of the Mexican Constitution (1917). This provision considered private property a privilege, redistributed lands in the form of *ejidos* and re-established communal ownership as 'social property'.[12] However, as this provision did not completely reach Poncitlán, the territorial, political and social structure remained the same. The following presidents distributed small quantities of land, but President Cárdenas, as a result of the growing discontent of peasants and indigenous populations, reallocated 45.4 million acres to 723,000 families (Haber *et al.* 2008, 30), primarily in order to hinder a forthcoming rebellion and activate capitalist agricultural plans (López 2007, 32). In Mezcala the restoration of communal land was crucial to

The Local Impact of Political Culture 39

Figure 1.1 Comunero.

preventing further threats; however, between 1930 and 1950, as a result of land redistribution its territory was reduced due to petitions of surrounding villages (Hernández García 2006, 110).

So in 1956 the community began a process of transforming their land into *Bienes Comunales* (Martínez Moreno 2012) in order to stop a border conflict with the neighbouring village of San Juan Tecomatlán; requesting that Mezcala's possession was recognised from time immemorial.[13] As a result, their land will be 'inalienable, imprescriptible and indefeasible' for the exclusive enjoyment of the community. In this context, *comuneros* narrate how an engineer arrived in Mezcala to establish the system of *Bienes Comunales*. As recalled by Don Miguel:

> An engineer named Esteban Covarrubias Jiménez came, I don't know if it was a political plan or we don't know, I was very young and came so people would be taken into account, the ones that Mezcala had, of people, to enrol it in a basic census so that this community was recognised in Mexico, and you see that we're all distrustful. Then, when that was done, the engineer took all these measurements, he charged for his work, or I mean that he was paid from Mexico just here they were going to give him a compensation of voluntary cents; I don't remember how this was exactly. So, given that not all of them compensated him as he said, they gave him the *Título* [*Primordial*] valuing what they were going to give of aid, and seeing that he became interested in the document because of those hardly where found here, only

40 *The Local Impact of Political Culture*

that *Título* they gave him. Then, once he advised the people, they said, the managers, 'Look gentlemen enrol your daughters, your sons, your wife or your spouse in the list because every person who doesn't appear in the basic census is going to be left out, he won't have a voice or vote, a day will come that the *comisariado* will name all the people he has, who is in the census' ... and you see that he has the look as a politician and you aren't getting there, 'well, the community is going to become a *ejido*' and no, it was not ejido, it was community so all could have a voice and vote. So at that time only those who got into the basic census were four hundred and six.

In effect, on August 2, 1959, the engineer Esteban Rubio Jimenez, who was the representative of the Department of *Asuntos Agrarios y de Colonización*, met with Donociano Jacobo Pérez, *Representante Comunal*, Malaquías Rosales G., *Secretario de la Comunidad* and Genaro de los Santos Paredes, *delegado municipal*, and all inhabitants and smallholders who responded to the call made two weeks before, in order to elect the *Representantes Censales de la Comunidad*.[14] Francisco González Baltazar and Concepción Santana de los Santos were appointed whereas in 1956 they were accused—together with the *delegado municipal*—of selling part of the community to the neighbouring village of San Miguel Zapotitlán.[15] In this context, this election is a first clue about the functioning of corrupt practices and internal problems within the community, since these subjects were acting as *caciques*, organising the political life of the community in favour of the PRI while engaging in the illegal sale of land.

Continuing with the narrative, two days later the *Censo General Agrario de Comuneros* was carried out.[16] It seems that the governmental representative possibly had the support of some inhabitants and the local priest, as Don Jacinto, a past president of *bienes comunales*, recalls 'they went door to door to tell them. For example, his house, they went to notify him and then, they ask them if they wanted to become *comunero*'. They invited all inhabitants irrespective of their age and gender; in fact, most of them remember being very young—the youngest 13 years old—and their parents were those who decided to include them. As experienced by Don Chava: 'no, I didn't decide, my father might have enrolled me, I don't know how this happened, but at the end ... I was in the census'. Others do not really know how they got into the process, as Don Felipe, another *comunero*, states, 'because I, too, without knowing "so, enrol me", and they enrolled me'; while others explain that enrolment occurred after a meeting, as the narrative of Don Fernando evidences, 'we went up to the hill, several people were not registered ... Then there they called the roll of the people who went, so those people who were called appeared in the census'. Besides, as this process included the measuring of their territory—the real purpose of their request—this engineer together with those willing to participate walked the boundaries of the community and established that it comprised 3,600.2 acres.

The agrarian authorities conducted a census where only 406[17] inhabitants of Mezcala obtained the entitlement of *comunero* and the right to vote. From that moment on, 398 males and only eight females[18] between the ages of 13 and 60

The Local Impact of Political Culture   41

were integrated into 'formal' politics. As Bastos identifies, only a half or a third of the community undertook the procedure to be considered *comunero* due to internal problems, political pressures or distrust (2011: 94). In fact, some inhabitants refused to participate due to fear of losing their land, as Don Salvador recounts:

> not all [the people] enrolled because they began to tell them not to sign up because the community was going to become 'agrarian' and they were going to take the land away. So the majority didn't enrol but those who signed up came in the list of the census.

Don Chava signals as culprits of this distress:

> the so-called *caciques*, the landowners, didn't allow people to enrol, right? They inculcated that if they enrolled, the community was going to become *ejido*, and many people didn't want it, so, just the few that included us on the list were those 306 [406] comuneros, no more.

The census could be counterproductive to local elites because the alienation of land would be harder to achieve; however, from this moment the state secured control of the community and established its clienteles. Paradoxically, this action is praised by *comuneros* who still remember President Cárdenas with respect and affection, materialised in the stamp of the *Comisariado De Bienes Comunales*. It was not until 1964 that their request appeared on the *Diario Oficial de Jalisco*, and it conferred a positive to President Luis Echeverría (1970–6), who signed the enactment of the *Resolución Presidencial* (1971).[19] Don Miguel's narration demonstrates this:

> The certificates of those who were registered in the census arrived, for all of us who enrolled and had a sentiment and collected our document, I have mine signed by the President of the Republic Luis Echeverría Álvarez.

From that moment a new hierarchy was established where, as perceived by José Luis, 'legally those 406 people are the owners of the community, others are considered settlers'. Borrowing the expression of Robert Andolina, Sarah Radcliffe and Nina Laurie (2005), a 'limited direct democracy' arose via the regulation of participation. The division of the population was no novelty; Martínez Moreno (2012) identifies in her thesis three tendencies associated with confrontations between *barrios* and the decisions to privatise land. However, since that moment such division was accentuated by not recognising all inhabitants as *comuneros* and excluding them from the elections of their representatives and the decisions in the community. Thus, as Don Chava notes, whereas some saw *comuneros* as meaning 'more political validity', other Mezcalenses 'said that how it was going to be possible that a few represented the whole village, the whole community'. In fact, the new organisation divided the community between those who complained of the

42 *The Local Impact of Political Culture*

disturbance of their traditional structure and *usos y costumbres*, and felt this action as a possible sale of their land, and those who believed they were protecting the land and helping the community, with some of them co-opted by the PRI authorities. As a consequence problems arose; as recalled by Don Salvador, referring to certain elections held during the mid-1970s:

> Oh, there was a problem, a big problem, but a big problem. They came and appointed a *comisariado*, then it was *comisariado*, and they brought people in, then the Secretary of *Reforma Agraria* came because they told him that they were not going to let them vote and all that, and he came. He said 'Look' and separate[d] people, 'look those who are not registered here and those who are registered here', so everyone was allowed to vote, they voted together anyway.

After that, a group of *comuneros* resorted to authorities in Poncitlán and Mexico City in order to claim the respect of the new authorities. Thanks to their affiliation with the PRI, the issue was solved—though after a slow and labyrinthine processing time, with the enactment of their certificates issued in 1980. Yet, not all *comuneros* collected them, as Don Salvador further narrates:

> they gave us the papers, brought them, distributed them and they came and said 'not to pick those papers up because the community was already in the "agrarian"'. Most [people] didn't want the papers, some have them but they were several who processed their papers but some don't have them.

Oddly municipal authorities aimed to prevent *comuneros* from obtaining their certificates as they foresaw a possible threat. Don Miguel remembers an ex-Municipal President trying to bribe him:

> 'We know that you have certificates from all over your community, why not give them to us? Look, we are going to give you 25 thousand pesos', at that time it was a fortune, 'With that money you can go build a house in Puerto Vallarta and get away from these snakes'.

Authorities sought to identify the subjects to whom they should address themselves, without caring about co-opting or defaming them, and increasing the tensions and divisions within the community.

In this context, most of the 406 *comuneros* were unaware of their new role, it took around 15 years for them to discover, as related by Don Indalecio, a *comunero* who migrated permanently in the 1980s, 'it was around the 56' when they carried out that census and until around the 70s, 72, when they used the first year the basic census to choose the commissary of there'. This new authority was not only in charge of creating agrarian documents, but was also responsible for decisions within the community to solve problems and safeguard the territory. Thus, the organisation of Mezcala changed from a single representative to the

Figure 1.2 Regular assembly.

Comisariado de Bienes Comunales integrated by 'a president, a secretary, a treasurer, the *Consejo de Vigilancia* and the *Asamblea de Comuneros*' (Martínez Moreno 2008, 59). The board, since then, has been made up of the first four and represents the *Asamblea General de Comuneros*, which is the highest authority, as explained by José Luis:

> The representative or president of *bienes comunales*, as it is now known, is the one that represents the *Asamblea* but does not decide for the *Asamblea*, but it's the *Asamblea* that is behind it. And he just executes the orders of the *Asamblea*.... It's a very balanced form of government because it doesn't fall to one side or the other. That is, he always sees what is best for the community.

The first president of *Bienes Comunales* was Antíoco Robles (1971), with an administration period of three years, and since then 13 boards—now 15—have managed the community (Martínez Moreno, 2012).

Representativeness at Risk? Fragmentation, Exclusion and Co-option

Politics within the community have become entangled with the inherited political culture in a way that facilitates the workings of neoliberal governance where exclusion, racism and fragmentation have been aggravated. In the past, elections seemed simpler; as Don Fernando recalls: 'they chose [the representative] democratically,

44 *The Local Impact of Political Culture*

there in a very big, leafy tree. I remember once I came, they said "look those who vote for X go there, those who vote for Y, and elections were like this, really quick"'. However, marginalisation already existed together with division and corruption. In fact, two groups existed and even fraud sometimes was committed. Don Fernando also remembers a representative of the *Confederación Nacional Campesina* (CNC),

> he was a former military, they took the box, it was a box … of votes, they took it away. After they said, X won, and the people quarrelled and were in conflict, and again there were two presidents of the community.

In line with the observations of María Aidé Hernández (2008), corporatism intervened in political processes and was part and parcel of fraudulent transactions while inhabitants were also forced to vote for the PRI. In any case, before the birth of *comuneros* things were far from perfect as the political culture had already made its appearance, and people were polarised possibly due to family confrontations.

Still, since the *Resolución Presidencial*, life in the community began to be managed by the new authorities—together with land, cultural and social organisation. *Comuneros* have their say in the assemblies that are usually held the first Sunday of each month in the *Casa Comunal* (inaugurated in 1982), with a second round the following Sunday if there is not an urgent matter. Here they discuss agrarian, civil, political and social issues, as well as community projects; the purpose of *comuneros* is to solve problems and to look after their territory and its population. In order to process any action or public work, the approval and authorisation of the *Asamblea* is first necessary; this means that the majority needs to agree. *Comuneros* are required to attend, but not all do so, while others do and to the present day do not know exactly what their functions are. Besides, as was earlier revealed, even though not all inhabitants were included in the census, the community supported them and the new organisation contained a representative percentage of them from the nine *barrios*.

Nonetheless, Mexico was characterised by a distinctive authoritarian mode that allowed regulated citizens' political activity. In effect, in Mezcala many *comuneros* supported the PRI and some of them were even affiliated to *Confederaciones*. This was a way to establish intermediaries and disconnect them from opposition (Fox 1994). For instance, Don Salvador, though he affirms he was not into politics, declared, 'just the only thing is that at that time I knew the governor, I knew the deputies, I knew … in Guadalajara'. His credentials opened doors for him and actually helped to mobilise processes and provide accountability in the village. The PRI formed relations of power and entangled the support of different parts of the community; people knew the benefits of their belonging to it. Along these lines, Rosalva Aída Hernández Castillo and Victoria J. Furio signal that corporatism not only entails 'institutional arrangements' for controlling population, but also pacts that can 'be used by those groups to develop counter-hegemonic practices and discourses' (2006, 129). As noted

The Local Impact of Political Culture   45

before, many *comuneros* functioned as *delegados*, and though most of them were affiliated to the PRI, they worked for their people.

In this context, *comuneros* increasingly fragmented; in fact, Bastos (2012) indicates that their division corresponds to those embracing 'progress', those fighting for a 'distributive justice' and those aiming for the protection of territory. Up to the present, this division has transformed; the postures of comuneros radicalised and reorganised them into two groups, as identified by Carlos:

> Historically something has been managed in the community that is the division. There are two currents inside. Previously *señores* [*comuneros*] mentioned that there were three currents within the *Asamblea de Comuneros*; now there are only two currents left. And those two currents are like the most conservative, the most everything; and the other is like the most open to the population.

This fragmentation also polarised with the pressure of the state to transform communal land into *ejido* (Martínez Moreno 2012). More precisely, I have noticed that all of them embrace the ideas of 'progress', 'modernisation' and 'development', but some are co-opted by the authorities and backed by a large number of institutions willing to welcome capital while expanding neoliberal governance.[20] Others maintain a 'traditional' autonomous posture combining the care of territory and an openness to integrate the rest of the community. Besides, despite the fact that some *comuneros* separate politics from the care of the community, the arrival and intervention of different political forces, in most cases, has affected their organisation by prompting them to follow another system and way of doing politics (Martínez Moreno 2008). In parallel, exclusion and racism are promoted and inhabitants are put into confrontation. Thus, on the one hand, affiliation to political parties has allowed some to work together; on the other hand, it has divided and weakened them and prevented them from fulfilling communal projects. In the words of Don Indalecio: 'some [say] "No, now we're going to work well" and then that cunt doesn't want to help because it's from the other party'. In this scenario, the *Asamblea* needs extra support to do the job in the community; thus, a group of young inhabitants engaged in the opening of spaces, such as assemblies, allowing up to 500 inhabitants to be integrated and consulted. However, even if they did not have voice and vote, 'people felt that the traditional authority at last recognised them as part of themselves', as Rocío, a leading young fighter, explains. This action empowered the community and gave force to *comuneros*, as described in Chapter 4.

In parallel, *jueces de barrio* as Carlos observes—'the true traditional government that existed',—were co-opted by the government with the support of the *invasor* of the hill *El Pandillo*,[21] transforming their character in the community. He narrates:

> Romo was in the government and he gave them a paper where it delivered and told them 'The Municipal Government of Poncitlán believes that such

46   *The Local Impact of Political Culture*

> person and such person is the *juez de barrio*' and already, they gave them like the.... Not as before, moral value that people said 'I chose him to represent myself and I'll support him'. But now the *Municipio* came and named a *juez de barrio* because he had influences or because he had ideas with a party.

José Luis also blames co-opted *comuneros* for losing this traditional figure:

> When this situation of carelessness comes to the community, even the same *señores* came to say, the *comuneros* 'no, that belongs to the city council' or they gave powers to the council about things that belonged to them in exchange of some money.

Moreover, the Municipal government, together with external subjects, profited from the division to manage the community and obtain benefits, such as power and land. Capitalists decompose social struggles by 'extending social surveillance' and instructing them (Kinsman 2006), and thus, *caciques* manipulate and even mediate through different kinds of rationales (Knight 2005). In this case, their political division has been based, following the ideas of Knight (1991, 101), on 'modernisers', those who allied with the ideals of the government, and 'traditionalists', those who opposed them. Therefore, regardless of the efforts of some *comuneros* and young supporters, 14 of them have been co-opted (Martínez Moreno 2012). Considering that an objective of neoliberal governance is to weaken resistance, the division of the population is boosted, in this case, through the opposition between 'traditionalists' and 'progressives'. In this regard, nowadays as this division persists some Mezcalenses have permitted the involvement of the government and the *invasor* in communal decisions (e.g. elections, trials, projects, use of land, etc.). Pedro explains:

> There is a group that says no to outsiders or that we must remove the man who invaded *El Pandillo* and the other group, the other position is defending their personal economic interests, that he stays or be silent or ignore things, not to follow the *Asamblea de Comuneros*, because there are personal interests from economic support, from influences, we see with the government, with lawyers, with judges, a lot of corruption as well.

In order to secure their interests, this faction of *comuneros*—together with the *invasor* and governmental institutions and authorities—have carried out some inherited practices of our political culture, such as fraud, *acarreo*,[22] vote buying and manipulation in the internal elections of 2008, 2011 and 2014.[23] In the elections of 2008, they allowed the triumph of Quintín Claro and the co-opted faction of *comuneros*. Fraud was committed due to the intervention of the Municipal government of Poncitlán, *Secretaría de Cultura Jalisco (SCJ)*, *Instituto Nacional de Antropología e Historia (INAH)* and *Procuraduría Agraria* allied with the *invasor*.[24] As this victory represented not only internal fragmentation

The Local Impact of Political Culture 47

and weakness but also an obstacle for legal procedures, the *Asamblea de Comuneros* sought to remove the elected authorities who were not acting under communal law; their actions lacked legality and were corrupted. In March 2009, *comuneros* disavowed their authorities and appointed a new board headed by Cirilo Rojas. It was a long and complex process; in contrast to how easily authorities, the *invasor* and their allies manipulate laws.

Notwithstanding, they achieved the recognition of this new board by state and agrarian authorities. However, the overthrown board maintained its links with the *Municipio*, INAH and the *Procuraduría Agraria* acting illegally and disregarding the *Asamblea*. It was a *doble comisariado*, since as noted by José Luis, 'at the end of the day, the Agrarian [*Procuraduría Agraria*] recognises Don Cirilo in a trial, but neither does he distances itself or ends, it plays dumb in ending the trial, to decree the end of Quintin'. As a matter of fact, in October 2009, the removed authorities in complicity with the government and the *invasor* broke into the *Casa Comunal* backed by the police, probably in order to steal the trial documentation and proof of the irregularities performed (Hipólito Hernández 2012, 102). In a newspaper interview (Del Castillo 2009), an inhabitant of Mezcala signalled that:

> Not only they're selling their body and dignity, but also they want to sell the body of others and our territory, within which is the heart of our people: the Island of Mezcala. They have a name, their pimp is the president of Poncitlán, Ramón Romo, but there are also Baltazar, *delegado* of Mezcala, Quintín Claro, Pablo Claro, Marcelo González, Mario Cruz and Guillermo Rojas. Characters that don't represent the community nor defend the communal interests.

The reality of Mezcala shows how political parties get engaged in the management of *usos y costumbres*, but more importantly, how the inherited political culture transcends political parties. More precisely, elites get involved co-opting and manipulating people regardless of the electoral competition pictured by political parties; *comuneros* are embedded in a game of power of local and external interests that operate through the rationale of neoliberal governance. In this setting, in the face of the illegal and coordinated actions performed, *comuneros* and young supporters organised an encampment outside the *Casa Comunal* willing to broadcast the abuses committed and prevent further violations. In this scenario, the Municipal government of Poncitlán was accused of collusion, but the *Ministerio Público*, the state prosecutor, refused to carry out the investigation (Hipólito Hernández 2012, 102).

Later, the next Municipal President, Carlos Maldonado Guerrero (2010–12), supposedly changed his approach by moving away from the *invasor*, ending the relationship with the INAH and SCJ and proposing several projects with the *Asamblea de Comuneros* (Bastos 2011, 2012, 2013). However, the truth is that corrupt, illegal and violent strategies persisted while the attempts to discredit the board of Cirilo and its supporters became more and more evident. These actions

48   *The Local Impact of Political Culture*

demonstrated how economic elites act together with the government according to their interests—and alongside those of the institutional network of power—as remarked upon by Carlos, 'that is, in a few words, the entrepreneur handles the city council and the city council came and manipulated [here]'. Accordingly, in 2011, the *Procuraduría Agraria* accepted the proposal of new elections launched by Quintín, ignoring its lack of legal standing and that they were due to take place before the end of the three-year administration of Cirilo. The *Asamblea* agreed to perform these elections in order to finish the argument, and they did not expect that fraud would go further. Don Chava explains:

> No, they were not normal, because the woman who came, the commissioner who came, was a *licenciada*, and no, it wasn't right … with legal basis, right? Because she managed the election, because it was done with the majority, but since she saw that the thing was wrong … we noticed that that *licenciada* came like in agreement with the man of *El Pandillo.*

In fact, vote buying and *acarreo* again took place supported by the *invasor* and with the help of the representatives of the *Procuraduría Agraria* (Bastos 2012, 237–8, 2013, 116–17), who supposedly came as neutral observers in order to grant legal effect to elections, as acknowledged by *comuneros*. Elections began late, and the representatives of the *Procuraduría Agraria* favoured co-opted *comuneros*, interfered in selecting the debate board, instructed the *Asamblea de comuneros* and ordered the repetition of elections arguing fraud. In this context, Itza, a young woman ex-secretary of the *Casa Comunal*, narrates:

> For example, in these elections it was revealed that many of them were paid by their votes. So they went for the people – because there are *comuneros* in Guadalajara who can't even walk – they go and bring them in private vehicles, they pay for their votes and just 'come and vote for the one', for whomever they [the bribers] want.

As noted before, *comuneros* are divided 'according to the man up there. Because he's buying a lot of people, with money he's buying people' (Don Chava 2012). The rumours between *comuneros* of vote buying multiplied to the extent that Don Fernando affirms that 'under the table, "there's your prize, your prize, your prize" and people who never came that day came and yes, one knows why they came'. So, from the 71 *comuneros* who participated in these elections, around 25 do not usually attend and are no longer bound to the community. Furthermore, currently, as *comuneros* are at least 70 years old, authorities and the *invasor* have taken advantage of this vulnerability securing them as their clienteles. However, this practice, in tandem with the ideas of Edgar Hernández Muñoz (2008), is not just about obtaining votes, but also the accompanying loyalties and feeling of protection that come with an often 'authoritarian' and 'paternalist' treatment. Adelo describes these co-opted subjects:

The Local Impact of Political Culture   49

These idiots, we call them there *lambiculos* [ass-kisser], that is, because they by kissing the ass to the powerful, the employee, always lower their pants and turn around and that, and with what? Says Rocío 'Motherfuckers don't know even how to steal, not even to grab five, just by patting [*sic*] their hands "this is my friend, what the fuck" '.

The benefits obtained by co-opted *comuneros* are scarce, only getting closer to power in an illusory way—as managed via the seductions of neoliberal governance; authorities abuse and discriminate while managing to dismiss *comuneros*. Thus, in these elections, Ambrocio Claro Paredes became the new *Presidente de Bienes Comunales* (2011–14) by only one vote. The winning board celebrated with the authorities while the rest of the *comuneros* worried about their land. The formula 'divide and rule' triumphed due to a scenario of poverty and uprooting. But, this second time, *comuneros* decided not to waste time and effort trying to remove the new 'elected' authorities, as it represented an obstacle to continue with the trial against the *invasor*. As explained by Don Fausto, a *comunero* who was previously Secretary of the *Asamblea*, 'on the one hand, it could, therefore, have been annulled it; on the other hand, it seemed it didn't suit us to lose due to the problem of the trial, so it could continue'. They believed that it does not matter who the representative is, since he must follow the decisions of the *Asamblea*. Later, they regretted it when the new president dumped the paperwork of the *Casa Comunal*, since he had already signed agreements with the *invasor*. As with the board headed by Quintín, assemblies were irregularly held, revealing the lack of commitment and the delaying and exclusionary tactics.

Inhabitants know that without the intervention of the *Procuraduría Agraria*, the results would have been different. The problem is not the division between *comuneros*, since it has always been present, but the external intrusion that reinforces the inherited political culture to serve the functioning of neoliberal governance. Although *comuneros* carried out several actions to confront this situation and managed to remove the representative of this institution, they regret not having objected and having been negligent. Besides, from that moment on other representatives have attended to all assemblies to monitor the proceedings. The *Procuraduría Agraria* is just a reflection of how the institutional structure of Mexico works, supporting informal power and performing a set of corrupted practices. In agreement with the observations of Bastos (2012, 247–8), authorities 'actively' or 'passively' support invaders, setting the legislation or allowing and encouraging the biased manipulation of laws, since the government is, in fact, interested in twisting the rule of law to favour investment and continue to politically and socially differentiate the population. Moreover, in Mexico institutions are neither representative of the interests and concerns of society nor protective of citizens and the bad behaviour of governors; rather, they interfere in the decision-making process to support economic and political elites. As signalled by Doña Guille, a migrant of the late 1970s who has recently been spending more and more time in the community:

50   *The Local Impact of Political Culture*

> In fact when we went to the *Agraria* so the *Agraria* backed us up, we thought we had the *Agraria* on our side.... But neither. That day we returned angry too; ... there it was made known that it's on their side.

The Municipal government and the *invasor* do not care about buying off authorities embedded in agrarian legal issues, and neither does it bother them to destroy documents; they are committed to privatising land in Mezcala while hardening economic, social and cultural differences backing neoliberal governance. Yet, right up to the present time, many inhabitants of Mezcala perceive *comuneros* as an authority, as individuals of great knowledge performing an important role, as Adelo exemplifies:

> It seems to me ... one of most dignified things, right? Fighting for, first, to preserve our status as an indigenous community, and then, of the history of Mezcala, right? And supporting, re-making it known for our children, right?

In this regard, Martínez Moreno (2012) signals that *comuneros* are recognised as such since they work for the people and continue to safeguard their territory without any payment and without complying with the state. Therefore, in spite of this scenario of corruption, a faction of *comuneros* persist in their fight, and although elections were continually postponed, in September 2014 they managed to establish a new board away from the interests of the *invasor* headed by Santiago Gonzáles Claro. They are carrying out several actions to confront the intrusion of external subjects, but more importantly, to deal with the inherited political culture that is ingrained in them, hoping to challenge the social and economic hierarchies that subjugate them to a life of misery, discrimination and dispossession. This is presented in the following chapters.

Conclusion

To sum up, the creation of the PRI represented the overall national experience, and meant, in the local instance, the reorganisation of politics. In Mezcala, two new political figures were implemented: *delegados* and *comuneros*. On the one hand, the former represented the 'official' authority, being elected through the *dedazo* and manipulated by the *Municipio*. Even though years have passed, *delegados* keep being appointed, have an exclusive intermediary role, lack power and have a strong relationship with the ruling party or the local/regional elite. More precisely, the *municipio* continues to be managed by the same *cacique* family, but has adapted to the new political pluralism by the use of diverse labels and different features. Moreover, in such a scenario, there is supposedly no such thing as ideologies and a disconnected political society; their links and role have been renewed, in the same way that informal power has been renovated in the new democratic era. In fact, in the context of a simulated democracy, authoritarianism and exclusion of citizen participation persist but now, it is harder to identify who is responsible. Besides, clientelism, fraud, corruption and

The Local Impact of Political Culture 51

corporatism are the base of the Mexican political system, which has allowed the prolongation of the *priísta* values, practices, methods and structure both institutionally and culturally. The discourse that portrays these habits as something from the past is thus challenged, showing the real face of democracy where social structures and distinctions are maintained.

On the other hand, considering that well-meaning individuals can become entangled in this setting, *comuneros*, recognised as the 'traditional' authority, do not escape this pattern of the Mexican political culture that creates barriers and challenges to reaching their objective: land conservation. However, since the beginning their creation was intended to respond to the dynamics and structure of the political system and to establish clienteles and institutional networks while reinforcing informal power. As a result the authenticity of the 'traditional' authority in Mezcala might be in question while the organisation of *comuneros* is increasingly deteriorating and facing a crisis of representation due to this inherited political culture, the inappropriate institutions and their reduction in number. Given this operational logic, not only political causes—such as authoritarianism and corruption—constitute the reasons why *comuneros* are losing power; cultural and economic sources, as analysed in the coming chapters, also play an important part. Besides, the population has increased and the ways of relating with the population have meant that inhabitants no longer feel represented by *comuneros*; Rocío describes:

> So, really, at that time it was a representation of the community, that is, they were mostly heads of family, and they represented a family. So they were the representation of the people. The problem now is that there is no strong representation, and it has ... detached itself, I believe, to a certain extent from settlers.

This situation is especially true for a sector of migrants and young people who ignore their role, and perceive them as obsolete, as enemies of 'progress' and even as *caciques*—as further narrated. *Comuneros* had the predisposition to serve the institutional networks of power, so it is no surprise that within neoliberal governance they experience a process of deterioration that is expressly driven by external subjects, political parties and institutions. In effect, the *Municipio* aims to weaken and end their organisation, and a first step is to stop assemblies from being held and to establish the *delegado* as the new authority. In addition, their age and illiteracy might exacerbate this process as possibly they might miss assemblies, find it difficult to understand or hear them or be hindered from performing legal actions. Here, it is important to mention that in 2012 there were only 137 *comuneros* alive, of whom 43 were migrants (Martínez Moreno 2012), and this number has further decreased. Most *comuneros* have died, and the rest are elderly, so, usually in assemblies no more than 50 *comuneros* meet mainly due to their age, health and location. In fact, the majority who regularly meet, that is, 20 to 30 *comuneros*, are those who keep protecting their territory and who have prevented others from performing illegal acts.

52   *The Local Impact of Political Culture*

Thus, despite the involvement of *comuneros* in the inherited political culture, their crisis of representation and the questioning of them as a traditional authority, without them Mezcala would be unprotected, become a no man's land, and as a consequence, their identity, culture and knowledge would also be at risk. Informal politics has been successful in fragmenting the community, but not at obstructing their mobilisation to defend their land. As underlined by Martínez Moreno (2012), the division of *comuneros* has not succeeded in the goal of the loss of land and, in fact, this is what keeps the community moving to protect their territory. *Comuneros* have preserved traditions, *usos y costumbres* and the territory, and, as José Luis argues, 'still are—whether the community wants it or not, people come with very modernist ideas and see them as obsolete; however, they remain key to the matter of community'.

Yet, inhabitants increasingly feel excluded and deceived, since the inherited political culture and its practices embedded in their form of government have served the workings of neoliberal governance, sustaining structures of power. They do not affect elections and politics exclusively, but expand to and comprise economic, social and cultural daily life experiences. From the national to the local there is an inherited political culture reproduced in relations, subjects, institutions and policies that perpetuate the same colonialist—and capitalist, as explored in the next chapter—dynamic and economic, social and cultural differences, which are propagated these days via the rhetoric of diversity and multiculturalism under neoliberal governance models and policies. And as will be examined more deeply in Chapters 4 and 5, it is even impressed into the language and representations, exacerbating exclusion, discrimination and racism.

Notwithstanding, their main task is 'to strengthen the organisation' (Rocío 2012), and the renovation of the census is seen as urgent and paramount to reinforce their *usos y costumbres.* They seem to be seeking to reconfigure their *usos y costumbres* as a true and authentic mechanism to overturn the effects of the inherited political culture, and rise up against local elites, diminish internal conflict and extend the inclusion and union of Mezcalenses, while confronting ultimately the current capitalist and colonialist dynamics. What is more, they are trying to make their voices heard, and improve the living conditions in the village, through an internal change from below. So, even if we might embody and be accomplices of such forms of domination, Mezcala demonstrates how negotiation spaces can be opened that influence the workings of the geographies of power. Both youth and migrants, as traced in the following chapters, in diverse forms, organise to deal with local, national and international processes damaging their government, livelihood, organisation, conditions, land possession and/or identity.

Notes

1 *Usos y costumbres* in the village, according to the Estatuto Comunal (2009), include the organisation of the 'traditional government' (*Asamblea General de Comuneros, Comisariado de Bienes Comunales, Consejo de Vigilancia, Jueces de Barrio, Delegado Municipal, Consejo de Primeros Comuneros, Comisión de Seguridad Comunal,*

The Local Impact of Political Culture 53

Capitanía de Puerto de la Comunidad de Mezcala, Comisión de Transparencia y Presentación), the management of land and commerce and the celebration of *fiestas*.

2 According to S. N. Eisenstadt and Luis Roniger (1981), patron-client relationships are 'patterns of interaction and exchange' that are characterised by their diffusion, unconditionality, solidarity, informality, voluntarity, verticality and inequality, and that therefore create contradictions within the functioning of power, coercion and obligation.

3 This political figure is supported by two *sub-delegados* or *agencias municipales* from the *barrios* of *La Cuesta* and *Ojo de Agua*.

4 In the words of Knight (2005), *caciques* are 'link-men' mediating between the upper and lower parts of society; but contrary to what he reveals, they are not exclusively those subjects with *puestos*, as, although they are usually institutionalised, they are also embedded in non-institutionalised procedures. Still, as Selee (2011) observes, these intermediaries maintain the functioning and life of the state at the same time that they 'deliver services, enforce the rule of law and respond to citizen demands'.

5 This means, the appointment of a successor by the president or other political authority.

6 Gavin O'Toole defines *camarillas* as the 'informal elite networks linked by personal loyalties'; these are 'subterranean' and allow 'politicians and public servants' to secure a good position by 'remaining loyal to a leading individual' while competition is taking place outside 'the public eye' (2010, 52).

7 This social relationship is based on the Catholic provision that *padrinos* are required to take care and protect *ahijados*. It is used, in fact, by political elites to obtain a diverse range of services, from financial, political, legal to personal (Nieto 2011).

8 In 2015, one Mexican peso equalled approximately US$0.06.

9 Webpage of Dulces Montes: www.montes.com.mx [accessed May 2013], and Milenio (2010).

10 Peña Nieto follows a hereditary process since he comes from a PRI family ruling in Estado de México while he is also *compadre* of Carlos Salinas de Gortari; this means, related to one another by, in this case, a Catholic link.

11 I take this concept from a conversation with Dr Jorge Alonso, who used the term referring to the normalisation of corruption, that is, to point out how corruption has become something natural, habitual and ordinary for Mexican citizens. Furthermore, corruption has expanded over our institutions and governors preventing citizens from finding political representation, while those ruling have been doing so through despotic practices and without solving the problems affecting society.

12 *Ejidos* are redistributed land with a legal personality to use them as a 'communal farm', but with the possibility of working them individually. Meanwhile agrarian communities entail the recognition of land possession since time immemorial and have a different form of organisation and government (Mackinlay and Otero 2006). None of them, due to the collective ownership of the land, could be negotiated and did not work as guarantee to acquire funding (López 2007, 31), though nowadays it is possible to sell land in *ejidos*.

13 *Memorandum de la Solicitud de confirmación de Bienes Comunales al Jefe del Departamento Agrario;* written by Félix Aquino Rojas and Simón Moreno Cruz, representatives of Mezcala; August 1, 1958.

14 *Acta de Elección de los Representantes Censales de los vecinos de la comunidad de Mezcala, municipio de Poncitlán, Estado de Jalisco*; signed by Esteban Rubio Jimenez, *Representante del Departamento de Asuntos Agrarios y de Colonización*, Donociano Jacobo Pérez, *Representante Comunal*, Malaquías Rosales G., *Secretario de la Comunidad* and Genaro de los Santos Paredes, *Delegado Municipal*; August 2, 1959.

15 *Petición de los vecinos de la comunidad indígena Mezcala;* written by Florentino Ramos Ruíz, Raymundo Ramos, Rosendo Ramos, Juan Sánchez, Esteban Baltazar R.,

54   *The Local Impact of Political Culture*

Atacio Pérez, Dario Moreno, Manuel Contreras Ramos, J. Jesús Baltazar and Eleuterio Ramos; June 12, 1956.

16 *Acta de Clausura de los trabajos censales verificado en la comunidad Mezcala, municipio de Poncitlán, Estado de Jalisco*; signed by Esteban Rubio Jimenez, *Representante del Departamento de Asuntos Agrarios y de Colonización*, Francisco González Baltazar and Concepción Santana de los Santos, *Representantes Censales de la Comunidad*, and Genaro de los Santos Paredes, *Representante Censal de la Autoridad Municipal*; August 4, 1959.

17 The documents state 408 *comuneros*, but there is a mistake as two names are repeated; this is the reason why Mezcalenses usually identify 406 rather than 408.

18 Before the agrarian regulation women in the community could vote freely, but usually, as noted by Gabriela Torres-Mazuera (2009), in Mexico women were excluded as *comuneras* since the agrarian law associated land possession with men. In this context, in Mezcala these *comuneras* had a limited participation in the activities of the *Casa Comunal* (Martínez Moreno 2012, 143).

19 This document proclaims Mezcala as social property, that is, imprescriptible, indefeasible and unalienable land for the exclusive use of the community.

20 From now on, I distinguish between co-opted *comuneros* and *comuneros*, those who have not been co-opted and continue to protect their land. However, *comuneros* can also refer to both, to 'all' *comuneros*. I have tried to be as clear as possible, but the reader must pay attention to avoid confusion.

21 I use *invasor* in order to respect the expression of respondents, and to emphasise how this figure is commonly known within the community.

22 This means that *comuneros* who had been absent for many years, living in the Metropolitan Area of Guadalajara, participated due to bribes and transportation given by the *invasor*. Bastos (2013) identifies that *comuneros* living in the United States also participated in this dynamic.

23 In the elections of September 2014, vote buying and *acarreo* of people from Tijuana took place; but it is not my intention to look deeper into this event as it happened outside the timeframe of this research.

24 All these governmental institutions had some interests at stake in the community with the promotion of tourism development and the celebration of the *Bicentenario* (Bicentennial Anniversary of the Mexican Independence), as analysed in Chapter 4.

References

Ai Camp, Roderic. 2000. *La Política en México*. 4th edn. Mexico City: Siglo XXI.

Anders, Gerhard, and Monique Nuijten. 2007. "Corruption and the Secret of Law: An Introduction". In *Corruption and the Secret of Law. A Legal Anthropological Perspective*, edited by Monique Nuijten and Gerhard Anders, 1–25. Hampshire: Ashgate Publishing Limited.

Andolina, Robert, Sarah Radcliffe, and Nina Laurie. 2005. "Gobernabilidad e identidad: indigeneidades transnacionales en Bolivia". In *Pueblos indígenas, Estado y democracia*, edited by Pablo Dávalos, 133–70. Buenos Aires: CLACSO.

Anguiano, Arturo. 2008. "México: contradicciones e incertidumbres de un proceso democrático trunco". In *La globalización y el Consenso de Washington*, edited by Gladys Lechini, 61–74. Buenos Aires: CLACSO.

Bastos, Santiago. 2011. "La nueva defensa de Mezcala: un proceso de recomunalización a través de la renovación étnica". *Relaciones* 32 (125): 86–122.

Bastos, Santiago. 2012. "Mezcala: despojo territorial y rearticulación indígena en la Ribera de Chapala". In *Jalisco hoy: miradas antropológicas*, edited by Renée De la

The Local Impact of Political Culture   55

Torre and Santiago Bastos, 223–56. Guadalajara, Mexico: Centro de Investigaciones y Estudios Superiores en Antropología Social – Unidad Occidente.

Bastos, Santiago. 2013. "La micropolítica del despojo: Mezcala de la Asunción en la globalización neoliberal". *Revista de Estudios e Pesquisas sobre as Américas* 7 (2): 105–34.

Bello, Walden. 2008. "La crisis global de la legitimidad de la democracia liberal". In *La globalización y el Consenso de Washington*, edited by Gladys Lechini, 139–52. Buenos Aires: CLACSO.

de Vries, Pieter. 2007. "The Orchestration of Corruption and the Excess Enjoyment in Western Mexico". In *Corruption and the Secret of Law: A Legal Anthropological Perspective*, edited by Monique Nuijten and Gerhard Anders, 143–63. Hampshire: Ashgate Publishing Limited.

Del Castillo, Agustín. 2009. "Cocas de Mezcala denuncian al gobierno de Poncitlán". *Milenio*, October 23.

Durán Matute, Inés. 2015. "Mezcala: construyendo autonomía. Balance de retos y propuestas frente al neoliberalismo". *Journal of Iberian and Latin American Research* 21 (1): 1–18.

Eisenstadt, Samuel N., and Luis Roniger. 1981. "The Study of Patron-Client Relations and Recent Developments in Sociological Theory". In *Political Clientelism, Patronage and Development*, edited by Samuel N. Eisenstadt and René Lemarchand, 271–95. Beverly Hills, CA: SAGE Publications.

Fox, Jonathan. 1994. "The Difficult Transition from Clientelism to Citizenship: Lessons from Mexico". *World Politics* 46 (2): 151–84.

González, Francisco E. 2008. *Dual Transitions from Authoritarian Rule. Institutionalized Regimes in Chile and Mexico, 1970–2000*. Baltimore, MD: The Johns Hopkins University Press.

Haber, Stephen, Herbert S. Klein, Noel Maurer, and Kevin J. Middlebrook. 2008. *Mexico since 1980, The World since 1980*. New York: Cambridge University Press.

Hernández Castillo, Rosalva Aída, and Victoria J. Furio. 2006. "The Indigenous Movement in Mexico: Between Electoral Politics and Local Resistance". *Latin American Perspectives* 33 (2): 115–31.

Hernández García, Adriana. 2006. "Mezcala: encuentros y desencuentros de una comunidad". *Espiral, Estudios sobre Estado y Sociedad* 12 (36): 97–128.

Hernández, María Aidé. 2008. "La democracia mexicana, presa de una cultura política con rasgos autoritarios". *Revista Mexicana de Sociología* 70 (2): 261–303.

Hernández Muñoz, Edgar. 2008. *Los usos políticos de la pobreza*. Toluca, Mexico: Colegio Mexiquense.

Hilgers, Tina. 2011. "Clientelism and Conceptual Stretching: Differentiating among Concepts and among Analytical Levels". *Theory and Society* 40 (5): 567–88.

Hipólito Hernández, Adrián Guillermo. 2012. "Mezcala: La lucha por la defensa del Cerro del Pandillo. Historia reciente de una resistencia contra el despojo". B.A. diss., Departamento de Historia, Universidad de Guadalajara.

Holloway, John. 2010. *Cambiar el mundo sin tomar el poder*. Mexico City: Sísifo Ediciones; Bajo Tierra Ediciones; Benemérita Universidad Autónoma de Puebla.

Kinsman, Gary. 2006. "Mapping Social Relations of Struggle: Activism, Ethnography, Social Organization". In *Sociology for Changing the World: Social Movements/Social Research*, edited by Caelie Frampton, Gary Kinsman, A. K. Thompson and Kate Tilleczek, 133–56. Halifax, Canada: Fernwood Publishing.

Knight, Alan. 1990. "Racism, Revolution, and Indigenismo: Mexico, 1910–1940". In *The Idea of Race in Latin America, 1870–1940*, edited by Richard Graham, 71–113. Austin, TX: University of Texas Press.

56 *The Local Impact of Political Culture*

Knight, Alan. 2005. "*Caciquismo* in Twentieth-Century Mexico". In *Caciquismo in the Twentieth-Century Mexico*, edited by Alan Knight and Wil Pansters, 1–48. London: Institute for the Study of the Americas.

Lewis, Vek. 2012. "Forging 'Moral Geographies': Law, Sexual Minorities and Internal Tensions in Northern Mexico Border Towns". In *Transgender Migrations*, edited by Trystan Cotten, 32–56. New York: Routledge.

López, Ann Aurelia. 2007. *The Farmworkers' Journey*. Berkeley, CA: University of California Press.

Mackinlay, Horacio, and Gerardo Otero. 2006. "Corporativismo estatal y organizaciones campesinas: hacia nuevos arreglos institucionales". In *México en transición: globalismo neoliberal, Estado y sociedad civil*, edited by Gerardo Otero, 135–53. Zacatecas, Mexico: H. Cámara de Diputados LIX Legislatura; Simon Fraser University; Universidad Autónoma de Zacatecas; Miguel Ángel Porrúa.

Martínez Moreno, Rocío. 2008. "La comunidad indígena coca de Mezcala, el sujeto de la historia en la defensa de la tierra". B.A. diss., Departamento de Historia, Universidad de Guadalajara.

Martínez Moreno, Rocío. 2012. "Tierra, historia y pueblo. Memoria y acción política en la comunidad indígena de Mezcala, Jalisco". Master diss., División de Estudios Históricos y Humanos, Universidad de Guadalajara.

Milenio. 2010. "Grupo Montes elaborará dulces para diábeticos". *El Informador*, September 6. www.informador.com.mx/jalisco/2010/231333/6/grupo-montes-elaborara-dulces-para-diabeticos.htm [accessed 17 May, 2013].

Morton, Adam David. 2012. "Stubbornness and Blindness: Understanding Mexico's Neoliberal 'Transition'". *NACLA Report on the Americas* 45 (4): 28–33.

Nieto, Nubia. 2011. "La socialización de las élites políticas mexicanas a través de la corrupción". *Análisis Político* 24 (71): no page numbers.

Núñez Noriega, Guillermo. 2006. "Los estudios de las masculinidades y la cultura política en México". In *Debates sobre masculinidades: poder, desarrollo, políticas públicas y ciudadanía*, edited by Gloria Careaga and Salvador Cruz Sierra, 377–91. Mexico City: Universidad Nacional Autónoma de México, Programa Universitario de Estudios de Género.

O'Donnell, Guillermo. 1994. "Delegative Democracy". *Journal of Democracy* 5 (1): 55–69.

O'Toole, Gavin. 2010. *The Reinvention of Mexico: National Ideology in a Neoliberal Era*. Liverpool: Liverpool University Press.

Olvera, Alberto J. 2010. "The Elusive Democracy. Political Parties, Democratic Institutions, and Civil Society in Mexico". *Latin American Research Review* 45 (Special Issue): 78–107.

Pansters, Wil. 2005. "Goodbye to the Caciques? Definition, the State and the Dynamics of *Caciquismo* in Twentieth-Century Mexico". In *Caciquismo in Twentieth-Century Mexico*, edited by Alan Knight and Wil Pansters, 349–76. London: Institute for the Study of the Americas.

Purcell, Susan Kaufman. 1981. "Mexico: Clientelism, Corporatism and Political Stability". In *Political Clientelism, Patronage and Development*, edited by Samuel N. Eisenstadt and René Lemarchand, 191–216. Beverly Hills, CA: SAGE.

Selee, Andrew. 2011. *Decentralization, Democratization, and Informal Power in Mexico*. Pennsylvania: The Pennsylvania State University Press.

Starr, Pamela K. 2010. 'The Two "Politics of NAFTA' in Mexico". *Law and Business Review of the Americas* 16 (4): 839–53.

Tamayo, Jaime, and Alejandra Vizcarra. 2000. *Jalisco: sociedad, economía, política y cultura*. Mexico City: Universidad Nacional Autónoma de México.

Torres-Mazuera, Gabriela. 2009. "La territorialidad rural mexicana en un contexto de descentralización y competencia electoral". *Revista Mexicana de Sociología* 71 (3): 453–90.

Warman, Arturo. 2003. *Los indios mexicanos en el umbral del milenio*. Mexico City: Fondo de Cultura Económica.

Zárate Hernández, José Eduardo. 2005. "Caciques and Leaders in the Era of Democracy". In *Caciquismo in Twentieth-Century Mexico*, edited by Alan Knight and Wil Pansters, 272–95. London: Institute for the Study of the Americas.

2 The Local Workings of a Global Political Economy

The privileged location of Mezcala allowed its inhabitants to live off the land and lake without really worrying about the lack of employment. For centuries, agriculture and fishing were the main survival and economic activities in the village; inhabitants grew corn and beans to survive all year round, while sowing other vegetables (cucumbers, tomatoes, green tomatoes, green beans, zucchinis, chickpeas and squash) and fruits (plums, mangoes, coffee, *zapote*, among others) helped in their sustenance. Besides, fishing of species such as *charales, mojarras* and *bagres* provided another form of living while the hill supplied the firewood to cook and a space to keep cattle. Even though Mezcalenses mainly used these activities for self-consumption, trade—either internally, or with neighbouring villages and Guadalajara—also played an important role in the community. Nonetheless, this situation changed partly due to the opening of the road in the 1950s that positioned migration as a fervent possibility.

Amazed by the unknown and the opportunities provided, Don Chava, Don Jacinto, Don Ramiro, Don Salvador, Don Fausto and Don Indalecio, were some of the *comuneros* who first experimented with migration through the Bracero programme (1942–64). They travelled with the hope of, as expressed by Don Fausto, 'making a fortune, supposedly … because here there was no chance, there was no work'. After that, a continuous flow was instituted, and in fact, as women transformed their role as workers, migration to the northern frontier and California was established as a common survival strategy for them too. For instance, in 1968 two sisters, Doña Vicenta and Doña Ino, migrated first to Tijuana and eight months later to Los Angeles. Doña Ino recounts:

> Well, at first we came because, you heard [people] saying that in Tijuana there was an opportunity to work. And, as in the *rancho* there was nothing just work on the fields … we used to help my dad in the fields, but work ended and there was no work. So then, it was hard because we went to school, but at school they demanded a pencil, notebook, even dresses for dancing, uniform when an event was coming … and my dad didn't have to buy us uniforms, and we said 'Oh! The situation is very hard'. My father twice got sick and didn't work…. But that was what made us come, the

poverty in which we grew up, and to see that my sisters, the youngest, were also going to suffer the same thing that we suffered.

Doña Vicenta usually worked as nanny or cleaner, while her sister was a nursing assistant. By the late 1970s, all their family was able to cross and joined them in this new life. Nowadays Vicenta spends half of the year in Mezcala selling candies to the kids outside her house near the *malecón*. Meanwhile, Doña Ino still lives and works in Los Angeles, awaiting her retirement to renovate a house that her parents bequeathed her and live half of the time in Mezcala. Like Doña Vicenta and Doña Ino, there are many Mezcalenses who have moved, either to Guadalajara, Tijuana or the United States. And while for many the reason to migrate is to experiment, to know, to adventure, most of them signal a context of neediness, of lack of employment, opportunities and money, and of a devastated economy.

As illustrated in this chapter, little by little, the role of land as provider declined as a result of the nation's socioeconomic processes, especially due to the broader tendencies of urbanisation and industrialisation. In this sense, we must recognise that the roots of migration do not lie exclusively in individual conditions or domestic factors such as unemployment, marginalisation, poverty and lack of progress. Rather, following the extended analyses of Portes and Walton (1981) and Saskia Sassen (1988), migration is a series of flows, induced mainly by economic forces, of certain sectors in nations connected by an international system. So here I link the micro and macro, and engage in a broader framework to understand the complexities, connections, inconsistencies and varieties of labour processes through policies, networks, practices and rhetorics, as lived by Mezcalenses within the context of neoliberal governance. By focusing on the workings of the political economy in this era, I aim to enhance our panorama of a local–global construction of unequal economic, political, social and cultural structures. The idea is to highlight the specificities and diversities of experiences, while building a common understanding of the effects of neoliberalism on the configuration of lives and spaces. For this, I make use of the concept of social capital, on the one hand, to provide insights and reflections on the continuous use of mechanisms of distinctions and the reproduction of hierarchies to understand the workings, networks and tactics of neoliberal governance; on the other hand, to bring into view the creation of support networks used as a survival strategy in the context of the unequalising consequences of capitalism.

In order to elaborate on this interconnection, first I present a brief historical context of the local setting and conditions, framed in a broader framework of political and economic changes that have fostered a readjustment of Mezcalenses' labour and social dynamics since the 1950s. Then I introduce the adaptation to the neoliberal model and its implications for the region and the community to illustrate how stratifications and a system of oppression are perpetuated via labour dynamics. Third, I move to tackle Mezcalenses' experiences in relation to agriculture, fishing, industries, migration and labour in the U.S.

60   *The Local Workings of a Global Political Economy*

These five subsections are intertwined to deeply comprehend the transformations and living conditions in the village; that is, how people organise their lives, practices and relationships in an era of neoliberal governance. Here I evidence how people passively and actively participate in these processes, but also I begin to outline how people aim to unite and defend themselves. In this sense, the aim of this chapter is to grasp how political economy is intimately intertwined in people's lives, assisting the functioning of a system based on inequalities, racism and exclusion and sustained by a rhetoric of 'development' and 'progress'. This will further help us in understanding the historical memory of Mezcalenses, which shows a continued awareness of being excluded, and in discerning the alternative projects and routes being constructed.

Looking for Work: A Longstanding Transnational Process

Although the change in the labour and social dynamics lived in the community could be traced to the colonial era, I take as a starting point the impact of the Green Revolution (1950s)[1] and the implementation of the Bracero programme (1942–64), since on the one hand, the introduction of agrochemicals in Mezcala made land infertile and agriculture no longer cost-effective (Hernández García 2006, 117). On the other hand, migration towards the United States in search of a new livelihood began to be promoted. In general, as documented by Ann Aurelia López (2007), this transformation into commercial farming provoked some negative effects, such as deprivation, privatisation and erosion of land, and exploitation, exclusion and migration of peasants. In view of that, in Mezcala agriculture transformed into an almost exclusive practice for those possessing land on the shore and on the islands, as cultivation was easier and cheaper. Moreover, at this time inhabitants opened a road to facilitate the conveyance and exchange of products to Poncitlán, Chapala, Ajijic and Guadalajara. This road offered new ways of earning a living; first, it allowed a large number of inhabitants looking for better salaries to work in Jamay and then, in the Metropolitan Zone of Guadalajara, especially in industries. As the young supporter, José Luis, explains:

> They arrived when the trail was opened below, they arrived those who [said] 'let's go to crop coffee', and they took people to cut coffee. That 'we are going to harvest sugarcane' and then, people like that in a short time started to see that they were making money. They earned some money and could have certain luxuries, so, it was like the door. Then, companies started to enter.

The installation of factories around the region began in the early nineteenth century (González Corona 1989, 12), and this later facilitated the establishment of the industrial zone in the Cuenca Lerma–Chapala–Santiago[2] and the development of means of communication and transport accelerating the industrialisation and urbanisation of the area (Durán Juárez, Partida Rocha and Torres Rodríguez

The Local Workings of a Global Political Economy   61

1999). Many multinational corporations in a wide range of fields, from food-stuffs and textiles to electronic and automotive industries, established themselves in the industrial park of El Salto at the outskirts of Guadalajara. But, it's not just capital that moves within the global economy; also ideas and people (Portes and Walton 1981), provoking the displacement of more people seeking new ways of earning a living. Inhabitants found jobs in these industries, causing in some cases the resettlement of complete families, but in other cases, they reached further afield, like the northern Pacific Coast.

Though some resisted migrating, as Mezcala and the region experienced rapid changes due to such economic developments, inhabitants were pushed to migrate. According to Hernández García (2006), it was during the 1940s that the U.S. government brought Mezcalenses to the strawberry fields in California through the implementation of the Bracero programme. However, I observe that it was during the 1950s that this initiative reached its peak in the community when many Mezcalenses suffered economically from the inundation of crops, as Don Chava recalls:

> There was no work here, and there was much ambition to go there, to the United States.... And then as the government, at that time, made an agreement with the United States because they were at war and sent people from here to raise the crops in the United States.

Active recruitment helped to broadcast the opening of economic opportunities among the population, but also to make movement easier and to some extent regulate the flow (Portes and Walton 1981). It was clear that the political structure and government influenced the characteristics of the immigration flow, establishing the work of braceros as a daily and steady livelihood. Under this programme, migration was regulated for men aged between 20 and 40 from marginalised communities in Mexico to work in the fields producing fruits, vegetables and cotton, and their task was 'to clean, to thin tomatoes, to thin beets, lettuce all that' (Don Indalecio 2013). Their contracts lasted 45 days with a possibility of renewal that highly depended on workers' willingness and luck. Braceros usually experienced harsh and exploitative conditions, being cheap labour; but this scenario still contrasted with the scarce earnings in the community. Don Fausto narrates his experience, evidencing these conditions:

> To the United States, all the braceros from Mexico made them rich, the United States, because they were at war, they paid us one peso [dollar] an hour, 75 I started to win the first time ... 75 cents of a dollar. The second time was a peso, a dollar per hour.

In this vein, in tandem with the observation of Harald Bauder (2008, 323), temporary foreign labour relegated migrant labour, guaranteeing the subordination of migrants, thereby ensuring the distinction within the labour market and the reproduction of economic privileges. The U.S. government had been aware of

62   The Local Workings of a Global Political Economy

the benefits of Mexican labour since the early nineteenth century (Calavita 1994) and even had a preference towards it due to cultural similarity, past experience, the relationship with employers and the character and temporality of their migration (Chavez 2013). Besides, the Mexican government also profited from braceros and their labour, and from corruption and bribery (Fitzgerald 2009). In fact, under the contracts it withheld part of their salaries for a fund, which in the end only a few braceros enjoyed.[3]

Afterwards, although the war was over, contracts continued, but braceros suffered a distorted image and discriminatory treatment (Stephen 2008). Meanwhile, a tendency to prefer undocumented workers spread (Stephen 2007), hence, corruption, illegality and rights violations increased together with the pressures of anti-immigrant groups (Délano 2011).[4] Although border control programmes began to operate, there was also a kind of complicity or 'indifference' on the part of the U.S. government towards illegal immigration (Calavita 1994). Nonetheless, as a result the criminalisation of the Mexican–American population increased (Hernández 2008), as did the abuse directed towards Mexican migration (Calavita 1994). In effect, as the Bracero programme ended (1964), some braceros were forced to return while others simply came back due to lack of employment, the difficulties in the process or realising that 'the United States is not for everybody' (Don Salvador 2012). A few continued to profit from job offers, but, as the programme had provided the impetus for illegal migration, 'many people left incautiously and crossed ... and many crossed' (Don Fausto 2012).

The continuity of the illegal migration flow, in tandem with the ideas of Portes (2012), was to some extent ascribed to the economic needs of the receiving country that was provided with cheap labour while it was also used as a political resource by the sender country to diminish economic pressures and social instability. More precisely, illegal immigration was politically manipulated to satisfy elites and allow their abuses. In this regard, the U.S. government acted as a promoter of these flows propelling migrants' vulnerability, partial border security and migration control measures, while it neutralised the efforts of sending countries to improve migrants' living conditions (Portes and Walton 1981, 57). Therefore, migrants experienced even lower salaries and harsher conditions, plus difficulties in getting a job and travelling. Don Indalecio remembers being caught three times as he tried to cross the border when contracts ended:

> At night they grabbed us and threw us out, we were already in Tijuana there. It was two, three in the morning and to look again for the *coyote* to come here, sometimes, in a few times no, if we didn't find him, we came another day, until the *coyote* put together several [people].

Beginning in the mid-1960s, the United States reworked its policies, internationalising its economy and settling a 'transnational space' that, as discerned by Sassen (1988), endorsed the circulation of workers, capital, goods, services and information. Still, border cities were receiving deportees, but also migrants who

The Local Workings of a Global Political Economy   63

aimed to cross; as noted by M. Laura Velasco Ortiz (2002, 237), they were absorbed by the *Programa de Industrialización Fronteriza (PIF)*.[5] Just like Doña Vicenta and Doña Ino, a number of Mezcalenses landed there, mainly in Tijuana. Indeed, usually women ended up in the Metropolitan Zone of Guadalajara obtaining urban jobs, predominantly as domestic workers, but as the zone did not provide the desired remuneration, they would try their luck in the northern frontier. Many worked in the fields or in the informal sector, providing services (e.g. nannies or domestic workers) or as street vendors. Don José remembers his experience when moving with his brother to Mexicali to re-encounter his mother:

> Days after we arrived they also fixed us some carts to sell shrimp, my other brothers tacos, that is, well, it's subsistence, still many people do it.

During this time, the situation of the Mexican countryside was affected as it privileged capitalist agriculture; for instance, in Jalisco, the boost of agribusiness and cattle raising stopped staples production (Tamayo and Vizcarra 2000, 27). In the village, agricultural production (e.g. corn and bean) deteriorated; Don Rogelio remembers his reason to migrate: 'little by little, the work crisis began, and ... we planned to come here [to the U.S]'. Concurrently, the industrialisation process in El Salto was propelled, especially through a governmental campaign highlighting the benefits of the zone to attract Foreign Direct Investment (FDI) (Durán Juárez and Partida Rocha 1990). So the industrial corridor immersed the zone in an accelerated and disrupted growth and capitalist urbanisation process while the populations along Lake Chapala were excluded from participating (Hernández García 2006, 106). In fact, they experienced water contamination, environmental degradation and fish shortages, since as observed by Don Chava, 'all the sources that supply the lagoon, come from Mexico, and from everything that the Lerma River comprises ... there are discharges from all industries and all that comes arrives here at the lagoon'.

In this sense, Sassen (1988) argues that capital mobility and mobility of labour are connected; so there is a close link between FDI and migration, since traditional forms of work, gender roles and ideas are disturbed, pushing people to migrate. In effect, Mezcalenses became aware of their exclusion from the benefits of urbanisation and industrialisation, as their main economic activities were damaged while only urban and maquiladoras employments were offered as means of survival. These conditions moulded migration flows of Mezcalenses, with Tijuana used as a *trampoline* to process a permit to enter the United States or to cross with the aid of *coyotes*, as the border had a low level of security. In this respect, Don Roberto, who crossed in 1972, reveals:

> In that time a *mica*, many times even without anything. I, they lent me a *mica*, when I crossed the line they didn't ask me a thing, nor I did show it. ... [It was] very easy, you just jumped one line and that's it, it was a wire more or less of the height of the television, simple, now it's ... a huge thing

64 *The Local Workings of a Global Political Economy*

and well protected with cameras.... Many people escaped through Tijuana, ... just folded their pants, it was very easy before.

Nonetheless, within the United States, surveillance was increasing; for instance, the immigration police were constantly moving and intercepting different points in the cities where undocumented migrants gathered, such as bus stops. Thus, migrants organised their life and movements to minimise the risks. For example, Vicente explains a typical working day when living in California during the 1970s:

> At three o'clock in the morning, we were awake to prepare our lunch, at four o'clock going hastily to the road. And we arrived before dawn, because the patrol on the junctions at six, seven were already there. So we left before, we arrived, threw, slept for a while, while it was dawn and then, to work.

Migrants have their methods and techniques, following the ideas of Lynn Stephen (2008), to avoid 'being seen'; however, they do not always succeed. In fact, many were caught when working as the U.S. immigration police ambushed workplaces; Vicente continues to narrate his experience in the chilli fields:

> There we were, the *migra* arrived, so come on. Many of us were picked up, we were hurriedly cropping, many of us passed [the time] like this. They say 'don't run!', they say 'keep cutting'. Many comrades who were undocumented didn't bring them because they didn't represent fear, and I don't know, it occurred to me to pass near an officer and he asked me, no ... straight away he realised. 'Come, let's go'. They brought us to Mexicali, but that time they were about twenty-something buses.

Those who kept trying usually did not encounter problems returning to the United States. But, those who were not willing to take the risks or were not as lucky returned to Mezcala or settled permanently in the northern frontier. Many though with a foot in the community, joined the patterns of those already established moving permanently to the U.S. At that time, the perception towards Mexican migration changed, as rather than being temporary and engendering a strong sense of belonging, such migration trends demonstrated how social networks stimulated migration by furnishing it with the necessary 'social infrastructure' (Massey 2009), and lowering social and economic costs. Mezcalenses constructed social networks across the border that provided social, cultural and psychological support, helping them in the crossing and adaptation processes and in keeping in contact with those left behind. Moreover, as argued by Karin Weyland (2004), in reference to Dominican migration, transnational networks helped individuals and families gain status, subsistence and reunification while impacting on their roles, dynamics and membership. In this regard, the Bracero programme consolidated the network building process, and allowed the establishment of what Stephen (2007) names 'translocal ties'.

The Local Workings of a Global Political Economy 65

Accordingly, relatives of immigrants were prompted to reunite, especially, as labour opportunities, and the positive influence of the 'American life', were emphasised. Moreover, migration became established as a family strategy in the face of a deteriorating local economy and persistent social exclusion; as the following passage of Doña Vicenta evidences:

> We thought about going back quickly, that we would go back but since my mom and my dad left [the community], and my dad also went to work in the fields and to the harvests of strawberry, grape and all that ... so we didn't come back.

People expected a better life, organised and settled in *comunidades satélite* throughout California according to their *barrios* of origin or families, in Los Angeles (mainly on Maple Street), San Diego, Sanger, Lancaster, Fresno, Modesto and Pomona, but later spreading further. Their networks created a form of 'social capital' that gave them security from the hostilities of the outside, so as not to be vulnerable to them. For instance, migrants served as intermediaries between employers and potential workers of the community. Don Rogelio recalls:

> I knew a lady there ... Lupe, she lived there along Maple [Street]. She says 'No, stay here' and that's it. And to get a job there, I was drifting and always a *concuño* [in-law] got me a job in a company of ... it was called 'Elixer', and there we were working.

The integration of migrants into the labour market, thus, depended on their community and familial networks and resources, allowing Mezcalenses to take up jobs as domestic workers or nannies, or in the fields or industries. However, even if social capital was used to respond to labour markets, as pointed out by Bauder (2008, 319), it can create survival strategies that take advantage of possibilities and create opportunities for change; but also leads to migrants being excluded from social networks that would provide better jobs. In this regard, social capital circumscribes the 'positions' and 'possibilities' of subjects (Siisiäinen 2000) and serves to reinforce the distinctions between them. In this context, the preference towards illegal immigration continued, so those who crossed kept a degraded and subjugated position. For its part, the Mexican government engaged in the well-known 'policy of having no policy' and consequently allowed the preservation of the status quo.

Therefore, although many obtained benefits and even employment letters to regularise their status, as pointed out by Leo R. Chavez (2013), employers benefited from these networks, cutting down time and money involved in recruiting new workers, and in their training and control. Migration constitutes a way through which the structures of economic domination are expanded while also allowing the survival of certain sectors; it shows how both dominant and subjugated groups are implicated in perpetuating inequality (Portes and Walton 1981, 65). What is more,

66   *The Local Workings of a Global Political Economy*

Mezcalenses joined U.S. labour on a position marked by their skills and resources but also by inequality and ethnic hierarchies that situated them on a lower standing. In effect, the 'ethnicisation' of workers justifies low wages and subordinated positions together with discrimination practices, that creates a labour hierarchy. Therefore, the promises of huge salaries were not completely the case; Don Rogelio also demystifies: 'As they said that here the money was swept with the broom. You said, "No, well, it's going to be good there, right?" but not, not here'. In fact, their salaries were low in comparison to those of native workers, being a kind of 'subsalary' based on exploitation and exclusion (Cypher and Delgado Wise 2010).

The 'New' Neoliberal Setting

In the era of neoliberal governance this situation exacerbated, and migrants were filling jobs in agriculture, and within industries and services in the U.S. that could not be relocated, while in the village their main survival and economic activities kept deteriorating and maquiladora jobs concentrated in the Mexican Silicon Valley were employing those Mezcalenses who stayed or moved to the Metropolitan Area of Guadalajara. In effect, the apex of *El Salto* arrived in the 1980s, as a result of coordinated actions of the Mexican and the U.S. governments who sought to internationalise the economy (Tamayo and Vizcarra 2000, 29), while fostering modernisation and development. The decision to 'open' the border was made under the pressure of IFIs and designed by the governments of 'core' countries through laws and treaties (Guillén Romo 2005, 163), given the possibility of economic disturbances and in the pursuit of new ways to promote capital accumulation. But, as pointed out by Immanuel Wallerstein (2007, 61), they pressed national governments to have in power persons they find 'acceptable', to embrace 'cultural practices' and to support their international leadership. An institutional structure and arrangements were in this way set up to regulate life, spaces and minds and enmesh people deeply into capitalist and colonialist relations and discourses; that is, the establishment of neoliberal governance.

In this regard, Sarah Babb (2001) identifies that, in the case of Mexico, neoliberalism comprises three sorts of institutional isomorphisms: mimetic, coercive and normative. That means, neoliberalism was applied through imitation of a model that is thought to be better planned; by force, implemented through the conditions of IFIs and the United States; and with the help and power of technocrats[6] who reshaped institutions and organisations. The policies promoted promised to overcome the economic crisis and achieve development, but showed how neoliberal governance works, creating institutional conditions to favour capital internationally, and grant their share to national supporters; thus polarising society even more locally and globally. Consequently, the outcomes in Mexico were, as summarised by Alicia Hernández de Gante (2010), an increase on debt, the contraction of the role of the state and the privilege of big corporations, but it also resulted in the privatisation of resources, the cheapening and flexibilisation

The Local Workings of a Global Political Economy 67

of labour and the upsurge of everyday violence. Moreover, U.S. companies affected Mexican agricultural production and the conditions of peasants, pushing them to work in the industrial zone or migrate.

In the region, neoliberal policies meant, in this way, the relocation of people, the devaluation of agriculture, the deforestation and contamination of the zone and the reification of natural resources. Mezcalenses were becoming used to another life, where they form part of a society increasingly polarised territorially, economically, socially and culturally. Vicente narrates how he adapted to this new setting and set up later in the industrial zone:

> I said, I'm going to work in that company, in the Hershey just two months, but you adapted, you adapt. You keep and keep on.... And you get a routine, and you don't look for other options. You know that every eight days or every fifteen days, you have your salary. And you're hoping for your savings fund, your vacation bonus, your holidays, and when you realise they already passed ten years.

Mexico's neoliberal restructuring—marked by the inherited political culture and IFIs assistance—boosted the power and accumulation of elite groups and set up a massive migration process (Cypher and Delgado Wise, 2010). Besides, since the U.S. represented the hopes and benefits of a 'developed economy', many decided to reach the other side of the border. Migrant networks continued to provide the information and channels needed, as Doña Ino explains: 'People began to arrive around the eighties, from the mid-seventies, the eighties, from then onwards more people came. Yes, because there were already more people here, so people were already having information that there were jobs'. Labour migration has been driven by colonisation, and thus it represents a movement away from peripheral zones reacting to the needs of industrial centres; but also, it is a modern movement of populations that seeks to 'take advantage of economic opportunities distributed unequally across space' (Portes and Walton 1981, 59). In fact, the peak of migration from the village arrived during the late 1970s and the 1980s, and responded not only to the networks, but also to the contact with the outside, new labour opportunities, the relocation of capital and different perceptions and aspirations.

Nonetheless, the impacts of labour migration were many for the U.S. and Mexican economies. As discerned by Raúl Delgado-Wise (2006), there was a reduction of the costs of production, an increase in consumption levels, the support of the U.S. economy and an detriment on wages; while, it hindered the Mexican economy of its most important form of capital accumulation and fostered the depopulation of the country. Besides, the economic demands were also accompanied by a restrictive sentiment seen, for instance, with the implementation of the Immigration Reform and Control Act (IRCA).[7] In the case of Mezcala, the status of Mezcalenses was regularised, leading to two outcomes: on the one hand, many who were continually travelling now settled permanently and were joined by their families; on the other hand, this action endowed the

68   *The Local Workings of a Global Political Economy*

U.S. government with a positive image and gave greater hope. Mezcalenses were attracted by the narration of 'marvellous' experiences, the unknown and the classic U.S. myths—as explained in Chapter 3. Therefore, the attempts to prevent illegal immigration were unsuccessful (Stephen 2007); henceforth problems arose, as a large number of newcomers were left outside the benefits and in lower and unprotected positions (Fox and Rivera-Salgado 2004; Martin 2003). 'Illegality', in fact, acts as a 'handicap' in their reception into the new society, subordinating migrants while appraising them for the obtention of citizenship and rights, that is, implicating them in 'the moral economy of illegality' (Chauvin and Garcés-Mascareñas 2012). An 'underground labour market' was established where the wages of the undocumented work force—and even those of legal Mexican migrants—decreased, and where labour was increasingly decided by 'social capital' and 'legal status' revealing a new form of discrimination (Phillips and Massey 1999).[8]

In this vein, Bauder (2008) argues that citizenship is a form of capital and a 'mechanism of distinction' that makes migrant labour more vulnerable and permits migrants' exploitation and exclusion. In effect, as labour markets reproduce social structures and hierarchies, revealing how labour is segmented by class and citizenship, but also by gender, race, ethnicity, nationality, sexuality, religion, etc., migrants are rendered subcitizens. Citizenship—formally and informally—strategically, thus, marks migrants as outsiders, through laws and policies moulded by the economic imperatives of neoliberal capitalism, to institutionalise difference and reproduce inequality and privilege. This perspective gives us valuable insights to understand the political economy under examination, providing a complete picture of the labour dynamics in the community, but more importantly, of the workings and motivations of a global system, the role of networks of power, the formal and informal practices and the rhetorics employed. The objective is to get a multifaceted and complete analysis of the functioning of the system, our own role and the channels opened that might help us to transform our political and economic situation. For this purpose, below I explore in detail this neoliberal restructuring in the daily life of Mezcalenses, taking five issues into consideration: agriculture, fishing, maquiladora employments, border control and labour in the US.

Surviving Through Agriculture?

President Salinas reinforced neoliberal policies and signed the North American Free Trade Agreement (NAFTA) aiming to re-establish the confidence of foreign companies, and boost the Mexican economy, the modernisation of the country, and the possibility of entering the 'First World'; but in parallel it weakened the 'political legitimacy' and increased economic inequalities within the country (Soederberg 2005, 182). Although the economic conditions of peasants deteriorated, in Mezcala agriculture still remains fundamental to their survival. Inhabitants continue to cultivate *chayote* throughout the year to sell, as well as corn and sometimes beans to live and eat all year. In this regard, Tomás, a migrant close

The Local Workings of a Global Political Economy 69

to Colectivo Mezcala, explains that people fish and sow for 'the need to do something, to support your family, right? Because actually you are only enriching a handful of people'. Their production has diminished, becoming almost exclusively a subsistence activity, as 'the field isn't profitable, isn't an earning, not a business' (Alberto 2012). Thus, though corn has always been used as a subsistence activity, progressively it no longer provides the same results, as Doña Guille, concerned by the living conditions in the community, identifies: 'They no longer say "we're going to sow to have corn for the year" as before, no, "to eat us a corn cob"'. Moreover, as the prices of corn diminished due to trade agreements, they do not find incentives to keep growing it. Vicente comments that he 'don't plant white corn, because there is no point, still *pozolero* corn sell for fifteen, sixteen, up to twenty pesos per kilo … and white, four, three, five at the most'. In brief, Don Gabriel, a peasant, recognises 'it's almost the same, to sow or to buy "ready-made" corn'.

Another example are *chayotes;* the zone of Lake Chapala still is one of the most important growing areas in Mexico; however, as Don Chava perceives, 'now they sow it everywhere, so that almost all the time the chayote is cheap'. Usually for a box of 30kgs they receive between five to 100 pesos, while in supermarkets normally *chayotes* are not less than five pesos per kilo. As illustrated by Utsa Patnaik (2008, 207) in the case of India, farmers (producers and consumers) are hit by neoliberal policies, since a reduction of prices does not mean a poverty drop but an unemployment rise as income is lowered. It is a vicious cycle; competitiveness appears to lower prices but in reality unemployment augments or at least the purchasing power of smaller producers is reduced, and then prices increase to compensate for the low input while farmers are immersed in deeper poverty. Pedro, a farmer, summarises the panorama:

> So, right now if the cultivation of the chayote also has its ups and downs for the prices, according to the supply and demand, like right now it's cheap, and there are also many plagues. It's no longer very affordable, gasoline [is] very expensive, whether for the irrigation engine, those pumps to water chayotes, fertilizers, fungicides, all that. Now people just do it to survive in some way.

The ideological component used by neoliberal governance makes us believe that the way markets act is outside the control of any state, institution or person, ignoring the domination and abuse of some subjects. A hegemonic rhetoric is endorsing a set of policies that hide relations of domination and make it appear as if there are no options.

In addition, as a consequence of the population growth, crops declined and the ones left were pushed towards the hills—areas not designated for this task—damaging the flora (e.g. *nopal* and *camote de cerro*) and fauna, and making their cultivation and irrigation harder. Besides, intermediaries or *troqueros*—whether or not from the community—have increasingly affected commercial trade by buying cheaply. In this context, the profit made by

Figure 2.1 Chayotes.

peasants in the community is low and restricted to subsistence level. As Alberto, a teacher in Guadalajara who travels every day, states: 'a peasant's salary is around 100 pesos, maximum 150 per day. Imagine, calculate a week how much he earns, six days of work. What if he has two, three children? What if he sends them to school?' Of course, as Tomás argued: 'there is something left because otherwise, they wouldn't be ... but not as it should be, clearly there neither is a reward to the effort that is invested and the work'. In this scenario, peasants try to save money by avoiding paying wages and establishing agriculture as a family activity. They also attempted to avoid intermediaries by creating a cooperative, but all their efforts were unsuccessful due to 'political matters' (Don Jacinto 2012), corruption and lack of organisation. After eight years, they managed to construct a warehouse and buy trucks, but failed to export anything and soon went out of business.[9] So, nowadays some try to sell their products directly in *tianguis* or use their crops exclusively for self-consumption.

Faced with this situation, the government assumed a paternalistic and populist approach as delineated in the previous chapter; and since 1993 it has provided subsidies (for example, fertilisers and seeds) through the *Programa de Apoyos Directos al Campo (PROCAMPO)* supposedly to help them to compete in staple goods production. However, as discerned by Don Fernando:

The Local Workings of a Global Political Economy   71

> The day they distributed PROCAMPO, they all had something to cheer about.... And it's a fraud because there are those who sow half a hectare and are reporting three and so, it's not legal and the government would do anything to have peasants with the mouth shut, 'hey, here there is support'.

As explored in the next chapter, these kinds of social programmes are not exempt from corruption and clientelistic practices, but they are also a way to alienate and keep control over the population. More precisely, as argued by María da Gloria Marroni (2008), focalised poverty alleviation programmes, by not tackling the structural conditions, have become a way to manage poverty. Thus, as prices rise, PROCAMPO silences discontent and co-opts peasants keeping social structures untouched. Within the greater panorama of neoliberal governance, the economic damages engendered appeared to be concealed; but the environmental ones, such as contamination and erosion of land, are harder to obscure. In this regard, many farmers in the community notice that 'land no longer wanted' (Don Gabriel 2012) due to, as Alberto explains, 'the chemicals, could be … the soil debilitated of nutrients, it can be the water of the lake that is very polluted with chemicals, we no longer know from where, or what led the field to stop being productive'. Environmental problems not only had an impact on agriculture, but, as presented in the next subsection, they also affected fishing.

The Disappearance of Fishing in Lake Chapala

The environmental degradation started to be felt by Mezcalenses in the 1960s when water from the lake stopped being suitable for consumption due to the high levels of pollution. As pointed out by López (2007, 187), the environmental consequences in the Cuenca Lerma–Chapala–Santiago have been manifested in a large amount of sediments, the drying of Lake Chapala and the high pollution produced by soil erosion, misuse, economic interests, industries, agrochemicals and lack of treatments plants. As well, some customs, such as swimming in and eating from the lake were impacted; Don Luis, a migrant, remembers he used to go 'straight to dive on the dock, because before the water was very clear, very clean. Now it's dirty'. Still their practices have not been completely abandoned, but inhabitants do not have the same and everyday approach to the lake due to the contamination and the frequent low level of the water.

As the lake was transformed into a dump deposit and had a low level due to the decreased rainfall and the excessive supply of water to the cities, it made 'fishing … sporadic, and right now fish is scarce in the lagoon' (Don Chava 2012). Contamination provoked the disappearance of fish species, their malformation and high toxicity, making the remaining fish in the lake noxious for health, and preventing people from surviving as fishermen (López 2007, 187–8). In this regard, Mezcalenses identify that different kinds of mojarras (*voladora, pinta, carbonera*) disappeared together with other species such as white fish, *bagre barbeta, popocha*, sardines, *cuchillo, boquinete* and *campamocha*. Contamination but also the introduction of foreign species provoked this fish shortage;

72 *The Local Workings of a Global Political Economy*

Don Salvador narrates that some decades ago, a man from Chapala arrived in the community:

> and said [to an inhabitant] 'hey, it's good to put a carp farm', 'okay', and they brought, I don't remember if they were 7 pots, 5 or 7 aluminium pots, big ones, full of little ones and they went inside [the lake] and emptied them. No, after a while it was an invasion; it was an invasion of mojarras.[10]

In addition, Don Jacinto finds that 'many accoutrements, such as *chinchorro*, *manguiadores*, nets ... damaged fish that came out on the shore of the lagoon'. These techniques were prohibited in Mexico, as even though effective, they were harmful to small fish, as explained by Don Fausto:

> Nets were what finished everything, because the charal arrived there, it got stuck, it couldn't go out and it was charal *enhuevador*, so it laid eggs sometimes in the same nets. Then they took out the nets and the roe was stuck and never moved, and ended dying. And fishing thus was terminating.

In fact, in 2009, there was an operation in Lake Chapala headed by the Comisión Nacional de Pesca y Acuacultura (CONAPESCA) where 1,800 fishing nets were confiscated such as *mangueadoras, agalleras* and *caniqueras* (El Informador 2010). Besides, before, they also prohibited their traditional techniques like *atarrayas* and *chichorros*. Don Fausto also remembers 'they forbade it then and some wanted to catch carelessly, but some of them, were caught and took their *chinchorro* away, fined them and finally stopped. And when the nets were introduced [*sic*], they also wanted to prohibit them'. Techniques kept damaging the fauna but the government did not provide any alternative, making fishermen fish in conditions of illegality. Besides, the local government recklessly overlooked the contamination of industries, as it seemed more concerned with the commercialisation of *charales* since it is the only fish in the lake that reaches national and even international markets.

Within this panorama, only a few Mezcalenses profit from the trade of *charales*, while most of them suffered economically from the absence of fish. Although in the village, fishermen depend on their 'fishing luck' (Pedro 2012) and some entrusted to *Santos* and others to the legendary figure of 'el Chan del agua',[11] actually 'there is no fish as before' (Don Rogelio 2013), and the few obtained are rarely sold on the outside. The profit is low, as Vicente argues, 'the kilo of tilapia ten pesos, right now some sell it at twenty-five'. But also, the fish shortage affected their daily life and practices; for instance, Carlos recalls: 'as a boy, they took you to the lagoon, if you were hungry, you would go there and grab the roe with your hand'. Nowadays, people are aware of the toxicity of fish; inconclusive studies have revealed that its consumption is believed to cause kidney and other diseases in a large number of inhabitants due to the content of heavy metals (De la Torre 2010; Ferreiro 2013). So, while corporations disregard environmental regulations, or abuse due to an absence of them, some inhabitants raise their voices to improve the environmental situation and their health.

The Local Workings of a Global Political Economy 73

Figure 2.2 Fishing boats.

As further expanded upon in Chapter 4, some Mezcalenses have extended their support networks to support their own claims, but also other struggles in different parts of Mexico. These efforts were manifested when the community organised the *Foro Nacional en Defensa de la Madre Tierra y la Autonomía de los Pueblos Indígenas* (National Forum in Defense of Mother Earth and the Autonomy of Indigenous Peoples) (2006), which united Mezcala with other indigenous communities to safeguard natural resources, environment, land, traditional medicine, autonomy and self-government (Alonso 2010, 318). Still a large number of families continue consuming fish, since, as explained by Rocío, 'they really depend on what the land gives them, of what the lake gives them, in other words, the food is the fish'.

Apart from this, the fish shortage has also affected Mezcalenses culturally, as can be surmised through the narration of Don Miguel, a fisherman:

> There is no longer because when it came out, when it went out to the *enhuevaderos*, like saying that stick there, the water was hitting there, the roe and when it was born [*sic*] it could be seen shining, in the night with the moon, it could be seen shining and on another day … one saw the roe, it was already white and it was not yellow and it was no longer the little eye of the charal and it would be because of the charal left, it went away.

In the daily life of Mezcalenses, fish has an important economic, environmental, nutritional, cultural and traditional significance; thus, they resist abandoning this

74   *The Local Workings of a Global Political Economy*

practice. So to complement this, many fishermen decided to explore the growing tourist sector, working in the cooperative of *lancheros* (boatmen) to transport tourists to the Island. However, they still experience harsh economic circumstances; Pedro explains:

> The *lanchero* [experiences] the same, because the inputs are very expensive, gasoline, the material of the boats are expensive too, it's a lot of investment to get the expenses. If you take two trips, 500 pesos, 200 for gasoline, 300 for your family, and 300 pesos to support a family all week, it doesn't get ahead.

Both farmers and fishermen continually resist abandoning their practices, getting a low remuneration in exchange, but securing their subsistence and the value of their traditions and identity. Some of them are surviving by combining both activities—agriculture and fishing—while also eking out a living through small quantities of cattle or whatever other work is available, from selling firewood to working in construction sites or as boatmen. What is more, often Mezcalenses resort to small family businesses or to informal jobs (for example, housemaids, gardeners, bricklayers and street vendors) in the surrounding areas. In this context, Pedro narrates his survival strategy:

> Although we do not complain of great thing, because little from one side and another, we have get ahead, either of the field, the sowing of corn, some orchard of plum, chayote we cultivate all year. And on the boardwalk selling a little bit of everything on Sundays, as a tour guide, DJ, soundman on weekends ... then, well at least to eat, to eat not as we want, but yes.

Their efforts, though, have not been enough to overcome their problems, pushing inhabitants to seek more and more alternative economic inputs.

Maquiladoras Accentuating Differences

Younger generations currently experience a lack of work in the community, and thus, as explained by Vicente, 'many people are going away due to the lack of employment'. There they receive better salaries, as Itza, a young woman, clarifies:

> They say '[the time] I'm slaving away here in the sun in this, well I better go to another place where they can pay me a little better and I study and work'. Besides, thoughts are now very different than before.

In fact, the inclusion of other ideas and values is pushing people to abandon agriculture. For instance, with the construction of the panoramic highway (2002), the access of Mezcalenses to the neighbouring areas including Chapala, Guadalajara and El Salto was easier, and this contact has been transforming their aspirations. As a Don Luis remarks:

The Local Workings of a Global Political Economy 75

Young people now say 'Why I? I don't want to be working on the hill'. Now what they do, what I see, that trucks always go. They arrive at night with the people, they hire them and they go to work to Guadalajara or any other place near there.

More precisely, in general the perspective of younger generations seems to be that these activities are retrograde and 'underdeveloped', and thus, aim to change their position as 'backward'. In this regard, young members of Colectivo Mezcala (2008) contend:

For this reason, we agree when the comrades say that neoliberalism hits us, because that, little by little, makes us leave the field alone, that we get ashamed of our roots and that we sell our land.

The manipulation of Mezcalenses' organisation and territory, and the transformation of their culture, production, communal life and *usos y costumbres*, has come along with neoliberal governance. Nonetheless, as working the land granted men the respect and honour of being 'providers', elders continue to cultivate, but the fields are turning empty as they get older. The youth are becoming ashamed of their practices and finding new economic inputs to satisfy their 'needs'; José Luis describes:

It's when the matter of economist progress comes. 'It's that here there are no sources of work, here there is no work, here you won't sustain yourself from the hill, you won't sustain yourself from chayote, you won't sustain yourself from this'. So young people feel so pressured that what they want is to have their pants, their shoes; they see the need of their family and leave.

By becoming enmeshed in urbanisation and industrialisation processes, people are hoping to get more profit in order to become part of the 'developed', 'modern' and 'high' society. The belief that material possessions equal 'progress' and 'modernity' is spread through a rhetoric that makes young people join maquiladoras. 'I believe there are two or three shifts, where constantly the trucks are entering carrying all those boys' (Don Roberto 2013), to work in the manufacturing industries, such as 'La Gama, San Mina ... SICSA ... FLEXTRONICS ... there are several' (Carlos 2012). Since the crisis of 1994,[12] the country kept attracting FDI (González 2008, 202–3), and, in this context, the Cuenca Lerma–Chapala–Santiago became home to at least 560 industries (Hernández García 2006, 103).

Many Mezcalenses have resorted to these maquiladoras established in El Salto; however, the problem, according to Tomás, is that these industries, 'they have a very brutal level of exploitation, I think they earn about six hundred pesos, six hundred and fifty a week, which in the end is nothing'. In fact not only have wages in the manufacturing sector in Mexico not really improved (Haber *et al.* 2008, 84), but, as José Luis discerns:

76   *The Local Workings of a Global Political Economy*

> companies come, look for really cheap labour, not even cheap. If in Guadalajara you're paid seven hundred pesos plus your vouchers; here they say, 'we are going to pay you seven hundred but from there they're going to reduce you the vouchers'.[13]

Besides, not all inhabitants can be hired by these companies, as they do not meet the requirements of age and education. Workers are rendered competitive through neoliberal policies of flexibilisation, deregulation and casualisation of labour.

At the same time, as noted before, labour markets reproduce the social structures since labour sectors are determined—as Alejandro I. Canales and Christian Zlolniski (2001) state—based on not only an 'economic logic', but also through 'social differentiation' (e.g. 'cultural', 'ethnic', 'demographic', 'gender' and 'immigration status'). So, although in contrast to earnings from agriculture and fishing, wages are higher, Mezcalenses still receive unfair salaries, have harsh labour conditions, lack social benefits and possibilities of union membership;[14] in short, they are 'disposable' and feel degraded. Moreover, as the economy in Mexico depended on transnational capital, U.S. companies expanded and profited, and consequently—as signalled by Velasco Ortiz (2002)—they differentiated workers on both sides of the border based on their salaries and stratification. So, while new inequalities, hierarchies and practices are being created, some Mezcalenses still praise these industries, perceiving them as providers of benefits. In this regard, Don Chava explains 'they are paid cheaply but at least there is a source of work' and, when I asked Don Salvador if these companies brought some benefits to the community, he asserted 'the benefits are only for workers, it's the strongest benefit the community now has'.

For Bourdieu, 'neoliberalism is the grand narrative of globalisation', a 'mythic inevitability' that employs euphemisms to force states to carry out certain actions (cited in Siisiäinen 2000, no page number). In this context, with the belief that privatisation and FDI would benefit people economically, Mexico adopted neoliberal governance models and policies, aiming to surpass 'underdevelopment' and achieve 'progress'. But, Mexico relinquished the national project in order to be incorporated into globalisation and meet the demands of markets by reducing times, improving quality, production and products (Guillén Romo 2005, 206–7), and thus managed capitalism outside of its boundaries interfering in further areas of daily life. Therefore, the presence of FDI in Mexico is linked to underemployment, modern consumption patterns and wealth concentration in upper classes (Portes 2012, 14). Furthermore, this has incurred a strong dependence, a high level of human and natural exploitation, and the extraction of benefits. Accordingly, as Ana Esther Ceceña (2011, 126) signals, the real characteristic of this model is the fight for the use and possession of territories that leads to the expulsion and recolonisation of people and their resistance, a topic expanded upon in Chapter 4.

That said, the practices of maquiladoras must be read in terms of a coordinated web of U.S.–Mexican interests, since local and global allies enjoy unrestrained

The Local Workings of a Global Political Economy 77

freedom, protection and profits and increase their power and influence in politics. In parallel, these industries perpetuate colonial relations, legitimising the right of exploitation and fostering what David Harvey (2007) calls 'accumulation by dispossession'.[15] In effect, neoliberal policies were designed to take power and resources away from lower classes, and grant them to national and international elites and their local allies. At the same time, there was a decrease in social spending and the privatisation of public services that kept fomenting migration (Blackwell *et al.* 2009), as illustrated in the next chapter. Besides, to some extent, rather than a transfer from the U.S. to Mexico, Mexico subsidises the U.S. economy via 'disaccumulation', reassigned social capital, subsidies and tax exceptions, while experiencing 'deindustrialisation', unemployment and underemployment (Cypher and Delgado Wise 2010).

Under the rationale of neoliberal governance, labour is rendered disposable and vulnerable, at the same time that inequalities and social stratification are exacerbated. Consequently, as with other indigenous communities in Mexico, Mezcalenses have relocated to sustain themselves and improve their quality of life. As observed by Tomás: 'If there was a fair payment I bet that many of us wouldn't have the need to leave our community, our village'. What shaped this path were, thus, international, national and local conditions and events; for instance, the growing demand of work in the U.S., the adoption of neoliberalism, and the devaluation of Mezcalenses' main economic activities. Migration of indigenous peasants and labour workers is, in this sense, a relief to economic pressures, but also 'collateral damage' of the restructuring of the global economy and of the workings of networks of power. Clearly, the political economy experienced in the community is becoming thoroughly transnational and entailing a new economic rationality. However, they try to skilfully respond to the changing economic and political circumstances making use of improvements in transportation and communication and of transnational social networks. Still far from an encouraging picture, by migrating they bear the burden of 'illegality', and thus, experience difficulties in crossing and poor conditions when arriving, as explored in the next subsection.

Controlling Borders and Managing Migration Flows

People, more than ever, have the need to cross the border for employment opportunities while the U.S. requires more and more cheap labour (McClennen 2011). However, at the same time, the crossing and the situation of migrants in the northern frontier became aggravated due to the reinforcement of military and security measures, such as *Operation Gatekeeper* (1994), and the Illegal Immigration Reform and Immigrant Responsibility Act (IIRIRA) (1996). Still some '"unwanted" immigrants' were accepted (Massey 2009); the aim of immigration policies is to control the flow rather than close the border (Portes and Walton 1981, 58; Stephen 2007, 28). National borders, in fact, act as mechanisms to reproduce the capitalist system by obtaining cheap labour via criminalisation, carrying out '*selective* enforcement' to benefit and protect economic groups

78 *The Local Workings of a Global Political Economy*

(Sassen 1988, 36–7 emphasis in original). This does not mean that, in parallel, people do not use borders as safety valves removed from the consequences of neoliberal capitalism —as argued in this book. Thus, the experiences of crossing the border fall in line with the period and tightened security measures, but also with factors marked by social difference, such as gender, nationality, ethnicity, sexuality, race, class, education and age. Juana shares her experience when crossing in the early 1990s, for example, 'I did suffered. They grabbed us like three times … But for one, as a woman, it's difficult because they take you out in the early morning hours'. Crossing the border is a unique and personal experience that also relates to the number of times and with whom a migrant crosses, plus the path and the method (Chavez 2013). For instance, Tomás narrates his experience with 20 Mezcalenses who were attracted to the fields of North Carolina with the promise of work in 1996:

> We were supposedly to be fine, they were going to give us a good accommodation and everything, but on the contrary … in the end it was only a lie. Yes, they gave us where to stay but they were in very deplorable conditions, it was like a cellar and there were only wooden boards without mattresses or anything, no pillows or blankets or anything, and that's how we slept. We didn't bring anything because obviously we didn't come with anything from there. So we were just with what we were wearing, we lasted like that a long time…. It didn't turn out to be true anything they said, that we were going to win apparently US$500 a week, what!? Not at all! No, no, no, we used to pick a bucket of 11 gallons of chillies. I think they paid about 35 cents, something like that. So it was very, very, very little money, and for that, I'm telling you, … they had us living there and they charged us for food, so obviously, the little we earned was more or less to pay only for food.

These campsites—as Stephen (2008) examines—have been bringing people from the most marginalised communities and forming a new kind of slavery. The experience of Tomás, in this manner, shows how borders reproduce capitalist structures, practices and rationales, and how inequality is manifested in different spheres and connected among locations.

Besides, security measures also damaged living conditions and fostered racism within the United States (París 2008; Stephen 2008, 203; Velasco Ortiz 2002, 80–1). In the context of 9/11 and the 'war on drugs', a change in the international relations between the United States and Mexico took place that accentuated these circumstances. In this context, the Mexican government displayed contradictory perspectives on how to deal with migration; on the one hand, it revealed a more 'proactive position' via institutions, programmes, groups and public opinion, and expressed concern around the widespread use of the anti-immigrant discourse, strategies and actions (Délano 2011), possibly due to its strong economic and political dependency on migrants—as analysed in the next chapter. Nonetheless, on the other hand, it continued to collaborate with the U.S. in border reinforcement and acted without really impacting the bilateral relationship

The Local Workings of a Global Political Economy   79

(Délano 2011). In any case, whereas in the past, as previously narrated, legal and illegal border crossing was simple and frequent, now immigration policies became more severe and migrants found it quite difficult to cross. In the words of Don Marcos, who settled in Tijuana: 'Now for the one that crosses, certain death'. In point of fact, the militarisation of the border determines which individuals can enter this space, not really diminishing illegal immigration but augmenting its dangers (McClennen 2011). For instance, migrants have kept using *coyotes* to cross the border, but as these have integrated into the drug trade networks, the path can be lethal. Tomás summarises this situation:

> It's dangerous on the Mexican side because cartels are taking over the line to cross. So many people, you hear that they are kidnapped, right? That is, for that part. And on the other hand, that here on the side of the United States, they have closed the main accesses, and force migration to go around in very big circles in the deserts and many people risk dying, to be left in the desert.

Additionally, *coyotes* exploit economically—rather than the past 300 dollars or so—according to Don Roberto 'right now a *coyote*, a person who crosses people, is charging between 8 thousand to 10 thousand dollars' and sometimes even resort to abuse and/or extortion of their families. However, the costs and dangers are not exclusively monetary but also physical, emotional and psychological (Hea Kil and Menjívar 2006). Since risks and prices increased, a reduction in the magnitude of migration has been provoked, as documented by Rodolfo García Zamora (2013). In the same manner, Mezcala has evidenced the discouragement of migration flows, seen in the stopping of return trips and illegal crossing; only a few cases were narrated of inhabitants still trying to cross, with a record of two disappeared persons. This situation is also the result of the inability of their networks to provide help and support for their fellow members. Don Santos, a migrant living in LA, explains this transformation:

> At that time for us, [it was] like jumping from here to the car, there in the street. It was very easy, easy, easy; no, no, no, not like right now, right now it's very difficult, no, no, no, you can't, and well I would recommend people not to move now.

Migrants from Mezcala, in fact, were discouraging migration indicating high risks, scarce job opportunities and a deteriorated U.S. economy. What is more, security policies have led to increased vulnerability (Marroni 2008), abuse, violence and racism (Hea Kil and Menjívar 2006), intolerance (Velasco Ortiz 2002), monitoring (Stephen 2008) and criminalisation of migrants (Hea Kil and Menjívar 2006; Hernández 2008); thus, undocumented or not, migrants find themselves constantly 'crossing the border' (Stephen 2008). Anti-immigrant sentiments persist and, as Chavez (2013) has documented, a form of nativism endures that targets immigrants—especially Mexicans—as a threat to national

80 *The Local Workings of a Global Political Economy*

security, sovereignty and the 'American life'. In this manner, mentalities on how to perceive immigrants in the U.S. are constantly adjusted, as explored in Chapter 5. In this sense, border security continues due to the racism it provokes, as it naturalises divisions and 'justifies' violence (Hea Kil and Menjívar 2006), but it also legitimises capitalism and the stratification and system of oppression that goes with it. Therefore, we should perceive these actions and policies in a context of two nations integrated into a world system, since there are multiple interconnected factors, actors and interests in the global–regional–local interface of power that must be acknowledged. So, in this era of neoliberal governance, a global system paradoxically perpetuates mobility together with class and ethnic stratifications; this is studied in the next subsection in regards to labour dynamics of migrants and the position they occupy in the U.S.

Migrants in the U.S.: Adapting to Labour Market Demands?

As mentioned before, Mexico became an exploiter and exporter of cheap labour (in manufactured products and in the migration of the workforce) establishing a subordinated integration of Mezcalenses into the renewed world-system structure. In this scenario, Mezcalenses left the community owing to the desire to improve their economic situation, find a job and fulfil their needs, as well as due to personal issues (e.g. family problems, diseases and deaths) and were supported by a transnational network while prompted by the sharing of classic 'American' myths and experiences. However, most of them ignored the process needed and the difficulties involved. For example, Tomás confesses:

> I came to dig out of the hole but without a fixed goal of what I was going to do, or what I wanted to do, or what I had to do, I just came and kept living here without any objective.

Moreover, in the context of the crisis of 2008, the U.S. damaged its reputation as the great provider of work. Don Marcos puts it: 'The United States is now very screwed-up, it's almost the same as all the towns here'. Migrants, thus, began diversifying their places of residency, due to labour demands and also by trying to find better paid jobs. As Doña Guille, a transient migrant, notes: 'Work has failed and many people have already moved and sometimes you don't know now where they are'. Migrants moved towards Arizona, Washington, North Carolina, Chicago, Utah, Oregon, Georgia and New York. However, this relocation has not always meant better salaries and opportunities, especially due to the absence of networks. In some cases migrants and their families were even pushed to return to Mexico since, as noted by Don José, a migrant in LA, 'the companies where they used to work closed and they went back'. Besides, the fields did not produce the same as before, and thus, 'people fought over work' (Doña Guille 2013).

In short, the crisis evidenced how neoliberal governance—especially as operationalised in the Mexican–U.S. transnational and migration interface—further

Figure 2.3 The border of opportunities.

reinforces capitalist structures. These structures of inequality and maldistribution are exhibited more generally among the population, but particularly among the migrants interviewed, in the deterioration of the workers' quality of life, the ending of social protections, a reduction in purchasing power, and the fostering of unemployment and lower wages. In this regard, Don Salvador observes that 'it's very difficult because there is almost no work'. Besides, payments are no longer as good as before; for instance, in maquiladoras Don José notes that 'at that time [1970s–1980s] it was good, right now not anymore, people don't make money there'. So, even if they usually earn more than double compared to the wages in Mexico, their income is insufficient, even more as prices of goods and services augmented. However, they still perceive increased possibilities that contrast with their possibilities in the community. As Alberto, who is also a liaison member of Club Mezcala, argues: 'In Mexico you work all day and partly eat ... and there not, there a few hours ... and you already secured the food for tomorrow'.

Furthermore, the crisis also affected other sectors and economies (Arenas Rosales 2010, 161), especially those that remarkably embraced the neoliberal model and maintained a deep connection with the U.S., such as Mexico. Hence, in order to overcome the impaired situation migrants established different temporalities of residence and altered labour dynamics by living and 'working on both sides' (Don Marcos 2013) and still some Mezcalenses continue to do it. The continuous immigration flows have split the labour market and created a

82   *The Local Workings of a Global Political Economy*

group of workers adapted to fulfil the needs of global capital, devaluing them and removing legal protections (París 2008). What is more, employers seek labour that adapts to their conditions, making them 'powerlessness' and 'profitable', and as a result, equating migrant workers to commodities (Sassen 1988) or 'human merchandise' (Cypher and Delgado Wise 2010, 155).

Mezcalenses experience this setting as their employment commitments absorb their time and lives. The jobs performed are varied, but usually, men and women join industries packing, cleaning, counting, assembling, mixing, sewing, garnishing, organising or supervising; or going to the fields to collect and pack harvests, while young people enter the service sector (for example, fast food chains and hotels). Aside from these activities, some provide services informally, as gardeners, bricklayers or nannies; employments that met the demands of the labour markets opening in 'global cities' (Sassen 2001, 1988). Chuy, a young returnee, narrates his experience after leaving school:

> I went to work at a hotel and from there to a restaurant, that's right of hamburgers, and as gardener again and basically that, in restaurants, hotels and as gardener. And sometimes I went with my dad to help him; he worked in what is here a building site, construction, right?

Within these jobs, migrants first perceive a change of pace, as Doña Guille experienced: 'I got up at four o'clock, at four thirty I left my house, in the morning; I arrived at five thirty at my house. It was a routine to go from Monday to Saturday'. Additionally, schedules are rough, for example, some of them have night shifts from 10 pm to 7 am, and in other cases, for 12 hours non-stop; Don Luis narrates his experience when working in a cookie factory:

> When I went out [of work] I was very sleepy and when I got to sleep in the day, I started to look at the brightness of the day and I couldn't sleep, just my forehead and my eyes hurt from here. So, I rested but very little.

Their lives took a radical turn as reported by Don Santos:

> Here, you walk with the clock, if you go to work you have to be at such times, the entrance at such time, whatever company, exit at such times … the other day in the morning the same, and like this, you go to sleep with the clock… and the clock, you're going to put the alarm to get up early for the reason that I don't want to be late for work.

Migrants subsist under rush schedules, and thus, frequently depend on family and *paisano* support for daily life activities, such as to ride to work or to take care of children. Moreover, migrants are required to perform hard, exhausting and high-demanding manual activities in a restraining and unsafe environment, Don Ramiro, a returned migrant *comunero*, argues: 'They are always hard jobs, more than you think, and there it's early'. For example, Don Luis talks about

The Local Workings of a Global Political Economy   83

working in the strawberry fields: '[I was] all day bent ... and very muddy', while, regarding sewing shops, Don Rogelio comments:

> I didn't like very well to do the machine, because my back hurt a lot ... or the *overlock* too, but it was damn hard there, and I looked at the women, men who earned more money, right? But it was a life ... and it's a very very ... arduous life.

Workers function as 'machines', and thus, many complain of health issues, whether these are problems related to eyesight or back pains. There are even cases of people being disabled after performing these jobs.

In addition, in line with the ideas of Stephen (2008), migrants feel constantly watched, trying hard every day to go unnoticed. Therefore, sometimes migrants overwork because they want to please their bosses or fear being fired, but also to improve their position, relationship and salary. In this regard, some migrants expressed how they excelled compared to the rest of workers because, as stated by Tomás, 'they have accustomed you to work hard, and you stands out in jobs because you put enough effort'. Still, they receive scarce benefits and their labour is mainly characterised by insecurity, irregularity and flexibility. Adelo describes his working year in northern California:

> I work by seasons at a cannery, it ends because the fruit of the season is canned, from there I go to one, they called it '*handler*' but that's also like cleaning nuts, they clean and dry them, and send them to packaging and when it's over I go to the field, to work on the field. Just two months and then I go to the window to get unemployment [funds].

What is more, due to their age many are no longer being hired, as expressed by Don Indalecio, a migrant comunero in his seventies:

> They don't give me work anymore, also you go to companies or wherever, they don't, they don't give us anymore. There are a lot of young people who do the job now, and as an old man, they no longer ... want you.

Thus, in the face of difficulties and reduced possibilities, many migrants do not hesitate to perform any work, in spite of conditions, schedules or lack of knowledge. As Don Santos explains: 'We are humble people who come to work in what they put us or rather what they give us as work'. Especially, undocumented migrants usually are subject to more abuses from employers, as Juana experienced: 'One in a job, one that isn't, is illegal. You tolerate discrimination, you don't speak the language, you don't have papers, there are many things, and you have to tolerate it because you need it'. Although many complain of Chinese and Korean employers, others find that Latinos are those who abuse the most, demonstrating how racist practices endure and are reproduced by the same members of marginalised communities, from local to national and even transnational

84　*The Local Workings of a Global Political Economy*

spheres. Hierarchies constantly adapt and are used and propelled onward by the neoliberal governance models and networks that underpin the social and economic order, as discussed in Chapter 5. Don José narrates an anecdote when working for a *gringo:*

> Once they came upstairs, they found me very sweaty, but because I was working hard, and nobody supervised me, I was in charge of that department, he says '*oh no José, we want you to enjoy your job, we don't want you to kill yourself*'.... And I say 'Wow!', if I were working for a Latino he would be saying with the whip, 'work, slave, work, slave', and this [guy] no, wow!

On balance, labour is not really determined by skills and an economic logic, but by social capital, migratory status and social differentiation. For instance, often employers offer to pay less than the minimum wage while being undocumented. Juana explains: 'There is still discrimination because I went to look for work there [Avalon Street], they want to pay a misery, like if they look at you very "low"'. Due to the working ambience many migrants might be constantly changing jobs, hoping to find an employer who will later help them to regularise their status but the time may never come for some of them to be supported in their application. In this vein, McClennen states that 'neoliberalism brings with it a cruel mentality that assumes that those who need aid are weak, that those who seek work are useless, and that those who demand help are dangerous' (2011, 175). Migrants wanted to escape from poverty and exclusion; however, they still struggle to have better conditions and to eliminate the new forms of racism and differentiation experienced. In effect, the position Mezcalenses occupy in U.S. society is decided based on their legal status, gender, race, ethnicity, class and origins. This logic operates in diverse contexts and within different subjects, moulding categorisations with novel features.

In this regard, migrants, in the era of neoliberal governance, subsidise the consequences of its policies, allowing the reproduction of inequalities and the expansion of capitalism. Accordingly, in line with the observations of Luis Eduardo Guarnizo (2003), the transnational character of migrants must account for not only the impact on the communities of origin and destiny, but also on the global macroeconomic processes and political economy. Moreover, Mexico was included in the new international division of labour, proving how the neoliberal model is a 'lose-lose' game for workers on both sides of the border, deepening the asymmetries within and between countries, while benefiting and giving control to U.S. capital and elite groups (Cypher and Delgado Wise 2010). Both economies—of the communities in Mexico and the United States—are impacted upon showing that there are 'winners' and 'losers' and thus, demonstrating how hierarchies interpenetrate and transnational structures and networks of power operate.

Unfortunately, any structural change in Mexico is averted due to the deep-rooted institutions—as detailed throughout this book. Meanwhile, in the U.S. by

The Local Workings of a Global Political Economy   85

2015, the efforts to provide appropriate migratory policies continued under debate, ranging from different proposals of comprehensive reform to isolated actions such as the Deferred Action for Childhood Arrivals (DACA) and the Development, Relief, and Education for Alien Minors (DREAM) Act. Although victories have been achieved, Martin (2010) explains that the aim of maintaining the status quo and the disagreement between economists over the effects of migration are preventing such comprehensive reform. Thus, in a context of co-option practices set by neoliberal governance, the successes of migrants are cast out and migrants, undocumented or not, more and more live a tense scenario entangled with criminalisation, massive deportations, anti-immigrant sentiments, racism, exclusion and marginalisation. Mezcalenses accept this situation as they might fear to claim their rights, while perceiving a (possibly slight) improvement in their living conditions and opportunities, bringing them closer to reaching the so-called 'American Dream'; as Don Santos discerns:

> We have survived there, because that is what one is doing, to survive more than to say 'I have a good job, I have this very good thing and this other'. And this is the life of Americans that we say; we're the 'American Dream'. What comes one to do here and, we come to whatever work they give us.

In this vein, Siisiäinen, following the ideas of Bourdieu, explains that 'social positions and the division of economic, cultural and social resources in general are legitimised with the help of symbolic capital' (2000, no page number). In this regard, 'development' has acted, as a 'fantasy' that makes migrants responsible for their conditions, discriminating, criminalising, blaming and misrepresenting them (Cypher and Delgado Wise 2010), but more importantly, seducing them to accept their position and situation and to perpetuate and broadcast a capitalist and colonialist rationale. However, as they are getting familiarised with the dynamics, the culture, the language and the structure of labour and social life in the United States, many are complaining and demanding decent and fair conditions and payments. In fact, migrants are increasingly organising and participating in unions, organisations and marches to stop their criminalisation, and to empower themselves to improve their conditions and claim their rights by making use of the pan-Latino identity. Migrants are creating support networks, and have also become highly politicised, opening spaces in U.S. and Mexican politics, advancing in the use of social capital as a survival strategy and scheme for change. Many of these issues are discussed in the next chapter.

Conclusion

To summarise, although Mezcala experiences the devaluation of its main economic activities, the land has not been completely abandoned and people continue to plant, catch or collect part of their daily food. Nonetheless, due to the development of means of communication and urban centres near the area, inhabitants are increasingly compelled to work in the cities, mainly in industries

86 *The Local Workings of a Global Political Economy*

in Guadalajara, Tijuana and the United States. This flow of people is informed, not only by economic forces that mark wage differences or opportunities, but also—following the ideas of Velasco Ortiz (2002)—by patterns of life, networks, measures and different historic processes taking place on both sides of the border. More precisely, Mezcala demonstrates that migration flows are moulded by an amalgam of economic, political and social conditions in origin and receiving communities, along with family and networks, migratory policies and the U.S. lifestyle and values.

In this regard, neoliberal governance shows a 'contradictory' modus operandi since, on the one hand, foreign industries in Mexico are growing their economic and political power and perpetuating colonial relations by exploiting displaced people from rural communities, who suffer the intrusion and costs of economic and political processes. On the other hand, in the U.S., elite groups profit from migrant labour, using security policies, and as result, a rhetoric that legitimates criminalisation, violence and racism but also migrants' economic, labour and social position. So, migration is being managed due to the increased dependence on this mobile population and their exploitation. In this sense, Mezcalenses, in the era of neoliberal governance, are being recolonised and relocated, as they are in the midst of a continuous fight for control of space, people, wealth, resources and power, as examined in Chapter 4. Therefore, we should acknowledge the increased dependence, needs and interconnections in this global system, but also, how exclusion is related to migration (Ruiz 2002) and the conditions of inequality in which it takes place (Castles 2010). This would lead us not only to address the local problems but also the structures of power and domination that connect the local with the global, thus forming articulated solutions that transcend times and spaces.

Under neoliberal governance, it is impossible for us to understand local realities outside the functioning of networks of power that allow local and global actors to form alliances and work together, and the complexities of a global system that perpetuates, reproduces and renews colonial and capitalist relations, stratifications, differentiations and disparities between and within countries. Moreover, territories are reconfigured; in Mezcala this is revealed not only through—as argued in the last chapter—a simulated political pluralism and the continuity of informal power, but also unemployment, poverty, inequality, migration, overexploitation, and power and wealth concentration, all of which reflects a national trend. So, while being deterritorialised, Mezcalenses' *usos y costumbres* and ways of life have been altered, thereby generating, following the ideas of Torres-Mazuera (2009), a 'new territoriality'. In here, the population is 'dispersed' and 'fragmented', and thus, agriculture and fishing are no longer the sole economic activities and *comuneros* the principal authority; different activities are carried out, and different subjects contest control. In the context of a post-agrarian territoriality where the *Municipio* has more power and interference through the *delegado*, the power of *comuneros* is breaking down, new institutions are introduced and negotiation is open to new subjects such as Club Mezcala, as examined in Chapter 3, while space is set aside for residency,

The Local Workings of a Global Political Economy 87

tourism and consumption purposes, as explored in Chapter 4. Furthermore, *comuneros* are pushed into worrying about social development, limited services and housing settlements rather than the low productivity of the land, fish shortages and environmental deterioration, which are also the focus of the next chapter.

The adoption of the neoliberal model, in its real and everyday guise, has transformed the landscape of Mezcala and the basis of community life and communal organisation, modifying peoples' relationships, routines, livelihood, customs, environment, practices, ideas, values, culture, health and nutrition. Ironically, in the face of such transformations, the promises of wealth and the entrance into the 'First World'—promoted by the associated discourse of 'development'—are increasingly distant and absent from everyday life. Mezcalenses must lean on their social networks and fight for the continuation of their *usos y costumbres*, the safeguarding of their identity and practices against the workings of a system based on inequalities, racism and exclusion and sustained by a rhetoric of 'development' and 'progress', a rhetoric that crosses frontiers and impresses itself on local forms. In this context, a first step towards the real transformation of the hegemonic economic order is to understand the functioning of networks of power, as presented in this chapter, but more importantly is to recognise how we reproduce and perpetuate such networks. This standpoint enables us to observe and take advantage of the small 'cracks' we make to dislocate capitalism, challenge democracy and development rhetorics, and start determining their life paths (Holloway 2010, 19), which is the rationale of the following three chapters.

Notes

1 The Green Revolution refers to the transfer and enforcing of agricultural technologies, such as hybrid seeds and toxic agrochemicals developed in the United States, into the fields, in this case, of Mexico, to promote agricultural growth and production (López 2007, 34–5). This initiative was key to the new agrarian policy adopted by the Mexican government in order to promote 'development' in the country under the Import Substitution Industrialisation model (Sonnenfeld 1992, 31–2).

2 Cuenca Lerma–Santiago–Chapala is made up of the adjacent territories of the rivers Lerma and Santiago and Lake Chapala. Its importance derives from the area ($130,000 \, km^2$) and the population (a fifth of the Mexican population) that it covers, making it one of the most important industrial shafts of the country (Durán Juárez, Partida Rocha, and Torres Rodríguez 1999).

3 In 2014, a demonstration of ex-braceros in Zacatecas took place in which protestors demanded their money back (Martínez 2014). In fact both the U.S. and Mexican governments and banks have been sued (Martin 2003). In Mezcala, ex-braceros have not received their money; the government has been profiting, either because of the lack of awareness of this situation, braceros' deaths or simply owing to the unresponsiveness of authorities.

4 Alexandra Délano (2011) explains that in parallel, Mexican–American organisations began to claim the rights of migrants, which were further embraced by the Mexican government in its attempt to protect the rights of Mexican migrants and enhance a nationalist position. This fact proves important for our argument as developed in Chapters 3 and 5.

88 *The Local Workings of a Global Political Economy*

5 In 1965 the PIF enabled U.S. maquiladoras to be established in order to improve social and labour conditions, but favouring foreign investment (Durán Juárez and Partida Rocha 1992, 244; Guillén Romo 2005, 202).

6 Technocrats are economists trained at top US Universities endorsed by the 'international community' that 'speak the same language' and have the same 'theoretical presuppositions' (Babb 2001, 214).

7 This policy aimed to reduce illegal immigration through legalisation, fines to employers and increased security (Phillips and Massey 1999).

8 There is an ongoing debate about the effects of IRCA on salaries, as the discussions between George Borjas and David Card evidence. See Philip Martin (2010).

9 The abandoned warehouse still exists and is available for anyone who wants to start the cooperative up again, but nobody has attempted to do so, as it requires strong investment and good organisation.

10 Since the beginning of the twentieth century, the introduction of species in Lake Chapala began with the carp (Ortiz Segura 2001). According to a newspaper report, by the 1970s Lake Chapala had 39 native fish species and six introduced when they began their disappearance (Info Rural 2007). Usually there is no precise data of how and who introduced these species, but Manuel Guzmán A. and John Lyons (2003) argue that it was a result of rural development policies. This shows a high degree of informality and a lack of protection and regulation by the Mexican government.

11 Exiquio Santiago Cruz narrates that in the 1970s a manatee was introduced in the lake to end the scourge of lily, but that people in the community saw

> that creature as something different, to such an extent that women began to make offerings as if it was something wonderful and special. And maybe they were right, because the fishermen did better when they were entrusted to the animal.
>
> (2003, 84)

Years later the manatee disappeared; nowadays, its figure only remains as a legend.

12 Following the ideas of Holloway, economic crises do not necessarily mean the restructuring of capital, but the fragmentation of 'social relations of capitalism' (2010, 265–6). Therefore, in Mexico there was a rearrangement of power relations that strengthen neoliberal governance.

13 Until 2015 salaries in Mexico were regulated by the minimum wage, depending on regions and activities. In Mezcala, the minimum wage was the lowest in Mexico, that is, 68.28 pesos per eight hours. This fact demonstrates a dynamic of internal colonialism through salaries.

14 As noted by Harvey (2007, 59), in the 1980s, Reagan abolished unions and diminished their rights allowing industries to move into zones with less union organisation and even outside the country, such as, for instance, Mexico. In Jalisco, in fact, Jaime Tamayo and Alejandra Vizcarra (2000, 37–8) observe there was an ineffective organisation of unions due to inhabitants' mainly rural origin, the presence of cottage industries and the dispersion and polarisation of the working class.

15 I understand this concept as a way by which wealth including environment, land, rights, labour and capital is being redistributed favouring the elite while perpetuating structures and hierarchies; some examples in Mexico are: the expulsion of peasants and indigenous people from their land, the privatisation of the *ejido*, the settlement of maquiladoras and flexibilisation of labour, the irruption into indigenous life and projects, the exploitation of mines, forests and rivers, the deficiencies and problems of the education system, and the foreign debt increase.

References

Alonso, Jorge. 2010. "La persistente defensa de la autonomía del pueblo de Mezcala como una creación de espacio público no estatal". In *¿Qué tan público es el espacio público en México?*, edited by Mauricio Merino, 311–46. Mexico City: FCE; CONACULTA; Universidad Veracruzana.

Arenas Rosales, René. 2010. "La caída financiera y automotriz del imperio estadounidense". In *La crisis capitalista y sus alternativas. Una mirada desde América Latina y el Caribe*, edited by Julio C. Gambina, 151–62. Buenos Aires: CLACSO.

Babb, Sarah. 2001. *Managing Mexico: Economists from Nationalism to Neoliberalism*. Princeton, NJ: Princeton University Press.

Bauder, Harald. 2008. "Citizenship as Capital: The Distinction of Migrant Labor". *Alternatives: Global, Local, Political* 33 (3): 315–33.

Blackwell, Maylei, Rosalva Aída Hernández Castillo, Juan Herrera, Morna Macleod, Renya Ramírez, Rachel Sieder, María Teresa Sierra, and Shannon Speed. 2009. "Cruces de fronteras, identidades indígenas, género y justicia en las Américas". *Desacatos* (31): 13–34.

Calavita, Kitty. 1994. "U.S. Immigration and Policy Responses: The Limits of Legislation". In *Controlling Immigration. A Global Perspective*, edited by Wayne A. Cornelius, Philip L. Martin and James F. Hollifield, 55–82. Stanford: Stanford University Press.

Canales, Alejandro I., and Christian Zlolniski. 2001. "Comunidades transnacionales y migración en la era de la globalización". *Notas de Población* 28 (73): 221–52.

Castles, Stephen. 2010. "Understanding Global Migration: A Social Transformation Perspective". *Journal of Ethnic and Migration Studies* 36 (10): 1565–86.

Ceceña, Ana Esther. 2011. "Postneoliberalismo o cambio civilizatorio". In *América Latina y el Caribe: escenarios posibles y políticas sociales*, edited by Theotonio Dos Santos, 121–31. Montevideo: FLACSO; UNESCO.

Chauvin, Sébastien, and Blanca Garcés-Mascareñas. 2012. "Beyond Informal Citizenship: The New Moral Economy of Migrant Illegality". *International Political Sociology* 6 (3): 241–59.

Chavez, Leo R. 2013. *Shadowed Lives: Undocumented Immigrants in American Society*. 3rd edn. Belmont, CA: Wadsworth Cengage Learning.

Colectivo Mezcala. 2008. *Mezcala es una comunidad indígena coca*. Mezcala, Mexico.

Cypher, James M., and Raúl Delgado Wise. 2010. *Mexico's Economic Dilemma: The Developmental Failure of Neoliberalism*. Lanham, MD: Rowman & Littlefield Publishers, Inc.

De la Torre, Adrián. 2010. "San Pedro y Mezcala: enfermedad y muerte, la pesca del día en Chapala". *La Jornada Jalisco*, September 28. www1.lajornadaguerrero.com.mx/2010/09/28/index.php?section=cultura&article=016n1cul [accessed September 30, 2010].

Délano, Alexandra. 2011. *Mexico and its Diaspora in the United States*. New York: Cambridge University Press.

Delgado-Wise, Raúl. 2006. "Migración e imperialismo: la fuerza de trabajo mexicana en el contexto del TLCAN". In *México en transición: globalismo neoliberal, Estado y sociedad civil*, edited by Gerardo Otero, 195–214. Zacatecas, Mexico: H. Cámera de Diputados LIX Legislatura; Simon Fraser University; Universidad Autónoma de Zacatecas; Miguel Ángel Porrúa.

Durán Juárez, Juan Manuel, and Raquel Edith Partida Rocha. 1990. "Empresas y contaminación ambiental. El caso del Corredor Industrial de Jalisco". *Cuadernos. Revista de Ciencias Sociales* (13): 37–45.

90 *The Local Workings of a Global Political Economy*

Durán Juárez, Juan Manuel, and Raquel Edith Partida Rocha. 1992. "Modelo económico, regionalización y nuevo estado mexicano (1940–1990)". In *El nuevo estado mexicano*, edited by Jorge Alonso, Alberto Aziz and Jaime Tamayo, 240–51. Mexico City: Nueva Imagen.

Durán Juárez, Juan Manuel, Raquel Edith Partida Rocha, and Alicia Torres Rodríguez. 1999. "Cuencas hidrológicas y ejes industriales: el caso de la cuenca Lerma-Chapala-Santiago". *Relaciones* XX (80): 100–29.

El Informador. 2010. "Destruye Sagarpa Jalisco dos mil artes de pesca prohibidas". *El Informador*, January 7. www.informador.com.mx/jalisco/2010/168378/6/destruye-sagarpa-jalisco-dos-mil-artes-de-pesca-prohibidas.htm [accessed March 17, 2014].

Ferreiro, Rebeca. 2013. "Construyendo ambientes enfermos". *La Gaceta Universitaria*, November 11. www.gaceta.udg.mx/G_nota1.php?id=14864 [accessed March 14, 2014].

Fitzgerald, David. 2009. *A Nation of Emigrants: How Mexico Manages its Migration*. Berkeley, CA: University of California Press.

Fox, Jonathan, and Gaspar Rivera-Salgado. 2004. "Introducción". In *Indígenas mexicanos migrantes en los Estados Unidos*, edited by Jonathan Fox and Gaspar Rivera-Salgado, 9–74. Mexico City: H. Cámara de Diputados LIX Legislatura; University of California Santa Cruz; Universidad Autónoma de Zacatecas; Miguel Ángel Porrúa.

García Zamora, Rodolfo. 2013. "Mexico's Experience of Migration and Development 1990–2013". *REMHU: Revista Interdisciplinar da Mobilidade Humana* 21 (41): 205–24.

González Corona, Elias. 1989. *El Salto, industria y urbanización de Guadalajara*. Vol. 15, *Cuadernos de Difusión Científica*. Guadalajara, Mexico: Universidad de Guadalajara.

González, Francisco E. 2008. *Dual Transitions from Authoritarian Rule. Institutionalized Regimes in Chile and Mexico, 1970–2000*. Baltimore, MD: The Johns Hopkins University Press.

Guarnizo, Luis Eduardo. 2003. "The Economics of Transnational Living". *International Migration Review* 37 (3): 666–99.

Guillén Romo, Héctor. 2005. *México frente a la mundialización neoliberal*. Mexico City: Ediciones Era.

Guzmán A., Manuel, and John Lyons. 2003. "Los peces de las aguas continentales del estado de Jalisco, México. Análisis preliminar". *e-Gnosis* 1.

Haber, Stephen, Herbert S. Klein, Noel Maurer, and Kevin J. Middlebrook. 2008. *Mexico since 1980, The World since 1980*. New York: Cambridge University Press.

Harvey, David. 2007. *Breve historia del neoliberalismo*. Madrid: Akal.

Hea Kil, Sang, and Cecilia Menjívar. 2006. "The "War on the Border": Criminalizing Immigrants and Militarizing the U.S.–Mexico Border". In *Immigration and Crime: Race, Ethnicity, and Violence*, edited by Ramiro Jr. Martinez and Abel Jr. Valenzuela, 164–88. New York: New York University Press.

Hernández, David Manuel. 2008. "Pursuant to Deportation: Latinos and Immigrant Detention". *Latino Studies* 6 (2008): 35–63.

Hernández de Gante, Alicia. 2010. "¿Éxito o fracaso del neoliberalismo?" In *La reconfiguración neoliberal en América Latina*, edited by Alicia Hernández de Gante and Adrián Gimate-Welsh, 119–53. Mexico City: Miguel Ángel Porrúa.

Hernández García, Adriana. 2006. "Mezcala: encuentros y desencuentros de una comunidad". *Espiral, Estudios sobre Estado y Sociedad* 12 (36): 97–128.

Holloway, John. 2010. *Cambiar el mundo sin tomar el poder*. Mexico City: Sísifo Ediciones; Bajo Tierra Ediciones; Benemérita Universidad Autónoma de Puebla.

The Local Workings of a Global Political Economy 91

Info Rural. 2007. "Jalisco primer productor nacional de charal". *Info Rural*, August 10. www.inforural.com.mx/spip.php?article10973 [accessed March 18, 2014].

López, Ann Aurelia. 2007. *The Farmworkers' Journey*. Berkeley, CA: University of California Press.

Marroni, María da Gloria. 2008. "La nueva migración rural a Estados Unidos en tiempos del neoliberalismo mexicano". In *México, de la utopía compartida a la nación dividida*, edited by Florencia Correas Vázquez, Carlos Figueroa Ibarra, Pedro F. Hernández Ornelas and María da Gloria Marroni, 135–54. Mexico City: Benemérita Universidad Autónoma de Puebla—Instituto de Ciencias Sociales y Humanidades "Alfonso Vélez Pliego"; Plaza y Valdés.

Martin, Philip. 2010. "The Research-Policy Nexus: The Case of Unauthorised Mexico-US Migration and US Policy Responses". *Population, Space and Place* 16: 241–52.

Martin, Philip L. 2003. *Promise Unfulfilled: Unions, Immigration and the Farm Workers*. Ithaca, NY: Cornell University Press.

Martínez, Víctor. 2014. "Exigen a diputados reactivar fondo para ex braceros". *NTR Medios de Comunicación*, January 21. http://ntrzacatecas.com/2014/01/21/exigen-a-diputados-reactivar-fondo-para-ex-braceros/ [accessed March 20, 2014].

Massey, Douglas S. 2009. "The Political Economy of Migration in an Era of Globalization". In *Internacional Migration and Human Rights: The Global Repercussion of U.S. Policy*, edited by Samuel Martínez, 25–43. Berkeley, CA: University of California Press.

McClennen, Sophia. 2011. "Life in the Red Zone or the Geographies of Neoliberalism". In *Cartographies of Affect: Across Borders in South Asia and the Americas*, edited by Debra A. Castillo and Kavita Panjabi, 165–90. Kolkata: Worldview Press.

Ortiz Segura, Carlos. 2001. "'Todo tiempo pasado fue mejor', o la pesca en el lago de Chapala antes de la desecación de su ciénaga". *Gazeta de Antropología* 17 (26).

París, María Dolores. 2008. "Estratificación laboral, migración transnacional y etnicidad". In *Migración, fronteras e identidades étnicas transnacionales*, edited by Laura Velasco Ortiz, 239–66. Mexico City: El Colegio de la Frontera Norte; Miguel Ángel Porrúa.

Patnaik, Utsa. 2008. "Teorías sobre la pobreza y la seguridad alimentaria en la era de las reformas económicas". In *La globalización y el Consenso de Washington*, edited by Gladys Lechini, 169–213. Buenos Aires: CLACSO.

Phillips, Julie A., and Douglas S. Massey. 1999. "The New Labor Market: Immigrants and Wages after IRCA". *Demography* 36 (2): 233–46.

Portes, Alejandro. 2012. "La inmigración ilegal y el sistema internacional. Lecciones de la reciente inmigración legal mexicana a Estados Unidos". In *Sociología económica de las migraciones internacionales*, edited by Lorenzo Cachón, 3–17. Madrid: Anthropos. Original edition, 1979.

Portes, Alejandro, and John Walton. 1981. *Labor, Class, and the International System*. New York: Academic Press.

Santiago Cruz, Exiquio. 2003. "El Chan del agua". In *Leyendas y personajes populares de Jalisco*, edited by Helia García Pérez, 83–4. Guadalajara, Mexico: Secretaría de Cultura del Estado de Jalisco.

Sassen, Saskia. 1988. *The Mobility of Labor and Capital*. Cambridge: Cambridge University Press.

Siisiäinen, Martti. 2000. "Two Concepts of Social Capital: Bourdieu vs. Putnam". ISTR Fourth International Conference "The Third Sector: For What and for Whom?", Trinity College, Dublin, Ireland, July 5–8.

92 The Local Workings of a Global Political Economy

Soederberg, Susanne. 2005. "The Rise of Neoliberalism in Mexico: From a Developmental to a Competition State". In *Internalizing Globalization: The Rise of Neoliberalism and the Decline of National Varieties of Capitalism*, edited by Susanne Soederberg, Georg Menz and Philip G. Cerny, 167–82. New York: Palgrave Macmillan.

Sonnenfeld, David A. 1992. "Mexico's 'Green Revolution', 1940–1980: Towards an Environmental History". *Environmental History Review* 16 (4): 28–52.

Stephen, Lynn. 2007. *Transborder Lives. Indigenous Oaxacans in Mexico, California and Oregon*. Durham, NC: Duke University Press.

Stephen, Lynn. 2008. "Vigilancia e invisibilidad en la vida de los inmigrantes indígenas mexicanos que trabajan en Estados Unidos". In *Migración, fronteras e identidades étnicas transnacionales*, edited by Laura Velasco Ortiz, 197–238. Mexico City: El Colegio de la Frontera Norte; Miguel Ángel Porrúa.

Tamayo, Jaime, and Alejandra Vizcarra. 2000. *Jalisco: sociedad, economía, política y cultura*. Mexico City: Universidad Nacional Autónoma de México.

Torres-Mazuera, Gabriela. 2009. "La territorialidad rural mexicana en un contexto de descentralización y competencia electoral". *Revista Mexicana de Sociología* 71 (3): 453–90.

Velasco Ortiz, M. Laura. 2002. *El regreso de la comunidad: migración indígena y agentes étnicos: los mixtecos de la frontera México-Estados Unidos*. Mexico City: El Colegio de México; El Colegio de la Frontera Norte.

Wallerstein, Immanuel. 2007. *World-systems Analysis: An Introduction*. Durham, NC: Duke University Press.

Weyland, Karin. 2004. "Dominican Women 'Con un Pie Aquí y Otro Allá'. Transnational Practices at the Crossroads of Local/Glocal Agendas". In *Dominican Migration Transnational Perspectives*, edited by Ernesto Sagás and Sintia E. Molina, 154–76. Gainesville, FL: University Press of Florida.

3 The Transnationalisation of Informal Power

Setting the Path to 'Progress'

On August 31, 2013, I was invited to attend the competition *Señorita Jalisco LA*, in Los Angeles Theatre, because Club Mezcala had launched a candidate to revive the impetus of its members, actions, networks and operation. That day two speeches marked me: first, the one by the Mexican Consul Carlos Sada who talked about how beautiful Mexico is and the need to achieve development; and, second, by Daisy Gonzalez, Mezcala's young candidate, who gave a speech on the 'American Dream' and how all of them have achieved it, as demonstrated by their presence in that beautiful building and important event. Like Daisy many migrants and their descendants have adopted this rhetoric into their life, but also have endeavoured to promote it into their community of origin through the ideas of progress. As a result, migrants have, in some sense, been gaining recognition within the community, being portrayed as subjects carrying 'American' values and respected because of their help in achieving 'progress'.

Like so, Mezcalenses are experiencing what Luis Eduardo Guarnizo identifies as 'transnational living'; this means, the reproduction of the community by 'social, cultural, political, and economic cross-border relations', which are shaped historically by different structures, actors, logics and hierarchies, and affect subjects in their multiple locations (2003, 667). Their lives are connected across space and time, and increasingly delineated by the ideas and values of modernisation, development and progress employed by different social, political, economic and cultural forces. Accordingly, in this chapter I address the function and spreading out of the rhetoric of 'development' and 'progress' in perpetuating structures, asymmetries and differentiations transnationally within the era of neoliberal governance. Here we must consider that the neoliberal project, by celebrating 'freedom, progress and individualism', has become a 'synonym of being American' and these values have become associated with 'Western civilization', influencing 'many domains of social life' while 'setting the normative standards of good citizenship in practice' (Ong 1996, 739). In this regard, most Mexicans have adopted certain cultural and social values, and thus, have integrated, internalised and perpetuated a hegemonic discourse, which aims to foster competitiveness within the global economy and impresses upon them ideas for entrance into the 'First World', into the category of 'developed' nations.

94 *The Transnationalisation of Informal Power*

Furthermore, many of them, by crossing the border and looking for a 'better life' and to reach the so-called 'American Dream', have connected with their communities of origin through economic but also 'social remittances', that is, in accordance with the definition of Peggy Levitt, the incorporation of ideas, identities, behaviours and social capital (1998, 927). In parallel, the Mexican government transformed migrants into 'heroic figures', while it sought to keep profiting not only from their labour and economic input, as noted in the last chapter, but also from their political and social potential. In this manner, in the era of neoliberal governance, new transnational agents are incorporated, and therefore, institutions adapted and informal channels expanded, reinforced and redefined. In view of that, this chapter brings together the place of both economic and social remittances through the use of informal politics, to demonstrate their impact on the ways of life and in reinforcing social structures and hierarchies both in the community of origin and broadly, among the workings of neoliberal governance.

More specifically, I aim to identify how the rhetoric of 'development' acts as an associated discourse used by neoliberal governance, driving inhabitants to bring into play these informal channels transnationally in order to improve the conditions in the village, while influencing their relationships, and ways of being and thinking. To begin with I contextualise the living conditions of Mezcalenses, especially apropos of health and education, by, on the one hand, narrating the current and persistent marginalisation and use of informal power in the village; and, on the other hand, exploring the myth of the 'American Dream' to grasp the flow of ideas and values that fostered the continuous movement of Mezcalenses to the United States, and their commitment to those left behind. Subsequently, in the third section, by following the emergence and development of *Club Mezcala de la Asunción*, I scrutinise the implementation of governmental policies and programmes to begin to complicate the expression of citizenship, but more importantly, the use of the rhetoric of development and progress by elites and a sector of migrants to shape the life and projects of Mezcalenses. For this purpose, I explore the institutionalisation of this transnational clientele attracted by the idea of sharing 'progress'. Next, I analyse the transnational political game in regard to *Programa 3x1* to appreciate the importance of migrants in both countries, the transnationalisation of the inherited political culture and the perpetuation of the marginalisation and abuse towards communities. Finally, through the example of a library project in the community I explore the reproduction of this game and its practices, but also the opening of new channels that allow the survival of the Club and the arrival of 'better conditions' to the village. In brief, this chapter is a reflection of the transnationalisation of informality and of social structures and hierarchies, but also an invitation to further debate the different interpretations of 'progress' and the paths and alternatives being constructed away from a capitalist and colonialist rationale.

Informality Managing Living Conditions in the Village

To the present day, rural and indigenous settlements have been mainly characterised by marginality as far as health, education and housing are concerned. This

Figure 3.1 Streets in the *Centro* of Mezcala.

national scenario can be observed in Mezcala where, as Vicente, a middle-aged inhabitant, notes, 'there are many people who really, hardly dress, eat and have a house, live in houses very insalubrious'. In effect, Mezcala experiences a high level of marginality, meaning that there are still houses without toilets, drainage, electricity, running water and floors; as Tomás, a migrant, observes, 'in La Cuesta we don't have drainage, we have to make [septic] tanks, and the water is given to us every third day only for two three hours'. Not only is the water service dysfunctional and irregular, but also other services such as health and education meet the same fate. Over the years inhabitants have been fighting for better conditions, either through communitarian work or negotiating with the government; yet there still is plenty of room for improvement and more necessities to be satisfied.

Concerning health, it wasn't until the 1980s that the community managed to get a small clinic constructed, but the service is deficient and the facilities remain the same, undersized and practically abandoned. As stated by Itza, a housewife, 'either it doesn't have a good service or doesn't have the medicine'. Due to the lack of doctors, medicines and proper facilities, or insufficient money to travel for medical care, to give birth, suffer from curable diseases and scorpion stings can be life threatening for inhabitants. Doña Ino describes this panorama:

> They take someone who is seriously ill or something, and sometimes [there is] no doctor, the doctor isn't working that day or if it's already night he

96 *The Transnationalisation of Informal Power*

doesn't open anymore, and they say, or if he opened sometimes there is no medicine that can be prescribed.... You can't trust, to say, someone is going to be sick at night and there is going to be a doctor there to take care of him, no. And the only thing they, those who can carry them to Guadalajara is where there is a hospital, so sometimes they manage to survive, and those who can't sometimes don't, no longer, don't last.

There is an institutional problem that highly affects the proper functioning of the healthcare system and that is also true for the education system. In fact, until the 1970s Mezcala only offered children the possibility to study the first three levels of primary school, 'El parvulito'. Children had few opportunities since education was deficient, of poor quality and inappropriate, and not all of them could attend. As a consequence, most of the population remained illiterate or migrated to find educational opportunities. Over time inhabitants negotiated with the government the creation of other educational levels, until they achieved the construction of the high school in the 2000s. Now Mezcala has a complete basic education system; but one that, as in other indigenous communities in Mexico, is still poor and inadequate; and yet not all children attend school. Just to contextualise, in 2010, 10.5 per cent of the population was illiterate and 35.5 per cent did not complete primary school in Mezcala (Sistema de Información Estadística y Geográfica de Jalisco 2012). Even though material conditions of schools are deplorable, the highest complaint is about how irresponsible, out-dated and low level teachers are. José Luis, an active defendant of the youth, denunciates: 'I do not know if they're the most dunce teachers that were found all over the country, or is intentionally, or is a punishment to Mezcala; but the teachers are good for nothing, really, the students don't learn anything'. Teachers are just part of the problem as they are immersed in the limited, deficient and corrupt education system where employment positions are negotiated.

Thus, as long as there is no institutional change and better conditions are not provided, inhabitants will continue to abandon school or migrate. José Luis also explains that 'the same bad education has left ... young people just to finish high school and go to work as bricklayers, to companies, to crop chayote; return to the same, as always'. Indeed, school is the most important 'ideological state apparatus', that instructs children in order to produce them as workers or peasants to fulfil their role within society, providing them just with the 'knowledge' needed (Althusser 2001).[1] The school aims to accomplish such alienation because, as pointed out by Tomás, a parent of three children:

it's part of a system, it doesn't suit them. It doesn't suit the government that you to think, it doesn't suit it that you rebel, it doesn't suit it that you protest for what they aren't giving you, for what they don't give you. Do you think it suits the corrupt ones that you know how to defend your rights?

The state will maintain these conditions to ensure the limitation of civic awareness and the endurance of corrupt practices.

The Transnationalisation of Informal Power 97

Indeed, as people are noticing the ravages of the system and are requiring better conditions, the government implements social programmes to silence discontent. In effect, after the consolidation of the PRI, social programmes were used to ensure support, obstruct discontent and guarantee the hegemony of the party. With the arrival of the neoliberal paradigm, the Mexican government embraced the discourse and agenda that IFIs spread into 'underdeveloped' countries, leading people to believe that the problem was the use of informal channels. However, informal practices were renewed through *social liberalism* that simulated an institutional change in a context of reduced social protection (Álvarez Yáñez 2008, 31); and further strengthened through social programmes that followed the guidelines of the World Bank. These programmes, in fact, must be read not only as responding to the logics of the state, but to the use of 'planning' to achieve 'progress', where institutions are shaped and people are rendered 'governable' subjects, in order to facilitate the imposition of norms, and to ensure the maintenance of social structures and the capitalist system (Escobar 1992).

In this regard, through these poverty alleviation programmes, the Mexican government has persisted with populist practices, dominating and privileging certain sectors through informal power, and thus, sustaining neoliberal governance. Accordingly, *Seguro Popular*, which provides health insurance to unemployed and informal workers, does not offer a good alternative to resolve health issues since families must continue to use the same deficient and corrupt system. For instance, inhabitants suffering kidney-related diseases, produced by the high toxicity level of the water, are not treated due to lack of information and funds (De la Torre 2010), while those who have this insurance are not covered (Ferreiro 2013).[2] Similarly, *Oportunidades* supports education by giving a monthly allowance to families in exchange for sending children to school; however, it disregards educational malfunction, the limited scope, low quality and inappropriateness of education, while this programme is shaped up by clienteles and corruption. In effect, inhabitants note that funds are irregularly distributed, which also raises suspicions about embezzlement and diversion of funds. Besides, sometimes the money is not intended to improve the living conditions of children; rather the programme operates as a family business; Itza clarifies: 'the majority is here almost only for the money, for what they're given and keep having [more] children'. In this context, the problems of such programmes are not only their reduced benefits and access, high costs, limitation of political participation and top-down design (Holzner 2010), but the legitimisation granted to the government that maintains the functioning and structuring of the system. In fact, these programmes have increased dependency while promoting alienation and exclusion. Itza also explains:

> Here you can have, there is work, but unfortunately people expect everything to be given by the *Municipio*. They want everything from the Municipio.... And they want everything for free. Right now, the programs of SEDESOL [*Secretaría de Desarrollo Social*] have given a lot of support here and I say 'oh well, that's good' ... but people should be taking advantage of it really well.

Figure 3.2 Distributing *Oportunidades*.

In this manner, corrupt and clientele networks absorb inhabitants under the promise of albeit little aid and misleading perceptions, hampering communal organisation and projects. In addition, social programmes are the channel through which political intermediation persists, allowing the emergence of local operators, who manage the relationships and allocation of funds. The population has their voice reduced to that of intermediaries, using informal negotiation while strengthening the power of local elites that trade political positions, money, favours, threats and bribes. To this effect, *caciquismo* is a form of 'clientelist' authority that carries out patronage, factionalism and violence (Knight 2005). Yet *caciquismo* needs to be understood beyond its strategic mechanisms and structural dimension in order to distinguish its extra-territorial and 'discursive' features (Pansters 2005), which allows the formation of networks (Hilgers 2011). In brief, social programmes are also used to gain popular endorsement, co-opt the population and attract electoral support by distributing minor benefits, creating networks and new pacts where corruption and clientelism are reproduced. In this regard, Chuy, a returnee, expresses that 'a lot of people [say] ... "No, I'm going to vote for the PRI, why? because it gave me a bag of beans, or because it installed me here my [aluminium] sheets"'.

In different degrees and forms political parties have used 'populist' measures to increase their clientele while destroying the state welfare system through neoliberal policies (Álvarez Béjar and Ortega Breña 2006) and fracturing society. Votes are a 'political weapon' (Hernández 2008) that entails the promise of

The Transnationalisation of Informal Power   99

improving living conditions, in a scenario of political manoeuvring and few channels of participation. This can be illustrated with an excerpt called 'The Circus Has Arrived' from the bulletin *El Ticus Insurgente* written by young inhabitants:

> The electoral campaigns arrive and we continue seeing the same scene as always, the candidates doing *maroma y teatro* [everything] to obtain your vote making you some very fanciful promises that we all know they won't fulfil. The change of government turns out to be only a change of master, and this implies continuing with the same misery and exploitation to give continuity to the privileges of the ruling class, the bourgeoisie.

For instance, in the case of the high school, Carlos, who is one of the writers of this pamphlet, remembers: 'Political parties brought us back and forth, "I'm going to help you, and if you support me in the campaign I'll help you build the high school"'. Accordingly, clientelism, as observed by Gastón Gordillo (2009) in the case of Formosa Argentina, must be understood not only as a set of imposed practices but also as the relations of power where people actively participate and are engaged in their reproduction and criticism.

Moreover, clientelism mixes symbolic and rhetoric elements to reinforce the functioning of these geographies of power. In this regard, *comuneros* are portrayed as enemies of 'progress' and 'development', leading the rest of the inhabitants to believe that—in the words of Alberto, a liaison member of Club Mezcala—'many programs have arrived and with a lot of cash, I'm talking about millions of pesos and that at the time if the team that is in *Bienes Comunales*, just say they don't agree, that program leaves'. Within this scenario, the government presents itself as a benefactor, whereas it is the one to divert the funds, to impede an improvement in quality of life and to maintain the exclusion of most of the population through its methods, policies and institutions. In this respect, Richard Snyder identifies the politics of reregulation, that is, the creation of 'new institutions for market governance', emphasising the political bargain between politicians, institutions and 'societal forces' taking place to establish policies and new 'exclusionary' and/or 'participatory' institutions in Mexico (2001, 195–6) to sustain the workings of neoliberal governance.

Despite this scenario, the high involvement and concern of inhabitants have combined to oppose governmental actions and find ways to cope by themselves, supported by their studies, relatives or knowledge. For example, Mezcalenses of *La Cuesta* organised and supported the creation of an additional health centre that is managed by a local family. Additionally, they are also pushing for better conditions, such as the construction of a hospital and of a university campus. In the meantime, some inhabitants, especially young people, keep migrating in search of work and education opportunities. Now, young people in the community have degrees in different fields, such as history, law, pedagogy, engineering, accountancy, psychology, medicine and nursing. The problem is that on graduation, opportunities to practise in the village are scarce; thus, they

100 *The Transnationalisation of Informal Power*

try their luck in other cities and villages or even in the U.S. In spite of this deterritorialisation, Mezcalenses do not want to leave the community stagnant and outside the benefits of progress, so they show attachment, give continuity to a sense of community, organise new ways to support the community while creating new expressions of citizenship, as discussed further on. Either locally, nationally or transnationally, they are negotiating improvements, confronting an indifferent government that seeks to absorb them through a clientele network. As shown in Chapter 1, informal power remains the principal way in which people and the state are linked; also in conjunction with institutions and social capital, Mezcala shows how this is readapted and renovated to address the current circumstances.

Mezcalenses Striving the 'American Dream'

Many Mezcalenses are crossing the border due to economic, political, social and individual factors, but also social constructions, and the influx of ideas and values have come to reinforce this flow. To begin with, Mexico and the United States have been erroneously constructed in opposition to each other (Heyman and Campbell 2007), because the idea of a corrupt and decadent South is necessary to uphold the notion of an honest and hardworking North (Anders and Nuijten 2007, 4). Within such a view, neither the connectedness nor the collaboration of both countries has been taken into account, creating a distorted image that has been reproduced internally over time. The idea of the 'American Dream' arises emphasising this binary opposition, being defined as a 'fantasy that helps maintain the structures of neocolonialism both inside and outside the country' (Rieger 2013, 7), reproducing hierarchies and legitimising white supremacy. Many Mezcalenses arrived in the United States seduced by the riches as portrayed by this dream, and shared this through the narration of 'marvellous' experiences; the elder Don Fernando explains how this began:

> The majority is in the United States because the first ones that go, the government also allowed it when the touted hiring of braceros arrived. The problem was that the firsts go and come and talk to them about the way of living, of eating, of working and the next time, more are encouraged, and more and more, and many didn't return, they started to stay, after a while they brought with them the family.

Although some did return and improved their living conditions in the village the truth is that the 'American Dream' has made people believe in the possibility of wealth and a better and easier life, and of climbing the economic and social structures. For instance, Don José narrates how he was lured by the U.S. lifestyle:

> My uncle Casimiro ... told us stories, always. When he was 15 years old he came as a bracero and said ... 'there, the United States is very practical. Everything is very good, if you want a coffee, you just open the hot water

The Transnationalisation of Informal Power   101

tap and you put the coffee and it's ready, and the bathroom and everything, everything very good'.

In line with the ideas of Portes, in Mezcala migration occurs, especially, due to the encouragement of a 'modern culture' and 'consumption cult' (2012, 12–13). 'Progress' and 'development', in this manner, are incentives to migrate due to the opportunities, benefits and services associated with living in a 'First World' country. However, not only have the stunning facilities and luxuries attracted them, inhabitants continually crossed with the hope of improving their living conditions back in the community. As Don Roberto, a migrant who arrived in the 1970s, shares: 'I came with the illusion of working, save some money, return to my village to buy a motor boat, and tools to continue fishing'. They also aspired to boost opportunities for their family members, inducing or bringing them to the U.S. to enjoy full benefits; for example Juana, a mother of four children, comments that she tells her oldest son:

> What I like about this country is that it has many opportunities for you. If you want to study, they lend you money, or they give you scholarships or whatever, and it's fine, everything depends on you, and you have to study, because it's good for you.

In short, Mezcalenses were encouraged by better salaries and employment opportunities, but also by the aspiration for development, seen in education, accumulation of capital and acquisition of material goods, while being supported by their network.

Therefore, as family members joined in, migrants settled permanently in the Los Angeles area, and in other *comunidades sátelite*, organising their transnational living. Their lives changed but this did not always mean their full incorporation via employment, family, economic capital, legal status, culture, education and language acquisition, with them remaining 'liminals', that is, as defined by Chavez (2013), outsiders living an uncertain and fearful life separated from U.S. society. So, as noted in the last chapter, while migration might represent some economic, social and political advantages, immigration control has sought to augment the risks and prices, and lower the benefits, provoking anti-immigrant sentiments and reproducing structures, practices and rationales to further exclude and outrage sectors of the society. Migrants are criminalised, which escalates their vulnerability and marginalisation, since, as documented by Sang Hea Kil and Cecilia Menjívar (2006), they are placed outside the legal order, allowing actions against them while authorities are exempt from obligations towards them. This affects their housing, education, health, employments, security, relations and subjectivity, pushing them to live underground and self-discriminate. In this context, Don Roberto expresses:

> Maybe the Anglo-Saxons have these services or ... they have more education, so one as Latino often comes from *ranchitos*, small villages that are

102 *The Transnationalisation of Informal Power*

not, we are not very prepared. So our culture is a little bit, not our culture, but our education is low. Many times we don't understand the message that the government wants to give us, the laws, and thus we're breaking everything that ... the Anglo-Saxon is used to its laws here.

Migrants were prepared to make some sacrifices hoping for a better future, but the U.S. was full of obstacles and eventually did not meet the expected life. For example, Doña Ino imagined that '[it was going to be] more money, the way of life was going to be better and I used to say, "if we're there we'll be able to better help our families financially" ... it wasn't what I thought'. Though experiences might vary, for Gretchen Levingston and Joan R. Kahn (2002) the lack of human capital and motivation was what affected successful incorporation to the 'American' life of the successive generations and limited the mobility of Mexicans. However, this perspective disregards the delineated complexities of labour, economics and social conditions and structures, while it contains a reduced dichotomic conception. Keeping this in mind, Mezcalenses have reached this 'better' life in some aspects, although in general, they have established themselves in marginalised and unsafe areas, and shared houses, paying rent, taxes, amenities and for food.

Migrants as subcitizens have restricted access, assuring in most cases a subordinated position, as for instance, in education. In addition, in tandem with the observations of Bauder (2008, 325) about informal citizenship, they are increasingly driven to express their loyalty and willingness to embrace cultural identity and adapt to the cultural conventions of the receiving country. These dispositions function as part of a system of distinction that is moulded by changed perceptions, particular practices and identity constructions, dimensions further explored in Chapter 5. As a result, many families perceive education in the U.S. as 'superior' compared to the one in Mezcala, and a path to success and to achieve the 'American Dream'. Therefore, many adjust their lives and future accordingly; like Tomás who decided:

> I'll stay here longer, is logical, because I want my children to grow up and prepare here, because if I go back to Mexico I won't be able to give them the education I can give them here, or the system gives them here.

For migrants, 'the basics to be able to start a life if you want to progress is to study the language' (Don Roberto 2013), but also education can give a better life to their children, gaining better remunerations and having the possibility to climb in the social structure. Migrants, even if some manage to fully enjoy it, often experience a poor and inadequate education but also, glitches mainly related to discrimination, economic impairment and distinct worldviews, values, languages and lifestyle that prevent the 'Dream' from becoming tangible (Hill and Torres 2010).[3] In fact, migrants of Mezcala have signalled as a problem the high demand of engagement towards parents and the expectations to provide children with the 'American-lifestyle' when having low incomes, few benefits and scarce

The Transnationalisation of Informal Power   103

labour support. As a result, a vicious cycle is created where migrants seem condemned to lower labour, economic, social and cultural positions via poor and marginalised educational access, support and achievement.

Similarly, regarding health services, they are often perceived as more 'advanced', but are also one of the hardest parts to achieve of the 'American Dream'. Most migrants are not provided with this service, and any medical care is a luxury they cannot afford. Under the mechanisms of neoliberal governance the responsibilities of the state are taken away, while migrants are portrayed as profiteers or even as parasites, in this case of the U.S. social services, reducing the resources available to the rest of the population. Therefore, even if the Mexican health system is deficient and of poor quality, sometimes it is praised compared to the one in the United States that is highly expensive and restricted.[4] Don Ramiro, a *comunero* who used to be a migrant, compares the two health services:

> When you get sick, don't think there is medicine, there [the United States] you go with a doctor but the *bills* come very expensive in money, very expensive, very expensive, so what one worked barely is to be paying them, paying them, paying them. And here, no, thanks to God, here we have everything, here you get your insurance, one feels a bit ill, and runs [to Guadalajara], I've never need it.

However, whether in the United States or Mexico, Mezcalenses struggle and migrants often are those assuming the economic costs in both locations. While citizenship in the U.S. might be seen as a door to accessing rights, to migrant mobility and inclusion, this is not guaranteed. In fact, citizenship is 'a system for exclusion and the reproduction of inequalities' (Gálvez 2013, 724). Hence, migrants still experience different forms of insecurity and racism, accentuated when they are considered illegal.

Still, even if the United States did not fulfil their expectations, it offered different lifestyles, jobs, opportunities and remuneration that impacted on life in the community of origin. Following the ideas of Velasco Ortiz (2002), the movement of people, objects, information and meanings create a network where adaptation and connection is facilitated for migrants. In this context, there was not a break in support networks, which persisted across frontiers to soothe their arrival and adaptation and as a bond toughened by their commitment to providing for their families. In this sense, migrants were advancing in the use of social capital as a survival strategy that also enabled the ones left behind to climb in the social structure by sharing the benefits; as Doña Ino expounds, 'even if there are no benefits for the workers or something, but at least they can send some money to their families every month for their sustenance'. Migrants are concerned about enhancing their families' economic situation in the face of the lack of state provision in Mexico regarding basic services; thus, most of them send money regularly; Don Ramiro narrates how he manages to survive:

104   *The Transnationalisation of Informal Power*

One sows its chayotes, sometimes you hit a good price, one is relieved and when not, you're getting at least for gasoline to water or your children, as you see luckily I have two in the United States, others are there in Tijuana, they're working, they have good jobs, in Tijuana. They work in these ... some with shoes, others in packing and others I don't know, what I know is that they don't leave me, they send me at least a few pennies.

Mezcalenses are finding additional funding sources, following the ideas of Massey (2009), employing some members abroad as temporary and even as permanent migrant labourers. In Mezcala remittances have come to constitute one of the main forms of economic support, as Don Chava, an elder, discerns: 'Like myself, I've that help, many here have that help too. Because there are many people there from here'. In this sense, for migrants of Mezcala, following the ideas of Debra A. Castillo and Kavita Panjabi (2011), family not only entails a network of support, but also represents the reason for their decision to immigrate while home is the beloved place where it is not possible to live but where conditions should be improved. Migrants have become 'perfect citizens', as noted by Dalum Berg and Rodriguez (2013, 653), who not only sustain themselves but also their families left behind, while the state is 'absolved of responsibility' (Gálvez 2013, 733). This fact has increased their dependence and continued to propel migration as the path towards a better life. Even now, a child's ideal is to grow up to migrate to the United States (Hernández García 2006, 123). In this sense, migrants, by assuming themselves as the bearers of the 'American Dream' and the rhetoric of 'development' and 'progress', might be also perpetuating the deterioration of the main local economic activities, the lack of the states' social responsibilities, cheap labour and exploitation, economic dependence, discrimination and aspirations to reach a 'modern life'; more broadly the dynamics of neoliberal governance that maintain the flow and structures unchanged.

In fact, despite migrants complaining of living stressful, pressured, exhausted and rushed lives, they commonly believe that, as Tomás comments:

materially you don't worry.... There's no need like when you lived there in Mezcala, it's very different because if you don't have something you go to the '*ninety-nine*', and you get something, you understand? No, it isn't that hard.

Thus, in general, although many Mezcalenses have come to realise that the 'American Dream' is an illusion, they have not disproved its myth, as they often perceive an economic advantage, since they can own material goods, as Chuy explains:

You live better [in the United States], because here Mexico, not only Mezcala is fucked up or maybe there is money but you see that only some want to be the beneficiaries.... As a cousin says here ... that there one pays rent and fucking everything, water and light, and I say, 'cousin, but there

The Transnationalisation of Informal Power 105

you pay for all that and you still have for some pants, to go to the movies, to go to eat, to go …'. And here one doesn't pay anything and there is no [money] for that. I mean, here how often one goes to the movies?

Paradoxically, migration establishes as a family survival strategy, being a source of income, but also a door to 'progress'. The economic flows brought about by migration allow new forms of consumption, and thus, migrants have become carriers of U.S. brand names, lifestyle and consumption ideology. They bring material goods, their cars and other luxury accessories and are concerned with investing in houses or businesses, since, in the words of Don Fernando, 'despite the life they had here, they have never forgotten Mezcala'. They are projecting a sense of their 'enhanced' life, expecting to reach social mobility within the community; however, their material life and values, ideas and relations brought might alter the landscape, act against the community practices, and accentuate in some cases economic, social and cultural inequality—as further explored.

Migrants are experiencing processes of deterritorialisation in parallel with processes of reterritorialisation. Mobility has not meant that Mezcalenses lose their sense of place; rather, inspired by the ideas of Escobar (2001), they experience the creation of boundaries and conceptions of affection and belonging through a continuous and persistent economic, cultural and social connection. Thus, on the one hand, economic remittances are a way by which migrants comfort themselves in the face of their absence and increase their connection with the community of origin, but also, by which they empower themselves, influence culturally, mobilise socially and economically, and thus, enhance their status. On the other hand, social remittances have been redefining the ways of thinking, their relationships and aspirations marked by the ideas of 'progress' and the myth of the 'American Dream'. While the effects on cultural practices, identity and sense of community are explored deeply in Chapter 5, the next section, through the lens of politics, addresses issues of citizenship more deeply, in order to recognise the impacts of such remittances on hierarchies and social stratifications.

The Transnational Institutionalisation of Informality

The Foundation of Club Mezcala de la Asunción

Being transnational has not meant being outside nation-state logics (Guarnizo 2003), rather, in some sense, to be used by national governments within the manoeuvring of neoliberal governance. In the case of Mezcala, migration has allowed the institutionalisation of a sector and the expansion of informality and networks of power and support. Migrants were already organised, but from the 1980s their organisation began to be regulated, as the priest approached them to aid in the chores of the church and to make collections for the deceased. From that moment on, the local priest extended links with migrants, while migrants united to support, raise money and promote infrastructure projects in their community. As the

106   *The Transnationalisation of Informal Power*

Mexican government perceived the influence of migrants in elections, it changed its passive role to improve their relationship and stimulate free transit (Velasco Ortiz 2002). This 'proactive' engagement served to legitimise its regime, control dissidence, enhance its interests in the U.S. and manage remittances, while responding, in some measure, to the pressures and needs of migrants (Délano 2011).

In this context, the Mexican government promoted dual citizenship, launched the *Programa Paisano* (1989) and propelled the creation of Hometown Associations (HTAs) through the *Programa para las Comunidades Mexicanas en el Extranjero (PCME)* (1990). However, by imitating the Church-inspired associations, which made migrants responsible for providing for their families (Fitzgerald 2009), the links with these migrants were institutionalised, and so was their support to their communities of origin. More precisely, as signalled by Matt Bakker and Michael Peter Smith, the Mexican government promoted migrants as 'extraterritorial citizens' while setting up the 'transnationalisation of the traditional corporatist strategy' (2003, 66–7). In this regard, HTAs have acted as national intermediaries embodying the inherited political culture. With this in mind, the government created the *Federación de Clubes Jaliscienses* (1991) in Los Angeles and the *Oficina de Atención a Jaliscienses en el Extranjero (OFAJE)* (1996). Additionally, in 1997, dual citizenship was legally recognised and used as a state approach due to the deteriorated conditions, and insecurities of its migrant population (Delgado-Wise 2006), and upon acknowledgement of the growing economic and political importance of migrants in both countries (Délano 2011). The extraterritorialisation of citizenship, thus, constituted a way to territorialise it and extend responsibilities to its migrant population and influence local issues and its relations with the United States. So, in 2003, the government transformed the PCME into the *Instituto de los Mexicanos en el Exterior* to keep supporting HTAs and help manage relationships with organised migrants. This meant via co-optation strategies a major control of remittances and indirectly a boost in migration, rather than the improvement of the conditions of migrants.

It was under these circumstances that migrants broadcast the benefits of being a club and their role as bearers of progress, inviting others to join. In 2003, Mezcala integrated to the *Federación de Clubes Jalisciences del Sur de California (FCJSC)*, and institutionalised a portion of them and their relationships. *Club Mezcala de la Asunción* was born in Los Angeles as a voluntary initiative of the president that included Mezcalenses who were already organised, had a close relationship and embodied knowledge, networks and trust among migrants. Through this association there was a shift from family remittances to institutional transfers. These transfers meant, following the ideas of Jonathan Fox and Xóchitl Bada (2008), that a limited transnational liaison was established, since only a few people acted as intermediaries between the global and the local. In this vein, their 'political transnationalism' was facilitated; that means, their actions were regulated by a minority, socially circumscribed, with juridical boundaries, which reproduced power structures (Guarnizo,Portes, and Haller 2003). Thus, similarly to *comuneros*, they became embedded in institutional networks of power serving the functioning of neoliberal governance. To this effect,

The Transnationalisation of Informal Power 107

migrants might participate and replicate structures and hierarchies in both countries with their alterations, variations and inconsistencies.

In spite of migrants' institutionalisation, as Pedro, a past liaison member, explains:

> although [the Club] is a non-profit organisation and as a civil association it can't [get] into religion and politics, but as almost, most [people] are Catholic, so, they have supported, they agree to [keep] support[ing] the matters of the church.

At the beginning people joined Club Mezcala mainly as a favour to the president, but, later, membership expanded through family relationships, and brought together a diverse group with different legal, economic and social backgrounds. People responded to the call for the benefit of their community, using people's affection, their ties and relationships, desires and sense of community. Don Santos relates: 'We decided to support to see if there was a change in our village, because when we came our village was a disregarded village'. The Club consolidated itself with approximately 24 board members, having the support of around 500 migrants from different cities in California: Sanger, San Diego, Fresno, Modesto, Pomona and Lancaster; and in Seattle, Washington. They contributed in different ways: recruiting support, buying tickets, organising events, lending equipment or donating food and money. However, their collective organisation and actions also established limits and social inequalities, since not all migrants participated due to their detachment from the community, economic impairment and work schedules, and also because the translocal network already constructed fostered hierarchies and divisions among migrants—differences between *barrios*, isolation, disagreements, and envy, jealousy and disdain—allowing only a minority to become the political intermediaries. Still, the president, Don José, felt supported and recognised that they were 'achieving great things because we were united and when one unites things are accomplished'.

Migrants proved that they do not detach, either spatially, culturally, economically or socially, from their community and their actions are consonant with the aim of either returning or, as José Luis says, 'thinking about their family, but they see it with the aim of sharing and they display it into something material that is good'. Accordingly, the Club enabled them to organise collectively and open a new public space to transform things in their community, especially as they share a common project of development and progress. In this sense, transnational political practices must account for a mix of dynamics, including the aims of migrants to have community recognition and support the people left behind; but also, to improve their own economic and social conditions, be incorporated into the elite strata, and gain rights. They are seeking a 'substantive citizenship' (Bakker and Smith 2003) or 'vernacular citizenship', as Alyshia Gálvez (2013) calls it, that goes beyond the one offered by the Mexican state and denotes how citizenship is constantly being negotiated, and how it is experienced, discussed, criticised and reinforced by migrants, as examined below.

108 *The Transnationalisation of Informal Power*

Programa 3x1: *A Transnational Political Game*

Initially the participation of Club Mezcala was limited to political support, as in the case of the highway that guaranteed its construction against opposing sectors in the village. In this respect, Don José narrates one of the visits of Governor Francisco Ramírez Acuña (2001–6):

> I told him that we wanted the highway to continue ... and I remember when he answered us, says, 'for my friends from Club Mezcala, I want to tell you that I already have funds allocated so that the highway continues'. So, like they listened to us more and like there was a commitment. He took us into account, and it was done. So, yes, to a large extent, the Club has influenced to make several changes.

In Mezcala the perception of migrants as 'heroes' was somewhat accentuated via the engagement in development projects. Accordingly, the local government realised that the political support from migrants could help them gain control and access to the community, while migrants also became conscious of their potential and power. Straight away Club Mezcala began to collect funds to carry out projects in the community. They arranged meetings, asked for contributions and organised events such as soccer tournaments and *kermesses.* The money gathered went to a bank account to be channelled and invested under *Programa 3x1*,[5] demonstrating how the inherited political culture crosses frontiers. In this programme there is a mutual agreement, as the state aims to channel remittances for public works and obtain electoral support while migrants need economic but especially political cooperation to achieve them.

However, this situation has resulted in permanent negotiations rarely won by migrants. The spaces of negotiation usually are events of the FCJSC such as *Señorita Jalisco LA*, where politicians and governmental authorities gather with migrants. Still, these spaces are exclusive and only a few can show their concerns and negotiate how to invest remittances; in fact, they constitute a way to buy access into politics. In this context, Club Mezcala's first public work was the rehabilitation of two kilometres of streets with ecofriendly pavement that also included running water and sewage. At that time, the Municipal President was Rodolfo García Becerra (2004–6). Don José speaks of the views of Club members towards him: 'We distrusted at the beginning, because in Mezcala we had about 35 years that no, that they had disregarded us, so in Mezcala there was nothing, there were no resources'. In spite of the institutionalisation of migrants, they rejected him, while also he ignored them. Soon he changed his attitude responding to the pressure from the authorities above, Don Santos narrates:

> Just when we started the Club that we were going to, when Rodolfo was president, he didn't want to know anything about the Club, nothing at all, Fox was the President, we were just a step short of reaching directly with Fox from here, the *Federación* [FCJSC] ... and he doesn't want and doesn't

The Transnationalisation of Informal Power 109

want … they talked to the governor, the governor then spoke…. 'This happens, they aren't appreciating Mezcala. They wanted to work through 3x1 and why are they not appreciating them?' … 'Get cracking', he said, 'because they're one step away from the President' he said, 'You're running on a wing and a prayer'…. On Saturday we had Rodolfo here.

Clientelism can involve participation and influence to negotiate proposals; but always determined and limited by the political context, relations and interests. In this sense, the administration of Vicente Fox was characterised by its concern and actions towards the amelioration of the relations with the U.S. and migrants;[6] and at the state level, as the PAN also ruled, the Club felt included, consulted and prioritised. In general, members of Club Mezcala felt supported with funds and in their initiatives, while also honoured locally with luncheons and small gifts. García Becerra gained their trust and even established good personal relationships, showing, in line with the ideas of Hilgers (2011), how patron-client relationships denote some kind of respect and 'friendship'. Meanwhile, members demonstrated their commitment to collaborate and continually collected money through fundraising events, raffles, personal donations and a bank loan, which, according to Pedro: 'for several years it had them, they say over there, "bound", because they had to pay interests'.

Within the community, however, some sectors were still opposed to their actions and were excluded from participating and expressing their opinion, creating tensions with the community. To improve this situation the president appointed a relative to be the liaison and the voice of the Club in the community and with the *Municipio*; the Club created a *Comité Comunitario* made up of two persons from each *barrio*, in charge of watching over, informing and communicating news about the works, and the priest promoted the Club, seeking its legitimation and approval. They managed to gain some support, as Doña Ino, another member, states:

Some of them are grateful to the Club, they say 'If it hadn't been you who started with the streets' they say, 'I think we would still be the same' they say, 'no, there wouldn't be more progress', they say, 'But thanks to the Club that began to fix those streets, ¿right? They had opened us a little bit the mentality that we can do something'.

Similarly to the case of el Rey del Tomate (Bakker and Smith 2003), members of the Club were regarded by a sector of the community as transnational subjects who exemplify the possibilities for Mexican migrants in the U.S., the 'American Dream', by sharing their success, helping them and bringing 'development'. In this context, *Programa 3x1* enhanced the image and perceptions towards migrants through both their economic and social (even cultural) input, while allowing them to be integrated into politics, functioning as 'good citizens' who were trying to gain some room to improve their own living conditions within the structures and dynamics set down by neoliberal governance. However, the political

110 *The Transnationalisation of Informal Power*

participation of migrants is shaped and limited and full political rights are denied (Bakker and Smith 2003). In this manner, migrants are valuable economic, political and electoral actors who got entangled in a new form of transnational citizenship that is framed in the strategy of 'neoliberal governance', exchanging status and power by political support, favours and management, serving the perpetuation and transnationalisation of clientelism and informal power and the marginalisation and abuse towards communities. For instance, presidents of clubs are public servants without a salary and all their duties represent time, effort and money; but, their actions are not only based on personal satisfaction, desires for development and kindness and love towards their community, but most of all, their participation aims to gain status and political influence. In fact, to be president of a club is usually seen as a first step to reaching upper political positions, either in Mexico or the United States, being crucial in learning how to behave as a politician. Don José narrates his experience:

> When I arrived here at the *Federación* [FCJSC], I looked at all the people on the board, the president, the vice president, well, like 'big men', and I felt so little as when I was in the village, but little by little I was having contact with them, I learned of them and there came a time when I felt like them, because I was on the board in several administrations.

Within clientelism subjects follow the rules of the game, adjusting their behaviour, values and beliefs to satisfy specific personal and collective needs. Thus, within the rationale of neoliberal governance, the time, effort and money invested were 'rewarded' by increasing the president's income and prestige, and improving his image, political influence, social status and economic situation in both countries. As he affirms, 'I have given a lot of time, dedication, funds too, but it has been given back to me'. Also other members of the Club experience a similar path, becoming highly implicated in informal politics, sensing that their status and power is elevated due to their growing influence in decisions and projects and their contact with authorities. As Don Santos demonstrates:

> In my life I never thought one day I would sit [at] the table next to the president ... sitting here, all the audience there, and I never in my life thought, because I had classified them ... we peasants and they arrived here ... that a president comes, a candidate for the presidency, wow!

These migrants were included partially in the life of authorities who are welcomed in the village with *banda, comida y fiesta*, as symbols of power, leadership, influence and reward. Accordingly, some of them came to feel that they had gained a voice and become part of the ruling elite; thus, in some way they are adding up to the structures of power. Following the ideas of Fox and Bada (2008) the Club gave a 'voice' to some Mezcalenses who did not have one before 'exiting' Mezcala, but such participation remains highly restricted while local political dynamics at large remain unchanged. So, in spite of their efforts,

The Transnationalisation of Informal Power   111

Club Mezcala got entangled in the inherited political culture and the national dynamics of power; but more broadly, in the channels set up by neoliberal governance and the reproduction of structures and hierarchies on a global scale.

However, we cannot negate how clubs might allow or enhance social welfare and its access, while also improving social capital and informal political participation (Duquette-Rury 2014). Therefore, it is not possible to neglect what the labour migrants do for their community of origin that might be creating a positive image against their *ausencia* (absence). But we can neither put aside the limitations nor problems, abuses and shortcomings of working through *Programa 3x1*, as well as the carelessness and deficiencies of such public services and the restrictions, obstacles and manipulations of the acquired political participation. For instance, whereas at the state level, the governor increasingly supported migrants and inaugurated three *Casas Jalisco* (2011–12); locally, as García Becerra left office, the next two Municipal presidents (2006–12) abandoned the Club limiting its political participation. In this respect, Pedro explains:

> With Ramón Romo ... he also said 'Forget the clubs, right now we aren't going to work with the clubs, we're going to work just as Town Hall', so [due to] the negativity of those two municipal presidents, Ramón Romo and Carlos Maldonado, we didn't work. And everything has brought, in any case, it has damaged the image and the morality of Club Mezcala especially of the people who are in the United States.

Club Mezcala continued to propose projects, such as the creation of a hospital/ clinic, and were willing to work, but the Municipal authorities were not interested. Meanwhile, the *Municipio* and the priest blamed the community, mainly *comuneros* and their supporters, for not succeeding in such projects nor reaching 'progress'. As Don Santos recalls:

> [The priest] said 'Look, I'm nobody to tell you anything' he says, 'but I see that this girl [Rocío] is putting us in a lot of trouble'. Rodolfo also told me.... 'There are many things that can be done here in the village', he says 'but, the bad thing is that we have many people who don't want [things] to be done. You try hard and all that'.... They aren't interested, or as we say vulgarly, they want it handed to them on a silver platter ... he told me 'this girl has put many obstacles'. For the hospital, they were among the first to say, 'we don't want an hospital here'.

On the contrary, *comuneros* were supportive and had a good opinion of migrants, in the words of Don Salvador 'they're fine.... We have to help them so that there is something, we progress something'. In this regard, as explained by Alan Knight (2005, 45), public works are sometimes obstructed by the same authorities in order to balance support between the two factions created, in this case, 'traditionalists' and 'progressives'. Don Marcos, a migrant in Tijuana, evidences this by saying that *comuneros* 'defend an integrity of Mezcala that is old-fashioned, right? They

112   *The Transnationalisation of Informal Power*

don't want progress; they don't want anything; that's what I perceive of them. So really people who are not *comunero* and who want progress are really different, act differently'. Public works are strategic actions where informal power is used occasionally to complete and other times to prevent their realisation, depending on the current political necessities. So while the problem was the lack of support of the *Municipio*, authorities wanted to wash their hands of responsibility by increasing distrust, misconception, division and internal problems to keep control and power over the community. This clearly reflected an example of the local functioning of a form of neoliberal governance.

Nevertheless, migrants later came to realise the lack of support of the *Municipio*, identifying in it the inherited political culture and the longstanding relations with Poncitlán that emphasise their exclusion, rejection, abandonment, marginalisation, discrimination and resentment, described in Chapter 5. For migrants, and indeed, for most of the population, the *Municipio* has never voluntarily supported projects to improve life conditions and development in Mezcala; rather, it has blocked several initiatives, and this time was not an exception. Authorities, as Alberto remarks: 'they see it on the political side. They don't really look for Mezcala to get better. No, no, "first let's look at our interests, if it's in our best interest we do it, if not no"'. This represents a battle between different local, national and transnational forces to obtain political benefits and increase their control over the area. Don Fernando notes:

> The government has always its strategies to keep power and so it continues to be. Now the municipal presidency to shut us up, comes and invests a little more but they press [it] in some way, I don't know if the government pressures those in the United States or those in the United States put pressure on the municipal government, because all the works that have been done, have been with tripartite contributions.

In line with the observations of Guarnizo (2003), within this 'transnational living' though some migrants might be empowered, they are not overcoming power asymmetries or eliminating inequalities, but, rather, conceding space for new forms of control and 'profit extraction', as delineated in Chapter 2. In fact, this goes beyond economic processes, since in this era of neoliberal governance, as demonstrated in this book, the political, territorial and cultural realms are subject to a similar dynamic. In this context, the political 'voice' gained by migrants was limited by the government trying to secure their loyalty, restrict intermediaries and channels of participation, manipulate projects and discourses, and fragment the community. What is more, as the Mexican government perceived how migrants can be a 'powerful lobby' to influence its relation with the U.S. (Fitzgerald 2009), their co-option together with the promotion to get involved in civil participation in the U.S. have become decisive. Clubs cannot engage in U.S. politics, so they do it 'individually'; for instance, some members by joining the *Consejo de Federaciones Mexicanas en Norteamérica (COFEM)* are becoming indirectly an important lobby for the Mexican government. This organisation, as Doña Ino explains:

The Transnationalisation of Informal Power   113

... helps the community, sometimes people need to fill out a form for citizenship, sometimes they want scholarships.... And they, for any political candidate who is going to arrive, they're always looking to see who is the candidate that gives us improvements, for us the Hispanics. And before this group was only of Mexicans, now we have even Guatemalans, Colombians, and from several Latin [American] countries.

Mezcalenses here are constructing a kind of citizenship in the U.S. by claiming their rights and the improvement of their living conditions. Furthermore, they might be challenging their classification as subcitizens, in a context where, following the ideas of Ong, 'the ideological formation of whiteness as the symbol of ideal legal and moral citizenship today continues to depend upon the "blackening" of less desirable immigrants' (1996, 742). Regardless of what their legal status may be, they seek to establish solidarities between Latin American people, and thus, might encourage the formation of a differentiated identity, as Hispanic or Latinos, that can have a valuable weight in politics—this is explored more deeply in Chapter 5 in relation to cultural and social incorporation. In this regard, Raúl Delgado-Wise (2006, 214) optimistically observes how migrants in the U.S. are promoting 'regularization of legal status, full citizen rights, the formation of a multicultural society' and even the opening of frontiers. Although this might be far from being obtained, by standing together as a Mexican/Latino community, they are favouring the position of the Mexican government.

However, 'transnational citizenship' is not only related to the actions of the sending country to extend citizenship rights (Chauvin and Garcés-Mascareñas 2012) and obligations, but also how migrants negotiate with authorities of both countries. Similarly, in this game of power, U.S. politicians know the importance of the Latino community and seek their support; for example, through COFEM. Don José, in this regard, signals that when 'Villaraigosa was campaigning for *Mayor*, we got involved, we went to his campaign centre and we were calling people, and when he won, it feels nice'. In this sense, the transnational character of migrants and their organisations affect both the U.S. and Mexico in the way they incorporate and participate and the expectations they might have of them. So migrants are challenging the boundaries of nation-state citizenship and becoming politically involved in both societies. They are advancing on their own 'transnational citizenship', that is, on other forms of membership construction and extension of rights involving cross-border communities and entailing 'state-based' and 'society-based' approaches (Fox 2005). On the one hand, they are willing to give back to their community and aiming to transform their exclusion; on the other hand, they are gaining new insights by which to integrate into U.S. politics and new commitments to improve conditions for Latinos. In effect, migrants have shown a double commitment, borrowing the concept of Xóchitl Bada, Jonathan Fox and Andrew Selee (2006), 'a civic binationality', where the focus is extended and reinforced from communities of origin to the U.S. society, seeking to establish their membership to manifest their

114   *The Transnationalisation of Informal Power*

concerns, speak up and improve conditions in both communities, and I would emphasise, to gain recognition inclusion and respect.

Migrants have been establishing their relations with the Mexican and U.S. governments, and transnationally, responding to the relationship between both countries and the historical political economic processes in a global context informed by and legitimised through the rhetoric of development. Therefore, migrants, although joining this kind of organisation and political action to resist their political, economic and cultural susceptibility, by so doing, directly or indirectly, mould politics and perpetuate the dynamics and practices of power in and between both countries. In this regard, Dalum Berg and Rodriguez's reworked concept of 'transnational citizenship' is of use, as it accounts for 'not only the actions of migrants and their organisations and the structuring activities of the state, but also the larger global forces which shape and produce these practices' (2013, 651). Like this, 'social and racialised exclusion' appears to spread transnationally (Dalum Berg and Rodriguez 2013) while migrants produce political subjectivities that articulate class, nationalism, citizenship, ethnicity and race across frontiers (Rodriguez 2013). In this manner, migrants have been altering—though also reproducing—structures and institutions in both countries, showing a redefinition of the terms by which the local and global connections are understood in this era of neoliberal governance. This implies how economies and societies are connected and how race is imbricated with other social structures marking the different forms of citizenship and their position within hierarchies; issues analysed in Chapter 5.

The Library: A Transnational Struggle for Power and 'Progress'

Under these circumstances, the organisation of Club Mezcala weakened, stagnated and lost supporters and funds. They were in crisis; members became demoralised and the image of the Club deteriorated. To deal with this situation, they appointed a new liaison member in Mezcala who commanded trust and a larger flow of money and mobilisation of support. The government still continued without supporting substantively, and it appeared that its abandonment was a punishment towards the community. Meanwhile, the economic crisis of 2008 accentuated the problems of the Club; members were affected by relocation, a reduction of their employment rates and the increase in housing prices and mortgages. Some were forced to abandon the Club or at least reduce their participation at events and encounters due to the need to prioritise their time and money, and the lost meeting spaces. In addition, the reinforcement of border security prevented the Club from getting new adherents. In this context, Don José explains that 'the recession came, the economy changed, many clubs ceased to exist, in fact Club Mezcala ... I continued to keep the membership and paying *liabilities*, but we were not active as before'. The functioning of the Club depends on the workings of the political economy that in turn affected recruitment and membership, but through its support networks it found strategies to resist and survive.

The Transnationalisation of Informal Power   115

However, this did not happen without confronting internal problems, due to the increased loss of interest, the fall-off in its actions, lack of support and economic and personal problems. Even the president announced his retirement, In fact, most board members were going to leave the Club, but were prevented from doing so by their interests, mutual commitments and the advice of the priest who signalled that this action threatened the relationships, power, respect and position of the Club. As Don José reports:

> He came and asked us to continue, he asked many people who had not approached the Club before, and they are doing it. So yes, the priest is supporting us, and has a lot of influence so that people follow his instructions.

For Club members the priest helped to avert their dissolution by enhancing their motivation and lessening internal problems; at the same time, he profited by maintaining the Church's political and social position and safeguarding his support and earnings via remittances.

In this context, Club Mezcala was not renewed, and continued under the same political dynamic, as Tomás narrates:

> Supposedly there was going to be a change of president of Club Mezcala, but there was a misunderstanding, I think the person didn't want to leave, he just wanted to rest for a while.... He explained there that he only wanted the position to last a bit longer, some years more, to be able to get into the board of directors of Clubs of Jalisco here. So it seemed to me that there was a lot of politics within that, do you understand me? In other words, this person has done a lot for the village and everything, but I felt that he was like just seeing his personal interest and not anymore, not towards the people.

Meanwhile, in the community, many Mezcalenses still refused to participate, and thus, members realised the importance of having *comuneros* on their side. Additionally, as young people engaged with *comuneros*, they also began to notice the importance of extending links with the Club through dialogue, cooperation and trust. At that time, *comuneros* and their young supporters had already planned a library, but Municipal authorities refused to support it. They shared this project with migrants who saw how it would go beyond superficial and infrastructure improvements and would provide educational support that could result in an opportunity for a 'better life' for those left behind. After that (2008) different sectors of the community began to press the government for the library's construction, until 2009–10 when, out of nowhere, in a meeting the FCJSC approved the library project that the president of the Club advocated for it. In fact, under Calderón's administration, the position of the Mexican government demonstrated the will for a closer pact with migrants and further exerted lobbying pressures (Délano 2011). Nonetheless, the process to consolidate the project was not exempt from confrontations, differences and obstacles. In this

116   *The Transnationalisation of Informal Power*

context, the project was adapted to the taste of migrants and the budget of the government. Carlos explains:

> Club Mezcala at that time insisted that let's do a project together, let's do this' and we said that 'we have projects, what we don't have is a lot of money to make them'. We had forged certain projects already. For example, we for the library, so we wouldn't spend so much [money], we had already managed that some architects made us the favour with the floor plans, with many things, and the studies of the soil and everything. And the Club members said yes, it can be done', and they said 'but you know that we work with municipal, state and federal governments. Are you willing to join them?' And we said 'no problem', right? The federal and state governments always provide their parts without asking, like that much, without much trouble. I always believe that the obstacles are here in the municipality. For example, this time with the library, the *Municipio*—now that Carlos Maldonado is there—he said that the library was not going to be done while that area hadn't changed the use of soil, that it was yielded and became part of the *Municipio*.

Comuneros donated some funds, but opposed the change of the use of soil, as they saw it as an attempt to expropriate their land, making it harder to finish the library and provoking disagreements with Club members who perceived it as an opposition to progress. This is a peculiarity of communal land; the government helps to construct the facilities, but provided that it is titleholder. Still the Club did everything in its power to begin the construction of the library, but, encountered several barriers and a degree of sluggishness, and, as noted by Alberto: 'the *Municipio* at the end just didn't sign, the Municipal President signed but another person from the *Municipio* had to sign and that person just didn't sign, so the library project fell to pieces'. Basically, the structures of the state are mainly driven by the exclusion from formal politics and inadequate institutions, while informal politics shows its complexity and power dynamics that block even the construction of a library. Therefore, for migrants the *Municipio* was obstructing the project and rumours spread that only the funds to be provided by the *Municipio* were lacking. Migrants were even afraid that the money already raised would get lost because 'as they leave, they take it' (Doña Vicenta 2012).

In this context, frictions and rumours spread in the community and migrants blamed the overall population for being alienated and supporting the Municipal President. As Doña Vicenta also discerns: 'I don't understand very well, but there are, I think, two parties or three parties, and almost the majority are on the president's side. So due to the president nothing is done because he says, "I got them tied"'. Fragmentation was propelled at a time when *comuneros* also confronted internal problems and the interference of the government and the *invasor*, and thus, when some inhabitants proposed to carry out the construction of the library autonomously, they did not manage to consolidate these plans. But as no project began, the image of local authorities was also further damaged.

The Transnationalisation of Informal Power   117

Mezcalenses complained about only receiving promises, excuses and lies; as Doña Guille, a migrant supporting *comunero's* struggle, recalls the words of the Municipal President:

> Supposedly [he said] that yes, he was going to help and that I don't know what else, and no, just blah blah blah, like everyone. When the time came, no, no, no, the 2x1 [3x1] won't actually happen; like implying that if we want a library we need to do it, something that is possible.

The opposition of the Municipal government demonstrated not only its wishes but also those of upper political spheres and the workings of the networks of power.

Within the Cub, demoralisation continued and migrants were withdrawing their participation, but in 2011, *Club Mezcala de la Asunción Tijuana*[7] emerged to inject energy and vitality into the Club through moral support, publicity, political energy and new ideas. They followed a reverse pattern, going from international to national levels, as their transborder relationship precipitated their association, and their family and friendship connections in Mezcala and Tijuana enabled them to organise and achieve the expected level of support. Meanwhile, Club Mezcala stopped negotiations expecting that with the new Municipal President things would change. In the words of Alberto: 'Today the PRI returns to the *municipio* and the hope of the *Hijos Ausentes* is that they resume the work'. They began negotiations as they were promised that the library would be the first project; evidencing that the quality of ties depends to some extent on the political party in power but more importantly, the continued and deeply rooted corporatism and the restructuring of power relations. More precisely, the reliance is on the patronage relationships previously established, pushing migrants to show a preference towards the PRI in a context of 'democratisation' and 'political plurality'.

Nonetheless, soon it was revealed that the library project had been manipulated for electoral interests. By August 2013, nothing was done but migrants began to mobilise to obtain the support of inhabitants. They attended the *Fiestas de la Virgen de la Asunción*[8] and began to promote the project, to collect signatures and to organise meetings in order to attract support, labour and money. With respect to *comuneros* and their supporters, the position of the Club towards them reflected internal problems as many continued to believe by the words of the priest that they were enemies of 'progress' and of public works. Finally, they were excluded, and no meeting was held with them. Conversely, the *delegado* was called upon, but kept his distance perhaps due to his closer relationship with the *Municipio*. In addition, following the advice of the priest, members decided to include three *jueces de barrio* from each *barrio* because, as Don Santos reported: 'They know the limits of their *barrio*, they know until where belongs to it, they know people so they're informed, and we're going to work this way'. Thus, in spite of what was observed in Chapter 1 on how the government sought to appropriate *jueces de barrio*, migrants succeeded in establishing a close relationship with them.

118   The Transnationalisation of Informal Power

At the same time, the Municipal President turned down any possibility of a meeting and, although he gave hope of visiting them in Los Angeles at the end of the month to attend *Señorita Jalisco LA 2013*, he did not show up. However, the dreams and hopes of members persisted thanks to the extended support and the possibilities seen in reaching 'progress', as Don Roberto comments:

> People are becoming open, I remember past politics, it seems that Mezcala was really slowed down by Poncitlán. So now they're becoming open, Mezcala's progress is being seen, and I tell my wife that if it continues like this, soon it will be a very flourishing, very prosperous village.

Moreover, members felt encouraged and empowered after Daisy, *Señorita Mezcala*, was elected *Embajadora Cultural*, while they also had more time to devote to the library project. Club Mezcala, thus, considered completing the library without the *Municipio*; as Don José claimed: 'We already thought that if it gets complicated, we leave the [municipal] president aside and we do it alone'. In this context, SEDESOL expressed its support to the president of the Club, and thereafter the Municipal President reconsidered and established an appropriate dialogue and in fact, announced his support. Unexpectedly, in September the construction began, after *comuneros* agreed to yield a portion of land of a quasi-abandoned social care centre of the *Sistema para el Desarrollo Integral de la Familia* (System for the Integral Development of the Family), as long as it was intended for the library. By doing so, even if possession of the land was maintained, they gave the control of the library to the *Municipio* and provided a way for the *Municipio* to gain more power over the community.

The expected inauguration date was December 20, 2013, demonstrating that when the government is interested, public works can be achieved quite rapidly. The construction company selected had a close relationship with the *Municipio*, and the budget was 4,057,332 pesos. Members negotiated to contribute with 625,000 pesos, while disregarding the high quote. They were aware of corruption, favouritism and diversion of funds, but negotiated within the system, giving corruption a positive value. In this sense, we must differentiate between different kinds of corruption; as Pieter de Vries observes, there is 'acceptable' and 'non-acceptable' corruption; that is, the corruption that serves 'to get the things done' and that which represents a 'spectacle that carries all sorts of enjoyments' (2007, 144). In this regard, Gabriela Coronado (2008) identifies how the hegemonic discourse has established informal polity as part of our Mexican culture, explaining that these practices might be judged inconsistently, being acceptable if they favour transnational sectors, governments and elites, arguing as she does, for 'cultural sensitivity', but being unacceptable when they are used as a 'survival strategy' by ordinary people. Moreover, corruption is not founded in our culture but upon unequal economic conditions and influential political systems (Heyman and Campbell 2007), and thus, it is negotiated and contextual (Blundo 2007).

In this context, the government sought to restructure its network of power to support dominance and work together with certain groups that benefit. Migrants

The Transnationalisation of Informal Power   119

were selected for this task as they represent an economic power, sending around 22,000 million U.S. dollars (2013) according to the World Bank, but also are becoming a rising political power. Therefore, by renewing confidence towards the PRI, elites want to retain control over the migrant population and remittances, and increase their political influence in a context of deteriorated international relations between the U.S. and Mexico. Hence, the government opted for the participation of migrants and encouraged HTAs, forecasting the existence of 800 clubs, carrying out 2,200 projects.[9] In fact, *Programa 3x1* was the second most funded social programme after *Oportunidades* (Duquette-Rury 2014) and in 2013 mobilised—according to SEDESOL—around 500 million pesos from the Federal government. Migrants are gaining force and influence, yet, as only organised migrant groups can participate in the programme, this results in partial and preferential empowerment.

Accordingly, migrants foresaw the urgency to collect money and their translocal network began to operate again, especially through Facebook. The Club required an urgent overhaul of the board, due to partial participation and devotion, low collection, a scarce number of supporters and increased level of confrontations; but, suddenly, Club Mezcala was reinvigorated and migrants' energy reactivated. They began to organise meetings, events and collections again, attendance to *kermesses* increased and support expanded towards other cities, such as Ceres, Pomona, Tijuana, San Diego, Sanger, Seattle and Oregon. The Club resorted to higher cooperation and loans while also, in the words of Don José, 'we're involving young people so that there is that energy and this continues'. Besides, their organisation was expanding to the secular side of the spectrum as the priest left the community. However, a lack of interest and opposition still persisted and some sectors continued to be excluded, and this limited their organisation and, in line with the ideas of Canales and Zlolniski (2001), restrained their networks of information and exchange and reproduced unequal structures and social problems.

Concurrently, in the community their organisation through *jueces de barrio* was producing results that worked against the inherited political culture. They coordinated a workforce in an exceptional fashion, while they also organised fundraisers.[10] Among Mezcalenses, the union was proving to be a force to revive and strengthen the search for better conditions and the possibility of obtaining the material and organisational resources to make these projects autonomously. Yet the government also demonstrated its efforts to absorb and control them, while benefiting from their contribution through the diversion of funds and cheap labour and materials. In any case, the inauguration took place on April 9, 2013, in an event where the Municipal government '*se paraba el cuello*' (showed-off) and SEDESOL appropriated the efforts. Without fear and measuring the risks, the president of Club Mezcala delivered a speech, declaring everything he 'should not' say about the *Municipio*. Later, he was compelled to apologise, but the *Municipio* still opposed the granting of the library keys to the community, blocking its functioning and any donations.

In the end members became highly indebted and demoralised and some withdrew their participation from the Club. But, oddly, in March 2015 the board of

Club Mezcala was replenished with atypical active members; Daisy took the lead while also other young migrants assumed positions, and a representative in Seattle was established.[11] In this scenario, whether by sheer coincidence or not, the library began to operate. Members are proud, to be sure; this project gave them personal satisfaction, reinforced the image and position of Club Mezcala within the community, and the possibility of a 'better' future. For migrants the library is a way—according to Don Santos—to give 'weapons to our children so that they study and know the culture, for example of our people, and know how to defend themselves before the world' and even—as expressed by Don Marcos—as 'the basis of progress, is the basis of knowledge', '[of] the development of peoples'. However, although the community welcomed this public work as it will give more opportunities to children, such a luxury was not well received, as it stands in high contrast with the landscape of the village and the living conditions of inhabitants. That said, migrants aimed to have a 'virtual library' just as in the United States; in the words of Don José: 'With the library we'll have the same service as any library here [the U.S.], it'll be equipped and it'll be very sophisticated'. By so doing, they placed the emphasis on having computers and the internet over books, disregarding the content of the library; this being reinforced as the *Municipio* assumed the library's management.

Following the ideas of Fox and Bada (2008), although in certain respects the library was intended to tackle a cause of exclusion, migrants directly and

Figure 3.3 The library.

The Transnationalisation of Informal Power 121

indirectly addressed the symptom, providing an image of 'wealth' and 'progress' rather than focusing on its functioning. Therefore, this library, a result of the workings of informal politics, must be seen as both a space where the neoliberal capitalist and colonialist system exerts itself, encompassing its actors, practices, knowledges and discourses, but also as something that could be reframed as a weapon against it. It is up to the community to negotiate the path the library takes; until now, the community has gradually gained control over it and given back the shape and purpose of the former project. There is still work to do to improve the functioning of the library and it also remains to be seen if their efforts continue and manage to complete new projects outside the state and even away from neoliberal governance. However, this fact demonstrates how Mezcalenses are advancing in the use of social capital as a survival strategy and scheme for change, this is looked at more deeply in the next chapter.

Conclusion

To conclude, the current situation in Mezcala shows that institutions and programmes do not solve either social problems or informality; on the contrary, they reinforce them. What is more, clientelism survives due to inequality and weak institutional structures, at the same time that the current social conditions are a cause and a result of it. So, even though clientelism might be a channel via which people can benefit from power, it is also a way to perpetuate domination and to prevent the dismantling of social hierarchies. This responds to the logic of neoliberal governance where concepts such as 'social transformation' and 'popular participation' are rendered negative serving 'social exclusion' and 'economic polarization' (de Sousa Santos 2009). The vices of the system are hard to change as citizens increasingly are seduced, absorb these practices and have their paths constrained by such methods. Accordingly, a real transformation of institutions, parties or policies has not been achieved; rather, citizens are being institutionalised but excluded from formal politics. Both within and outside the community the inherited political culture endures and reproduces itself even at a transnational level, as Club Mezcala demonstrates. Despite being a response from below, it reiterates and makes use of structures of power and transnationalises informal power, serving as an institutional channel to regulate the relations with migrants under the workings of neoliberal governance.

This scenario exemplifies how neoliberal governance, as noted by De Angelis, is a new form of 'governmentality' or 'biopolitics' that integrates different powers and uses tactics for the management of networks and life (2005, 243–4). In the case of migration, through the creation of HTAs and *Programa 3x1*, politics has been reorganised as the Mexican state perceives migrants as a channel for administering population, social welfare, wealth, labour, national identity, foreign relations, the environment and power for personal or clientelist benefit above and beyond the interests of society. As observed in Mezcala, transnational citizenship entails strategies of the state that are persuasive, coercive, and corrupt, and sideline and limit popular participation. Moreover, it includes larger

122 *The Transnationalisation of Informal Power*

global forces that comprise the ideas of 'development', 'progress' and 'modernisation'; as for instance, economic and social remittances that transform the village in order to provide 'First World' facilities, have services and duplicate U.S. spaces, increasing the 'value', 'prosperity' and 'development' of these. As Vicente notes:

> those who come from Los Angeles, bring another mentality, 'because we went to Long Beach', I don't know what the fuck, 'there this and that'. They now want to put a Disneyland here in Mezcala and [have] only those [ideas]. They forget the values, traditions, *usos y costumbres*.

Members of Club Mezcala have an idea of development informed by hegemonic discourses and associated with urbanisation and their lifestyle in the United States, that is inhabiting local spaces, as presented in the following chapter.

To this effect, the 'American Dream', in spite of its contradictions, has positioned a group of migrants as the bearers of 'progress' and more 'cultured' practices and values influencing life not only economically but also politically, socially and culturally. Here it is evidenced how, adding up to the ideas of De Angelis (2005), neoliberal governance articulates 'the power to coerce' with the 'power to seduce' in favour of accumulation through the normalisation and universalisation of market values and the co-optation of subjects, projects and struggles to improve life conditions and reach social justice. In view of that, the 'American Dream' goes in hand of migration policies and governmental actions since, on the one hand, the U.S. government keeps attracting 'dreamers' from the margins to reinforce their economic and political position, while social structures are being transnationalised. On the other hand, the Mexican government profits from this rhetoric to maintain the control and management of people and resources. For instance, Club Mezcala is displaying a symbolic power that is exploited by the government to spread informal politics transnationally, while taking advantage of the desires of migrants to transmit the long-awaited 'progress', plunging them into a battle to take credit and to obtain immediate benefits in the form of capital of various kinds. Within these geographies of power, migrants—as Esteva (1992) would say—are dreaming someone elses' dreams of development, rather than their own; at the same time, that fragmentation is further accentuated, dividing 'traditionalists' from 'progressives'.

In this vein, as evidenced by Club Mezcala, communal tradition and social and political links with the village of origin are the basis of their social reproduction. In fact, through them there is a continuous transfer of political, economic, material and ideological assets that creates new forms of social relations marked by economic and sociocultural inequality and separation. Nonetheless, Club Mezcala is an example of HTA development that also evidences its distinctiveness (for example, communal organisation, personal relationships and the application of *usos y costumbres*), which has allowed its survival for almost 15 years in the face of political, economic, legal, cultural and social difficulties. Accordingly, migrants are gaining influence and importance on both sides of the

The Transnationalisation of Informal Power   123

border, constructing other expressions of citizenship that allow them to open spaces of negotiation, to push for the improvement of conditions, while troubling the governmental management of the population and the local workings of neoliberal governance. Additionally, within the community the Club is gaining influence and profile while seeking to establish itself as a transnational communal engagement. Although this collaboration has not been free from problems, clashes and disagreements, it evidences the potential and power to work with *comuneros* and *jueces de barrio* in order to reinforce the vitality and strength of their organisation and obtain a voice to pressure governments, resist abuses and distribute the progress truly want.

Notes

1 The function of education in relation to the hegemonic ideology is discussed in Chapter 5 to emphasise its links with identity construction and discriminatory policies.

2 In 2010, the government did not believe that these two variables were related, and only provided information about consumption, but no alternatives (Saavedra Ponce 2010). Furthermore, while some doctors highlighted contaminated water as the possible cause, the government refused to provide information and to support research on the matter, as argued for by the doctor Felipe de Jesús Lozano Kasten, a researcher on heavy metals in humans, since such research might affect the economic interests of certain groups (Ferreiro 2013). This situation was aggravated in 2016 when the University of Guadalajara denounced how in the neighbouring villages of San Pedro Itxicán and Agua Caliente there is a large number of inhabitants, especially kids and young people, suffering from kidney-related diseases; and blamed contaminated water as the cause since traces of heavy metals were found in their urine (González 2016; Alatorre 2017). The government still does not act.

3 Illegal migrants can study English, vocational courses and elementary, middle-high and high school; but, as broadcast with the Dreamers mobilisations (2012–13), they cannot enrol in college nor have financial aid for it, regardless of whether they have lived in the U.S. since being infants. In this regard, educated in the U.S. with the aspirations of any other young person, undocumented youth face educational and labour obstacles to reach their 'American Dream' (Chavez 2013). Victories have been achieved; DACA has given work permits and social security numbers to some of the undocumented youth while, specifically in California, the DREAM Act approved in 2011 opened up their possibilities in education. Although these actions were far from being truly inclusive, their situation menaces to get worse with the actions President Trump is taking against them.

4 Seth M. Holmes through interviews with indigenous Mexicans in the U.S. concluded that 'ethnicity', 'legal status' and 'social class' marked the 'disparities in health status and health care experiences' (2006, 1787). In 2010, President Obama carried out a much-debated health reform under the Affordable Care Act, which made the expansion of coverage possible, but overlooked crucial issues, such as the rising costs and the quality of care (Wilensky 2012), and the disparities mentioned in 'gaining access to high-quality care' (Barr 2011, 273). Meanwhile, the Mexican government carried on with the social programme, 'Go Healthy, Return Healthy', to advance the promotion, prevention and attention of health issues related to migrants; this being a strategy to obtain the support of migrants and expand the clientele network.

5 The *Programa Migrante 3x1* consists of the economic support of the three levels of government (Federal, State, and Municipal) so that for every peso donated by a Club

124 *The Transnationalisation of Informal Power*

each party gives another. The money goes towards a project for the benefit of the community and is managed by SEDESOL

6 The interests at stake were crucial for the Mexican economy (investment, tourism and remittances); thus, the government stopped promoting anti-Americanism and fostered a friendly perception (Starr 2010, 844). To this effect, Fox briefly established a bilateral agenda, though still favouring the economic and geopolitical interests of the U.S. (Delgado-Wise, 2006); and later, in 2005, he succeeded in granting the right to vote from abroad, demonstrating the interest of the Mexican government in migrants maintaining dual ties.

7 This Club is partially independent from the one in Los Angeles; they manage their own funds but support the same projects, have similar approaches, dynamics, values and ideas and follow the same president, though they have a president too and send the money directly to the representative in Mezcala.

8 Migrants organise convoys or buses to travel together to the patron-saint *fiestas;* and it is believed that more than 1,000 migrants attend, as the *Catholic News* documented (Agren 2007). Accordingly, the priest established a day in this celebration dedicated to migrants, *día de los Hijos Ausentes.* Migrants, mainly members of Club Mezcala, organise and pay for this celebration, while the Municipal government and the priest exploit this day to secure the alliance with migrants and to gain their political and economic support. Chapter 4 explores more deeply the alliance between the Church, migrants and the state, and Chapter 5 addresses the power of the priest to mould Mezcalenses' perceptions.

9 *Tercer Informe Trimestral* 2013 – *Programas de Subsidios del Ramo Administrativo 20, Desarrollo Social* to abide by the *Ley de Transparencia y Acceso a la Información,* can be consulted online at the SEDESOL website [accessed July 2014]: www.sedesol.gob.mx/work/models/SEDESOL/Transparencia/InformesPresupuestoEjercido/Tercer_Informe_Trimestral_2013.pdf

10 In Mezcala inhabitants engage in communitarian work through *jueces de barrio,* a more relaxed version of *tequio* but where payments may or may not exist.

11 It was the first time that the board and the role of many members changed, demonstrating how younger generations are getting involved and helping the reproduction of the community, increasing awareness of abuses, rejecting past deals and strengthening the chances of working autonomously.

References

Agren, David. 2007. "Faith, Family, Public Works keep Mexican Migrants' Ties Strong". *Catholic News Service,* August 31. http://catholicreview.org/article/work/economy/faith-keeps-mexican-migrants-ties-strong – sthash.bI4tQCoe.dpuf [accessed June 25, 2013].

Alatorre, Karina. 2017. "Encuentran metales pesados en orina de habitantes de Poncitlán". *La Gaceta Universitaria,* January 30.

Althusser, Louis. 2001. *Lenin and Philosophy, and Other Essays.* New York: Monthly Review Press.

Álvarez Béjar, Alejandro, and Mariana Ortega Breña. 2006. "Mexico's 2006 Elections: The Rise of Populism and the End of Neoliberalism". *Latin American Perspectives* 33 (2): 17–32.

Álvarez Yáñez, Leonel. 2008. "Las fuentes teóricas de la democratización neoliberal en México". *Utopía y Praxis LatinoAmericana* 13 (42): 11–34.

Anders, Gerhard, and Monique Nuijten. 2007. "Corruption and the Secret of Law: An Introduction". In *Corruption and the Secret of Law. A Legal Anthropological*

The Transnationalisation of Informal Power 125

Perspective, edited by Monique Nuijten and Gerhard Anders, 1–25. Hampshire: Ashgate Publishing Limited.

Bada, Xóchitl, Jonathan Fox, and Andrew Selee. 2006. Al fin visibles. La presencia cívica de los migrantes mexicanos en los Estados Unidos. Washington D.C.: Woodrow Wilson International Center for Scholars, University of California.

Bakker, Matt, and Michael Peter Smith. 2003. "El Rey del Tomate. Migrant Political Transnationalism and Democratization in Mexico". *Migraciones Internacionales* 2 (1): 59–83.

Barr, Donald A. 2011. *Introduction to U.S. Health Policy: The Organization, Financing, and Delivery of Health Care in America*. Baltimore, MD: The Johns Hopkins University Press.

Bauder, Harald. 2008. "Citizenship as Capital: The Distinction of Migrant Labor". *Alternatives: Global, Local, Political* 33 (3): 315–33.

Blundo, Giorgio. 2007. "Hidden Acts, Open Talks. How Anthropology Can 'Observe' and Describe Corruption?" In *Corruption and the Secret of Law. A Legal Anthropological Perspective*, edited by Monique Nuijten and Gerhard Anders, 27–52. Hampshire: Ashgate Publishing Limited.

Canales, Alejandro I., and Christian Zlolniski. 2001. "Comunidades transnacionales y migración en la era de la globalización". *Notas de Población* 28 (73): 221–52.

Castillo, Debra A., and Kavita Panjabi. 2011. "Introduction". In *Cartographies of Affect: Across Borders in South Asia and the Americas*, edited by Debra A. Castillo and Kavita Panjabi, 1–50. Kolkata: Worldview Publications.

Chauvin, Sébastien, and Blanca Garcés-Mascareñas. 2012. "Beyond Informal Citizenship: The New Moral Economy of Migrant Illegality". *International Political Sociology* 6 (3): 241–59.

Chavez, Leo R. 2013. *Shadowed Lives: Undocumented Immigrants in American Society.* 3rd edn. Belmont, CA: Wadsworth Cengage Learning.

Coronado, Gabriela. 2008. "Discourses of Anti-Corruption in Mexico: Culture of Corruption or Corruption of Culture?" *PORTAL Journal of Multidisciplinary International Studies* 5 (1): 1–23.

Dalum Berg, Ulla, and Robyn Magalit Rodriguez. 2013. "Transnational Citizenship Across the Americas". *Identities: Global Studies in Culture and Power* 20 (6): 649–64.

De Angelis, Massimo. 2005. "The Political Economy of Global Neoliberal Governance". *Review (Fernand Braudel Center)* 28 (3): 229–57.

De la Torre, Adrián. 2010. "San Pedro y Mezcala: enfermedad y muerte, la pesca del día en Chapala". *La Jornada Jalisco*, September 28. www1.lajornadaguerrero.com. mx/2010/09/28/index.php?section=cultura&article=016n1cul [accessed September 30, 2010].

de Sousa Santos, Boaventura. 2009. "Governance: Between Myth and Reality". *RCCS Annual Review* 0: 1–14.

de Vries, Pieter. 2007. "The Orchestration of Corruption and the Excess Enjoyment in Western Mexico". In *Corruption and the Secret of Law: A Legal Anthropological Perspective*, edited by Monique Nuijten and Gerhard Anders, 143–63. Hampshire: Ashgate Publishing Limited.

Délano, Alexandra. 2011. *Mexico and its Diaspora in the United States*. New York: Cambridge University Press.

Delgado-Wise, Raúl. 2006. "Migración e imperialismo: la fuerza de trabajo mexicana en el contexto del TLCAN". In *México en transición: globalismo neoliberal, Estado y sociedad civil*, edited by Gerardo Otero, 195–214. Zacatecas, Mexico: H. Cámera de

126 *The Transnationalisation of Informal Power*

Diputados LIX Legislatura; Simon Fraser University; Universidad Autónoma de Zacatecas; Miguel Ángel Porrúa.

Duquette-Rury, Lauren. 2014. "Collective Remittances and Transnational Coproduction: the 3x1 Program for Migrants and Household Access to Public Goods in Mexico". *Studies in Comparative International Development* 49 (1): 112–39.

Escobar, Arturo. 1992. "Planning". In *The Development Dictionary. A Guide to Knowledge as Power*, edited by Wolfgang Sachs, 132–45. London: Zed Books Ltd.

Escobar, Arturo. 2001. "Culture Sits in Places: Reflections on Globalism and Subaltern Strategies of Localization". *Political Geography* 20: 139–74.

Esteva, Gustavo. 1992. "Development". In *The Development Dictionary. A Guide to Knowledge as Power*, edited by Wolfgang Sachs, 6–25. London: Zed Books Ltd.

Ferreiro, Rebeca. 2013. "Construyendo ambientes enfermos". *La Gaceta Universitaria*, November 11. www.gaceta.udg.mx/G_nota1.php?id=14864 [accessed March 14, 2014].

Fitzgerald, David. 2009. *A Nation of Emigrants: How Mexico Manages its Migration*. Berkeley, CA: University of California Press.

Fox, Jonathan. 2005. "Unpacking 'Transnational Citizenship' ". *Annual Review of Political Science* 8 (June): 171–201.

Fox, Jonathan, and Xochitl Bada. 2008. "Migrant Organization and Hometown Impacts in Rural Mexico". *Journal of Agrarian Change* 8 (2 and 3): 435–61.

Gálvez, Alyshia. 2013. "Immigrant Citizenship: Neoliberalism, Immobility and the Vernacular Meanings of Citizenship". *Identities: Global Studies in Culture and Power* 20 (6): 720–37.

González, Mariana. 2016. "Agua caliente … y tóxica". *Proceso Jalisco*, July 2.

Gordillo, Gastón. 2009. "La clientelización de la etnicidad: hegemonía partidaria y subjetividades políticas indígenas". *Revista Española de Antropología Americana* 39 (2): 247–62.

Guarnizo, Luis Eduardo. 2003. "The Economics of Transnational Living". *International Migration Review* 37 (3): 666–99.

Guarnizo, Luis Eduardo, Alejandro Portes, and William Haller. 2003. "Assimilation and Transnationalism: Determinants of Transnational Political Action among Contemporary Migrants". *American Journal of Sociology* 108 (6): 1211–48.

Hea Kil, Sang, and Cecilia Menjívar. 2006. "The "War on the Border": Criminalizing Immigrants and Militarizing the U.S.–Mexico Border". In *Immigration and Crime: Race, Ethnicity, and Violence*, edited by Ramiro Jr. Martinez and Abel Jr. Valenzuela, 164–88. New York: New York University Press.

Hernández García, Adriana. 2006. "Mezcala: encuentros y desencuentros de una comunidad". *Espiral, Estudios sobre Estado y Sociedad* 12 (36): 97–128.

Hernández, María Aidé. 2008. "La democracia mexicana, presa de una cultura política con rasgos autoritarios". *Revista Mexicana de Sociología* 70 (2): 261–303.

Heyman, Josiah McC., and Howard Campbell. 2007. "Corruption in the US Borderlands with Mexico: The "Purity" of Society and the "Perversity" of Borders". In *Corruption and the Secret of Law. A Legal Anthropological Perspective*, edited by Monique Nuijten and Gerhard Anders, 191–215. Hampshire: Ashgate Publishing Limited.

Hilgers, Tina. 2011. "Clientelism and Conceptual Stretching: Differentiating among Concepts and among Analytical Levels". *Theory and Society* 40 (5): 567–88.

Hill, Nancy E., and Kathryn Torres. 2010. "Negotiating the American Dream: The Paradox of Aspirations and Achievement among Latino Students and Engagement between the Families and Schools". *Journal of Social Issues* 66 (1): 95–112.

The Transnationalisation of Informal Power 127

Holmes, Seth M. 2006. "An Ethnographic Study of the Social Context of Migrant Health in the United States". *PLoS Med* 3 (10): e448.

Holzner, Claudio A. 2010. *Poverty of Democracy: The Institutional Roots of Political Participation in Mexico, Pitt Latin American Studies*. Pittsburgh: University of Pittsburgh Press.

Knight, Alan. 2005. "*Caciquismo* in Twentieth-Century Mexico". In *Caciquismo in the Twentieth-Century Mexico*, edited by Alan Knight and Wil Pansters, 1–48. London: Institute for the Study of the Americas.

Levingston, Gretchen, and Joan R. Kahn. 2002. "An American Dream Unfulfilled: The Limited Mobility of Mexican Americans". *Social Science Quarterly* 83 (4): 1003–12.

Levitt, Peggy. 1998. "Social Remittances: Migration Driven Local-Level Forms of Cultural Diffusion". *International Migration Review* 32 (4): 926–48.

Massey, Douglas S. 2009. "The Political Economy of Migration in an Era of Globalization". In *Internacional Migration and Human Rights: The Global Repercussion of U.S. Policy*, edited by Samuel Martínez, 25–43. Berkeley, CA: University of California Press.

Ong, Aihwa. 1996. "Cultural Citizenship as Subject-Making: Immigrants Negotiate Racial and Cultural Boundaries in the United States". *Current Anthropology* 37 (5): 737–62.

Pansters, Wil. 2005. "Goodbye to the Caciques? Definition, the State and the Dynamics of *Caciquismo* in Twentieth-Century Mexico". In *Caciquismo in Twentieth-Century Mexico*, edited by Alan Knight and Wil Pansters, 349–76. London: Institute for the Study of the Americas.

Portes, Alejandro. 2012. "La inmigración ilegal y el sistema internacional. Lecciones de la reciente inmigración legal mexicana a Estados Unidos". In *Sociología económica de las migraciones internacionales*, edited by Lorenzo Cachón, 3–17. Madrid: Anthropos. Original edition, 1979.

Rieger, Joerg. 2013. "Introduction. Crossing Borders in the Postcolonial Empire: On Deep Solidarity in the Americas". In *Across Borders: Latin Perspectives in the Americas Reshaping Religion, Theology and Life*, edited by Joerg Rieger, 1–25. Lanham, MD: Lexington Books.

Rodriguez, Robyn Magalit. 2013. "Beyond Citizenship: Emergent Forms of Political Subjectivity amongst Migrants". *Identities: Global Studies in Culture and Power* 20 (6): 738–54.

Saavedra Ponce, Viridiana. 2010. "Para Petersen, los casos de San Pedro y Mezcala son ironías de la estadística". *La Jornada Jalisco*, September 29. www1.lajornadaguerrero. com.mx/2010/09/29/index.php?section=cultura&article=016n1cul [accessed September 30, 2010].

Sistema de Información Estadística y Geográfica de Jalisco. 2012. *Diagnóstico del Municipio de Poncitlán*. Guadalajara, Mexico: Gobierno de Jalisco.

Snyder, Richard. 2001. *Politics after Neoliberalism: Reregulation in Mexico*. New York: Cambridge University Press.

Starr, Pamela K. 2010. "The Two "Politics of NAFTA" in Mexico". *Law and Business Review of the Americas* 16 (4): 839–53.

Velasco Ortiz, M. Laura. 2002. *El regreso de la comunidad: migración indígena y agentes étnicos: los mixtecos de la frontera México-Estados Unidos*. Mexico City: El Colegio de México; El Colegio de la Frontera Norte.

Wilensky, Gail R. 2012. "The Shortfalls of 'Obamacare'". *The New England Journal of Medicine* 367 (16): 1479–81.

4 Tourism

A Fight to Define Progress

In Mezcala, as delineated so far, the scenario is beset by the terms of ambition for power, wealth and control; the characteristics of the territory, such as the proximity to the lake, the biodiversity of the hills, the fertility of the soil, the abundance of natural resources, the beauty of the place, and the favourable temperate climate increase the interests and envy of national and international outsiders to possess Mezcalenses' land. When I interviewed Don Miguel, one of comuneros' most fervent defenders of the community, he explained to me that this is a tendency widely performed by elites over indigenous communities; he said that 'they look at you like a nobody, to all indigenous communities, there the government wants to get in their way and fuck up the land, the mines, water springs, the cattle, clearly for that matter, but to help them?' Mezcalenses, in this way, are being recolonised and relocated to create space for residency, tourism and consumption purposes. So, while their territory is suffering deforestation, contamination and the reification of natural resources, they experience internal fragmentation, the deterioration of their main economic activities, migration, limited basic services and poor living conditions.

In this sense, in agreement with the ideas of Bastos (2013, 123–7), an important ideological force exerts itself: as seen in promises of progress, job creation and an economic spill-over of private initiatives, all framed by a 'false' and 'perverse' discourse that obscures the dependence of those proposing new economic ventures to combat the continued existence of poverty—in the land and labour markets. So inhabitants are being absorbed by this logic, and as consequence, might legitimise the meddling of external subjects. For instance, Doña Vicenta argues that as people say:

> it's an indigenous people, they don't let people to get in, people to enter to buy land. I say that if people entered to buy ... Mezcala would be more ... there would be more trade ... people wouldn't be as we are, that we don't have much to eat.

Elites are getting involved in the community via the inherited political culture, institutional networks of power and the rhetoric of 'development' and 'progress', serving the functioning of neoliberal governance. So, in parallel, they are triggering

Tourism: A Fight to Define Progress 129

new aspirations and visions, often contradictory, informed by hegemonic discourses and associated with urbanisation and a 'modern life', that shape their own projects.

Given this background I remember that Adelo narrated to me his radio participation in order to reveal the real objectives of the 'development' promoted through elites' plans:

> Someone called [a radio listener] ... 'no, I don't know the feeling that it provokes in me these retrograde people who instead of always walking forward always go backwards', and I replied to him 'no, so you must be one of the investors that is around there', I said 'but we want progress, not the kind of progress that you think is progress, we want the progress for the people, not your progress ...' and the commentator says 'and for you, what is progress? What kind of progress do you want for the people?', -'For our people, we want good schools.... A hospital, and things that for me are progress and not your progress, your progress is to fill ... your pockets with money passing over the people'.

In the era of neoliberal governance, territory cannot be seen as something fixed, as a sole geographic area, since it entails institutions and subjects embedded in a larger scale network that continually negotiate development and structure society. Therefore, we should endeavour to rethink our perception of space in the life of transborder subjects and multisited communities, which are connected by people, labour, ideas, goods, values, affect and power. For this matter, space must be considered as 'relational' (Massey 2005); but without neglecting a permanent dialectical tension between 'absolute' and 'relative' space and how it is experienced, conceptualised and lived (Harvey 2005).

In view of that, the present chapter investigates how tourism is sought, legitimised, and implemented by expanding upon the articulation of different social relations that contest the management of lives and territory in Mezcala. However, here, I not only reflect on how meanings are internalised, but more importantly, on how place provides people with meanings and identities (Escobar 2001; Massey and Jess 1995; Streibel 1998) that might help to elaborate alternatives (Escobar 2001; Johnson 2012). In effect, territories are a place where power is contested (Lefebvre 1991); there is a space of control where hegemonic capitalist and colonialist trends, now embodied through neoliberal governance, seek to rule but also where alternatives to capitalism and modernity are being designed. This chapter, thus, expands previous analyses of tourism in Mexico by connecting the local and the global through the location of subjects, institutions and methods involved in the land problematic, envisaging how neoliberal governance is imbricated in lives and territories subjectively, materially, symbolically and rhetorically. At this juncture I am especially interested in breaking down the discourse of 'development' in order to advance its acclimatisation; revealing the possibilities therein created through local knowledges.

130   *Tourism: A Fight to Define Progress*

For this purpose, first I explain the land conflicts framed by the property market and tourist industry demands, through the associated ideas of 'development', 'modernisation' and 'progress'. This section is divided in two in order to, first, provide a historical context to capture the continuity in a rhetoric framed upon the colonial past and second, narrate the current problematic that has meant the strengthening of the alliance between economic and political powers. Following this, I trace the intensification of confrontation between the networks of power and the networks of solidarity created by *comuneros* and young supporters. For this, I begin to narrate the emergence of opposition within the community to the elites' development and tourist plans. Next, through the analysis of the appropriation of space and the endorsement of tourism by the *invasor* and the state, I examine how they use the rhetoric of 'development' to legitimise their actions and shape the life and visions of Mezcalenses, but more importantly to support the capitalist—and colonialist, as expanded in the next chapter—system and a way of life that perpetuates structures and hierarchies. Finally, by analysing the proposal of *turismo comunitario* (community tourism), I ponder how new meanings to development are being shaped and other ways of being, thinking and living are being proposed, taking up the 'traditional' way of life.

'Development': Clearing the Path for Tourism

New or Old Planning, Projects and Tactics?

Following Mexican Independence, elites adopted the ideas of 'progress', 'modernisation' and 'development', and governors reinforced them as synonyms of foreign capital, economic growth and novel practices to propel urbanisation, industrialisation and the tourist industry. In fact, 'the faith in progress' emerged to give sense to the new dominant norms and institutions; it was a 'moral power' justifying inequality and Western values and acting against traditions and peoples considered to be 'an obstacle to the expansion of the market, industry and the modern state' (Sbert 1992, 193–7). In the Chapala region, that meant the endorsement of industrialisation and the handing over of the control of commerce to foreign capital and the consolidation of tourist development, since the end of the nineteenth century (Talavera Salgado 1982). This situation affected native populations, and in fact, as noted before, the development of the roads in Mezcala (1940–50s) signified an easier path for land invasions.

Later, as a result of land entitlement decrees by agrarian authorities, *comuneros* were advised to distribute the territory between them, but, on the contrary, they allowed inhabitants to enjoy and use land (Martínez Moreno 2008), bringing about irregular distribution and settlement at the same time that invasions continued. Besides, the government established access and control in the community through the perpetuation of political culture and informal politics, whose legacy was vividly outlined in Chapter 1. In addition, threats continued in the region as President Echeverría had a strong interest in the development of the industrial zone, *El Salto* (González Corona 1989, 64) and also purchases in

Tourism: A Fight to Define Progress 131

the neighbouring villages multiplied (Del Castillo 2009). In this context, it is worth noting that oddly in the *Resolución Presidencial*, the islands were excluded, so one cannot help wondering what the real intentions of this decree were.[1] Nonetheless, some *comuneros* refused to ally with the government, quarrelled and opposed their plans and residential tourism, and appointed themselves as the heirs of the protection of the territory.[2]

The threat of privatisation increased when President Salinas carried out the liberalisation of the country far beyond requirements. In this context new institutions, such as the *Procuraduría Agraria*, the *Tribunales Agrarios y* the *Registro Agrario Nacional* were created and the *Programa de Certificación de Derechos Ejidales y Titulación de Solares (PROCEDE)* was launched in 1992. Thereafter, PROCEDE was accepted by the neighbouring communities, and one can presume that around that time, this programme and its counterpart which addressed itself to communities, *Programa de Certificación de Derechos Comunales (PROCECOM)*, also arrived in Mezcala. The programme promised a higher value of land, the possibility to sell and to be incorporated into the development of the country. Many people in reality were led by the possibility of reaching progress, but, inspired by the ideas of Escobar (1992, 132), this was part of a development planning that meant domination and social control and helped in the configuration of underdevelopment. Indeed, this programme obscured taxation, dependency, alienation and dispossession of land carried out;[3] Don Miguel remembers how its deployment threatened the community:

> Some engineers arrived promising PROCEDE to Mezcala because they were very poor, PROCEDE helped with many things, even with cattle, money; we just needed to say yes and sign the document, but since we're indians we refused ... and some did want it because they wanted money, cows, chickens; they were giving all that.

Some *comuneros* realised how agrarian authorities were trying to trick them, so they rejected the programme in order to secure the preservation of the community, their own role and the future of younger generations. Their objectives were not only economic and political, but also social and ideological, impacting on the configuration of the community, and more importantly, leading to what David Harvey (2005) identifies as an 'uneven geographical development'. In effect, to serve the workings of neoliberal governance, places are interconnected in unequal ways, displaying geographies of power that structure hierarchies and inequalities and frame our local experiences (Massey 1995). In this way, the division and confrontation among *comuneros* was taken further, as seen in a *comunero*'s narration recalled by Chuy:

> He told me that when PROCEDE first arrived ... that a *comunero*, one of the interested ones, also threatened him with death, because he didn't let them enter.... He said to him, 'how am I going to let PROCEDE enter after my ancestors fought with their life and shed their blood, so I suddenly want

132   *Tourism: A Fight to Define Progress*

to sell the village'. Because if PROCEDE enters, it means selling the village ... and that the interested party said 'no, look, they're going to bring a lot of help and all that shit, and now they're going to take all them away from us'. But no, they never took them away.

PROCEDE and PROCECOM promised many things, and some people came to believe that, as Don José, a migrant, comments apropos of land regularisation, 'there is no progress because people don't want to invest there as they don't have guarantees'. But these programmes aimed to expand clientelism and corporatism, while looking to privatise lands in the hands of national and international capitalists and to commodify natural resources.

In this manner, wealth is redistributed from lower classes to upper, speculative and unproductive classes backed by a legal and financial power structure that concurrently encourages the commodification of society and the environment, that is, the 're-establishment of the class power' (Harvey 2007). In this regard, within the era of neoliberal governance, the Mexican government has been firming up the relationship with the business elites; including Mexican business conglomerates and multinational corporations to promote tourism (Clancy 1999), and new sectors, especially those made up of U.S. executives (Ai Camp 2006). However, as Knight (2005) points out, the liberalisation of the country was not only a strategy from the top down as interests and subjects from all levels benefited; it also served to develop patron-client relationships. Furthermore, as observed by Carmen Martínez Novo (2010), there is no real separation between imperialism and *caciquismo* and between colonial and neoliberal practices. In effect, colonisation is being renewed in this era of neoliberal governance, as transnational corporations supported by local governments and elites are embodying colonisers who destroy and dispossess the native population without regard for the environment (Schabus 2005, 519).

Like this, Mexican governors have associated progress with the U.S. values and assets, permitting the increasing entrance of foreign capital into the country with the help of economic elites. Lured by the 'American' lifestyle Mexican elites were hoping for economic spill-overs, but, their arrival meant not only the embracing of Western values but the disturbance of economic activities, the transformation of society and culture and the exacerbation of local problems, as outlined in Chapters 2 and 3. In the region, this manifested with the development of the industrial zone of *El Salto* and the boosting of the shores of Lake Chapala as one of the main retirement destinations of U.S. citizens in Mexico (Sunil *et al.* 2007, 491). In fact, the Lake Chapala area has become an 'American place'; more precisely, in tandem with the observations of Torres and Momsen (2005) for the case of Cancun, it is a 'tourist bubble' where U.S. retirees can feel at home and reproduce consumption patterns and behaviours. Consequently, these retirees have come to influence local practices, cultures and values, while being oblivious to the local reality, which underscores disparities spatially, socially, culturally, economically and occupationally between them and the native population (Torres and Momsen 2005). In Mexico, thereby, the colonial past endures

Tourism: A Fight to Define Progress 133

through the national development paradigm and the impetus of tourism, due to the alliance between local, national and international elites that allowed unrestricted and irresponsible exploitation and appropriation of human and natural resources while also expanding violent and coercive measures.

Furthermore, through an economic rationality, spaces are being transformed into new 'business opportunities', presupposing the knowledge of people's desires to collaborate and yield the management of resources, territories and lives (Leff 2005). This rationalisation has given other meanings, functions and organisation to territories and nature according to capitalist ideals of progress (Ceceña Martorella 2009, 198–9). In Mezcala this can be clearly seen as the state governor, Alberto Cárdenas Jiménez (1995–2001), from the PAN ensured the settlement of an entrepreneur from Guadalajara, Guillermo Moreno Ibarra (GMI), through the pretext of a reforestation programme and via corporatist and corrupt connections (Alonso 2010b, 316), and an alleged close relationship between them (Paredes 2012). In addition, he found local support, a *prestanombres* (straw party), Crescenciano Santana that 'allowed' him to appropriate ten acres of *tierras de uso común* in 1999.[4] He fenced it off, established guards and constructed a mansion at the top of *El Pandillo*. Although some *comuneros* expressed dissatisfaction and asked for explanations, from the beginning it was demonstrated that the chosen techniques of GMI were dishonesty and bribes.

The president of the *comuneros*, Santiago de la Cruz, therefore, was accused of being negligent and of not carrying out immediate actions; rather, he signed a sale document without consulting the *Asamblea*. As Don Luis, a migrant, observes: 'He made a mistake, but he knew what kind of mistake. "Well, when I get out of here, when I leave here, it's your problem. Meanwhile, the money is mine"'. Nonetheless, four *comuneros* opposing this action were accused of illegal deprivation of liberty and imprisoned for three months (Bastos 2012, 231, 2013, 113) because 'the man has levers, has money' (Francisco 2013). Still *comuneros* sought legal advice and decided to establish a trial even though they were warned that 'trials are time-consuming, last long and many times, in court, those who have money win' (Don Chava 2012). This evidenced how, within the working of neoliberal governance, co-option and division is promoted to benefit networks of power, commodifying territories, controlling population, perpetuating inequalities and hierarchies and provoking endless political, economic, social and cultural consequences.

Reinforcing Tourist Development

The collusion with economic elites went further than expected with the arrival of the PAN to the presidency that also bolstered the tourist industry. At the state level, the governor, Francisco Ramírez Acuña (2001–6), also affiliated to this party, colluded with the *invasor* and, as Vicente Paredes (2012, 89) an inhabitant of the community observes, their good relationship added force to the promotion of tourism and land privatisation in the region. In 2002, Ramírez Acuña supported the construction of a 'panoramic highway' to connect Mezcala to the

134   *Tourism: A Fight to Define Progress*

town of Chapala and other neighbouring villages. By means of advertising, the government used children to justify their intervention towards 'progress', and consequently, their actions favouring tourism; but more importantly, they did so in order to maintain the status quo. This tactic reflected, following the ideas of Nederveen Pieterse, how development can be promoted in a way that entails human and social development (basic needs, education, health, and so on) (1998, 345); in this way, it pushes Mezcalenses to endorse the proposal since it is seen as a first step to ending their marginalisation—clearly an action following the tenents of neoliberal governance.

Nonetheless, the opposition of some *comuneros* and inhabitants who foresaw potential threats became manifested as well. Still the project moved ahead and as a result, as explained in Chapter 2, the easy and rapid access of people facilitated new kinds of labour and migration that impacted on the practices, values, organisation and ideas of the community. In this regard, the young supporter Carlos discerns that the changes in the village were due to 'the proximity to, it could be said, places a bit more developed'. Furthermore, while this work represented a bond with the city, it also constituted the opening up of the village as a strategic area for residential and cultural tourism. Martínez Moreno (2008) documents how this highway prepared the terrain for tourism setting aside a part of the territory with high potential for housing developments. In fact, while at least five housing developments were planned in the lands before Mezcala (Martínez Moreno 2008, 43–5) the Municipal President García Becerra also showed interest in transforming the place into a cultural and ecological tourist attraction. For example, in the *Plan Municipal de Desarrollo Rural Sustentable (2005)*, he declared that:

> Poncitlán deserves more attention in the development of the ecotourism sector, since it has a potential not yet exploited, but already recognised by the inhabitants themselves and because of whom we are fortunate to work in it, but, above all, the determining factor to carry out change in their communities and activities is undoubtedly the people; people who have been vastly exploited and abused and whom we have today the great opportunity to serve and, if possible, to accompany.

This statement and plan reflected the institutionalisation of sustainable development, assisting in maintaining the 'status quo' (Nederveen Pieterse 1998, 365) and constituting a way to 'sustain' development (Esteva 1992, 16). More precisely, sustainable development—as pointed out by Enrique Leff (2005)—acts as a 'smokescreen' to sustain 'economic rationality' and to provide frames flexible enough to maintain the economic growth level; in so doing, such development prolongs the appropriation and damage of natural resources while sharpening the differences between and within countries.

In addition, while executing the plans to open land to tourist capital in 2005, the Municipal government of Poncitlán, together with the SCJ and INAH, revealed the project for the archaeological restoration of the major Island of

Mezcala, as part of the celebrations of the *Bicentenario* (Bicentennial Anniversary of the Mexican Independence) celebrated on September 16, 2010. Soon it came to light that there were many irregularities in the proposal to rapidly transform *the heart of the community* into a tourist attraction by changing the use of soil and, as Vicente denounces, 'form a trusteeship ... that will be administered by people from outside and where they'll charge to enter'.[5] As well, it is believed that the aforementioned reform of the Constitution of Jalisco was made for the government to dispossess the community, and to appropriate and control their territory favouring certain economic groups and institutions. Indeed, authorities profited from a legal paradox to reject the power and authority of *comuneros*, and undermine their legal personhood. The works began, disregarding the population and their practices, positioning inhabitants as an obstacle to tourism and thus, advocating the need to embrace the discourse of 'progress', to enjoy the benefits by being temporal labourers, sellers, security guards and gardeners. In this way, following the ideas of Rafael Sandoval (2009), they were dispossessed from their territory to transform them into private property for tourism purposes but granting the benefits only to a small privileged political and economic sector.

Aside from this, the architect Cuauhtémoc De Regil (2009), an employee of INAH Jalisco, disclosed the interests at stake and the corruption which was unleashed that disregarded the commodification of cultural heritage. In this context, the government encouraged a form of 'cultural tourism' transforming inhabitants into 'folkloric objects', while privatising their land and improperly reconstructing the ruins (Alonso 2010b: 320–2). What is more, tourism, as in the context of Quintana Roo, was evidenced to be supported by a construction of 'otherness' that allows sustaining class and ethnic differentiations and hierarchies internally and externally (Pi-Sunyer 2002), 'rooted in colonialism' (Torres and Momsen 2005, 326). So, we were witnessing how the commodification of a space transforms its economic, social, cultural and historical values, while impressing on it a new interpretation and representation according to the needs, structures and plans of neoliberal governance. In this manner, Mezcala is being transformed into a tourist destination, being constructed for the interests of outsiders, not only physically, but also through the marginalisation, control and artificial representations of Mezcalenses, their territory, history and culture, representations that are further internalised.

Additionally, during this period, the threats of PROCEDE/PROCECOM did not disappear, and the government even launched the *Plan de Ordenamiento Territorial de Mezcala* (Territorial Arrangement Plan) in 2006 to change and control the use of soil. This was accompanied with proposals such as the *Cordón Verde*, that is, the delimitation of tourist zones along Lake Chapala, that, as recounted by Vicente: 'It was going to be controlled by the government. Supposedly, because within them, the same businessmen or the same politicians ask the government: "I want that zone for blah blah blah", and they keep it'. In this sense, the alleged ecological protection zones would later be granted to elite members; therefore, developmental plans follow clientele interests, allowing land grabbing, the boost of commodification and the transformation of spaces

136 *Tourism: A Fight to Define Progress*

and their representations. Attempts did not stop here, in 2008, with the collaboration of the environmental Non-Governmental Organisation (NGO), *Instituto de Derecho Ambiental (Idea)*, they aimed to institute a training programme comprising the use of land and natural resources, tourism and defence of territory without consulting the *Asamblea General de Comuneros* (Torres 2008). This not only reflected again the institutionalisation of 'alternative development', but also how NGOs, in a neoliberal governance setting, might function to 'promote neoliberal state and business values and agendas' (De Angelis 2005, 240). In effect, neoliberalism manifests as another stage of developmentalism where, as observed by Nederveen Pieterse, institutions recommend to people what to do to achieve 'modernisation, nation building, progress, mobilisation, sustainable development, human rights, poverty alleviation and even empowerment and participation' (2000, 182).

Likewise, the refurbishment of the *malecón* took place and manifested as a strategy to transform the area into a tourist attraction and render as commodities everything it contains, such as the space, people and resources. Again the government sought the support of certain sectors by promoting the ideas of 'progress' or distributing economic benefits. The *malecón* was inaugurated after more than five years of work and multiples glitches, including diversion of funds, debts, corruption, fabrications, use of inappropriate materials and incomplete works. In effect, in 2011, in the official press release (Solís), the *Secretaría de Turismo Jalisco* (STJ), Aurelio López Rocha expressed:

> His desire for 'this being just the start' of something—since he said, this *malecón* is 'the first of many works' planned for this area of the entity—that means 'a daily effort' through which Mezcala 'becomes increasingly attractive', where the visitor 'finds services' and there is 'an economic spillover' that impacts on 'the livelihood and dignified life' of the community.

Elites were aiming to set up a private, exclusive and capitalist form of tourism that benefits only a few families and endorses a higher presence of foreigners, and thus, were promoting and adjusting colonialist structures. Under these circumstances, many Mezcalenses have been absorbed and incorporated into such dynamics of neoliberal governance through the inherited political culture, disregarding their responsibility to safeguard territory and report any issue involving land and resources grabbing. They are not only embracing governmental tourist's proposals but also its ideals of 'progress'; as the following passage of Don José, a board member of Club Mezcala, evidences:

> Previously, there on the Island, there were only chayote crops, of green beans and everything was forgotten, the walls were damaging. Who came to rescue this was Rodolfo García, talking about Rodolfo García Becerra is pride, and what he has done, he has done it for the community, because when he started many people opposed and said he was going to take the Island. But how is he going to take it? If you can't, but the changes he made, I think they are to be valued and appreciated.

In fact, some inhabitants argue that public works are used to improve the image of the government, distribute bribes and favours and as a form of embezzlement. As Don Fernando, a combatant *comunero*, explains: '[They're] a way through which the government justifies itself and expresses that we're investing in the historic village of Mezcala, but it doesn't invest rather they keep it [the money]'. Like so, they managed to thwart community spirit, increasing its fragmentation and modifying the sense of place, ownership and control. They carry out partial projects and aim to change the use of land to increase the power and presence of authorities over territories and societies. In fact, keeping in mind the ideas presented in the last chapter, public works represent personal and political interests, and thus, sometimes the government prevents, blocks or slows them down. Neo-liberal governance demonstrates, in this way, the endurance of an inherited Mexican political culture that cooperates to uphold, but also to transform, the social absorption and neoliberal economic agenda enacted by the rhetorics of 'development', 'modernisation' and 'progress'.

Networks of Solidarity[6] vs. Networks of Power

The Energies of Resistance

Tourism has brought about the transformation of the territory, changing labour, values, practices and organisation, but it has also co-opted and seduced population, accentuating divisions, and boosting foreign invasions and state planning. This has provoked, as unveiled in this section, struggles for appropriation and defence of space. Mezcala has become a 'transnational space', following the insights of the study of Torres and Momsen (2005), mediated by a multiplicity of social relations across all levels, where inequalities and imbalances are reproduced and the local reality is indelibly reshaped. However, in line with the observations of Pi-Sunyer for Cancún, Mezcalenses are not passive recipients of this development incursion, and thus, Mezcala contains 'spaces of negotiation and contestation' and an 'environment for the elaboration of modes of geographic imagination' (2002, 217). As space is relational, as noted before, it thus has an ideological finality, being constructed, lived, imagined and represented differently and in interaction (Massey 2005).

In this sense, here lies the importance of place, since Mezcala is a distinctive and contested place built by interconnections that provide different meanings and identities that might explain their location but also their survival strategies. Place entails, in the words of Escobar, 'the location of a multiplicity of forms of cultural politics' (2001, 156), that is, the struggles over meanings and representations in order to transform social relations and redefine power (Alvarez, Dagnino, and Escobar 1998, 8). In Mezcala, therefore, on the one hand, elites might try to enforce a fixed narrative, but as this space is filled up with history, memory and a sense of place, Mezcalenses are elaborating their own, and thus, visualising alternatives to the marginalisation, exploitation and commodification of the community. In this regard, Mezcalenses' knowledge and identities can contribute to changing the meanings of culture, territory, politics and economy.

138 *Tourism: A Fight to Define Progress*

Therefore, even if *comuneros* have been integrated into state logics and culture, many have remained steadfast in the protection of their territory and found supporters. This started to materialise in the early 2000s, when *comuneros* no longer had the same capacity to oppose and PROCEDE and PROCECOM's threats of privatisation were strongly felt. Three young inhabitants organised in a movement called 'Jóvenes unidos contra PROCEDE' (Young People United Against PROCEDE) with the support of other inhabitants, especially women, in order to step up against it. Rocío, one of these young fighters, remembers:

> We had our banners and the ladies were shouting 'Assholes, you're going to sell the community and everything!', and that assembly was won by three people, that means that they almost accepted PROCEDE.

Little support was necessary to put *comuneros* on track and motivate them to keep fighting against land privatisation. But, as these young inhabitants realised that weakening and fragmentation was expanding among *comuneros*, they widened their organisation and understanding about agrarian problems while enhancing their pride in being indigenous. This group later led to the creation of Colectivo Mezcala (2003), which brought together around ten young inhabitants, some of them university students in Guadalajara. They gathered together based on their sympathy with Zapatista ideas and shared concerns produced by neoliberal capitalism (Alonso 2010a, 18). Besides, they were supported by academics from Guadalajara, with whom they created the Seminar Series of Social Movements of the region, and the *Frente Zapatista* from whom they learned the similarities between communities in Chiapas and their own experience, but also, the value of and the need to join forces with their local authority. Some *comuneros* joined due to family connections, but also as a result of their attendance at a meeting of *La Otra Campaña*.[7] *Comuneros* found several coincidences with the Zapatista movement and other indigenous communities, so enmeshed themselves to the indigenous national struggle through the *Congreso Nacional Indígena (CNI)*.[8] These alliances empowered the community and their claims, while they also supported a creative process towards the elaboration of proposals and actions to safeguard their lands and traditions opposing predatory capitalism and moving away from traditional politics and state power, but more importantly, to vindicate their communal organisation and autonomy.

Although at the beginning Colectivo Mezcala was not entirely accepted by *comuneros* due to the different perspectives and the lack of social legitimacy attributable to their age and gender, from that moment on, they opened up their doors and a series of collaborative actions began. One of their first actions was the organisation of the *Foro Nacional en Defensa de la Madre Tierra y la Autonomía de los Pueblos Indígenas* (2006), which drew in other sectors of the community that showed interest in supporting their claims and struggle (Martínez Moreno 2008). In addition, these young inhabitants broadcasted the importance of *comuneros*, while also opening assemblies and integrating voices of other sectors claiming to be excluded from decisions, as noted in Chapter 1.

Comuneros were backed by a large number of inhabitants who participated either by protesting, discussing, acting and, later, working with them. In this way, in 2007 *comuneros*—together with young supporters—managed to expel a motocross club, *Enduro MotoClub*, which was using the hills in Mezcala with the authorisation of the Municipal President, Ramón Romo (Martínez Moreno 2008). They also succeeded in charging the Municipal government for the unauthorised extraction from sandbars (2009), allocating these funds towards the construction of the library, as narrated in the last chapter.

Furthermore, they stood up, organising several events and declarations against privatisation and the trampling of authorities over their history, celebrations, values, authority and territory, and deceptions enacted through the discourse of 'progress' and via the promotion of tourism. Basing themselves on their history, they articulated their fight, while they were passing and sharing their responsibilities. For instance, Itza, a member of Colectivo Mezcala, expresses:

> Something curious that almost all elder *comuneros* mention is: 'Don't leave the lands, don't abandon them, because they want to divide them, they want to split them to sell them to the rich'.

For these fighters, their territory has permitted the reproduction of their culture, and their fight is invoked in these terms, as one of them denounces, see Martínez Moreno (2014). Therefore, thanks to their efforts, inhabitants increasingly believed that 'to be *comunero*, to defend the land, to safeguard the land not only it's up to *comuneros* rather it's a task for the whole population' (Rocío 2012). Accordingly, these young Mezcalenses began a process to renew the census of *comuneros* in order to reinforce their role, the struggle to defend the land and the quest for autonomy, while *comuneros* welcomed new people to achieve new projects and to be the new intermediaries in the negotiation of better conditions. In this manner, *usos y costumbres* were adapted, and inhabitants were assessed to become *nuevo comunero*; at the same time, the history, values and authority were transmitted, reinforced and recreated to prevent the dissolution of the community, its appropriation by external powers, and to achieve the degree of autonomy sought. Accordingly, the role of *comuneros* and the long struggle for land were revalorised since, as Felipa expressed, 'they are the archaeological gems of our village. They teach us to listen, learn, remember, live, defend our history and our land' (Moreno 2010, 170).

Comuneros are engaged in a historic fight over land and the conservation of the community, enhancing the role of territory and thus opening more communication channels. So, first, together with young fighters they began working from 2006 on the *Estatuto Comunal*, the internal regulations, in order to protect and regularise their territory and organisation in environmental, cultural, social, economic and political spheres.[9] They also walked the borders of the community with the aim of teaching how to recognise their territory and take care of it. Later, they organised a public consultation (2008) that, although not concluded, served to interact with inhabitants, to understand their needs and concerns about

140   *Tourism: A Fight to Define Progress*

territory, work, tourism, migration, representativeness and practices. Like so, Mezcalenses were renovating their sense of place; that is, as defined by Streibel (1998) on how they live and experience places and their multiple relationships with it, thus combining the symbolic with the concrete. Furthermore, senses of place are part of the 'politics of identity' since they establish distinctions, disparities and differences with other groups, influencing our interpretations of them in parallel with the construction of ourselves (Rose 1995, 103–6). The sense of place that this group of Mezcalenses embody, therefore, contrasted to the one that elites want to create through tourism; as it is partly delineated away from the criteria of others, and aims to construct their own identities and alternative meanings to the hegemonic ones.

Thus, with the aim of further encouraging younger generations to identify with their land, to make them commit, they organised history workshops. Here, territory was portrayed as a blessed, free and open place, full of history, identity and tradition to be protected as a legacy of their ancestors and to ensure their own future, home, security and livelihood. In effect, by understanding the current problems in the community and becoming familiar with the avenues available to defend the land, their purpose was to coordinate further actions. In this regard, the historical awareness reached such a degree that it has been equated to an obstacle to the capitalist system (Moreno 2011). More precisely, these workshops provided other forms of socialisation where people visualised the possibility of a system change and to become the agents of their own history through their actions, desires and commitments. *Comuneros*, together with these young inhabitants, have thus created their own public space where they discuss their needs, boost their identity and defend their rights (Alonso, 2010b: 334); that contrasted from the one opened by migrants as they have even produced other forms of knowledge to disrupt the hegemonic order. In this sense, Mezcalenses have connected their political struggle with the possibility of their claims being realised.

'Progress' Violating and Subjugating Mezcalenses?

The confrontation with the government and the *invasor* became more violent as the opposition towards the elites' development plans strengthened. This especially intensified from 2006 in the context of the 'war on drugs'. This war, determined by the U.S. government (Alonso 2011), guaranteed the benefits of business elites and foreign groups (Delgado-Ramos and Romano 2011, 93) while it accentuated direct confrontation and promoted neoliberalism and infrastructure projects (Carrillo Nieto 2014). Along these lines, Escobar (2004) argues, violence is 'constitutive' of 'development', and, thus, the internal wars and displacements help to 'free up' these regions for transnational capital, favouring the interests of the hegemonic world order, disrupting identities and forming 'cultures of destruction'. This war thus surfaced as a course of neoliberal governance, where there is no regard for human and social costs, which are too often—if conceived in any terms—understood as negative externalities that prolong exclusion, violence and repression.

Tourism: A Fight to Define Progress 141

In view of that, some Mezcalenses blamed the collusion of the government, the *invasor*, the police and *narcos* for this violent scenario, demonstrating how organised crime has captured institutions, affecting inhabitants, who are thrown into the midst of their arrangements while being repressed. For instance, as noted in Chapter 1, the police, rather than serving the community, accept bribes and get involved in corruption protecting those offering the best reward.[10] What is more, in a neoliberal governance setting, the higher military presence in the country, as observed by Gilberto López y Rivas (2005, 111), was accompanied by co-option and integration of different subjects into paramilitary forces in order to end resistance, impede autonomy projects and to some degree, shore up support for the imperial project of the United States. In this context, since 2008, the *invasor* armed his *prestanombres* together with a group of around 20 men who have been intimidating people who approach the invaded zone.

However, *comuneros*' visible opposition and growing support from social movements, academics and the media only increased. They created a network of solidarity that shows how social actors are expanding their space of political struggle, changing the conception of globalisation, using it from below and increasing their chances to succeed through their increased organisational capacity. In this way their internal and external links allowed the community to survive and oppose many of the state and elite's actions. *Comuneros* and young supporters, informed by the experience of neighbouring villages and other social movements, kept broadcasting the negative impact of the governmental programmes and projects and the intentions of the *invasor*. The rallying cry was expressed in a statement by Colectivo Mezcala (2008):

> Land for us is of great significance, because in it is our history and our work, now with neoliberal governments their attempts to implement PROCEDE have been constant, since we are neighbours of a lake, the largest of the country, and one that also hosts many gringos and entrepreneurs who want to turn our house into a golf course.

Given this background, Bastos (2012; 2013, 112) signals that GMI's plans aim at integrating Mezcala into the land market of the shores of Lake Chapala while Mezcalenses are transformed into an exclusive form of 'sellers of workforce'; and that such plans correspond with a broader trend of accumulation by dispossession. Through illegal paths land is expropriated to settle a form of residential tourism that entails the elevation of status of national and international foreigners, but the persistent subordination of Mezcalenses. However, via the reproduction of the inherited political culture and its practices, and the use of formal and informal routes of power within the community, as narrated in Chapter 1, a faction of *comuneros* was co-opted by the *invasor*. Bastos (2013, 115–16) identifies this as the 'communitarian capture' where the subordination of a local sector is sought in order to support the interests of an external power, which creates an 'institutional paralysis' and transforms this issue into a conflict between *comuneros*. Accordingly, Don Miguel expresses regarding the invasion:

142 *Tourism: A Fight to Define Progress*

Men with balls that were not interested had to claim it, we're just cowards, if you'll forgive the expression, that for a miserable 500, a thousand pesos we sell ourselves and eat out of their hands. And why is that? Lack of courage, of spirit of those ancestors [who] gave their lives to ensure that we're a free community.

Capitalists use local authorities as their loyal promoters to enforce neoliberal policies that seek to make communal lands available to the private market and 'help' indigenous people to overcome their 'backwardness' (Bastos 2013, 126–7). In this way, the conflict over land has not be an exclusive form of 'cannibalism' between *comuneros*, as Bastos (2012) argues, but among the whole community and families; as pointed out by Carlos, 'he puts us into a fucking family conflict; in a context where we reject them, they reject us. We can no longer frequent our own families for the same reason'. In effect, the *invasor* profits from the disadvantages of the community, buying cheaply and offering infrastructure development and employment, or as many Mezcalenses affirm: 'The *invasor* knew how to enter making use of the need of its inhabitants' (Chuy 2012). In sum, as noted by Pedro: 'His intention was not purely good, to help people, rather it was double-edged, to appropriate land'. This fact follows the logic of the oppression and domination, as described by Don Fernando:

Look, the truth is that people who have the power are the ones who have the economic resources and somehow are going to extort people who lack the resources, and especially when there is a lack of culture and misery forces us into this situation.

Héctor Díaz-Polanco (2005) uses the term *etnofagia* to refer to the strategy of seducing indigenous people into the institutional network that serves the interests of the neoliberal project through economic and sociocultural appeals (for example, development), while also stressing differences and provoking the weakening of movements or organisations. The promises of a better future, capital inflow and individual benefits attracted Mezcalenses to accept the entrepreneur's 'help', at the same time that the idea of 'economic progress' pushes forward; as the following commentary of Don Roberto demonstrates: 'There are places, many outlooks that if some millionaires came to Mezcala, they would build their houses in the most beautiful places like the case of this man [GMI]'. In effect, some Mezcalenses, as in the case of some migrants, were further attracted through the ideological power of the priest who got involved in the land problematic.[11] They justify the *invasor* and his actions as he represents 'modernity' and the possibility to 'progress' through the boost of residential tourism, seen as the impetus to bringing benefits and overcoming the 'traditional' lifestyle.[12] No wonder Don Roberto defines progress as follows:

Progress would be that people have more flexibility in the economic sphere, because with respect to Mezcala, to say 'how pretty Mezcala is' and have whoever is not from there be tempted to go and visit, he or she will be considered a tourist. Therefore a town where there is tourism has income, there is an economy for people whether they have their *changarritos*, their stores, that sell their products ... whether that be a soda, sandwiches, tacos, whatever. Then I think that Mezcala by changing its structure is going to spread the word that Mezcala, it can be said that it is a picturesque town like Chapala, I mean, because Chapala is a small town but one walks inside that little village and it's like an American city, and tourists that arrive there buy their products and that is money that stays there, right?

Thus, these migrants represent a diaspora that, nonetheless, in some measure distances itself from territorial concerns and displays an ideological repositioning, giving new meanings to territory and welcoming public works and external intervention. As the following passage of Don Marcos, a migrant, evidences regarding invaders:

If they're peaceful people and they're good people, and they want to help the village, they should leave them. Land there is many, and if you bought it and did it that way it's okay, but simply they should support the village. I don't see it as something bad....

The large migration flow provoked by uneven development is not only leaving empty spaces that can be appropriated, but, more importantly, is impacting on community projects, strategies and ways of living through economic and social remittances and by meddling in political matters and endorsing different ideals and values. In this way, Mezcala could be transformed, as noted before, into a space for the production and consumption of U.S. retirees and national elites, where the wealth generated increasingly empowers these sectors economically and politically, and inequality and segmentation based on race and class are propelled as a result.

The *invasor*, like this, is encouraging a form of unequal exchange to favour trade with upper classes and foreigners supported by his connections, and making use of the inherited political culture and the rhetoric of 'development'. In fact, the *invasor* found a way to justify his violent and fragmentary actions through this discourse, as observed in an email addressed to the *Centro para la Justicia para la Paz y el Desarrollo (CEPAD)*:

All of this in order that society as well as authorities and members of our community can manage to overcome the *stalemate* that it has experienced for decades.

(Moreno Ibarra 2011, emphasis added)

Furthermore, in a 2010 interview, he stated that 'it was necessary to train militarily people from the same community and that his goal was to save "indians" from those who opposed the development of the village' (Guillén 2014). In this

144　*Tourism: A Fight to Define Progress*

context, paramilitarisation increased with the forming and arming of a group of 40 women known as *Las Agüilas del Pandillo*, who, for instance, in November 2011 disturbed an assembly in order to lobby *comuneros* to accept a reforestation programme called *ProÁrbol* (Colectivo Mezcala 2012). In this way, all the strategies, such as corruption, bribes, manipulation, twisting of laws, criminalisation, intimidations, coercion, violence and ideological subjugation used by GMI at local and state levels have protected him and slowed down the agrarian judicial process, to advance the development of the tourist–residential project. Likewise, as opposition of *comuneros* and young supporters became established, more violence was triggered, from threats and gunshots to the imprisonment of ten *comuneros* and inhabitants who were charged with property damage. It was evidenced in the process of these legal prosecutions that, as noted in Chapter 1, informal relationships and practices have been redefined, renewed and readapted making it harder to identify the subjects involved.

In this scenario, inhabitants needed to choose between allying with the *invasor*, or, if opposing, to face repression. Indeed, the neoliberal rationale has attempted to inculcate individual responsibility for freedom and wealth (Harvey 2007, 73), acting against communal values and collective goals, while at the same time portraying individuals as incapable of 'progress' and 'growth' and passing on the idea of one path to reach 'development'. Some Mezcalenses are in this way driven to forget their roots, their community, their history and their identity in exchange for money to satisfy immediate needs, being ideologically subjugated to the ideals of progress embodied by GMI. They are imagining another community where tourism and development are equated with local opportunities and upward mobility rather than with marginalisation, exclusion and out-migration. So, 'many of them [comuneros] have persisted with the idea of progress but the wrong one' (José Luis 2012) and thus, the emergence of a strong movement of opposition is hampered. But as history gives meaning to the resistance of *comuneros* (Martínez Moreno 2012) and young supporters, it keeps them standing by, being ready to '*que corra el sangre*' (to spill blood), as some of them express. In fact, throughout these years the position and identity of *comuneros* and their tenacious opposition have been reinforced in spite of the attacks and transformations provoked in their territory, practices, values and organisation.

They have held multiple actions, such as: the encampment (2009), their participation in the national *Marcha por la Paz* (2011), and the denunciations against the *invasor* and its paramilitary force before state institutions. In addition, they have been supported by media to broadcast the real situation while opening new spaces of collaboration and mobilisation; as for instance, Adelo's radio participation previously mentioned. This demonstrates not only the growing role of media as a political actor but also the possibility to challenge its 'corporate control', to borrow the expression from Kinsman (2006). What is more, as young fighters have become media producers they have disseminated the problems faced and the importance of their local authority, values and territory within the community. In effect, the appropriation of media and public spaces has, in line

Tourism: A Fight to Define Progress 145

with the ideas of Juan Francisco Salazar (2002), given people the possibility of having greater control over economic, political, social and cultural processes through the exchange of perceptions, negotiation of identities and the request for action and debate. Thus, for instance, by organising independent channels, such as, the newspapers *El Ticus Insurgente* and *El Ingobernable*, electronic articles, social media, and radio transmission, information is travelling between families and across borders, impacting on local knowledges and consolidating a trans-local and reinforced movement of Mezcalenses who are coming together to defend their community. Although such efforts have had their ups and downs through a counter-hegemonic use of hegemonic instruments, they help their political struggle to resist domination and decide their own destiny.

However, in spite of denunciations and actions, a fire in the hills occurred signalling the *invasor* as the possible responsible party, while later, a new governmental programme was disclosed, the *Fondo de Apoyo para los Núcleos Agrarios sin Regularizar* being the new image of PROCEDE that presented itself as a reforestation and environmental programme trying to trick communities into granting concessions of land. Thanks to their informed and cautious opposition and the transnational solidarity network, they confronted and averted land regularisation; yet, throughout the years the *invasor* has overrun more land.

Maintaining the Fantasies of the Nation via the Appropriation of Space

Meanwhile, the government kept on working in the Island using inadequate methods, materials and guidelines, and benefiting from co-opted *comuneros*. It used symbolic and rhetorical avenues to sustain itself and its allies; for instance, they carried out the reconstruction—and not the restoration—of the archaeological remains, as some Mezcalenses claim. In this regard, Don Fernando discerns: 'They disfigured [the ruins], supposedly we are in the modernisation era'. In fact, in general, *comuneros* perceived that invaders on their Island had a different vision, or, as Moreno (2010, 171) recounts:

> [A comunero] asked us: 'Have you seen what the man with no control is doing [on the Island]?' And we said no, that we saw the land, the blood, the history of our insurgents. Don Chava laughed and said, 'Yes, me neither, I don't see anything other than what you see'. But the truth is that there is something different, and that's what the sick man sees, thinks and does, that we don't.

The problem with this disease, to extend the metaphor implicit in this citation, is that it has the power to transmit this vision, and thus, *comuneros* asked young inhabitants for their help to stop its spread (Moreno 2010). In spite of all the efforts and actions of *comuneros* and their network of solidarity, authorities kept seeking to commodify the Island while changing the meaning of their history and territory, as denounced in a declaration:

146 *Tourism: A Fight to Define Progress*

It is foolish for us that they are using the heroic struggle of our insurgent parents to change the meaning of this communal space. For this reason.... *On the Island of Mezcala no tollbooth or any other charging mechanism will be installed for people who visit our Island, this is because we consider that it means the beginning of the privatisation of a communal space and the commodification of our hearts as people.*

(Comunidad Indígena Coca de Mezcala 2009, emphasis in original)

Considering that the commodification of space is pivotal for the construction of the modern nation-state (Alonso 1994), elites were creating a space for their business while keeping alive national fantasies, as Carlos explains:

They aimed to reconstruct this type of history because it's tourism that gives them financially more money, right? They don't reconstruct history as it is, because the true history doesn't favour them, as well as the fact that it doesn't provide them with badass buildings so as to attract people who go there to learn the history.

In contrast, in line with the observations of Alonso (2010b, 2012) and Bastos (2011a, 2011b), Mezcalenses remember the battle of *insurgentes* as a victory and a symbol of pride and identity that sustains the defence of territory. This was explicit in a declaration made by *comuneros* in 2007 to commemorate the event:

Every November 25, our history together with our dead, our ancestors, walk around the village, the lake, the Island, come out and whisper in our ear the care we must have for our territory, our heritage. That is why, here in the indigenous community of Mezcala, the land is not for sale, rather we defend it, because it's the closest memory that unites us with them. Also, the dead come to remind us that we are the legitimate owners of the more than 3,600 hectares of Territory, in addition to the possession of the Island of Mezcala. And that just as they did, we have to take care of it and defend it, that is, what they did in ancient times we have to do it now and that also the attempts to take away the land that has belonged to us for more than 500 years, just like yesterday, we have them now.

(Comunidad Indígena de Mezcala 2007)

In this sense, whereas the Island and its remains helped to reinforce a history of victory, by transforming this place new historical meanings could be given, reinforcing the power of dominant groups over history, myths and community. Indeed, history is a repeated imagined narrative (Carter 1987, XV) and the construction of places might involve 'a renewal of history-making skills' (Escobar 2001, 169). Here, the government aimed, inspired by the ideas of Alonso (1994, 382–98), to transform a place embodying a local autonomy into a 'homogenised and nationalised domain'; more precisely, into 'heritage', where official history makes the 'presence of the state' evident in daily life, and the state secures its

Figure 4.1 Comuneros shocked by the reconstruction.

ownership as the 'custodian', and thus, the representation of space is imbricated with 'ethnic formation and inequality'. This matches our prior arguments on how inequities are reproduced physically, symbolically and pragmatically via tourism, but what I want to emphasise here is how places are reconstructed to serve specific aims, emptying their history and transforming them into resources, being a strategic tool of domination of neoliberal governance.

With this in mind, spaces are socially constructed perpetuating categorisations where indigenous cultures might be portrayed as 'backward', and opposed to progress, being relegated to something of the past, in parallel to being reduced to folkloric elements. In this regard, Mezcala has shown two main representations as a place of 'rebel' indians or a historical enchanted place where the state, following the insights of Nelly Richard in regard to post-dictatorship Chile, aims to construct a memory that is a 'monument' (a fixed past), or a 'document' (the 'objectification of the truth') (2000, 275). Thus, although the state's representations of people and culture can be challenged, the problem is how they tend to expand and shape our knowledge prolonging forms and structures of power worldwide. Actually, these images are well matched with *indigenismo* and the general processes of state formation, but also congruent with 'the economics of transnationalism' (Pi-Sunyer 2002, 227). Hence, this scenario showed a tendency to transform the community into people without history or voice and to

148 *Tourism: A Fight to Define Progress*

ascribe national memory to their territory while sustaining the capitalist and colonialist logic exerted via tourism.

However, Mezcalenses are challenging ideological constructions, categories, meanings, representations and market arrangements; and thus, are engaging in cultural politics. Therefore, different scenarios seem possible, in line with the ideas of Leff (2005), through the emergence of 'politics of place, space and time' manifested in the struggles over identity, autonomy and territory in which people might seek to maintain cultural practices but also reconstruct and create new identities in order to exert their right to be different and autonomous, recuperate control over their territories, resist being riven by the economic rationality, and thus, to be the creators of their future. In effect, place is fused with the 'politics of identity' where Mezcalenses, taking the ideas of Richard (2000) further, via a struggle over meaning and cultural validation through difference based on history and territory, they glimpse alternatives, paths from which to articulate their claims and survive. These are, nonetheless, entangled with obstacles, tricks and contradictions that seek to absorb them into the logic of the system.

Within this context, the opposition of *comuneros* and young supporters strengthened, especially as the celebration of the *Bicentenario* approached. Either due to this conflict or because the restoration was not ready, in 2010 the planned governmental commemoration did not take place and the community celebrated as usual the 'Día de los Insurgentes de la Isla de Mezcala' (Day of the Insurgents of the Island of Mezcala). Nevertheless, authorities persisted in their plans and, two years later in November 2012, they appropriated the celebration of the Bicentennial Anniversary of the *Lucha y Defensa de la Isla de Mezcala* (Struggle and Defence of the Island of Mezcala), imposing a schedule of events, including a Mass and a military spectacle.[13] *Comuneros* quarrelled before the municipal and state governments and institutions; however, they only received an invitation to negotiate after the conclusion of the celebrations by the Director of Internal Affairs of the *Secretaría General de Gobierno del Estado de Jalisco*, who threatened, 'just don't ruin things for me this weekend'. Through their solidarity network, they managed to prevent the attendance of the governor, and dispel the enthusiasm about these festivities, but the celebration proceeded, and was followed up with an elitist presidium and over 100 soldiers who riddled the place, limiting public dissent and opposition. Moreover bribes were offered to inhabitants, increasing fragmentation and co-option in the community, and supporting a favourable image of the government.

In this vein, in a way similar to the observations of Sandra Garabano for the case of Chile, these kinds of events 'can strengthen or shatter the myths, narratives and histories that form the archive of any nationality' (2012, 344). There is a formation of 'scenarios' by the state to perform a 'modernist project of development', as Rosario Montoya identifies in the Sandinista state in Nicaragua; here 'national subjects' assume a role and are active participants in the creation of marginal populations to hold national identity, and construct the state (2007, 73–4). In this regard, subjectivities are being shaped, and Mezcalenses are embedded in a fantasy that masks, upholds and naturalises a national capitalist

Figure 4.2 The militarisation of the Island.

scenario cast in the image of modernity/coloniality. Actually, in tandem with the arguments of Garabano (2012), in this celebration there was a mixture of a discourse of 'modernity' and 'progress' that encountered inequality and the reality of impoverishment of the community, demonstrating both opposition and co-option to the national project and elites' development and tourist plans. In effect, through this celebration and the multiple associated actions, the government performed symbolic appropriations and propelled internal conflicts to incorporate Mezcalenses into a national project in order to seize and transform their territory. Consequently, the exclusion, discrimination and misrepresentation of Mezcalenses and indigenous people were reinforced, marking their interactions, experiences and identities with power imbalances.

In brief, within a scenario marked by the performance of neoliberal governance, Mezcalenses are enjoined to comply with the state and market logic, while the Mexican government reinforces this by recreating itself, staging the scenario of a multicultural modern country and establishing, as argued in the first chapter, a simulated democracy, pursuing the co-option of opposition and resistance. Besides, in tandem with the proposal of Harvey (2007, 185–6) about the contradictory argument of the neoliberal project, I observe that at the same time a vision of democracy and justice is touted; violent and corrupt actions maintain class hierarchies undisturbed, supported by the ideas of achieving 'progress' and

150 *Tourism: A Fight to Define Progress*

'development'. In this context, recently, a *diputado* from the PRI, Victor Díaz Palacios, declared that 'the cost of modernity must be paid. There is no single modernisation that hasn't paid a cost, either regarding the environment or human rights. All, absolutely all of us must pay a cost, but there is no alternative' (Ortega 2013). Locally, this logic is reproduced, for example, as a former Municipal President of Poncitlán mentioned in an interview performed by Bastos (2009):

> Mezcala has always been a bit of a clash, different ... historically it has been so, there no PROCEDE initiative has been implemented, none. They have been very traditional, I don't know why. The development of the country, of the zone, could go much further; we have to generate wealth for the inhabitants.

There is a move towards the elimination of obstacles against elites by arguing the need for the development of the country and the people, even though in reality uneven development is exacerbated. Within this era of neoliberal governance, elites are looking for their socio-political empowerment, emphasising it physically, materially, symbolically and rhetorically. Accordingly, they have been blaming indigenous communities for their failure to achieve 'development' and act accordingly. Therefore, as noted before, authorities have broadcast the idea of *comuneros* and their supporters as enemies of 'progress'; Don Fausto, a *comunero*, argues: 'many [inhabitants] say "you're against benefits", it isn't that we're against them, it's that they didn't do things right'. The rumours that portray *comuneros* as out-dated, uneducated, 'primitive' or '*atrasados*' (backward) spread among inhabitants while tourism was seen as beneficial. For instance, following the same logic as authorities, Alberto, a liaison member of Club Mezcala, explains that for migrants:

> [tourism] is seen as a benefit. Benefit, not for them, but benefit for those who sell something. They don't see anything negative, obviously we know that it'll always be that, the more people enter there will be changes, there must be changes either for better or worse. That's the law.

People's aspirations and desires are being transformed, influencing the construction of their identities and the negotiation of their position through out-migration (Torres and Momsen 2005), but also, via in-migration. More precisely, Mezcalenses by bringing distinct temporalities and spatialities create new connections and exchanges that impact on the construction and interplay of their identities. These identities do not only respond to capitalist interests or national fantasies, some are used by people for their survival and/or for recognition and respect, but this is explored in the next chapter.

However, going back to the point of this chapter, paradoxically Mezcalenses are being contained within two forms of marginalisation via migration, as summarised by Don Marcos; 'in Chapala there are only gringos living there ... and

Tourism: A Fight to Define Progress 151

people from Chapala are living here in the United States'. Here out-migration means being expelled by elite's plans and subordinated in the receiving society and in-migration means being positioned as servants of foreigners. In this regard, as previously delineated, the elites' projects in Mezcala support and go hand in hand with the workings of a political economy, while they also evidence the vindication to reach a 'modern life'. Like so, political actors are seeking the reorganisation of territory and the control of society together with that of nature and land, clearing the path for foreign capital, housing developments and tourism via corruption, criminalisation, public works, governmental programmes and invasions. In this sense, Martínez Moreno (2014, 42) denounces:

> The problem is not tourists, rather all the capitalist interests that are pursuing an attractive market for capitalist enrichment. Their banner is progress, however they constantly forget that this progress is built on our lands and culture.

There is an alliance between capital and political power that is seeking control and to change the meaning of territory, to legitimise their actions and find local support by making use of informal politics and violence, and taking advantage of the marginalisation of inhabitants and the discourse of 'development'. Within the working of neoliberal governance, there has been a reorganisation of powers that stress authoritarian forms and use the inherited political culture and the rhetoric of 'development' to dominate and manipulate local actors serving a global objective and allowing the repression and criminalisation of opposition movements, but more importantly, the justification and perpetuation of a system based on economic and cultural hierarchies.

The community is left fragmented and violated while new invaders are allowed to become imbricated in the game; and in this way, following the argument in Chapter 2, a new territoriality is being delineated, where different subjects are contesting the transformation of the land at the whim of 'development'. In this context, the government and its allies have hindered the participation and integration of *nuevos comuneros* while serving themselves of irregularities, corruption, partiality, complicity, economic manipulation, twisting of laws, fabrications, larceny, institutional and procedural lethargy and deadlocks, as witnessed in the agrarian and criminal trials.[14] *Comuneros* and young supporters still do not give up and organise different events, actions and denunciations to make their situation visible, to find support and to exert pressure.[15] They have become dangerous for elites' plans and thereby, to the functioning of this system by resisting and defending their territory by recalling their history and identity, as Don Jacinto, an elder, explains:

> There are some [inhabitants] who understand this, and say 'no, the territory can't be modified nor can't there be other owners here either' and the generations that come after us have no need to suffer the consequences of those [actions] they haven't committed, that [in] the previous war, [our ancestors]

152 *Tourism: A Fight to Define Progress*

bought the territory by being charged two prices, one with money and another with blood, so the blood can never be erased and that's what we're always fighting for.

As Johnson argues, 'storied places', that is, how we forge places associating them with histories and create meaning and culture, are a way to glimpse alternatives (2012, 831). In this sense, as previously demonstrated, their past struggle maintains its meaning by viewing the defence of territory through an uninterrupted continuity. So, territory and history inspire people to mobilise against capitalist and colonialist projects, and shape their identities to construct their futures. Many Mezcalenses continue to protect their territory against the lures raised by neoliberal governance, and thanks to their solidarity network they are unmasking the consequences of the predatory development and progress. They are seeking their self-determination carrying out parallel actions and promoting their own alternatives and projects using their knowledges and practices while maintaining their sense of place, organisation, cultural identity and collective memory/history.

Working for a Redefinition of Progress

So far it has been evidenced that *comuneros* and young supporters are not antitourism, hence they are not 'against progress'; they are simply against those in whose name/interest it is sought. They are aware of the abuses performed by the *Municipio* and how—as noted before—the Municipal government negotiates downward only with key (pre-selected) subjects for the allocation of funds for public works and services, often resulting in projects managed at the whim of elites. However, some Mezcalenses have engaged and succeeded in their negotiations with the government to stop the incursion into their land, demonstrating their influence and an altered use of informal practices. Besides, through their actions and collective projects they are creating new spaces to find solutions to their problems, taking up the 'traditional' way of life, designing new perspectives on how to collaborate and conceiving a different kind of progress. So they have found strategies to enhance their living conditions and solutions to their daily problems not through democratic paths but rather, as an inhabitant expressed for a newspaper interview (Torres 2010):

> [We are working] from an autonomous perspective and not using the governmental handouts, because we don't want the Municipal government to show off saying that it does work, when we are the ones who have done everything, all the work.

Autonomy is a daily practice to satisfy community needs and build a different society (Hernández Navarro 2009, 55–6). In this regard, in Mezcala they have resorted to different methods such as the use of transnational 'informal' relations and working through *barrios*, as in the case of a road to take their crops out,

Tourism: A Fight to Define Progress 153

showing how their relationships, union and organisation across borders can be the force of change. Furthermore, they have embraced a 'reflexive development', where people think about the problems caused by 'development' and are managed through popular participation (Nederveen Pieterse 1998, 367–9). In fact, Mezcalenses have been designing their own *Plan de Ordenamiento Territorial* while keeping in mind many proposals to improve the image, the services and conditions in the village, such as footpaths, a university campus and a hospital. More importantly, they are also conceiving productive projects, such as creating community kitchens and restaurants and a campsite, reactivating the *chayote* cooperative, the construction of a hotel, planting fruit trees, building *pozos artesanos* and fishponds. Despite the obstacles and problems, this shows how, following the ideas of Holloway (2010), the multiple small or larger daily actions in the community are 'cracks' creating a path that disrupts neoliberal governance. Let's now turn to the project of *turismo comunitario* to appreciate how they are doing this and how they aim to create employment by profiting from their resources and using their collective forms of organisation.

The Project of 'Turismo Comunitario'

Young fighters have perceived that the government is responsible for the poor living conditions, due to their fierce opposition to land regularisation, and notice how the community presses on for the realisation of works—as in the case of the library—and the *Municipio* profits from or blocks these efforts. In this context Carlos expresses that 'they always speak about progress, right? They say, "they impede progress, they don't want progress". However, I now believe that the issue is a bit the opposite in regard to them'. Moreover, these young fighters have comprehended the importance of capitalism in embracing the widespread idea of 'progress', as José Luis, a member of Colectivo Mezcala, comments: 'Capitalism has had great power among all peoples, communities, and has been created as a basic need. And from there, it's established as progress: you have [resources], there is; you don't have, there is not'. Therefore, they embrace *zapatismo* and communal values, joining *comuneros'* struggle and understanding their opposition through the fear of dispossession, dissolution and degradation of their land and the endurance of informal power. These young inhabitants are aware that the community has the capability to 'be autonomous, and not always appeal to a government. You can work and you can make money doing a lot of things' (Itza 2012). They are elaborating other forms of relating with the state while disclosing the tricks and glitches of neoliberal governance, especially the rhetoric of 'development'. Carlos, a young inhabitant involved in this project, explains:

Many people saw it that way, right? 'If we aren't indigenous, we can't get projects that the government might offer us for social development', right? However, I have understood that it isn't through the kind of development or the charity that the State offers us to develop as such. By ourselves we can

154 *Tourism: A Fight to Define Progress*

develop these projects without its support. So, now, they aren't useful for me at all.

The case of Ajijic has illustrated to them how communities along Lake Chapala are being dispossessed from their lands, and experiencing disruption to their organisation, labour, subsistence activities, sovereignty and practices. Thus, they see restaurants and hotels as a façade and see how inhabitants from being owners fall adrift, struggling to find new housing, jobs and incomes while their territory is fenced off supposedly for security reasons. Accordingly, *comuneros* together with young supporters declared:

> We have already seen that progress doesn't arrive when the rich invade your lands, as in the case of the village of Ajijic, where progress arrived with North Americans, but there are only misery-level servant jobs, and now landlessness. So we want tourism, but as long as we're the owners, not the servants. We're not against progress as the businessmen, the government tells us, but we want a kind of progress that doesn't exclude us. So we support the gas station, but if the owner is the people, we support the hotels, restaurants, huts, everything, as long as we handle them by ourselves.
>
> (Asamblea General de Comuneros de la Comunidad Indígena de Mezcala 2008)

To this effect, new perceptions and ways of action are being promoted against the neoliberal logic and people informed on how to defend land autonomously. For instance, they took the example of the community of San Pedro Atlapulco, Estado de México to design their proposal for tourism that reinforces the 'sense of community' (Rocío 2012), maintaining their self-sufficiency and defending their territory, history and resources. So via *turismo comunitario* these young Mezcalenses have aimed to demonstrate how communal life is not preventing the creation of employment, the arrival of tourism and the improvement of conditions of the village and its inhabitants.

The youth worked together building the place *Paraje Insurgente*, a communal dining area that began to publicly operate in August 2013. This project comprises different cooperatives, such as *pulque*, baked goods, preserves and sauces, organic agriculture and a regional food restaurant; however, it is also a space for meetings, workshops, exhibitions and cultural activities that support the struggle of *comuneros*. In effect, its aim is to allow different groups to have a place for selling their food and products, exemplifying what Jorge Santiago Santiago calls 'solidarity economy'; that is, a form of economy based on collective labour under solidarity and communal guidelines, to respond to their current situation of poverty and marginalisation, which is a consequence of their 'structural and historic exclusion of capitalism in its neoliberal phase' (2009, 222). Thus, these young fighters are proposing to be the owners of their work to the benefit of the community, seeking a form of development based on coexistence and equal relationships, and using local avenues and resources.

Tourism: A Fight to Define Progress 155

Figure 4.3 Paraje Insurgente.

They are not providing a recipe to overcome the system in its entirety, but, rather, through their solidarity networks and communal actions they are redefining progress according to a communal—and autonomous—perspective; as José Luis claims: 'I consider that the progress of peoples is in the effort of each individual within the interest of their community.... Speaking about a sustainable economy in the sense of sharing, that means, walking hand in hand'. In this sense, these young inhabitants are furnishing new meanings while strengthening the defence of their territory and proposing to control their economic, but also their cultural lives. They are doing so by being owners and beneficiaries of tourism, working away from the government and creating conditions to avert the impairment of their economic activities, their residency, and that of their organisation, history, identity and territory. José Luis also explains:

> The project of the Colectivo is a form of *turismo comunitario*, that is, to include deprived people, so that they can see by themselves that it's possible to carry out tourism and that you don't need to have a terrace, or some tables, to sell something, you can do it by knowing your history, by defending your customs and traditions. It's to realise that the land is yours, there for fighting for; we know that the issue comes from another side, to offer what the community produces.

156   *Tourism: A Fight to Define Progress*

What is more, they propose to better integrate visitors and strengthen the internal organisation; Carlos explains:

> It's a form of educational tourism where you not only educate the person who visits and eats, where ... you not only show your history to them, but also make them commit to the preservation of that history within them.... The function of this *turismo comunitario* is to strengthen as well the entire history of the community's internal population.

They have been organising their materials and training themselves in collaboration with other indigenous communities, academics, teachers and social movements. By so doing, they are constructing tourism according to their context and necessities. Accordingly, they have planned to receive both local and external visitors in agriculture, fishing, and history workshops; in camps, historic walks and visits to the Island. However, their focus is on the community, aiming to receive younger generations, to spread local knowledge and transmit the care, identity, values, history, organisation and defence of the community. This collective and autonomous project is thus based on their own understanding of the world, on the community's long tradition of organisation, values and knowledge, and on historical, territorial and, as analysed in the next chapter, ethnic claims to be conveyed.

In this way, they are constructing autonomy; that is, as defined by Durán Matute, the ability 'to decide, create new open spaces, transform relations of power, establish solidarity and collective action, build a new institutional structure and change the relations between state and society and between society and nature' (2015, 8), thereby challenging the workings of neoliberal governance and changing their experiences of oppression.[16] Yet there is not a single way to understand autonomy since it is deeply contextual, and thus, it is through the 'dialogue and negotiation' in local realities that the form it takes is decided (Gasparello and Quintana Guerrero 2009). Therefore, these young people are offering a vision from a communal base, not only to prevent the *invasor* and authorities from dominating lives and territory, but also to re-engage with the importance of their territory, history and identity in relation to their labour. Rocío explains:

> We are in the fight against a fucked up economic model that is winding us up and that is because, although it's people from the community, the individualist scheme and all of that's already there. So, we said that if we didn't do a project that would guarantee the [sense of] community, we would reach a time when, even if it were people from Mezcala, there would be, how can I tell you? ... Even the space would be privatised.

In a community where work is a need, they want to redefine labour by transcending its division and halting its capitalist reproduction. So, although they are not offering easy money nor the possibility of becoming rich, they are proposing a

Tourism: A Fight to Define Progress   157

new form of employment that is more equitable and in agreement with their communal values; as Chuy describes: 'Even [to earn enough] for a soda, right? Not to buy a car, right? But enough not to, perhaps, to not migrate and not to sell their land'. This matches the proposals of Holloway (2010), that is, to stop the increase in the 'monetisation of social relations' of neoliberalism, to recover the power of making and doing, but also to reject the denial of their humanity, to be precise, to fight 'fetishism' through 'dignity' in order to allow change and stop reproducing the dominant structure and create new social relations.

On balance, up to the present times, *Paraje Insurgente* does not run all the activities, but has attracted visitors who are entranced by their food, organisation and projects. Besides, as these young people are committed to distributing benefits to all the community, they are sharing their ideas, values and organisation and hoping that others will launch their own projects creating more forms of self-employment and benefits for Mezcalenses. They are transforming the economy in order to create better conditions and move away from the forms of accumulation and development set up by neoliberal governance. In this sense, autonomy, following the ideas of Zibechi (2006), is a process in construction from below to transform the relations of power outside and inside communities, working towards their liberation and challenging the pre-existent structure of domination, but also giving rise to different models according to the local needs.

By so doing, these young Mezcalenses want to remedy aggressions, dependency, exclusion and submission to the economic and political order. Inspired by the work of Raquel Gutiérrez Aguilar (2009, 357–8), their actions thus can be identified in two ways: first, as 'siege' (*cerco*) because their opposition is immobilising dominant arrangements physically, geographically and politically; and, second, as an 'outlet' (*fuga*), since they are trying to escape collectively from the state meanings and practices. So, even if they still articulate to some extent their demands within the system, they are doing so by reshaping informal power through the values of unity, solidarity and consensus. In this manner, young fighters have not closed the door to negotiations with the government and do not escape the deleterious effects of constant communal problems. However, they are exemplifying new understandings of modernity, development and progress and forms of state practices, and how their reorganisation, empowerment and networks can challenge neoliberal governance, and even be the engine of change.

Conclusion

Although there are wider channels and possibilities within the context of an informal system, the room for manoeuvre is reduced if our position is not well established. In view of that, the *Municipio* has made pacts with the economic elite to weaken and fragment the political organisation, culture and resistance of Mezcalenses, while also seeking to revitalise the power-holder's image to sustain their rule. In effect, Mezcala exhibits the different methods that have been unleashed showing the complexity, inequality and violence of informal politics

158　*Tourism: A Fight to Define Progress*

within the establishment of a new territoriality. Mainly, elites use the discourse of 'development' and 'progress' to protect their own interests and for the reproduction and survival of interconnected local–regional–global hegemonic structures. It is an *etnofága* strategy that drives people to assimilate (into) this discourse, welcomes neoliberal values and impedes the creation of alternatives, showing how people passively and actively participate in the courses of action of neoliberal governance.

However, as the promise of economic flow or trickle down from elite proposals does not arrive, Mezcalenses are beginning a quest to confront the system that excludes them while giving rise to different perspectives of progress. Some have started exploring new forms of negotiation and democratic participation, as demonstrated in Chapter 3, but others have decided to draw autonomous paths and challenge the passivity promoted by such democracy and elaborate a new understanding of progress, as Colectivo Mezcala exemplifies. Moreover, young inhabitants, together with *comuneros*, have mobilised, resisted, and challenged their position and role, and in doing so, have formed a network of resistance based upon solidarity. In this manner, *comuneros*, backed up by a larger sector, have reinforced their organisation, identity and history while responding to the constant territorial threats; indeed, it is from this contentious terrain in the duelling divisions around visions of territory and culture, and their value and purpose, that such a reinvigoration has been made possible. They are fighting through a consciousness of their historical memory and identity, the revalorisation of land and 'traditional authority', living and constructing a history of resistance.

In this context, in the face of global and local powers acting together in this phase of neoliberal governance, Mezcalenses are trying to inhibit their advance, questioning and in some measure refusing the dominance of capital and the state. They are creating their own economic and political project based on their local reality and sustained on a network of *anti-power*,[17] re-establishing intermediaries, reshaping informal power, using local knowledges and integrating others into the conversation. *Comuneros* with young supporters are negotiating their position within the world system, while they provide new avenues to conceive their ways of being, thinking and living. For this, they use their own institutions and processes, but are also creating new forms of social, economic and political relations that, nonetheless, encompass their own conflicts and contradictions, tracked in the chapters before. On this view, we might accept our locations within the system, not for the purpose of its mere reproduction, but in order to manoeuvre from such positions and forge degrees of autonomy as practice and relation, from our own spaces and places. What this means is to speak up, oppose and actively make decisions, using the institutionalised forms as little as possible, and when doing so employing a counter-hegemonic use of hegemonic instruments.

The proposal, then—as pursued by youth aligned with *comuneros*—is, in tandem with the ideas of Mónica Gallegos (2012), to look towards the actions that will allow us to decide our destiny, to analyse (and enact) our daily autonomous

Tourism: A Fight to Define Progress   159

practices, while we recuperate spaces and test other forms of interaction, creating another world by living in it. In view of that, tourism is being redefined according to the needs and values of the community. The example provided of *turismo comunitario* is far from ideal, as it involves different positions and interests, thus, entailing inconsistencies, conflicts and regressions. They are not going 'beyond development' or creating 'alternatives to development'; however, in pursuing these avenues, inhabitants are working towards a redefinition of progress, which involves a creative process of meaning construction that is based on collective participation, communal values, history and identity, as well as the defence, conservation and use of territory. So while young inhabitants are resolving their local issues and daily needs, they are also vindicating the assaults of the past 500 years. They are trying to design their own life paths, being the creators of their future and strategies according to their knowledges, capabilities, location, history, culture and experiences, while challenging state representations, generating new meanings from hegemonic rhetoric and calling out for an institutional change and transformation of social relations away from the organisation of neoliberal governance. However, a real transformation is far from being evident if the colonial legacy of structural violence keeps framing mentalities; the next chapter addresses this issue.

Notes

1 It seems that this was no accident, but, rather that the previous representatives González Baltazar and Santana de los Santos were bribed by the engineer of the *Departmento de Asuntos Agrarios y de Colonización* to accept this larceny.
2 The first president of *Bienes Comunales*, Antíoco Robles, rejected the bribes offered and initiated the claim for the recognition of the Island (1974), but authorities managed to flip the story, accusing him and advocating his prosecution. He managed to put a stop to this accusation, thanks to the support of other politicians, while Francisco Sanabria, the last representative, also accused, had to flee the community until proving his innocence
3 Inhabitants, due to being an indigenous community, do not pay *predial*, i.e. land taxes, they only are committed to giving a symbolic donation to *comuneros*. By accepting PROCEDE their properties will be regulated; that is, measured and charged according to their location, area and value, bringing in an important income for the Municipal government and endorsing the seizure of their proprieties.
4 *Tierras de uso común* means land managed, guarded, cared for, controlled and owned by the *Asamblea General de Comuneros*, and used exclusively for harvest and cattle, and not for residential purposes nor parcelled due to its flora, fauna and significance.
5 Even though in 1997 the islands were recognised as part of the territory of Mezcala through the *Acta de Deslinde y Amojonamiento Definitivo*, the government acted as if it was Federal property rather than communal land.
6 Here by using the concept 'network of solidarity' I aim to emphasise how networks are being created to overcome capital accumulation, and thus, move away from the identification of their efforts as merely 'social capital'.
7 *La Otra Campaña* was, as summarised by Alonso (2006, 17), a new proposal of the Ejército Zapatista de Liberación Nacional (EZLN) on how to do politics from the left and from below, opposing capitalism and neoliberalism, proposing a new national plan and constitution, and respecting the different struggles and actors. This proposal aimed at detachment from political parties, dominant groups and from any seizure of power (Caudillo Félix 2011, 112).

160 *Tourism: A Fight to Define Progress*

8 The CNI was founded in 1996 and includes one of the largest percentages of indigenous people in Mexico, integrating most of the leaders that emerged with the Zapatista rebellion and supporting the more radical postures (Hernández Navarro 2009, 35). It is also an organisation independent of the state and political parties that aims to create autonomies outside the state institutionality.

9 This collective initiative approved in 2012 comprises key articles, such as: the establishment of requirements for voters, the ownership and management of islands and shores, compulsory consultation for any public work or governmental project, and the prohibition of selling and inheriting land between and to foreigners.

10 It is worth noting that Mezcalenses are often the ones enlisting in the police or the Mexican army as these are seen as opportunities to end their longstanding exclusion. This fact demonstrates how they suffer not only from direct violence but also structural violence, as defined by Johan Galtung (1969), that results from the inequality in power and living conditions endorsed by institutions and the economic and political system.

11 As noted in Chapter 3, the priest has been positioned as a point of liaison in the community, representing another form of *caciquismo* where the government profits by ensuring order is not altered and 'development' is promoted.

12 This contrasts with the collaboration of other migrants who have been warning of the threats of land regularisation, supporting communal projects and, in some cases, even sending money to pay the lawyer defending the community in the agrarian trial.

13 One of the main events was a regatta called '*Copa Gobernador*' (Governor's Cup), showing how the imposition and celebration from above is in every single symbol and form of rhetoric.

14 In spite of the legal support and backing provided by academics, organisations, social movements, politicians and media, the ten accused in September 2011 were found guilty. Until November 2015 they were found not guilty in the criminal trial. In addition, although after 15 years the resolution of the agrarian trial turned out to be positive for the community, the *invasor* appealed in the *Tribunal Superior Agrario*. Although, this time, *comuneros* and young supporters managed to prevent the outcome of elections favouring the *invasor*, not much time passed before the court ruled the agrarian trial in his favour, prolonging the timeframe while revealing the complicity of judges. Until the present, no final judgment has been issued. The community is placed at a crossroads in terms of the next steps, as Mezcalenses experience, in the words of Jorge Alonso, the perversion of dispossession, because now the *invasor* is legally considered *comunero* and might turn this invasion into an 'internal' issue.

15 In spite of this adverse scenario, they have achieved significant victories. For instance, in 2014, after seven years of working, three widows were legally recognised as *comuneras* and voted in the elections supporting *comuneros*. This fact is in line with the opening of participation that has allowed women and young inhabitants to increasingly get involve in the management of the community.

16 In this article I detail the multiple projects carried out and mechanisms employed by *comuneros* and their young supporters to protect their territory, enhance their identity and history, and strengthen their organisation.

17 Anti-powers, following the ideas of Holloway (2010), are found in the dignity of daily social relations, allowing people without power through '*el grito*' to make evident their disagreement with the current capitalist world-system state of play—glossed as a *falso mundo*—and through the posture of '*la crítica*', to end fetishisation and break the established forms of social relations. This is connected to the proposal of Zapatistas, *mandar obedeciendo* (lead by obeying), which, according to Alonso (2012, 156), means a different kind of power that liberates people without imposing new rulers.

References

Ai Camp, Roderic. 2006. *Las elites del poder en México*. Mexico City: Siglo XXI.

Alonso, Ana María. 1994. "The Politics of Space, Time and Substance: State Formation, Nationalism and Ethnicity". *Annual Review of Anthropology* 23: 379–405.

Alonso, Jorge. 2006. "La Otra Campaña Zapatista". *Asian Journal of Latin American Studies* 19 (2): 5–36.

Alonso, Jorge. 2010a. "La lucha contra el neoliberalismo por medio de la autonomía comunal, el caso de Mezcala, Jalisco". *Autonomia y Emancipación*. http:// autonomiayemancipacion.org/la-lucha-contra-el-neoliberalismo-por-medio-de-la-autonomia-comunal-el-caso-de-mezcala-jalisco-jorge-alonso/ [accessed September 2011].

Alonso, Jorge. 2010b. "La persistente defensa de la autonomía del pueblo de Mezcala como una creación de espacio público no estatal". In *¿Qué tan público es el espacio público en México?*, edited by Mauricio Merino, 311–46. Mexico City: FCE; CONACULTA; Universidad Veracruzana.

Alonso, Jorge. 2011. "La guerra perdida contra los narcos y las otras guerras". *Envío* (349).

Alonso, Jorge. 2012. "Hay que perder el miedo a pensar desde la autocrítica". In *Hacer política para un porvenir más allá del capitalismo*, 139–66. Guadalajara, Mexico: Grieta Editores.

Alvarez, Sonia E., Evelina Dagnino, and Arturo Escobar. 1998. "Introduction: The Cultural and the Political in Latin American Social Movements". In *Cultures of Politics, Politics of Cultures. Re-visioning Latin American Social Movements*, edited by Sonia E. Alvarez, Evelina Dagnino and Arturo Escobar, 1–29. Boulder, CO: Westview Press.

Asamblea General de Comuneros de la Comunidad Indígena de Mezcala. 2008. Declaratoria de Mezcala. Mezcala, Mexico.

Bastos, Santiago. 2009. "Interview with Municipal President". Poncitlán, July 15.

Bastos, Santiago. 2011a. "La comunidad de Mezcala y la recreación étnica ante la globalización neoliberal". *Revista CUHSO* 21 (1): 87–103.

Bastos, Santiago. 2011b. "La nueva defensa de Mezcala: un proceso de recomunalización a través de la renovación étnica". *Relaciones* 32 (125): 86–122.

Bastos, Santiago. 2012. "Mezcala: despojo territorial y rearticulación indígena en la Ribera de Chapala". In *Jalisco hoy: miradas antropológicas*, edited by Renée De la Torre and Santiago Bastos, 223–56. Guadalajara, Mexico: Centro de Investigaciones y Estudios Superiores en Antropología Social – Unidad Occidente.

Bastos, Santiago. 2013. "La micropolítica del despojo: Mezcala de la Asunción en la globalización neoliberal". *Revista de Estudios e Pesquisas sobre as Américas* 7 (2): 105–34.

Carrillo Nieto, Juan José. 2014. "Contrainsurgencia en México: neoliberalismo y guerra (2006–2012)". In *Movimiento indígena en América Latina: resistencia y proyecto alternativo*, edited by Fabiola Escárzaga and Raquel Gutiérrez Aguilar, 395–403. Mexico City: Universidad Autónoma Metropolitana – Unidad Xochimilco; Centro de Investigaciones y Estudios Superiores en Antropología Social; Benemérita Universidad Autónoma de Puebla; Centro de Estudios Andinos y MesoAmericanos.

Carter, Paul. 1987. *The Road to Botany Bay. An Essay in Spatial History*. London: Faber and Faber.

Caudillo Félix, Gloria Alicia. 2011. *Movimientos indígenas en América Latina. Liderazgos, discursos y utopías*. Buenos Aires: Elaleph.

Ceceña Martorella, Ana Esther. 2009. "Autonomía y control de los territorios en América Latina". In *Otras geografías. Experiencias de autonomías indígenas en México*, edited

162   Tourism: A Fight to Define Progress

by Giovanna Gasparello and Jaime Quintana Guerrero, 195–212. Mexico City: Redez tejiendo la utopía.

Clancy, Michael J. 1999. "Tourism and Development: Evidence from Mexico". *Annals of Tourism Research* 26 (1): 1–20.

Colectivo Mezcala. 2012. "Arrecia acoso contra comuneros". *El Ingobernable*, January.

Comunidad Indígena Coca de Mezcala. 2009. Declaratoria de la comunidad indígena coca de Mezcala, Jalisco. Mezcala, Mexico.

Comunidad Indígena de Mezcala. 2007. Cada 25 de Noviembre. Mezcala.

De Angelis, Massimo. 2005. "The Political Economy of Global Neoliberal Governance". *Review (Fernand Braudel Center)* 28 (3): 229–57.

De Regil, Cuauhtémoc. 2009. "Mezcala, patrimonio desprotegido". *Crónica de Sociales*, February 4. http://cronicadesociales.org/2009/02/04/mezcala-patrimonio-desprotegido/ [accessed May 21, 2013].

Del Castillo, Agustín. 2009. "Disputan tierras de la ribera de Chapala comuneros y extranjeros". *Milenio*, March 23. www.milenio.com/cdb/doc/impreso/8549402?quicktabs_1=2 [accessed September 12, 2013].

Delgado-Ramos, Gian Carlo, and Silvina María Romano. 2011. "Political-Economic Factors in U.S. Foreign Policy: The Colombia Plan, the Mérida Initiative, and the Obama Administration". *Latin American Perspectives* 38 (178): 93–108.

Díaz-Polanco, Héctor. 2005. "Etnofagia y multiculturalismo". *Memoria* 200 (October).

Durán Matute, Inés. 2015. "Mezcala: construyendo autonomía. Balance de retos y propuestas frente al neoliberalismo". *Journal of Iberian and Latin American Research* 21 (1): 1–18.

Escobar, Arturo. 1992. "Planning". In *The Development Dictionary. A Guide to Knowledge as Power*, edited by Wolfgang Sachs, 132–45. London: Zed Books Ltd.

Escobar, Arturo. 2001. "Culture Sits in Places: Reflections on Globalism and Subaltern Strategies of Localization". *Political Geography* 20 (2001): 139–74.

Escobar, Arturo. 2004. "Development, Violence and the New Imperial Order". *Development* 47 (1): 15–21.

Esteva, Gustavo. 1992. "Development". In *The Development Dictionary. A Guide to Knowledge as Power*, edited by Wolfgang Sachs, 6–25. London: Zed Books Ltd.

Gallegos, Mónica. 2012. "¿Más allá del capital y del Estado? Cuatro pro(a)puestas por la vida y un comentario (que intenta recoger pontencialidades y pensar la descolonización)". In *Hacer política para un porvenir más allá del capitalismo*, 113–26. Guadalajara, Mexico: Grieta Editores.

Galtung, Johan. 1969. "Violence, Peace and Peace Research". *Journal of Peace Research* 6 (3): 167–91.

Garabano, Sandra. 2012. "The Brilliance of Progress: People, Nature and Nation". *Journal of Latin American Cultural Studies: Travesia* 20 (4): 343–54.

Gasparello, Giovanna, and Jaime Quintana Guerrero. 2009. "Otras geografías: autonomías en movimiento". In *Otras geografías. Experiencias de autonomías indígenas en México*, edited by Giovanna Gasparello and Jaime Quintana Guerrero, 259–84. Mexico City: Redez tejiendo la utopía.

González Corona, Elias. 1989. *El Salto, industria y urbanización de Guadalajara*. Vol. 15, *Cuadernos de Difusión Científica*. Guadalajara, Mexico: Universidad de Guadalajara.

Guillén, Alejandra. 2014. "Comunidad Coca de Mezcala recupera territorio". *Más por más GDL*. http://masgdl.com/maspormas-gdl/comunidad-coca-de-mezcala-recupera-territorio [accessed October 14, 2014].

Tourism: A Fight to Define Progress   163

Gutiérrez Aguilar, Raquel. 2009. *Los ritmos del Pachakuti. Levantamiento y movilización en Bolivia (2000–2005)*. Mexico City: Sísifo Ediciones; Bajo Tierra Ediciones; Benemérita Universidad Autónoma de Puebla.

Harvey, David. 2005. *Space of Neoliberalization: Towards a Theory of Uneven Geographical Development* Edited by Hans Gebhardt and Peter Meusburger, *Hettner-Lectures*. Munich: Franz Steiner Verlang.

Harvey, David. 2007. *Breve historia del neoliberalismo*. Madrid: Akal.

Hernández Navarro, Luis. 2009. "Movimiento indígena: autonomía y representación política". In *Otras geografías. Experiencias de autonomías indígenas en México*, edited by Giovanna Gasparello and Jaime Quintana Guerrero, 33–61. Mexico City: Redez tejiendo la utopía.

Holloway, John. 2010. *Cambiar el mundo sin tomar el poder*. Mexico City: Sísifo Ediciones; Bajo Tierra Ediciones; Benemérita Universidad Autónoma de Puebla.

Johnson, Jay T. 2012. "Place-based Learning and Knowing: Critical Pedagogies Grounded in Indigeneity". *GeoJournal* 77 (6): 829–36.

Kinsman, Gary. 2006. "Mapping Social Relations of Struggle: Activism, Ethnography, Social Organization". In *Sociology for Changing the World: Social Movements/Social Research*, edited by Caelie Frampton, Gary Kinsman, A. K. Thompson and Kate Tilleczek, 133–56. Halifax, Canada: Fernwood Publishing.

Knight, Alan. 2005. "*Caciquismo* in Twentieth-Century Mexico". In *Caciquismo in the Twentieth-Century Mexico*, edited by Alan Knight and Wil Pansters, 1–48. London: Institute for the Study of the Americas.

Lefebvre, Henri. 1991. *The Production of Space*. Translated by Donald Nicholson-Smith. Oxford: Basil Blackwell Ltd.

Leff, Enrique. 2005. "La geopolítica de la biodiversidad y el desarrollo sustentable: economización del mundo, racionalidad ambiental y reapropiación social de la naturaleza". Seminario Internacional REG GEN: Alternativas Globalizaçao, Rio de Janeiro, Brasil, October 8–13.

López y Rivas, Gilberto. 2005. "México: las autonomías de los pueblos indios en el ámbito nacional". In *Autonomías indígenas en América Latina: nuevas formas de convivencia política*, edited by Leo Gabriel and Gilberto López y Rivas, 47–111. Mexico City: Plaza y Valdés.

Martínez Moreno, Rocío. 2008. "La comunidad indígena coca de Mezcala, el sujeto de la historia en la defensa de la tierra". B.A. diss., Departamento de Historia, Universidad de Guadalajara.

Martínez Moreno, Rocío. 2012. "Tierra, historia y pueblo. Memoria y acción política en la comunidad indígena de Mezcala, Jalisco". Master diss., División de Estudios Históricos y Humanos, Universidad de Guadalajara.

Martínez Moreno, Rocío. 2014. "La lucha actual de la comunidad indígena coca de Mezcala, Jalisco". In *Movimiento indígena en América Latina: resistencia y proyecto alternativo*, edited by Fabiola Escárzaga and Raquel Gutiérrez Aguilar, 40–6. Mexico City: Universidad Autónoma Metrópolitana – Unidad Xochimilco; Centro de Investigaciones y Estudios Superiores en Antropología Social; Benemérita Universidad Autónoma de Puebla; Centro de Estudios Andinos y MesoAmericanos.

Martínez Novo, Carmen. 2010. "The Making of Vulnerabilities: Indigenous Day Laborers in Mexico's Neoliberal Agriculture". *Identities: Global Studies in Culture and Power* 11 (2): 215–39.

Massey, Doreen. 1995. "The Conceptualization of Place". In *A Place in the World?: Places, Cultures, and Globalization*, edited by Doreen Massey and Pat Jess, 45–85. Oxford: Oxford University Press.

164 *Tourism: A Fight to Define Progress*

Massey, Doreen. 2005. *For Space*. London: SAGE Publications.

Massey, Doreen, and Pat Jess. 1995. "Introduction". In *A Place in the World?: Places, Cultures, and Globalization*, edited by Doreen Massey and Pat Jess, 1–4. Oxford: Oxford University Press.

Montoya, Rosario. 2007. "Socialist Scenarios, Power, and State Formation in Sandinista Nicaragua". *American Ethnologist* 34 (1): 71–90.

Moreno, Rocío. 2010. "Mezcala: la isla indómita. Las luchas por la tierra y la isla de Mezcala hoy". *Desacatos* 34: 170–4.

Moreno, Rocío. 2011. "La experiencia de Mezcala. Jóvenes e historia, una fatal combinación para el sistema capitalista". *Desinformémonos. Periodismo de abajo*, November. http://desinformemonos.org/2011/11/jovenes-e-historia-una-fatal-combinacion-para-el-sistema-capitalista/ [accessed November 4, 2011].

Nederveen Pieterse, Jan. 1998. "My Paradigm or Yours? Alternative Development, Post-Development, Reflexive Development". *Development and Change* 29 (2): 343–73.

Nederveen Pieterse, Jan. 2000. "After Post-Development". *Third World Quarterly* 21 (2): 175–91.

Ortega, David. 2013. "Reforma Energética traerá graves consecuencias sociales y ecológicas, 'pero no hay de otra', dice diputado federal poblano". *Periódico Central*, December 13. www.periodicocentral.mx/2014/nacional-seccion/reforma-energetica-traera-graves-consecuencias-sociales-y-ecologicas-pero-no-hay-de-otra-dice-diputado-federal-poblano [accessed July 5, 2014].

Paredes, Vicente. 2012. "Historia y comunidad indígena de Mezcala de la Asunción, Jalisco, invadida y humillada por autoridades de los tres niveles de gobierno". In *Mezcala: la memoria y el futuro. La defensa de la isla en el Bicentenario*, edited by Santiago Bastos, 89–92. Guadalajara, Mexico: Centro de Investigaciones y Estudios Superiores en Antropología Social.

Pi-Sunyer, Oriol. 2002. "Space, Power, and Representation in Yucatán". In *The Spaces of Neoliberalism: Land, Place and Family in Latin America*, edited by Jacquelyn Chase, 213–35. Bloomfield, CT: Kumarian Press.

Richard, Nelly. 2000. "The Reconfigurations of Post-dictatorship Critical Thought". *Journal of Latin American Cultural Studies: Travesia* 9 (3): 273–82.

Rose, Gillian. 1995. "Place and Identity: A Sense of Place". In *A Place in the World?: Places, Cultures, and Globalization*, edited by Doreen Massey and Pat Jess, 87–132. Oxford: Oxford University Press.

Salazar, Juan Francisco. 2002. "Activismo indígena en América Latina: estrategias para una construcción cultural de las tecnologías de información y comunicación". *Journal of Iberian and Latin American Studies* 8 (2): 62–79.

Sandoval, Rafael. 2009. "La lucha por la defensa del patrimonio cultural implica hoy la lucha contra el despojo, la explotación y la opresión capitalista". Foro de Defensa del Patrimonio Cultural de los Trabajadores del INAH, Mexico City.

Santiago Santiago, Jorge. 2009. "Construcción de alternativas en las prácticas pequeñas: economía solidaria". In *Otras geografías. Experiencias de autonomías indígenas en México*, edited by Giovanna Gasparello and Jaime Quintana Guerrero, 213–28. Mexico City: Redez tejiendo la utopía.

Sbert, José María. 1992. "Progress". In *The Development Dictionary. A Guide to Knowledge as Power*, edited by Wolfgang Sachs, 192–205. London: Zed Books Ltd.

Schabus, Nicole. 2005. "Autonomía indígena: status quo o desafío". In *Autonomías indígenas en América Latina: nuevas formas de convivencia política*, edited by Leo Gabriel and Gilberto López y Rivas, 493–540. Mexico City: Plaza y Valdés.

Solís, Ricardo. 2011. "Buscan incentivar el turismo en Mezcala con su nuevo malecón". *La Jornada Jalisco*, August 7. www1.lajornadaguerrero.com.mx/2011/08/07/index.php?section=cultura&article=010n1cul [accessed March 20, 2014].

Streibel, Michael J. 1998. "The Importance of Physical Place and Lived Topographies". National Convention of the Association for Educational Communications and Technology (AECT), St. Louis, MO, February 18–22.

Sunil, T. S., Viviana Rojas, and Don E. Bradley. 2007. "United States' International Retirement Migration: The Reasons for Retiring to the Environs of Lake Chapala, Mexico". *Ageing & Society* 27 (4): 489–510.

Talavera Salgado, Francisco. 1982. *Lago de Chapala. Turismo residencial y campesinado*. Mexico City: Instituto Nacional de Antropología e Historia.

Torres, Raúl. 2008. "Idea recibirá un mdp para un proyecto que nos excluye: indígenas de Mezcala". *La Jornada Jalisco*, January 9. www1.lajornadaguerrero.com.mx/2008/01/09/index.php?section=sociedad&article=007n1soc [accessed May 10, 2013].

Torres, Raúl. 2010. "Habitantes de Mezcala sacan adelante su pueblo sin "limosnas" del gobierno". *La Jornada Jalisco*, November 17. www1.lajornadaguerrero.com.mx/2010/11/17/index.php?section=cultura&article=012n1cul [accessed November 18, 2010].

Torres, Rebecca Maria, and Janet D. Momsen. 2005. "Gringolandia: The Construction of a New Tourist Space in Mexico". *Annals of the Association of American Geographers* 95 (2): 314–35.

Zibechi, Raúl. 2006. *Dispersar el poder. Los movimientos como poderes antiestatales*. Guadalajara, Mexico: Taller Editorial La Casa del Mago; Cuadernos de la Resistencia.

5 Identities Across Borders
Legitimising or Challenging Stratifications?

On June 23, 2009, Dr Santiago Bastos invited me to attend a meeting with Gabriel Martínez, Head of the Department of the *Comisión Nacional para el Desarrollo de los Pueblos Indígenas (CDI)* (National Commission for the Development of Indigenous Peoples) in Jalisco. One of the subjects we discussed was in regard of the non-recognition of some indigenous groups in the context of the enactment of the *Ley sobre los Derechos y el Desarrollo de los Pueblos y las Comunidades Indígenas del Estado de Jalisco* (2006). He expressed the view that self-identification was problematic and made it difficult to census, so the 'requirement' for the CDI was to speak an indigenous language. So, when we discussed the issue Mezcala faces with the Island, he said that they were not able to help them since there is no recognition of Mezcalenses as indigenous. While authorities were denying and disregarding them, however, the community was elaborating different actions and claims to confront this situation. For instance, in 2008 they wrote a letter to the United Nations Commissioners for Human Rights on the Rights of Indigenous People where they declared:

> We want to inform you that in our community, the Mexican state does not recognise the Coca people, they say that the Cocas are over and that we are just a people, that is, we are not indigenous because, as we do not have either the language or the clothing, we cannot be indigenous anymore. Our people, our elders laugh at the words of the government, because we do not need its approval to tell our children, to the population in general, that our people come from a long time ago and that what we have, our territory, our islands, our forest, our traditional authorities, our dances, celebrations [and] customs are the inheritance of our ancestors. However, with these arguments is that they begin to get into our lives; first because it hinders them that we are indigenous, and then that our land is communal.

Comuneros and young supporters, in fact, organised multiple events to broadcast the actions the government and elites were carrying out against them and their territory. For example, they profited of the celebration of the Day of the Territory, that is, the day when water and land was recognised as their own by the Spaniards through the enactment of the *Título Virreinal*, to make clear statements against the

Identities Across Borders 167

government and transmit to younger generations the knowledge and importance of territory. I remember on February 5, 2009 hearing the voice of different *comuneros* in the Island, claiming the recognition of their territory, traditional authorities, rights and the legitimacy of the *Título Virreinal*, and calling for the union of the community, for the force of the youth and not to give up their fight. Thus, it was no surprise when Itza, a young supporter I interviewed, declared:

> [Even if] they tell us that we don't exist, that we aren't as we say we're, I believe that it's something we carry in the blood. No, there's no reason to be able to say 'I'm going to give you recognition here, what you're or what you aren't'. If they say 'well, you aren't an indigenous community', ultimately, for them we aren't. But I say, there are many, many things that are proven, which are completely the opposite.

Mezcalenses are fighting in a game they did not choose, their struggle being not only for material needs but also entailing cultural and identity claims; that is, *identity politics*. Actually, from the time of the Spaniards' arrival to the era of neoliberal governance, Mezcala has been experiencing several processes that have amplified the scale of the modifications and alterations to the ways of being of its dispersed population. Economic, political and cultural processes have impacted on the delineation of their identity. In effect, ethnic/racial identities have been moulded by processes of global capitalism, hegemonic discourses, state practices, but also within local realities, showing their multiple manipulations and the global–local connections.

In this regard, cultural identity should not be considered something exclusively derived from the past but also from the future; it is 'always in process' through our 'memory, fantasy, narrative and myth' and entails 'the different ways we are positioned and position ourselves' (Hall 1990, 222–6). Therefore, we must consider that Mezcalenses have multiple identities and might live and interpret them differently, and also assume and use them depending on interactions, relationships and context; identities constantly interplay across space and among different communities. That said, identities cannot be reduced to social location or positioning, as the state situates us in multiple ways to favour its own agenda, applying identifications that categorise and classify us, often criminalising sectors based on race, ethnicity and economic standing (Sánchez 2006). So, in order to have a better understanding of identities, it does not suffice to identify discourses and positions; one needs to analyse relations of power and assess under what circumstances the discourses were produced and received (Widdicombe 1998), and thus, identities formed. Furthermore, one must examine how subjects imagine, construct and create their communities.

Accordingly, the purpose of this chapter is to explore the notions of indigeneity in the contemporary period and understand the different forms of identity construction by establishing Mezcalenses' political, economic, social and cultural relations to the present. Therefore, first, I take up the discussions about the configuration of the national ideology and identity, to reprise its impact on lived

168   *Identities Across Borders*

experiences, showing how people construct identities and internalise identifications that might legitimate social structures. Second, I analyse how migration is not only related to the transnational organisation, exchanges, connections and transformations of time and place but also to how multiple identities and relations are reshaped and constructed through the transnationalisation of discourses and structures of ethnic/racial classification. In the third part, I examine how identity is a resource for Mezcalenses; thus, I focus on how indigenousness is revived and dignified in a sort of ethnogenesis to urge their struggle for territory, their sense of community and even their autonomy. Finally, I scrutinise the paradoxes of ethnogenesis, signalling, on the one hand, how elites have aimed to appropriate it and be the ones to determine the 'authenticity' of Mezcalenses; and on other hand, how the dignification of indigenousness can transnationally expand the networks of solidarity, form a movement of opposition and be a survival strategy. The objective, thus, is to perceive how identities are lived and used, created and recreated, represented, negotiated and contested, affirmed and denied, imposed and resisted, influencing the perceptions and definitions of ourselves and our interactions with others, but, above all, the construction of society.

Enclosing the Power to Name: The Internalisation of Hegemonic Discourses Perpetuating the Status Quo

As argued in the Introduction, Mezcalenses have experienced indigeneity through the fraught interfaces of *mestizaje, indigenismo* and *neoindigenismo* in state practices and discourses. In this regard, we should consider that ethnicity is part of the projects of the nation-state formation that create 'hierarchized forms of imagining peoplehood'; thus, the construction of internal others helped maintain the self-identity of the modern Mexican nation-state (Alonso 1994, 390–1). In this vein, Pansters argues that 'the state has always invested much in its political, administrative and economic strength, but also in its imaginary and ideological powers' (2005, 360). These kinds of rhetorical legacies, thereby, only pull apart words from realities, maintaining and stressing asymmetries and disclosing the complexity of a network of power. In Mezcala, in this sense, indigeneity has been constructed entailing the internalisation of hegemonic discourses, and thus, the propagation of self-discrimination and racism, as analysed below. What is more, 'indigenousness' is reconstructed by 'mestizo-ness' (Wade 2005), from its articulation to non-indigenous forms, practices or subjects (De la Cadena and Starn 2009). Therefore, identities emerge in interaction (Barth 1969; De Fina 2003), and in connection to lived experiences. In this way, they are structured in a game of power, at the same time that social reality is defined.

In this regard, John Comaroff and Jean Comaroff (1992) note that the identity assigned to a group from the outside differs from how it is assumed from the inside. This means that identities are not merely imposed, bargained over or assumed, rather that identities are always constructed in relation to another or others, either endorsing, negotiating or denying their assertions. More precisely,

Identities Across Borders 169

identities are mediated by power; they are sites from whence we negotiate our standpoints and conditions, although not under equal circumstances. Here the distinction proposed by Rosaura Sánchez between positioning and positionality becomes valuable, identifying: the first as one's location, which, for her, is 'structurally determined', 'discursively mediated' and 'relational' while the latter is ideological, referring to reflexivity, our 'imagined relation or standpoint relative to that positioning' (2006, 38). Accordingly, as a consequence of their ethnic identity many Mezcalenses complain of being historically placed in a subordinated position, always serving, mistreated and not respected. Respondents comment they are often called *chantes, indios*, but also, *nacos* or *huarachudos* and this is usually accompanied by adjectives such as *menos, tontos, sucios, patarrajada* e *ignorantes*, and discrimination and mistreatment based on their physical appearance, features and origin. In this sense, until the present day, the government has tried to classify them by delineating their ethnic identity, and imprinting it with a negative perception. For instance, when I asked Carlos, a young fighter, if he knew he was indigenous since being little, he explained to me:

> We used to go to Poncitlán or you went to Poncitlán [and you heard] 'the *chantes*, the *indios*, the this and that, are coming', so, this influences a lot. So, that's why many didn't consider themselves indigenous or didn't tell you they were indigenous. However, in you, you know that you are, right? And many for that matter refuse to say that they are indigenous. Because the indigenous is always a symbol of the lowest, the dumber, the most all of this, right?

In this regard, interests have determined 'where' Mezcalenses should be located, and thus, many Mezcalenses have become ashamed of their origin and have felt 'behind the times' and 'underdeveloped'. What is more, up to the present day, the *mestizo* rhetoric prevails giving hope to indigenous people to overcome their position, revealing the difficulties to undo, borrowing the expression of Alonso, 'its "accents" of conquest and inequality' (2004, 460). So, some of them have been denying the indigenous identification and dream about their 'whitening' or '*mestizaje*', as noted before. In this sense, the distinction between identity and identification is also valuable; Sánchez (2006) argues that identity entails a 'self-reflexive critique', it is 'agential' and 'cannot be reduced to social location or positioning', whereas identification is 'a relational and discursive process' that not only entails designation but also negation based on relations of power. Thus, as identifications are lived realities, indigeneity for Mezcalenses has appeared in their personal histories and relationships and daily experiences, being kind of a 'brand' that shaped their collective identity. In this vein, as noted by Bastos (2011b, 98), the term *indio* gave them, on the one hand, the consciousness of a relationship based on subordination and exclusion, but on the other hand, a motive for pride.

Even so, indigenous identity has not been the sole one present in Mezcala (e.g. *campesinos*), but others did not erase their subordinated position as indigenous people; for instance, Don Salvador recalls the words of a Municipal

170 *Identities Across Borders*

President when his son made a request for funding '[he] said "how annoying! I already told you that for those *indios huarachudos* there is not even water and you're still fucking with me"'. The national group uses markers of difference to legitimise their ruling vis-à-vis the hegemonic system and has persuaded them to follow its rules. As noted before, neoliberal multiculturalism has limited cultural rights and recognition, while it grants limited space to raise their demands and achieve collective empowerment (Hale 2002). The government is creating the image of an 'indio hyper-real', as defined by Guillaume Boccara and Paola Bolados (2010), a model subject that does not make up the real and lived experiences of indigenous people and obscures their struggles and claims. The elite does not respect them as collectivities; instead it favours individual rights while it continues to have the power to name, regulate and structure the population to maintain hierarchies, inequalities and perceptions.

In this vein, the new legal framework clearly does not recognise cultural diversity, let alone give it voice; in reality, differentiated identities must at least be negotiated, thereby being a mechanism of neoliberal governance. As argued by Rosaldo (2006), it is not only a matter of choosing our belonging to a group, but of whether or not this is accepted. In this regard, even if, as noted before, *comuneros* and young supporters might not care whether in the eyes of the Mexican state they are considered indigenous, they showed a degree of concern. For instance, in 2013, thanks to their solidarity network they organised a meeting in *Paraje Insurgente* with some *diputados*, which expressed their willingness to transform the Jalisco State Constitution in order to end the disavowal of Mezcala. Up to now, no reform has been approved and the position of Mezcalenses has radicalised further. Meanwhile, indigenous people are still considered subjects in need of assistance, which fosters co-optation and dependency and exercises formal and informal modes of prejudice and discrimination.

Moreover, ideologies, consciously or unconsciously, provide the 'mental frames' to validate, sustain and develop that everyday and institutional oppression (Pérez Huber and Solorzano 2015, 303). In this vein, Gall (2002) observes that *indigenismo* (and *mestizaje*) left an ideological legacy in our Federal institutions to maintain national unity but via recourse to racism, which might also mould people's lives and minds. Given a scenario of neoliberal governance, the position and actions of the elite are being justified through *neoindigenismo*, ensuring that Mezcalenses are kept in the margins, at the same time that racism and hierarchies are reproduced and a larger system of domination perpetuated. More precisely, the position of the *Municipio* is informed by the social and racial structure constructed since colonial times while the inherited political culture serves to emphasise and misuse these categorisations.

In this context, borrowing the concept of 'microaggressions' from Critical Race Theory, I see how everyday acts of racism that inform our institutions and lives are arising from racial assumptions and master narratives (Delgado *et al.* 2012). Actually, whereas racism based on somatic indexes has not completely disappeared in the region, in tandem with the ideas of Knight (1990), it has also been sustained by other factors, such as the assertion of indigenous as backward.

Therefore, over the years the opposition of 'indigenous' versus 'modernisation', 'urbanisation', 'literacy', 'development' and 'progress' has persisted, and ethnic and class stratifications have become accentuated. Through these ideas, upheld by neoliberal governance, elites control populations, exercise diverse forms of racism and discrimination, limit voices and prevent direct representativeness while they continue co-option and manipulation. Rocío, the history student and young fighter, explains this in regard to *delegados*:

> The assholes arrive there, and the first thing they tell them, and you can ask this to some of those who have been *delegados* ... 'stop being an indian, you bastard, you have to modernise yourself, you have to do what the *Municipio* does'.

As a consequence, the mentalities of oppressed groups are also being delineated and in fact, as previously observed, usually *delegados* serve the *Municipio* and disregard the needs and issues of the community accentuating the fragmentation between 'progressives' and 'traditionalists'. Here, in tandem with the observations of Martínez Novo, 'tradition is associated with racial discrimination of colonial origin and modernity with greater democratization' (2006, 53), and also with 'development'. Thus, in a context of an ingrained inherited political culture, a past Municipal President, when narrating how due to the opposition of *comuneros* programmes do not arrive, affirmed in an interview with Bastos (2009): 'There are times when they are so traditional that they slow down the development of the community'. As a matter of fact, in Mezcala two 'official' identifications interplay; on the one hand, Mezcalenses are portrayed as despicable, submissive and gullible, preventing the improvement of their condition, and on the other hand as rebels and aggressive, living in open confrontation. Although the latter, as noted before, has been resignified as a motive of pride, both characterisations show how colonial images persist, though they have changed over time, portraying them in opposition to the values of 'modernity' and 'development'.

Therefore, racism, as a daily practice and ideology, not only is ingrained in elites, *caciques* or public servants, but it has also reached such a degree that it has even been absorbed by the same indigenous communities that are condemned by it (Knight 1990). In this regard, Mezcalenses are driven to embrace hegemonic discourses and practices, especially to disdain their 'traditional' authority in seeking their path to progress. José Luis, a young fighter, elucidates:

> People that way, I tell you, see it at their own convenience, [they] say 'well, their ideas and all that are already obsolete; they're already behind'. Yes, but beforehand they don't give up to them [comuneros] because they know that when comuneros give up the type of use of land, then the indigenous community is over.

Even though Mezcalenses do not completely disdain their authority, they might reproduce practices, structures and hierarchies in their private life. In effect, the

172   *Identities Across Borders*

machineries of neoliberal governance have been obscuring their vision, and affecting their *usos y costumbres* and paving the way with obstacles to their practices and construction of an alternative way of life. In view of that, Mezcala shows an adaptation and adoption of new practices around the national project according to the rhetoric of multiculturality and 'development' endorsed by the capitalist system, which is internalised by the same members of the community. These discourses continue to categorise people within different structures, making the intersectionality of social divisions clear, such as gender, class, race and ethnicity, which are crossed by different proportions of 'economic disadvantage' and 'status subordination' of their experience, and where individuals are traversed by multiple categories (Fraser 2003). In this manner, the position subjects occupy within society is marked by this functioning, inciting the interplay of a multiplicity of identities, as discussed and exposed with the ensuing case of transnational migrants.

The Transnational Community: An Interplay Of Multiple Identities

Ethnoracial Stratifications Crossing Borders

As narrated in Chapter 2, since the early twentieth century many Mezcalenses have left the village looking for better opportunities, and when doing that took with them selected memories connecting and detaching from their home community. In this regard, their place of origin is continually recalled as a treasured place, their territory as a fertile and holy land. For example, Don Roberto, a migrant in LA, describes the hills:

> Gosh, they're beautiful! ... One descends to the Comal, it's the region that it's named the Comal because it's full of pines. And in every season there is grass, grass that looks as a machine has cut it, but it's because in the day those who have cattle are eating and are swallowing the grass, and that's why it looks pretty nice. In rainy seasons there are streams that one looks at like a paradise, I used to like it a lot. We used to go and play during the Children's day, they took all the primary school, and we had a good time there on the tour playing football, or anything we could, on the banks of a stream, on the trees that are moved by the wind, it sounded like it whistled, like someone was talking to us, so so beautiful up there.... And up there, you go around by car because it's flat and even, there are no cliffs, there are no boulders, so there is a place near there, the Comal, which takes you back to the dinosaur years.

Territory entails both a delineated physical space and an appellant (utopian) imaginary that is used to reaffirm ties, identity and distinctiveness. In Mezcala it is interwoven with the past, possessing both identity and political value that surpasses borders. In this sense, as Comaroff and Comaroff argue,

Figure 5.1 Mezcala: a treasured place.

even where some, most or even all of a people do not actually live on it, it has the capacity to serve as a politico-legal alibi, as a sheet-anchor for ethno-capital, and as a space from which to speak, to assert subjectivity, to claim exception.

(2009, 81)

So migrants evoke a common past and kinship links, coming together in order to feel less stressed and abandoned, aiming to reproduce their life back in the community while finding survival strategies. Upon arrival in the United States, they organised and settled in *comunidades satélite*, which mainly gather families or members of *barrios* together, also mapped out in Chapter 2. However, they were shocked by the new lifestyle, as Doña Ino narrates:

It was very, very difficult to arrive in a country where we did not even speak the language.... And as we arrived the bread that they ate here was not even like the one we used to eat, they ate wheat bread with, it looked like sesame seeds, something like that, and oh no! Everything they ate was very difficult, but little by little we became accustomed.

Therefore, as they recreated the community of origin, they tried, if possible and desired, to eat similar food, speak Spanish, organise celebrations and social

174 *Identities Across Borders*

events, work in the fields, marry other Mezcalenses, transmit values and practices and visit the village.[1] Yet their daily routine was substantially modified and they missed their families, their homes, the land, the language, the food, the traditions, their lives back in the community, or, as Don Luis shared: 'Tears came to my eyes, because I said, "I'm far from my village"'. Moreover, while their network helped them to soothe their establishment, they found it hard to adapt to this unknown place and support their families left behind. And as not all were able to return, some established transnational families while others founded their family nuclei. But, even if this meant better opportunities and living conditions, it also signified in some cases that new generations grew up disconnected from the community.

As argued in Chapter 3, migrants have adapted their lives, trying to overcome cultural differences and avoid feeling isolated and outsiders to U.S. society. They have done so without losing their territorial reference, relationships, and contact (for example, through telephone calls, social media, emails and videos). In this sense I remember Francisco, a migrant who has not been able to return since 1991, who nostalgically asserted, 'Maybe in a couple of years, we'll be able to finally visit our village. Right now we only see it in video'. These videos are taped and sent by his family who still lives in the community, proving that, in line with the observations of Canales and Zlolniski (2001), a complex flow of people, goods, money, labour, symbols and information is allowing the settlement of transnational communities. Mezcalenses in this way organise their economic, social and cultural lives across frontiers. They demonstrate —following the observations of De la Cadena and Starn (2009)—how they neither occupy a single and defined territory, nor is their identity exclusively local. Beyond the political organisation of migrants, thus, Mezcala established itself as a 'transnational community'. The transnational quality of these communities implies that origin and residence countries are linked through relationships based on kinship and *paisanaje*, creating another temporality and spatiality by integrating new places and processes (exchanges, organisation and communications) into their communal life (Velasco Ortiz 2002).

Hence, migrants—though not all—brought over time their sense of community with them, providing a feeling of belonging to those geographically away. In this regard, following the ideas of Stephen (2007), subjects are connected simultaneously to multiple locations and communities extended, and hence construct their identities accordingly; Mezcala has multiple homes that are 'discontinuous' but connected through different material, social and symbolic resources articulating their indigenous identity. Mezcalenses have organised themselves within and across borders, incorporating discourses and redefining the conception of territory, membership, community, identity and politics. They have multiple identities that are constructed, lived, internalised and performed differently. What is more, globalisation is fostering homogeneity and differentiation at the same time (Morán Quiróz 1997; Speed 2002). We are living 'glocal' lives, being incorporated into larger or global economic, cultural and political systems (Eriksen 2001) and thus, our local identities are being reconstructed and redefined appropriating non-traditional elements and discourses (Hernández Castillo and Nigh 1998).

Identities Across Borders   175

What is crucial in these 'global–local' connections is how they perpetuate ethnoracial stratifications. As temporality and spatiality are extended, migrants perceive their condition at the bottom of a social structure within the new context as a continuation of the position lived in the community. In line with the ideas of Fox and Rivera-Salgado (2004, 11–12), the economic, social and political exclusion they face, although it is embodied differently in the U.S. than in Mexico, entails the same processes related to lower positions, racist practices and absence of rights. In effect, people when arriving in the United States were assessed, positioned and stereotyped within the structure and hierarchies of the 'American' society (Ong 1996). In both societies Mezcalenses have been placed as internal others to sustain the national culture, but also a global system and structure. However, depending on how they cope with the dominant society, they mould their status of subcitizens—although exceptions might exist. In effect, Mezcalenses' racialisation began in Mexico, retaining with them a memory of exclusion and degradation, of lack of opportunities and discrimination, although with a possibility to change it. Chuy, the young returnee, links his experiences across borders:

> They use a lot that word, *wetback*, which means *mojado*, so it didn't bother me at all, at all, at all, because I knew that was what I was; that's what I'm. So here when they call me indian it doesn't sadden me at all, at all, at all. But what makes me sad is the way they say it, like '*pinches indios*' [bloody indians] because they don't consider us as anything else!

Even though the representation of indigenous people as subordinated subjects prevails across frontiers establishing their 'material' and 'symbolic' circumstances (Velasco Ortiz 2002, 255), in this case, migrants have not expressed being discriminated against for their indigenous identity in the U.S; the lack of evident features (e.g. language and dress) might have contributed. In effect, Mezcalenses are ignored as indigenous in their multiple settings; racism, though with variation, is reproduced by negating them their indigeneity in the United States and being appraised, reduced to and treated as Mexicans, as *mestizos*. Moreover, as traits or social and cultural practices are evidenced, they might be racialised and subject to discrimination. Don Roberto shares an experience:

> We went together, all the family, and right from Mezcala, and we were going to the beach ... Venice Beach, and the Americans were there sunbathing with their shades and the girls with their bikinis and all that; and we went in *fila india* [single line], we [had] our watermelon here, our lunch bags. When they saw that we parked taking over a space, we felt bad because they all left, like implying that we don't fit in there.

Recognised or not as indigenous, Mezcalenses absorb a degraded position while experiencing difficulties competing in societies that enhance 'modern' principles.

176 *Identities Across Borders*

Migrants were promised better conditions, but not all knew the path to reach them and found that relations of power and rigid categorisations remain. They were embedded in racist views, especially in regard to political exclusion, economic marginalisation and social discrimination. Thus, migrants subordinated by their class and ethnic position suffer multiple discriminations, not only in the sense that such forms of discrimination are exerted in different spaces but also in that they suffer from being inscribed in several categories.

Indeed, at the beginning of the twentieth century both Mexico and the United States, as studied by Alexandra Minna Stern (2009), used eugenics, though in different forms, to racially categorise their population. They designed policies for demographic management and outlined the national identity in a way that sustains the country position vis-à-vis the international order and structures of white supremacy. In this case, Mexicans in the U.S. at that time were already seen as a labour force and many were subject to a lack of rights due to their portrayal as 'Indian' (Stephen 2007). Therefore, 'Mexican' was classified as a race category, labelling this population as 'non-white' and 'foreign' while promoting immigration policies, border control and supporting negative stereotypes, towards them; and, this left a 'lasting imprint' (Stern 2009). In addition, the reception of migrants has deeply depended on international relations showing how unequal power relations between Mexico and the United States impact upon the life of migrants and the ways they can be accommodated legally and collectively (Dalum Berg and Rodriguez 2013).

In this context, as unveiled in Chapter 2, after 9/11 national security policies affected migrants in the U.S., but more importantly they structured mentalities on how migrants were perceived, criminalising them and creating a social class without legal protection. Border militarisation also impacted upon the construction of identities (Hea Kil and Menjívar 2006) and revealed the production of state dominion based on exclusion tactics, where citizenship facilitates the 'conceptualisations' of 'us' and 'them', in their entitlements and belonging, according to legal but also racial stipulations (Gálvez 2013, 725). Besides, in an era of neoliberal governance, migrants experience not only the violences of the border, but also, a new scenario of exclusion and unfavourable conditions, from unwanted jobs to low wages and lack of benefits, opportunities and services. This has resulted in their being constantly reminded about their 'difference' (Stephen 2008) and not having much contact with 'Americans', since, Doña Ino, a migrant, senses:

> [Americans] prefer not to live among Latinos, to move farther and that's it. They prefer to go to schools where there aren't many Latinos, right? But I think that's normal, because everyone wants the best for their children.

Although this might not be the only reason for such division, they are aware that 'Americans' and 'Mexicans' do not mix, perpetuating racism, self-discrimination and their location at the bottom of the ladder. In this context, even if usually migrants express that their lives have improved in the United States with respect to economic conditions and opportunities, they still are victims of racism and

Identities Across Borders   177

live a daily life of discrimination and confrontation embodied in the poor conditions experienced by them and set in relief to those of 'Americans'. The 'land of freedom' is not experienced by all migrants, so while some are subjects of rights and obtain (though scarce) benefits and protections from the receiving country, others continue to fear for their lives, and, as such, they take their precautions to avoid making an inappropriate move, even gaining a traffic ticket, as they could be deported. Francisco, a migrant living in south-east LA, shared with me when I asked him how he gets along with 'Americans': 'we don't mess with them. Here we live only with *morenos*, we don't mess with them: they talk to us, we talk; they greet us, we greet them. We don't relate so to not have conflicts or problems'. In fact, when arriving in the United States the promise of legalisation prompts them to behave as 'good illegals' as a form of regularising them, but also allowing migrants to further claim their belonging (Chauvin and Garcés-Mascareñas 2012, 247–9). Migrants feel constantly observed trying hard to go unnoticed, and thus, prefer to live indoor lives and reduce their relationships and recreational spaces to those provided by other Mezcalenses.

Migrants: To Remain Mezcalense in a 'New Modern' Setting

The promotion of 'ideal' migrant citizens in both countries leads them to find a place within their receiving country that might be closer to the 'white' standards. As presented in Chapter 3, migrants view the 'American life' as having greater validity, working hard to adapt, and hence, to 'whiten' and facilitate racial and cultural acceptance and their mobility. In this regard, Hill and Torres (2010) argue that at the beginning of the twentieth century education served to assimilate immigrants into the U.S. culture, but that up to the present day, it privileges Euro American culture, subsuming Latino cultures. In fact, in certain moments English has proved to be related to better jobs and salaries, and even to neutralising the effects of being 'illegal' (Phillips and Massey 1999, 243). Accordingly, in line with the observations of Richard Alba (2006), the dominance of English and other cultural characteristics not only shows where the opportunities in the mainstream society lie, but also the willingness of migrants to be incorporated into U.S. society. Therefore, migrants seek their integration through the respect shown towards their rules, the use of the language, practices, values, and via education and political participation. Don Roberto comments in relation to this:

> I don't feel at a disadvantage, because maybe yes, before yes, because of the fact that I didn't speak English or couldn't understand it, but I think that we are fighting for that daily, competing. Not competing but trying to have that education for the sake of adapting to the American life. So, what I mean by adapting to the American life and following its rules, I make reference to this because once we experienced awful discrimination.

Regardless of the widespread and increased use of Spanish, English is privileged over Spanish, since migrants feel that, upon acquiring English the effects of

178 *Identities Across Borders*

racism decrease while a door to a better life is opened. Many Mezcalenses, hence, following the renewed rationale embodied by neoliberal governance, see in transnational migration the possibility to adhere to a more 'advanced' culture, sensing the possibility to progress and secure better opportunities for their families and, as a consequence, the chance to climb in the social structure while transforming themselves into 'modern' subjects.

However, even if some might negate in certain contexts their Mexicanness or Mezcala-ness, this does not mean that their assimilation has erased their 'ethnicisation'; rather it has resulted in the phenomenon of *pochismo*. That is, to show their 'additive cultural hybridization', the feeling that they are taking the best of both worlds (Fitzgerald 2009, 138). In this context, within the community, migrants' language, clothes and manners become social remittances that are adopted by many inhabitants who are amazed and attracted by the transformations. This fact also generates a perception with regard to migrants based on distrust, revealing a fear towards the outside and towards mixture, many being concerned with the social and cultural transformations that might damage local practices and values.[2] Notwithstanding, in general, migration, in the words of Pedro:

> is now more common, … [so] I see them [migrants] twith pleasure, more at parties, with pleasure like when you see a friend, or you see a family member or relative, then yes … they see them in that sense, with pleasure, 'welcome to your village'.

As noted before, the priest has also played an important role in shaping Mezcalenses' perceptions, and thus, in the community, the celebration of the *Hijos Ausentes* is, in fact, the prevailing representation.[3] As Carlos, a young fighter, describes:

> People don't see them like that, as something bad.… On the contrary, many of them [say] 'they're concerned, even though many of them haven't even been here for years', and we talk about twenty years there that they haven't come. And yet they're sending money from over there so that Mezcala can develop things in its community.

Inhabitants in general are proud of the achievements, efforts, sacrifices and support of migrants allowing them to be enmeshed in the community as active translocal members. They have been gaining the respect and admiration, receiving praise for their economic help, and even for the status and values obtained. However, in a similar vein to the observations of Fitzgerald (2009, 3), migrants are seen through a paradoxical lens, as 'heroes' providing economic support and enhancing material conditions, being 'agents of modernisation' shown in their cars, houses and luxuries, but also, as 'traitors' for leaving behind their land and people. In this sense, Carlos also shares an excerpt of a conversation with an uncle who lives in the U.S: 'It has always been the claim towards my uncles "and why do you live there? Why did not you stay here?"'. Although some migrants break their relationship with the community, many are aiming to demonstrate that they think of their families and the community and are trying to make real their presence, and thus have resumed their commitment with the village independently or through Club Mezcala.

By feeling part of this imagined community, Mezcalenses in their multiple locations share a sense of community. So, multiple locations and experiences together with economic and social dynamics have provoked the adaptation, recreation, reproduction, reinforcement and/or revalorisation of their own ethnic identity and *usos y costumbres*. The community is recreated as a cross-border interaction experiencing a simultaneous process of deterritorialisation and reterritorialisation, and thus being Mezcalense means constantly crossing multiple boundaries. In this context, Mezcalenses have established living spaces, such as those provided by Club Mezcala, that not only reinforce their relationship between themselves and their place of origin, but also demonstrate their shared values. Thus, in spite of the fact that Club Mezcala seems to follow a conventional pattern, the influence of their *usos y costumbres*, their collective action, and connections, values, practices and relationships is quite evident. This can also be seen in different actions, such as migrants' participation in *cargos* (duties)[4] and *fiestas*, the emphasis on communal effort and compassionate collaboration. However, in parallel, frictions and problems (e.g. the division among inhabitants and *barrios*) are being reproduced, as seen in the past chapters. In effect, migrants—in this era of neoliberal governance—are trapped between being a tool of domination and of reproduction of hegemonic rhetoric, and being a strategy of opposition and empowerment, as presented next.

Migrants Between Nationalist Tactics and Transnational Empowerment

As noted before, some migrants have rejected the authority of *comuneros* and considered them ignorant, *atrasados* and enemies of 'progress' due to their customs, education, practices and land management. What is more, they have blamed cultural traits of inhabitants for not improving living conditions and not reaching 'development', not exclusively regarding economic and social matters, but also in the political and cultural spheres. In this vein, responding to the broader rationale of neoliberal governance, they imitate or renovate the structures of power, stratifications and the status quo both within the community and with external subjects. Accordingly, some migrants have assumed themselves to be the agents of 'American' values and lifestyle, acting over the community informed by their experience in the United States, but also by their relationship and dependence on local subjects, such as the Municipal President and the priest; in this sense even power flows between them.

Migrants engage in different actions as they sense that they owe something to the community in Mezcala and want to show that they have not forgotten their origin, values and duties. For some of them remittances, donations and co-

180 *Identities Across Borders*

operations are equated to love and loyalty towards the community. In the words of Don Marcos, a migrant in Tijuana: 'Those of us who donate and all that, we only do it those who really love our village and those who don't really want it, the village, well, they don't help at all'. In this sense, for migrants such work is a kind of 'affective labour' that, as defined by Michael Hardt (1999), produces immaterial gains, such as 'a feeling of ease, well-being, satisfaction, excitement, passion—even a sense of connectedness or community'—and thus, representing a potential for the reproduction of life but also for autonomy and liberation. Therefore, in general, migrants maintain their contact and commitment, keeping in mind, most of the time, to return and aiming to uphold membership, rights and land in the name of their identity, loyalty and investment. So, migrants are looking for a place and to be recognised, like Francisco:

> At least we already contribute our bit. If we're there, we have the honour, or at least they won't tell us 'You didn't cooperate, you don't appear in the list and you're already here in the village'.

Migrants, in fact, represent a diaspora from both communities. Therefore, *comuneros* have been discussing the role migrants should have, and have established many regulations in their *Estatuto Comunal (2009)* to protect their values and practices in order to secure their identity and territory.[5] However, there is a tendency to adapt to new circumstances, keeping migrants connected and even later incorporating some of them through the renovation of the census. In this sense, the strong bond, the economic and social remittances, the information, and cultural practices of migrants transform life, relations and structures in the village, while migrants integrate the political culture and social relationships of the village into their organisation and life in the United States.

Club Mezcala, therefore, exemplifies a case of 'transnational association'—as defined by Canales and Zlolniski (2001)—that seeks the empowerment and defence of the rights of community members on both sides of the border. The Club, against the use given by neoliberal governance, has acted as an institutionalised channel via which political demands in Mexico and the U.S. can be raised. Accordingly, Club Mezcala provides spaces and interactions to reinforce their affection, sense of community and identity towards the community and Mexico, while also promoting political and economic ties. Still, the Mexican government grants membership and extends the sense of community, so migrants keep their gaze towards Mexico. As mentioned earlier, the Mexican state shows its imaginary and ideological power through HTAs and other nationalistic tactics (e.g. dual citizenship), aiming to wash its hands of social and economic responsibility, while assisting its economic and political objectives, and lobbying and controlling national identity. This has been possible through the integration of a sector as the intermediary that has also proven to be a social support and has transmitted the Mexican culture and values to the US-born generation.[6] But the government is promoting a stereotypical and romanticised definition of migrants—framing them as *paisanos*—to maintain its dominion and sustain the economic, political and social order unaltered.

Identities Across Borders 181

Moreover, as U.S. citizenship does not reduce the transnational participation (Portes 2012), 'migrants are encouraged to become American while maintaining their *mexicanidad*' (Fitzgerald 2009, 33). For example, Doña Ino affirms: 'Although I already have the citizenship, I still consider myself Mexican and I have my roots there'. However, as nation-states are bringing their citizens and immigrants into their cultural and political projects in order to contend for hegemony (Kearney 2004, 218), one can observe how both nation-states are willing to extend their power beyond frontiers, implementing strategies that impact on the process of identity formation, moulding their national community and citizens (Fox 2006). In that account, the United States has constructed a homogenous ethnic category, as argued before, making Mexicans suffer from policies and practices that portray them as undesirable subjects and a threat to the 'American values'. The United States is willing to exercise the power to define itinerant populations, constructing its own characterisation and imposing its own identifications to grant partial rights in order to preserve structures and hierarchies today promoted and oftentimes reinforced by neoliberal governance.

So many Mezcalenses have still been unable to change their legal status and the perception of society, or to fulfil the 'American' stereotype, and thus have not succeeded into their incorporation to U.S. society. Migrants, regardless of their legal status and experience, are treated as permanent foreigners or even as degraded subjects, and thus most of them have ended up constructing a differentiated identity, joining Latinos. As evidenced in the following passage shared by Don Roberto: 'more is the attack of one as a Latino as they hear me speak and then I'll notice that they're making fun of me ... I don't feel frustrated, but yes I have noticed the insults'. This pan-ethnic identity as Latinos is traversed by class, ethnic and racial stratifications (Ong 1996) and has been the subject of an anti-immigrant sentiment marked by assumptions of 'social evolution' and 'progress' (Chavez 2013, 208). However, while, in line with the ideas of Weyland (2004, 155), they became part of a 'transnational system of stratification', in parallel, this pan-ethnic identity serves to challenge the state formation, and enhance their position, allowing migrants to profit from their achievements and the power of their network.

Taking up the discussion in Chapter 3 about transnational citizenship, migrants—together with other Latinos—following the ideas of Rosaldo and Flores (1997), have been working on their 'cultural citizenship', that is, to empower themselves, to have the possibility to defy hegemonic discourses about citizenship while claiming and expanding rights that would allow them to be different but still accommodate themselves in relation to the nation-state. Furthermore, Ong takes 'cultural citizenship' to the subjective field to point out that it involves 'a dual process of self-making and being-made within the webs of power linked to the nation-state and civil society' (1996, 738). In this regard, Latinos are engaged in different forms of civic and political participation that might seduce them into becoming another mechanism of neoliberal governance, but which might also challenge this rationale. For instance, some members participate in COFEM or political campaigns, constantly negotiating and pushing for

182   *Identities Across Borders*

projects while doing so in reference to their identity and belonging in both countries.

In this regard, migrants in the diaspora might embrace their Mexicanness more fiercely but this does not mean that they are not critical of the nation-state and questioning of concepts such as citizenship and community. In effect, migrants, in this way, although directly or indirectly supporting the reproduction and reinforcement of the structures of power across borders, are challenging state-defined identities, thus, hierarchies while delineating possibilities for social change. In this case, migrants might identify as Americans, Latinos, Mexicans or just Mezcalenses, fighting and bargaining to obtain memberships and rights, to construct themselves and experience and practice such identities in a variety of ways. Migrants might create and structure their projects, feelings and identities according to different places simultaneously (Ruiz 2002, 95). In this sense, identities steadily fluctuate, as migrants live a complex and ambiguous sense of belonging/belongings with respect to these 'imagined' and 'constructed' communities—in the words of Don Rogelio: 'We belong there, we belong here'. Due to their connection with both places, many migrants have not constructed a sole transnational identity; rather, their identities have become fluid across spaces. Don José identifies: 'When I go to Mezcala, I feel good, happy, pure Mexican. When I get back here, I'm American'. Instead of living in a tension between assimilating or resisting, Mezcalenses embrace, negotiate, define and experience multiple identities according to the context, impacting their membership, rights and position in their multiple locations.

Consequently, as signalled by Fox (2005), the concept of 'cultural citizenship' falls short by not accounting for the cross-border interactions. In effect, any consideration of citizenship, in tandem with the ideas of Stephen (2007), is not only concerned with how migrants claim rights, recognition and public space based on their contribution to the country they live in, but also to their country of origin and community. In brief, citizenship should be based on differences and account for the political participation that people sustain simultaneously and across borders. Moreover, as subjects work out and take part in relations of power, citizenship should be also related to the processes established with each nation-state or hegemonic system that entail those identities. In this vein, transnational citizenship, as presented in Chapter 3, might account for the reproduction of structures and hierarchies in both countries following the historical political economic processes and showing how race is imbricated with other social stigmas, apparent even in our subjectivities. Thus, with different degrees and features Mezcalenses embody, ascribe, interpret and live these identities. In this setting of neoliberal governance, hence, it is not really a matter of citizenship or legality but how they can accommodate themselves in their multiple locations with the stigmas they carry and the mentalities constructed from their multiple identities.

Therefore, we need to go beyond a conceptualisation or juridification of citizenship, and transform our ways of thinking about territory and belonging, and thus, identity. This requires that we consider identities as complex, flexible,

Identities Across Borders 183

contextual, multiple, with vested interests and, thus, always changing. Identities are linked to different groups at the same time, being subjective, creative and motivated, so we need to grasp identities through the connections and dynamics that merge or separate them. What is more, identities are always open, fluid and dynamic, being inseparable from our positioning but also strategic (Sánchez, 2006). Hence, we need to understand identities as constructions in relation to the outside, on how we are treated and identified and with respect to how we want to be treated and integrated into the receiving culture. This means that Mezcalenses are cosmopolitan subjects who amalgamate elements from different places, allowing them to make claims in different positions and move within different local spaces. In the current era, migrants might challenge the jurisdiction over rights, benefits and membership of both countries, and even those of the community, while resisting their categorisations. Within this liminal space we are witnessing a process in which identities coexist, are adapted and recreated, and positionalities enhanced, defying how nations aim to control identities and maintain positionings, while trying to change their realities. This might prove useful for the development of our final argument.

The Dignification of Indigenousness

Indigeneity and the Value of History

Although identities might be delimited by hegemonic processes, elite discourses and relations of power, and might serve to perpetuate ethnic/racial hierarchies, they can also help to disassemble them, as evidenced by the following analysis of ethnogenesis. But, before delving into how identity is strategically used by Mezcalenses, we should recall that Mezcala is a case where indigenous identity was maintained in spite of losing the 'external markers', and adapting to the political setting of the Mexican nation-state. In this regard, in Mezcala ethnic identity is related to the history of possession of and being residents in a territory; in tandem with the observations of Bastos (2011a, 2012) it is something that furnishes them with memory, meaning and cohesion and is not much related to the cultural difference. Thus, in general, indigeneity is assumed by means of external labels and physical appearance, but more importantly, by their territory, origin, history, blood and/or *usos y costumbres.* In this sense, inhabitants consider themselves indigenous, though 'maybe they don't know what kind of people; yet they do know that the people is ancient, it's a community different from those around the Rivera' (Rocío 2012).[7] Vestiges, petroglyphs and cave paintings, and also values, practices, organisation and celebrations—which embody other knowledges, perceptions, relations and timeframes—are just some elements that serve to reinforce this. Nonetheless, there are many meanings being created about what it is to be indigenous nowadays.

To this effect, *comuneros* and other inhabitants construct their identity over their origin and blood, and the history of resistance that accompanies, from the *Título Virreinal* to the *Resolución Presidencial.* Although history has many

184　*Identities Across Borders*

versions and episodes, its veracity and precision is not necessary; rather its importance resides in the sentiment that incites the ingraining and propelling of an identity based on the possession and defence of territory. For instance, Chuy explains: 'one comes ... from an indigenous people, a warrior [one]. Not anyone will say, "no, I'm not from there", knowing that one starts with the blood'. They romanticise the past, making the limits between myth and history unclear while preventing the elites' voice from dominating. In fact, for them, in a similar vein to the observations of Daniel Cooper Alarcón made for the case of Chicanos, 'myth is just a different kind of authority' (1992, 57). Over the years, local history has been orally transmitted or learned by an auto-didactic method since 'this village is very studious, is keen on history' (Don Miguel 2012). In this way, they reinforce their sense of community, exalt the pride of being indigenous, the defence of territory and a long history of attacks and discrimination.

These knowledges are confined in networks and discourses of power, but also are used as a tool for people to defend themselves. For example, every 25th November, on the Anniversary of the struggle of the defence of the Island, they have been organising the *semana de la resistencia*, to create, through a range of events, a common feeling among the community of the importance and safeguarding of their territory, as was stated in a pamphlet distributed a propos of this celebration in 2009:

> The *fiesta* of the insurgents is a date in which the community gathers, remembers, narrates and discusses how, since ancient times, our people has resisted constant attempts to deprive it of its territory, but also of how it has defended itself.

History is complex, but they recuperate, adapt and rewrite it to reinforce and reconstruct their identity and political positions. In this sense, it builds a sentiment strong enough to protect the territory and impress on them their resistant nature. Vicente, a supporter of *comunero's* struggle, comments:

> If the Insurgents fought, in defence, ... against the damage done by the Spaniards in burning the village, wanting to subdue them, taking away their territory, so to speak. If they did that, we're willing too. It's a clear example that we must continue, fighting for what we have because we all know, the majority, that was a, it's a legacy that they left us, it's a territory that they fought for, bought, it can be said. And they have defended it and it's ours, as the *Título Primordial* says, it's from immemorial times and is ours forever.

Land strengthens ethnic identification, either by reference to the historical memory it contains or the emotional attachments; at the same time, this historical memory reactivates and recreates itself. For instance, the Island is perceived as a site where they 'preserve the memory of our [their] people and reaffirm our [their] identity as an autochthonous group' (Comunidad Indígena de Mezcala 2007). So *comuneros* make use of indigeneity to stress their political position of

Identities Across Borders 185

defence of territory and autonomous life, to be recognised as authorities and transcend the fragmentation provoked by the meddling of external subjects. In effect, the word *indio* or *indígena* amalgamates their culture, organisation, territory and history; they are aware of its racist nature, and in spite of the agendas orchestrated by neoliberal governance, it is used strategically to defend their interests and change their position within the system. Identities are linked to the past and origin as well as part of our agenda and ways of envisaging the future. In this sense, they are negotiated and delineated according to the context and subjects involved.

Mezcalenses, in this way, still are conscious of their indigeneity, their attributes and roots: 'Our colour, my colour doesn't lie, right? We are really indigenous and thus 100 per cent' (Don Marcos 2013). Nonetheless, they are also aware of time changes, influences, impositions and connections, as a Don Miguel, the fervent *comunero*, explains: 'It was impossible to keep all these traditions throughout the years, but anyway that doesn't take away our drive and determination to keep being indigenous until death'. However, increasingly, this identity is becoming problematic as they absorb the hegemonic discourses and 'integrate' to the 'national culture', showing its ironies, as observed in the following statement by Alberto:

> Indigenous ... just because the title says it: 'Indigenous Community of Mezcala', but I repeat, the basic, basic element of an indigenous community is its language and custom, its clothing, so there only customs remain, and very few and very few.... Because everything *se mestizó.*

In this context, *mestizaje* proves not to amalgamate different cultures and create equal positions (Lopez 2002) nor tear up hierarchies, unequal power relations, and differences (Wade 2009, 237). As follows, as menaces of land commodification arrived, the *comuneros*' authority faded and the community fragmented; Colectivo Mezcala sought to change this panorama. In line with the observations of Bastos (2012, 2013), when the internal renovation of the *Asamblea de Comuneros* was taking place, they launched a proposal for transforming their identity from 'Mexican indigenous' to one pertaining to the Coca people, giving them historic rights over land in order to legitimate their fight to protect their territory and possess self-government, rights and autonomy, as investigated in the next subsection.

Ethnogenesis and Indigenous Knowledges (IK) Working Together

Mezcalenses, through ethnogenesis, have been able to transmit, reinforce and create knowledges to sustain their struggle. However, not for all does the Coca origin make much sense, as in the case of the *comunero* Don Salvador: 'Well, they say we are indigenous Cocas, that's what I don't understand, why Cocas?' Still, inspired by the analysis of Alonso (2010), this assumption and revitalisation strengthened and redefined their identity, their resistance and struggle, their

186 *Identities Across Borders*

authority, their projects and opposition to the neoliberal model, as well as to the social composition and developmentalist rhetoric displayed by its form of governance. That is why that to find out if identities are 'true' is not central; rather, to see how they are used, their intentions and reasons (Antaki and Widdicombe 1998) and even their achievements are what concern the community. Thus, one of the first steps was to broadcast and reinforce their indigenous identity and sense of community, their values and care for the territory. History workshops were organised that, as presented in Chapter 4, served to link inhabitants and their authority, but also to create social capital that aims to disband the relations of power, while opening spaces and widening solidarity (Durán Matute 2015). The efforts of these young inhabitants did not conclude there and, in 2008, they organised history workshops in *barrios* in order to inform inhabitants of their Coca origin, and study their tools and history to defend themselves.[8]

These workshops were further accompanied by a public consultation, which included, among the questions asked, 'why are we an indigenous community?' In spite of the fact that attendance was low and the public consultation was not conclusive, these actions came to reinforce their struggle, mobilisation, memory and identity, and some even embraced the 'Coca discourse'. So, as Martínez Moreno (2012), asserts, *comuneros* and young supporters transmitted history to create a collective memory where specific events are dignified, rights and duties reinforced and land defended. More precisely, they were carrying out a creative process of ethnogenesis to defend their territory and fulfil their own projects to improve life conditions. On this point, López y Rivas (2010) drew the link between autonomy and identity, the former being a tool used to strengthen or restore the latter, its institutions, knowledges, beliefs, heritage and land through the claiming of rights and the retrieval of territory, culture, authority, social relations, values and lifestyle. In addition, this identity and history granted continuity to their fight, as observed in Chapter 4, with them challenging the system while becoming the agents of their own history. Young fighters and *comuneros*, in this way, believed in the need to approach younger generations, as they perceived them as increasingly detached from the community, largely due to the poor education system. As outlined in Chapter 3, inhabitants experience a marginalised, low-level, discriminatory and exclusionary education system where teachers do not have a grasp on their reality, and disdain their population and its knowledge. Accordingly, they merely teach 'official' history; Carlos expresses:

> It's a pressure that the government voluntarily and involuntarily exercises through institutions, right? They tell you 'you're going to study history' and they bring you here a history program and they force you to study the *Niños Héroes*, right? You learn this history so well that you forget that of your people. So it's like a double-edged sword of the state, so if you forget your history, you don't know anything about Mezcala anymore.... It's a way for them [we] lose our land, it's a way of changing the use of land, to allow privatisation, because you're going to forge the ideas of private property within a community.

Since the 1920s, in line with the already examined national discourse of *mestizaje*, education has sought to instruct indigenous people and stimulate in them a national sentiment (Knight 1990) with the image of *mestizos* as 'the core' and 'the future' of the country (Alonso 2004, 478). What is more, as analysed by Lopez (2002), education has been the tool used by the government to try to transform indigenous people into *mestizos* by providing a positive image of national identity. In this regard, education keeps excluding the vision, needs and proposals of indigenous peoples while it also encompasses the methods to 'modernise' them. In some ways, the government is teaching them 'what it is to be indigenous', separating knowledge from experience, and in consequence, attacking Mezcalenses' identity and culture while pushing for their abandonment to ascend in the social structure. In fact, some Mezcalenses have adopted the 'official' discourse that portrays education for indigenous people, in the words of Eduardo Sojo, director of INEGI, 'as a way out of the exclusion and discrimination to which they have been exposed for years' (Cruz Vargas 2012). In this sense, it is no surprise that Don Roberto argues when talking about education that 'we need to open ourselves, like other peoples, to what the culture of Jalisco and Mexico has been, but I think that it's going to be achieved [through education]'.

In contrast, young fighters are betting on the use of their own knowledges passed on by *comuneros*, seeking to provide another kind of education against the ideological function of mainstream education that incites assimilation, exclusion and discrimination towards different kinds of knowledges. Like this, they challenge the idea of how economic and cultural dependence are related and reject the ideas propelled by neoliberal governance that ironically devaluate them and limit their creative ability to design their own projects. Their aim is to create new meanings, practices and projects and reinforce among the population their identity, *usos y costumbres* and culture, organising, transmitting and reshaping values, history, practices and worldview. Hence, *comuneros* and young supporters, for instance, decided to organise—with academics of the University of Guadalajara and teachers of a primary school—workshops for children of the community in order to reinforce the local identity and recuperate the historic memory. This pedagogy exemplified a kind of cultural praxis, showing how situated knowledges and their transmission in education among indigenous groups achieve certain political ends.

Here, the concept of Indigenous Knowledge (IK) is useful as it brings out how inherited knowledge, especially in reference to 'historical interpretations', gives sense to their lives, to 'who they are', to 'how they perceive the world' while finding solutions to the community problems (Ortiz 2007). This is why the result of the workshops went beyond educational matters, that is, towards the production of a book entitled *Mezcala ¡Se querían llevar la isla!* (Mezcala, they wanted to take away the Island!), written and illustrated by children of the community to narrate the struggle in the Island performed by the *insurgentes*. This action had a political, social and cultural impact, since it was an effort against the working of neoliberal governance in order to prevent the loss of their

Figure 5.2 Children exploring the island.

memory and detachment from the territory of younger generations, while contextualising their current struggle.[9] In tandem with the ideas of Patricio Ortiz (2007, 117), IK is 'a form of meaning construction of the subordinate' and 'becomes a counter-hegemonic narrative' pushing critical thinking, resistance and identity construction. IK are finding new ways to be transmitted, but also find themselves recreated in parallel to Mezcalenses' identity. For instance, Colectivo Mezcala (2008) denounced:

> In this country being indigenous is an evil, because even to date they call us *naco* or *chantes*, that is happening today, they continue to abuse us for our roots, our ways of speaking, our colour, but now, we ask what do you mean by indian? If you want to offend or praise us, well now we are proud of being indigenous.

They are creating emancipatory and vindicating practices while gaining political voice. Furthermore, Mezcalenses are being pushed to rethink who they are, the position they occupy and their relationships with others and in the world, generating new meanings and spreading the pride of their identity, as Pedro, a proud inhabitant, demonstrates:

> There has always been such discrimination, as well. But, now one values things and feels proud, doesn't feel ashamed, on the contrary, [it's] an honour to be from Mezcala ... and to be of indigenous origin.

Little by little the Coca discourse has extended via workshops, internet, pamphlets, dialogues, talks and media, being heard and sometimes adopted (or at least indigenousness). Following the ideas of Holloway (2010), with this effort they are transforming the negative perspective towards them by challenging the origin of the classification and creating an 'anti-identity' based on what they 'do' and not on what they 'are'. More precisely, they are providing an identity that is not merely based on the other but on their history and struggle, in order to have control over their lives, reverse the effects of categorisations and structures of power that further advance through neoliberal governance regimes, and build autonomy. They are advancing in agency; however, by doing so they are moulding their history in a way that not only challenges power, but also can legitimise it.

The Paradoxes of Ethnogenesis

Global Networks and Powers Determining 'Authenticity'

As narrated in the last chapter, *comuneros* and some inhabitants, in the context of the restoration of the archaeological remains in the Island, felt wounded and feared being excluded from *the heart of the community* and its commodification. The government and its partners reconstructed the Spanish prison rather than the fort of the *insurgents*, in parallel rumours spread 'saying that they were going to take away the Island, that we just were not going to be the owners of the Island' (Doña Ino 2013). They sent a message of repression, and trampled on Mezcalenses' authority, history, values, territory and identity while evidencing how internal colonialism persists in moulding minds, behaviours, practices and discourses. By chance, this Island, as Paredes (2010), an inhabitant supporting *comuneros,* narrates, is locally known as the *Isla indómita* where *indígenas indómitos* gave their life to defend it. So, they stood up arguing that they are the legitimate owners, demonstrating, in a way similar to the portrait of the *indio indómito* given by Boccara and Bolados (2010), how they are active defendants of their territory, identity and rights, resisting the hegemonic order and aiming to be recognised as subjects deserving a better life.

In this context, their indigenous identity and struggle showed continuity, but also, as narrated in the past chapter, joined the voice of opposition towards state repression, inadequate wealth distribution, lack of services, corruption and more generally, the neoliberal project. Both class and cultural demands crisscrossed, being guided by their relationships and alliances with Zapatistas, other indigenous communities, social movements and academics. In effect, by embracing indigeneity Mezcalenses were able to unite, speak up and work together with a broader base of support in order to confront the state and change their own realities, enhancing their position and rights. In this vein, Stavenhagen asserts that the right to self-definition has become a matter of 'cultural identity', and often one of 'honour'; moreover, redefined over time, being indigenous nowadays can be a 'political instrument in a disputed social space' (2001, 386). So, while

190 *Identities Across Borders*

becoming part of an 'imagined' collectivity and adapting a novel identity, this right to self-definition reinforced their historical right over land, and their claims for self-government and autonomy.

It, thereby, demonstrated how this identity could be a political tool and option against the working of neoliberal governance. *Comuneros* and supporters, as noted before, reworked their identity strategically arguing in terms of 'authenticity' and 'legitimacy' to protect their land and sustain their claims. The Coca discourse thus adapted itself to a pan-indigenous globalised identity, at the same time to their forms of thinking, to their needs and agendas. It gave continuity to their national and local identification and own identity, though it also impacted on the perceptions of their selves and their community. They assessed their documents and recuperated their history of struggle and possession, but also availed themselves of laws and different mechanisms, such as the Convention 169 and human rights, giving a counter-hegemonic use to hegemonic instruments to enhance their positioning. In this regard, Mezcalenses, even if they might internalise hegemonic discourses, also use them for their own purposes, constraining and empowering them at the same time.

In spite of all their efforts, the government continued with its plans and soon it was revealed that, regarding the project of the Island, 'they don't do it to bring to light the history ... they do it only for economic purposes, to profit' (Tomás 2013). Therefore, the government resignified and appropriated their history and even later, the Coca discourse. Like this, within this process of ethnogenesis, it was demonstrated that the disputes over 'authenticity' have meant artificial constructions that might challenge or reproduce the hegemonic order and system. In effect, the co-option characteristic of neoliberal governance was in evidence, showing how ethnic identities can be used according to political and economic interests in certain times and spaces to sustain dominance, where recognition and negation, inclusion and exclusion go hand in hand. There were two clear examples of how this happened; first, in the *grito de independencia* the names of the *insurgentes* were incorporated clearly with the aim of justifying governmental actions and the intervention in the Island, while giving a positive image of sympathy. Second, in the appropriation of the celebration of the Bicentennial Anniversary of the *Lucha y Defensa de la Isla de Mezcala*, a speech of 'being Coca' was delivered by a co-opted member of the community, while the community was being dispossessed from their festivities, history and land and being pulled into informal channels.

In this regard, the study undertaken by Comaroff and Comaroff (2009) sustains the idea of how culture and capitalism, identity and the market have been working together for a long time, making us rethink the division between 'authentic' versus 'non-authentic'. Thus, Mezcalenses—following the rationale of neoliberal governance—navigate between the notions of 'authenticity', since on the one hand they are denied recognition and rights, while on the other hand, the state manages to exploit a stereotyped perspective on them; as revealed with touristic promotion by the STJ:

Identities Across Borders 191

This is a village that declares itself with a fully indigenous population, which is captured in its rich customs and people proud of their roots.[10]

In order to promote tourism, the government, following the tenets of neoliberal multiculturalism, reinvigorates a market perspective of their indigeneity that entails their subordination and updates past classifications. So there is a tension between romanticisation and degradation; they are praised and condemned at the same time. This clearly connects with our analysis made in Chapter 4 in regard of representations and appropriations of space within the tourist industry. Therefore, taking further the ideas of Díaz-Polanco (2005), the plurality of cultures serves the reproduction and expansion of capital (*globalizante* and *etnófago*); as some differences are included and 'respected' whereas those representing social conflicts are ignored or eliminated through the 'seduction' to the hegemonic culture and, more specifically, to 'progress'. In this regard, paradoxically, some Mezcalenses have found in governmental tourist projects a source of community pride, as Pedro explains:

> now they're not that ashamed anymore, I believe that people who are ashamed are now minimal. Yes, but because now Mezcala, with the Island and with the own village, the boardwalk, now people [say] that's so nice, right? Being of Mezcala.

However, by linking, tourism, progress, pride and belonging, they might reinforce elites' representations and plans. All these insights concur with the ideas presented in the Introduction about the functioning of the operational logic embodied by neoliberal governance, and with the critical observations about multiculturalism and *neoindigenismo* as supporting mechanisms.

In this context, elites keep trying to integrate indigenous people into pre-existent institutions and channels in order to 'modernise' them and sideline their demands (Hernández Navarro 2009, 47–8). Thus, as Mezcalenses develop an oppositional identity, in a setting of neoliberal governance, they have sought to absorb it through a strategic response where their collusion and the link between racism and economic oppression has become explicit, as has the rhetorical opposition between 'progress' and 'underdevelopment'. Power purports to reduce something to nothing (Grossberg 1996, 96), proving how the neoliberal project has a limit of tolerance towards difference where conflictive ones are attenuated, if necessary, through repressive methods but in an adapted form of internal colonialism that articulates also international and transnational methods of control, as observed by González Casanova (2006). This was clearly evidenced with the collusion of the *invasor*, but also, as the government tried through its multicultural rights agenda to legitimate, perpetuate and expand their dominant and violent actions, and integrate a sector via informal politics, as previously illustrated. Besides, a *neoindigenista* framework by moulding the attitudes and practices of the civil and political society accentuate inequalities to maintain the system unaltered.

192 *Identities Across Borders*

In consequence, what damages the community is the impairment and manipulation of their history, organisation, identity and territory through an intervention that reinforces the inherited political culture, emphasises personal benefits, and perpetuates dependence and 'status quo', not the non-recognition per se. So, while some members have become accomplices of the state, racism—together with the discourse of 'progress' and 'development'—has accentuated the disarticulation and fragmentation of the community and the weakening of their authority due to the desire of being incorporated to the dominant society. Yet it is necessary to see how indigenous identities might help to fight against the state and the system, and how they might emerge at all, given the socioeconomic logic of neoliberal governance (and neoliberal multiculturalism) at play. Furthermore, being Mezcalense in multiple locations adds complexity to how they define their ethnic identity, and its importance resides in how they cross multiple borders and are projected in the different locations in which they are living.

A Brief Look at the Use of Indigeneity North of the Border

Identities entail subjective and contextual processes, and thus, have different meanings and features. In this regard, in general the knowledge of migrants about the community is mainly informed by other kinds of myths, such as the legend of la *cueva del toro* and the practice of *brujería*.[11] Indigeneity is not a rigid notion, but, rather, is open to interpretations that are marked by the subjects' own experiences. Besides, their perception towards indigenousness has been influenced by the rhetoric of *mestizaje* that also north of the border erased indigenous heterogeneity constructing a folklorised Aztec Indian (Alonso 2004). Hence, despite recognising their indigeneity, 'being indigenous' remained a subjugated positioning, allowing, as Martínez Novo (2006) argues, colonial images to persist in immigration contexts, and showing the ability of racial structures to cross borders. For instance, Don Roberto explains how indigeneity is used:

> They consider us indigenous due to our traits, but there is already a lot of [people from the] new generation with mestizo traits. So I say that we're opportunistic because [if] something is convenient for us to say, I, for example, I want to go and cut down a tree and I won't ask permission because I know they don't fine me because it's indigenous land, right? But in other aspects … I don't want to be an indigenous, because, for example, so that I can reach the level of all the villages around there.

Although many migrants have been seduced and coerced, some others have engaged in the possibility to reverse the effects of neoliberal governance employing their identity. As the Coca identity and rhetoric grew stronger, it reached the point that encouraged migrants' curiosity and learning, reshaping and enhancing the indigenous identity. For instance, Tomás, a proud migrant Mezcalense, claims:

I'm indigenous, 100% indigenous. That I don't have a loincloth doesn't mean that I'm [not] indigenous, I'm still indigenous and I'm going to die indigenous, and my children are indigenous because we come from there. A *nopal* [cactus] although it's planted in the United States, it'll always be a *nopal*; and we remain being *nopales*.

This action, together with that of the celebrations of the *Bicentenario*, propelled in them the sense of being indigenous and of being Mezcalense, though at the beginning it little fomented the adoption of the Coca identity. In this context, *Señorita Mezcala* paraded LA in a 'traditional dress' made by hand by her family using materials direct from Mezcala that stressed the importance of its territory and identity. Meanwhile, other migrants further studied their history and transmitted it, even uploading a Spanish and English version on the internet. Again its veracity was unimportant and migrants adapted their own versions helping to reinforce their link with the community, justify the possession over territory and reaffirm the pride of being 'authentically' indigenous and of a never conquered land. As affirmed by Doña Ino when I asked her if she considered herself indigenous: 'Yes ... Now in some way it gives me more pleasure to know that yes, we're from an indigenous community'. Media again was used as a counter-hegemonic tool where Mezcalenses organise around their shared collective identity while a deeper analysis of their situation was encouraged. Even solidarity and autonomous and communitarian work increased, as might be further demonstrated by the novel organisation *Unidos por La Cuesta* (2015) that has close links with Colectivo Mezcala. In this regard, what migrants' identity shows is not a process of 'scaling up' (Fox 2006), rather of 'scaling down' as the local identity becomes a symbol of pride and the history gains terrain. Don José who migrated in the 1970s explains:

[Migrants from Mezcala] used to say that they were from Guadalajara, that well, it was also because it was a little village that small that nobody knew it, but now it's well known, if you go into YouTube or into the Facebook webpage, there are only things from Mezcala. And I believe that people right now feel proud, at least I'm proud to be from Mezcala.

However, to reaffirm their identity as indigenous does not mean that the other identities disappear, given what has been sustained here; that is, that identities are used and interact depending on the context and the purposes at play. Besides, indigeneity has multiple meanings; it is a gathering of possibilities; and migrants impress on it their own peculiarities. Moreover, as transnational migrants take with them a conception of collectivity, homeland and identity, they might reinforce their activism and claims, and open spaces to renew their indigenous identity and their survival strategies (Blackwell *et al.* 2009). For instance, some migrants deploy their indigenous identity to exalt positive features, bring them together, advance their projects, oppose the *Municipio* and/or legitimise the bond with the community. They are brought closer to *comuneros* and to the community as a

194 *Identities Across Borders*

whole, where they redefine ethnicity and reinforce the sense of community, this being a mode of individual and collective survival. Thus, subjects with distinct backgrounds, experiences and ideologies are amalgamated with a common purpose, that is, to end the longstanding subordination and exclusion.

By articulating migrants' position with the claims of *comuneros* and young supporters, Mezcalenses can become a transnational movement of opposition to the neoliberal project, challenge the state and elites' complicity, and address the roots of their conditions. External, but more importantly, internal networks of solidarity are crucial to ending global inequalities and hierarchies and navigating the geographies of power. In this sense, Mezcalenses, in all their contradictions and ambiguities, still do not give up and engage in a fight over meaning through the use of their indigeneity. Like this, they delineate a collective identity based on their transnational experience and ties, advancing in what Hale and Millamán (2006, 282) identify as 'cultural agency'; that is, the pursuit of social change through creativity and the emphasis on difference to end 'internal hierarchies'. Mezcalenses are challenging the objectives of neoliberal governance by giving new meanings to what it is to be indigenous nowadays, making the discrimination suffered evident in its multiple locations and varied configurations, while renewing their past with their identification as modern subjects. Nonetheless, it remains to be seen if this identity consolidates itself as a transnational subversive identity, or merges itself into the state discourses, and more broadly, into the machineries of neoliberal governance.

Conclusion

In this 'democratic' era of neoliberal governance, Mezcalenses have been driven to be part of a transnational process of informalisation accentuated by the fact of being stereotyped subjects equated with profits rather than rights and having scarce channels of action. Thus, being Mezcalense has multiple locations and implies identities that interplay, but also positionings that accompany them. Whether as indigenous people or migrants, what Mezcalenses are experiencing is a system of differentiation that crosses borders and eras, impressing itself on local forms. It is in this context that stereotypes cannot be formally overcome and prejudices overturned, and identities become part of the processes of neoliberal governance, being disarticulated while a set of imaginary changes are offered, realities ignored, voice and participation restrained and subjugation and domination maintained. It is true that processes of nation building and state practices, global politics and capitalist economics, constructions of alterity and hierarchies, class and ethnicity, hegemonic discourses and networks of power, but also own experiences and subjectivities, history and future, networks of solidarity and counter-hegemonic practices, and struggles and claims mediate what is to be Mezcalense nowadays.

As this chapter has shown, identities—within the workings of neoliberal governance—are constructed and reconstructed through a subjective process marked by relations, practices and discourses that intersect in institutionalised

Identities Across Borders   195

and non-institutionalised locations, external and internal spaces, and manifest in local and global forms. Thus, in Mezcala class and ethnicity, territory and diaspora, participation and imposition, and struggle and negotiation cannot be separated; they are interwoven and mutually inscribed. In this vein, depending on circumstances, subjects negotiate and decide upon their identities; even further, they actively mould them in parallel with the construction of social realities. So, in assorted ways Mezcalenses seek to manage their identities and identifications incorporating different features, understandings and goals but without losing their connection with the collectivity. They aim to end the colonial legacy of discrimination and transcend their subordinated status and positioning experienced on different levels, places and forms. They are placing their difference and identity in a political sphere where it seems possible to transform their local realities. Identity, in spite of Mezcalenses' contradictions and ambiguities, can constitute agency, serving both individual and collective objectives; it can change our location and challenge hierarchies and structures of power, to gain control of our realities and construct other relations and ways of being, thinking and living away from neoliberal governance.

In this sense, identity politics has to do with participation and dialogue, and, as Alcoff (2006a, 8) would say, with the possibility to construct a 'united front'. Yet we need to see this process, not as bottom-up or top-down (Martínez Novo, 2006; Sánchez, 2006), but, rather, as involving complex and intertwined relations from the local to the global that shape identities and our perceptions and uses them in paradoxical forms. Besides, although engaged in identity politics, Mezcalenses' struggles are not really for recognition but for equality, respect and dignity. Identity is only used to secure a better position and establish more possibilities of action. Nonetheless, we should not disregard that agency is embedded with power, and thus, Mezcalenses do not represent a romanticised version of indigenous people claiming social justice and democracy. Furthermore, their struggle is not necessarily a threat to the capitalist system, but as Mezcalenses have proven, by getting involved in global/local struggles they can transcend particularities and build social change through alliances and a management of identities marked by difference. Mezcalenses, in this way, are dreaming, as Doña Ino shares:

> 'It's a dream that I want everyone to be the same' and I say, 'well, the dream of us is the same'. We're going to focus on the dream of Martin Luther King, it's the dream that Mezcala really has a good change now.

And this change, as Tomás envisages, 'with the support of us [migrants] here and the work of those from there we can achieve it'.

Clearly, another mode of organisation and participation that is inclusive, fair, consensual and horizontal based on dialogue, recognition and respect, should be brought to bear. What is more, following the ideas of Fraser (2003, 93–4), a 'nonreformist reform' strategy should be pursued; that is, in the form of policies that satisfy redistribution and recognition in ways that also entail an institutional

196 *Identities Across Borders*

change. This includes an end to discourses and social structures that sustain exploitation, discrimination and oppression to finally build an understanding across differences. Therefore, it is not enough to name and construct concepts; neither suffices to open and refurbish legal spaces. In this sense, law and social sciences, though important spaces of dispute, are inconsequential if the roots of colonialism are not pulled out of our mentalities, practices and cultures. Being aware of this is a first step to eradicating or at least partially dismantling hegemonic values and discourses rooted in our minds and actions, in our culture, identity and lifestyle, in our relationships, institutions and governments that perpetuate, in the era of neoliberal governance, imbalances, exclusion and intolerance, and legitimate a capitalist world system cast in the image of modernity/coloniality.

Accordingly, Mezcalenses confront internal conflicts and interests, remain intermingled in the network of power, encountering hegemonic and national discourses and policies. However, in their own struggles and methods, by adapting, resisting, negotiating and reworking their indigenous identity, in varying degrees, they are achieving the strengthening of the sense of community and reinforcing communal ties while agreeing on the need of union and progress in the community. To this effect, their transnationalisation of networks can become an important force to challenge the power of the state, dismantle the institutional structure, transcend political representations and deconstruct ethnic and economic hierarchies marked by colonialist social constructions. In this sense, the recreation of their ethnic identity, or I would rather say, the dignification of their indigenousness, entails contradictory perspectives while it shows how identities, in line with the observation of Speed, are both 'strategic' and 'authentic' (2002, 221–2), as well as involving unity and diversity. This identity project can thus be seen as a transnational survival strategy, a framework to work for the welfare of Mezcalenses, to transform their realities, end fragmentation, defend the land and, more importantly, change perceptions, transgress stratifications and exclusions performed, and redefine the labels, identifications and brands imposed.

By ourselves we cannot change the meanings of our identities, but we can do it collectively (Alcoff 2006b). The risks of reverse outcomes are there, but Mezcalenses do not give up, and are deploying their capacity to denounce, confront, and unite for life, territory and dignity. In this way, wondering whether or not they are 'authentic' and 'legitimate' indigenous people becomes irrelevant in the sense that the importance resides in how people manage identities and negotiate their locations with others. It is in this context that identities should be understood as ambiguous, contradictory, convoluted, dynamic, in permanent tensions between fluidity and fixedness, between past and present, subjective and interactive, inheritance and experience, positioning and positionality, location and dispersion. Therefore, the questions of how to define and who gets to define indigeneity, as complicated as it is, might be elucidated by listening to the narratives, histories, experiences, perspectives and horizons from those who live this identity.

Notes

1 It is interesting to relate this to the observations of Wade that point out how 'non-white Latinos' have 'higher rates of endogamy' and poorer life-chances, especially in respect to 'education' and 'income' (2009, 233).

2 For instance, the problem of gang members who are deported shows the transformation of the community and spreading of their expressions, practices, organisation and perceptions. It also demonstrates the reproduction of this sort of violence, exclusion and racism. However, as the case of Chuy who has joined the fight of *comuneros* reveals here, this situation is more complex and thus further studies on this matter are needed.

3 As well, in the U.S., for instance for Club members the Catholic Church represents a point of contact, refuge, support and action. In line with the observations of Levitt (2008)—religion links people across space, facilitates and informs their socialisation and organisation into the receiving country and prolongs their participation and visibility in their country of origin. Nonetheless, at the same time, the contact of migrants with other faith organisations is prompting others to detach from Catholicism, impacting culturally and socially, while causing internal problems.

4 *Cargos* in the community can be both those managed by *comuneros*, meaning a public service, and those managed by inhabitants, especially regarding communitarian projects and celebrations. Migrants only engage in the second one.

5 *Comuneros* enacted a section about the organisation and participation of *Hijos Ausentes* in the *Estatuto Comunal (2009)* to regulate their involvement while recognising their rights and duties as any other Mezcalense.

6 It seems that the coming generations, although they might advocate to be recognised as 'American', will keep embracing their Mexicanness and also their Mezcala-ness, and their commitments as the recent appointment of *Señorita Mezcala* as the new president of Club Mezcala evidences the persistence of transnational efforts by second generations.

7 An example of how this is lived is offered by the wrestler Ringo Mendoza 'el indio de Mezcala'.

8 Other efforts are seen in the making of videos, such as the documentary 'Voces emergentes' made in collaboration with the Universidad de Guadalajara to show how inhabitants address what it is to be indigenous, and the meaning of their territory to reinforce their identity while broadcasting the current situation lived.

9 This effort did not conclude with the book, but continued in the workshop 'Pintando tu historia' organised by young fighters where the aim was to reinforce the history of the community while prompting them to think critically. Nowadays, this duty is arranged in workshops and activities carried out in *Paraje Insurgente.* Another example might be the library that, as stated in Chapter 3, can further be consolidated as another form of IK.

10 Webpage of Portal Turístico, Gobierno del Estado de Jalisco: capturaportal.jalisco. gob.mx [accessed November 2014].

11 Priests in Mezcala have been portraying the local practices as *brujería* in order to legitimise Catholicism, dismantle opposition and represent inhabitants as ignorant, and this has shaped the perception of some migrants while sustaining hierarchies.

References

Alba, Richard. 2006. "Mexican Americans and the American Dream". *Perspectives on Politics* 4 (2): 289–96.

Alcoff, Linda Martín. 2006a. "Reconsidering Identity Politics: An Introduction". In *Identity Politics Reconsidered*, edited by Linda Martín Alcoff, Michael Hames-García, Satya P. Mohanty and Paula M. L. Moya, 1–9. New York: Palgrave Macmillan.

198 Identities Across Borders

Alcoff, Linda Martín. 2006b. *Visible Identities: Race, Gender, and the Self.* Oxford: Oxford University Press.

Alonso, Ana María. 1994. "The Politics of Space, Time and Substance: State Formation, Nationalism and Ethnicity". *Annual Review of Anthropology* 23: 379–405.

Alonso, Ana María. 2004. "Confronting Disconformity: 'Mestizaje, Hybridity, and the Aesthetics of Mexican Nationalism'". *Cultural Anthropology* 19 (4): 459–90.

Alonso, Jorge. 2010. "La persistente defensa de la autonomía del pueblo de Mezcala como una creación de espacio público no estatal". In *¿Qué tan público es el espacio público en México?*, edited by Mauricio Merino, 311–46. Mexico City: FCE; CONAC-ULTA; Universidad Veracruzana.

Antaki, Charles, and Sue Widdicombe. 1998. "Identity as an Achievement and as a Tool". In *Identities in Talk*, edited by Charles Antaki and Sue Widdicombe, 1–14. London: SAGE Publications.

Barth, Fredrik. 1969. "Introduction". In *Ethnic Groups and Boundaries: The Social Organization of Culture Difference*, edited by Fredrik Barth, 9–38. Oslo: Universitets Forlaget.

Bastos, Santiago. 2009. "Interview with Municipal President". Poncitlán, July 15.

Bastos, Santiago. 2011a. "La comunidad de Mezcala y la recreación étnica ante la globalización neoliberal". *Revista CUHSO* 21 (1): 87–103.

Bastos, Santiago. 2011b. "La nueva defensa de Mezcala: un proceso de recomunalización a través de la renovación étnica". *Relaciones* 32 (125): 86–122.

Bastos, Santiago. 2012. "Mezcala: despojo territorial y rearticulación indígena en la Ribera de Chapala". In *Jalisco hoy: miradas antropológicas*, edited by Renée De la Torre and Santiago Bastos, 223–56. Guadalajara, Mexico: Centro de Investigaciones y Estudios Superiores en Antropología Social – Unidad Occidente.

Bastos, Santiago. 2013. "La micropolítica del despojo: Mezcala de la Asunción en la globalización neoliberal". *Revista de Estudios e Pesquisas sobre as Américas* 7 (2): 105–34.

Blackwell, Maylei, Rosalva Aída Hernández Castillo, Juan Herrera, Morna Macleod, Renya Ramírez, Rachel Sieder, María Teresa Sierra, and Shannon Speed. 2009. "Cruces de fronteras, identidades indígenas, género y justicia en las Américas". *Desacatos* (31): 13–34.

Boccara, Guillaume, and Paola Bolados. 2010. "¿Qué es el multiculturalismo? La nueva cuestión étnica en el Chile Neoliberal". *Revista de Indias* LXX (250): 651–90.

Canales, Alejandro I., and Christian Zlolniski. 2001. "Comunidades transnacionales y migración en la era de la globalización". *Notas de Población* 28 (73): 221–52.

Chauvin, Sébastien, and Blanca Garcés-Mascareñas. 2012. "Beyond Informal Citizenship: The New Moral Economy of Migrant Illegality". *International Political Sociology* 6 (3): 241–59.

Chavez, Leo R. 2013. *Shadowed Lives: Undocumented Immigrants in American Society.* 3rd edn. Belmont, CA: Wadsworth Cengage Learning.

Colectivo Mezcala. 2008. Mezcala es una comunidad indígena coca. Mezcala, Mexico.

Comaroff, John, and Jean Comaroff. 1992. *Ethnography and the Historical Imagination.* Boulder, CO: Westview Press.

Comaroff, John, and Jean Comaroff. 2009. *Ethnicity, Inc.* Chicago, IL: The University of Chicago Press.

Comunidad Indígena de Mezcala. 2007. Cada 25 de Noviembre. Mezcala.

Cooper Alarcón, Daniel. 1992. "The Aztec Palimpsest: Toward a New Understanding of Aztlán, Cultural Identity and History". *A Journal of Chicano Studies* 19 (2): 33–68.

Identities Across Borders 199

Cruz Vargas, Juan Carlos. 2012. "Indígenas en el abandono total: INEGI". *PROCESO*, August 7. www.proceso.com.mx/?p=316419 [accessed August 27, 2013].

Dalum Berg, Ulla, and Robyn Magalit Rodriguez. 2013. "Transnational Citizenship Across the Americas". *Identities: Global Studies in Culture and Power* 20 (6): 649–64.

De Fina, Anna. 2003. *Identity in Narrative. A Study of Immigrant Discourse*. Amsterdam: John Benjamins Publishing Company.

De la Cadena, Marisol, and Orin Starn. 2009. "Indigeneidad: problemáticas, experiencias y agendas en el nuevo milenio". *Tabula Rasa* (10): 191–223.

Delgado, Richard, Jean Stefancic, and Ernesto Liendo. 2012. *Critical Race Theory: An Introduction*. 2nd edn. New York: New York University Press.

Díaz-Polanco, Héctor. 2005. "Etnofagia y multiculturalismo". *Memoria* 200 (October).

Durán Matute, Inés. 2015. "Mezcala: construyendo autonomía. Balance de retos y propuestas frente al neoliberalismo". *Journal of Iberian and Latin American Research* 21 (1): 1–18.

Eriksen, Thomas H. 2001. *Small Places, Large Issues: An Introduction to Social and Cultural Anthropology*. 2nd edn. London: Pluto Press.

Fitzgerald, David. 2009. *A Nation of Emigrants: How Mexico Manages its Migration*. Berkeley, CA: University of California Press.

Fox, Jonathan. 2005. "Unpacking 'Transnational Citizenship'". *Annual Review of Political Science* 8 (June): 171–201.

Fox, Jonathan. 2006. "Reframing Mexican Migration as a Multi-Ethnic Process". *Latino Studies* 4 (1–2): 39–61.

Fox, Jonathan, and Gaspar Rivera-Salgado. 2004. "Introducción". In *Indígenas mexicanos migrantes en los Estados Unidos*, edited by Jonathan Fox and Gaspar Rivera-Salgado, 9–74. Mexico City: H. Cámara de Diputados LIX Legislatura; University of California Santa Cruz; Universidad Autónoma de Zacatecas; Miguel Ángel Porrúa.

Fraser, Nancy. 2003. "Social Justice in the Age of Identity Politics: Redistribution, Recognition and Participation". In *Redistribution or Recognition? A Political-Philosophical Exchange*, edited by Nancy Fraser and Axel Honneth, 7–109. London: Verso.

Gall, Olivia. 2002. "Estado federal y grupos de poder regionales frente al indigenismo, al mestizaje y al discurso multiculturalista. Pasado y presente del racismo en México". In *Etnopolíticas y racismo. Conflictividad y desafíos interculturales en América Latina*, edited by Carlos Vladimir Zambrano, 47–72. Bogota: Universidad Nacional de Colombia.

Gálvez, Alyshia. 2013. "Immigrant Citizenship: Neoliberalism, Immobility and the Vernacular Meanings of Citizenship". *Identities: Global Studies in Culture and Power* 20 (6): 720–37.

González Casanova, Pablo. 2006. "Colonialismo interno (una redefinición)". In *La teoría marxista hoy. Problemas y perspectivas*, edited by Atilio A. Borón, Javier Amadeo and Sabrina González, 209–434. Buenos Aires: CLACSO.

Grossberg, Lawrence. 1996. "Identity and Cultural Studies: Is That All There Is?" In *Questions of Cultural Identity*, edited by Stuart Hall and Paul Du Gay, 87–107. London: SAGE Publications.

Hale, Charles R. 2002. "Does Multiculturalism Menace? Governance, Cultural Rights and the Politics of Identity in Guatemala". *Journal of Latin American Studies* 34 (3): 485–524.

Hale, Charles R., and Rosamel Millamán. 2006. "Cultural Agency and Political Struggle in the Era of the Indio Permitido". In *Cultural Agency in the Americas*, edited by Doris Sommer, 281–304. Durham, NC: Duke University Press.

200 *Identities Across Borders*

Hall, Stuart. 1990. "Cultural Identity and Diaspora". In *Identity: Community, Culture, Difference*, edited by Jonathan Rutherford, 222–37. London: Lawrence & Wishart.

Hardt, Michael. 1999. "Affective Labor". *Boundary 2* 26 (2): 89–100.

Hea Kil, Sang, and Cecilia Menjívar. 2006. "The 'War on the Border': Criminalizing Immigrants and Militarizing the U.S.–Mexico Border". In *Immigration and Crime: Race, Ethnicity, and Violence*, edited by Ramiro Jr. Martinez and Abel Jr. Valenzuela, 164–88. New York: New York University Press.

Hernández Castillo, Rosalva Aída, and Ronald Nigh. 1998. "Global Processes and Local Identity among Mayan Coffee Growers in Chiapas, Mexico". *American Anthropologist* 100 (1): 136–47.

Hernández Navarro, Luis. 2009. "Movimiento indígena: autonomía y representación política". In *Otras geografías. Experiencias de autonomías indígenas en México*, edited by Giovanna Gasparello and Jaime Quintana Guerrero, 33–61. Mexico City: Redez tejiendo la utopía.

Hill, Nancy E., and Kathryn Torres. 2010. "Negotiating the American Dream: The Paradox of Aspirations and Achievement among Latino Students and Engagement between the Families and Schools". *Journal of Social Issues* 66 (1): 95–112.

Holloway, John. 2010. *Cambiar el mundo sin tomar el poder*. Mexico City: Sísifo Ediciones; Bajo Tierra Ediciones; Benemérita Universidad Autónoma de Puebla.

Kearney, Michael. 2004. *Changing Fields of Anthropology: From Local to Global*. Lanham, MD: Rowman & Littlefield Publishers, Inc.

Knight, Alan. 1990. "Racism, Revolution, and Indigenismo: Mexico, 1910–1940". In *The Idea of Race in Latin America, 1870–1940*, edited by Richard Graham, 71–113. Austin, TX: University of Texas Press.

Levitt, Peggy. 2008. "Religion as a Path to Civic Engagement". *Ethnic and Racial Studies* 31 (4): 766–91.

Lopez, Felipe H. 2002. "The Construction of Mexican Identity". *Rutgers Law Review* 54 (4): 989–98.

López y Rivas, Gilberto. 2010. "Tesis en torno a la autonomía de los pueblos indios". *Rebelión*. www.rebelion.org/noticia.php?id=106782 [accessed May 2, 2012].

Martínez Moreno, Rocío. 2012. "Tierra, historia y pueblo. Memoria y acción política en la comunidad indígena de Mezcala, Jalisco". Master diss., División de Estudios Históricos y Humanos, Universidad de Guadalajara.

Martínez Novo, Carmen. 2006. *Who Defines Indigenous? Identities, Development, Intellectuals and the State in Northern Mexico*. New Brunswick, NJ: Rutgers University Press.

Morán Quiróz, Luis Rodolfo. 1997. "Cosmopolitismo, migración y comunidades transterritoriales: cultura global y culturas locales". *Espiral, Estudios sobre Estado y Sociedad* 7 (9): 21–46.

Ong, Aihwa. 1996. "Cultural Citizenship as Subject-Making: Immigrants Negotiate Racial and Cultural Boundaries in the United States". *Current Anthropology* 37 (5): 737–62.

Ortiz, Patricio Rodolfo. 2007. "Intercultural Bilingual Education, Indigenous Knowledge and the Construction of Ethnic Identity: An Ethnography of a Mapuche School in Chile". PhD diss., Cultural Studies in Education, University of Texas.

Pansters, Wil. 2005. "Goodbye to the Caciques? Definition, the State and the Dynamics of *Caciquismo* in Twentieth-Century Mexico". In *Caciquismo in Twentieth-Century Mexico*, edited by Alan Knight and Wil Pansters, 349–76. London: Institute for the Study of the Americas.

Identities Across Borders 201

Paredes, Vicente. 2010. "Mezcala: la isla indómita. Las luchas de los insurgentes en Mezcala". *Desacatos* 34: 167–70.

Pérez Huber, Lindsay, and Daniel G. Solorzano. 2015. "Racial Microaggressions as a Tool for Critical Race Research". *Race, Ethnicity and Education* 18 (3): 297–320.

Phillips, Julie A., and Douglas S. Massey. 1999. "The New Labor Market: Immigrants and Wages after IRCA". *Demography* 36 (2): 233–46.

Portes, Alejandro. 2012. "Convergencias teóricas y evidencias empíricas en el estudio del transnacionalismo inmigrante". In *Sociología económica de las migraciones internacionales*, edited by Lorenzo Cachón, 101–15. Madrid: Anthropos. Original edition, 2003.

Rosaldo, Renato. 2006. "Identity Politics: And Ethnography by a Participant". In *Identity Politics Reconsidered*, edited by Linda Martín Alcoff, Michael Hames-García, Satya P. Mohanty and Paula M. L. Moya, 118–25. New York: Palgrave Macmillan.

Rosaldo, Renato, and William V. Flores. 1997. "Identity, Conflict, and Evolving Latino Communities: Cultural Citizenship in San Jose, California". In *Latino Cultural Citizenship: Claiming Identity, Space, and Rights*, edited by William Vincent Flores and Rina Benmayor, 57–96. Boston, MA: Beacon Press.

Ruiz, Martha Cecilia. 2002. "Ni sueño ni pesadilla: diversidad y paradojas en el proceso migratorio". *Iconos: Revista de Ciencias Sociales* 14: 88–97.

Sánchez, Rosaura. 2006. "On a Critical Realist Theory of Identity". In *Identity Politics Reconsidered*, edited by Linda Martín Alcoff, Michael Hames-García, Satya P. Mohanty and Paula M. L. Moya, 31–51. New York: Palgrave Macmillan.

Speed, Shannon. 2002. "Global Discourses on the Local Terrain: Human Rights and Indigenous Identity in Chiapas". *Cultural Dynamics* 14 (2): 205–28.

Stavenhagen, Rodolfo. 2001. "Derechos humanos y derechos culturales de los pueblos indígenas". In *Los derechos humanos en tierras mayas. Política, representaciones y moralidad*, edited by Pedro Pitarch and Julián López García. Madrid: Sociedad Española de Estudios Mayas.

Stephen, Lynn. 2007. *Transborder Lives. Indigenous Oaxacans in Mexico, California and Oregon*. Durham, NC: Duke University Press.

Stephen, Lynn. 2008. "Vigilancia e invisibilidad en la vida de los inmigrantes indígenas mexicanos que trabajan en Estados Unidos". In *Migración, fronteras e identidades étnicas transnacionales*, edited by Laura Velasco Ortiz, 197–238. Mexico City: El Colegio de la Frontera Norte; Miguel Ángel Porrúa.

Stern, Alexandra Minna. 2009. "Eugenics and Racial Classification in Modern Mexican America". In *Race and Classification. The Case of Mexican America*, edited by Ilona Katzew and Susan Deans-Smith, 151–73. Stanford, CA: Stanford University Press.

Velasco Ortiz, M. Laura. 2002. *El regreso de la comunidad: migración indígena y agentes étnicos: los mixtecos de la frontera México-Estados Unidos*. Mexico City: El Colegio de México; El Colegio de la Frontera Norte.

Wade, Peter. 2005. "Rethinking Mestizaje: Ideology and Lived Experience". *Journal of Latin American Studies* 37 (2): 239–57.

Wade, Peter. 2009. *Race and Sex in Latin America*. London: Pluto Press.

Weyland, Karin. 2004. "Dominican Women "Con un Pie Aquí y Otro Allá". Transnational Practices at the Crossroads of Local/Glocal Agendas". In *Dominican Migration Transnational Perspectives*, edited by Ernesto Sagás and Sintia E. Molina, 154–76. Gainesville, FL: University Press of Florida.

Widdicombe, Sue. 1998. "Identity as an Analysts' and a Participants' Resource". In *Identities in Talk*, edited by Charles Antaki and Sue Widdicombe, 191–206. London: SAGE Publications.

Conclusions

The research that formed this book has been quite a journey. Feelings of impotency and faith, frustration and joy, scepticism and optimism have popped up along the way. I have traced the hopes of Mezcalenses for 'democracy' and a voice, for a better life and the protection of 'traditional' forms, to reach the 'American Dream' and improve life conditions, for economic spill-overs and autonomous organisation, for recognition, respect and dignity. These desires have not only made evident the differences between members of the community, their contradictions and ambiguities, their fragmentation and internal problems, but also demonstrated how lives and territories have been largely and indelibly shaped and controlled by hegemonic rhetorics and elites' plans. In effect, through the establishment of clienteles, and the co-option of community members, and more precisely, via the setting up of a simulated democracy, the voice and paths of Mezcalenses are being constrained. At the same time, the discourses of 'progress' and 'development' have been fragmenting the community through dispersion, new forms of employment, invasions, the development of the tourist industry, and transformations of lifestyles and values.

In this context, a form of neoliberal governance, as delineated along this book, is set in place. Multiple subjects, actors and institutions from the local to the global sphere have been identified as working to sustain elite dominion and capitalist expansion. This entails a transnational collaboration of institutions sustained by the rhetoric of 'development' and the use of an inherited political culture that privileges informal power and accentuates economic, social and cultural differences in order to obtain the control of lives and territories. In this way, the community is manipulated and exposed to corrupt and violent, but also subtle and institutionalised, strategies. In view of that, *comuneros* have been split between 'progressives' and 'traditionalists', and this division has expanded among the whole population. Mezcalenses are living a new territoriality where different subjects contest the control of territory, transforming it at the whim of 'development'. Within this scenario, the complexity, inequality and violence of informal politics are revealed, as well as the perpetuation, reproduction and renewal of colonial relations, stratifications, differentiations, and disparities between and within countries.

Accordingly, Mezcala is implicated in these geographies of power exemplifying how neoliberal governance shapes the lives, projects and identity of most

Conclusions 203

remote communities, while furnishing a local support of such a dynamic. This can be seen, for instance, in how economic and social remittances are transforming the practices, organisation, values and aspirations in the village while paradoxically and concomitantly reinforcing social structures and hierarchies based on the ideas of 'progress'. Politics work together with economic dynamics, all of which are framed by the discourse of 'development', for the management and exploitation of the diasporic population. But, this does not mean that there is neither an active or passive collaboration of Mezcalenses to sustain the migration flow, or more broadly, the workings of neoliberal governance. In effect, as argued in this book, neoliberal governance simultaneously articulates coercion and seduction (De Angelis 2005) to reinforce the economic and political positions of countries and of elites, transnationalising social structures and sustaining the control and management of people, spaces and resources. Moreover, the place's quality as a diasporic community suggests multiple scenarios of exclusion due to different conditions of inequality. These circumstances point to an 'intersectionality' of social divisions in a global setting of neoliberal governance that protects the interests of elites within the global–regional–local interface of power. As a result, either Mezcalenses are compelled to absorb discourses, ideas and values that maintain these social structures and integrate themselves into such dynamics, or, if they oppose them, they face criminalisation and repression, which in turn leads to their delegitimisation and stigmatisation.

In this sense, Mezcala is a transnational space mediated by a multiplicity of social relations across all levels that put the community at risk of fragmentation and dissolution, through the management of local authorities, labour, development projects, land ownership and identity. The recolonisation and relocation of Mezcalenses provokes a heightened vulnerability that increases the possibility of residential and cultural tourism in the community through the intervention of the government and the *invasor*. In Mezcala, therefore, the desirability of land puts into play the commodification and exploitation of space and history, of nature, culture and people. In this context, elites have been using different tactics towards a simulation in the improvement of the inhabitants' living conditions and a kind of upper social mobility. So while Mezcalenses, their actions, demands and thinking are rendered invisible or institutionalised, a national project outlined by multiculturalism and *neoindigenismo* has acted as a supportive 'folklorising strategy'. This kind of social project aims to maintain a portrayal of indigenous people as something from the past and 'underdeveloped', while it also romanticises some elements of their cultures and emphasises the 'diversity' of the Mexican culture. Accordingly, through the makeover of this strategy that manages and appropriates difference, national elites keep imprinting meanings and representations onto spaces and people that are consonant with 'national history' in order to sustain an imagined community, obscure power imbalances and racism, and allow the rationalisation of territory—all of this on behalf of neoliberal governance.

Under this scenario, we need to consider that the community does not relate to territory in the same way as it did before. Moreover, Mezcala is a heterogeneous

204   *Conclusions*

and dispersed community that is enmeshed in internal conflicts and unequal relationships. In this manner, Mezcala is being constructed through disputes and negotiations between its members. Mezcalenses are real people; *comuneros*, young supporters and migrants are complex subjects who occupy different positions and visualise a variety of projects. Hence, this book has traced the varied experiences, knowledges, anxieties and strategies shared by these Mezcalenses enmeshed in the geographies of power. On the one hand, some members of the community have been absorbed by a dynamic of political power play and the promise of economic spoils, in which they try to negotiate and overcome their position through personal endeavour and community support. For instance, Club Mezcala has been using and producing a form of social capital to diminish the vulnerability of migrants and even of those left behind; yet, as an association, it is still immersed in a structure of exclusion and distinction. On the other hand, another sector has come to challenge this setting through the formation of a solidarity network that allows them to pursue autonomous projects. Colectivo Mezcala has exemplified this path, and, in parallel, provides evidence of how its members are seeking to overcome the obstacles set by a capitalist world system cast in the image of modernity/coloniality. Each group still entails different perspectives and embodies their own contradictions and ambiguities, but in general terms they have delineated a similar objective: to improve the living conditions of Mezcalenses. Accordingly, the community uses different forms of safety valves for the confrontation between its proposal and that of neoliberal governance, outlining paths for survival and even going beyond survival by constructing autonomy.

Hence, despite internal contradictions and conflicts, the inherited political culture, economic damage and the crisis of representation, *comuneros* still embody a form of governance that guarantees, or at least seeks to act on behalf of, the conservation of the land. Furthermore, *comuneros* are passing their responsibilities, values, worldview, practices and identity onto new subjects in order that they continue to stand up and resist. Therefore, young inhabitants are emerging as a force of change by creating a solidarity network and new forms of participation, and making use of local knowledges, history, values, their sense of community and of place, their territory, authority and identity. In effect, Colectivo Mezcala is challenging state representations, redefining social relationships and constructing their own meanings about economic and political processes, the community, the places and the self. Together with *comuneros* they are building autonomy and opening paths towards their futures while supporting their identity and territorial claims. Moreover, within and beyond the global system, they are constructing another world, transforming their own daily reality while vindicating their struggle against colonial forms of oppression and halting the advance of local, regional and global powers in the era of neoliberal governance. In effect, through the dignification of indigenousness, they are creating a powerful discourse that upturns state representations and social, ethnic and economic hierarchies; that is, the effects of the inherited political culture, and mostly products of modernity/coloniality.

In fact, Mezcalenses in their multiple scenarios not only have been marked by a position of 'subcitizens'; more importantly, as investigated in Chapters 2, 3

Conclusions 205

and 5, citizenship—within the workings of neoliberal governance—has acted as a mechanism to sustain exclusion and distinction, to manage labour and population, to strengthen the hegemonic culture, gain economic and political support, or as a way to limit popular participation and rights. In some cases Mezcalenses are accepting and in other cases challenging these conceptions of citizenship. For instance, migrants are constructing other expressions of citizenship, going beyond the boundaries of the nation-state, becoming politically involved in both societies, claiming belonging and expanding rights that would allow them to be different, but still accommodate themselves. Meanwhile, Colectivo Mezcala is teaching us a lesson that combines different forms of action, using statist and non-statist channels and a network of solidarity via which they might overcome political and economic problems but also social structures that discriminate and marginalise them. Against a system of differentiation that structures societies across eras and frontiers, identities have emerged as avenues of agency for individual and collective objectives. Indeed, among Mezcaleneses, identity is a cohesive and creative strategy to improve life conditions and build social change; it is a first step towards a broader construction of autonomy that aims to stop the looting, abuses, exclusion, dependency and fragmentation historically suffered. In this respect, although Mezcalenses directly or indirectly support the reproduction and reinforcement of the structures of power across borders, they are launching important proposals and projects while challenging state-defined identities, and hence, their position within the system.

Elites feel threatened by the strength they are gaining and thus launch constant attacks waiting for the death of the last *comunero* that would release Mezcala from title holding and eventually allow it to be considered as 'vacant land'. In fact, external actors abuse and manipulate the community, place into confrontation and weaken the population, while such entities also inhibit Mezcalenses' efforts in order to establish their own times, spaces, relationships and practices. Still, Mezcalenses keep in mind a range of projects, becoming aware of the potential of different sectors to work together and of the importance of giving younger generations the tools to keep defending their territory. They are aware that their union can defend the community, their traditions, organisation and government, and accomplish their projects, improve living conditions, gain a voice and respect, and even construct and vindicate paths whereby they work on their own form of development. As Pedro, an inhabitant, argues: 'Here we have to apply the word "communal", that is, the one for the other ... all in common, all united and supported, that would be the objective'. So, as Doña Ino, a migrant, asserts: 'progress would be for them [inhabitants] to trust that things can be done but united'.

In this way, by reaching a transnational level, their identity project can, in truth, offer a way to transform the terms by which the community engages or not with the current world system. Not surprisingly, recently a banner stating 'The Coca People of Mezcala doesn't dream about world change, dreams about people gaining consciousness, since if the Coca people gain consciousness dreams are no longer needed' has been placed in multiple events. Mezcalenses

206 *Conclusions*

are on their way to exemplifying a 'transnationalism from below', building up the argument of Smith and Guarnizo (1998) and Delgado-Wise (2006, 195), where spaces of resistance are created and hegemonic structures, rhetoric, identifications, representations and meanings challenged. In effect, by renewing the relationship with the community, new generations both in Mexico and the United States are showing a continuity of commitment to protecting it. On the one hand, as I have argued, Colectivo Mezcala demonstrates a clear and defined path that pursues the construction of autonomy, while on the other hand, Club Mezcala offers a more complex setting since they must swim against the current of institutionalisation and co-optation.

To be sure, *comuneros* have given their life for the territory, and although many have died without experiencing the benefits of their struggle, younger generations are proving that it has not been in vain through their identity and communal projects. So even if they do not truly provide disconnected alternatives from the system rationale, local communities that face a stark system of exclusion on a daily basis are providing an example for others to follow. In effect, as the possibilities of working together augment—recently evidenced with the dialogues established between young members on both sides of the border—they might create alternatives across borders that challenge the actions and practices of neoliberal governance. Therefore, in spite of differences between *comuneros*, young inhabitants and migrants, they are all evidently active subjects, agents of their history and future, who show marked dispositions to dialogue and unity among themselves while they seek to recuperate communal organisation, values and practices. As actors and agents, they are taking up their own experiences and constructing a cohesive and intricate diasporic community through their sense of place and of community, through their identity and solidarity. They are advancing a form of 'cultural politics', inspired by the ideas of Hernández Castillo and Furio (2006, 124), by creating new meanings, reconstructing collective identities, destabilising the social order, setting up new social relations and challenging power to achieve local demands in multiple and ever more complex locations.

However, as the project of the library has shown, the co-option of members, the meddling of networks of power and inequality still endure within the community. So, too, (previous) forms of programme management, establishment of standards and the use of discourses and practices of *neoindigenismo* and *desarrollismo* continue to alter communal projects. Democracy works as a political illusion to sustain 'development', while the inherited political culture endures, following the ideas of Alvarez,Dagnino, and Escobar (1998), affecting the remaking of cultural politics. In point of fact, as neoliberal governance is maintained by a set of formal but also informal institutions, in order to tackle it at its root, it is not enough to transform existing institutions. Rather, what is required is the creation of new and distinct ones that challenge the current political system, the structure and relations of power and transcend the inherited political culture. In effect, although informal networks have proven to be a mechanism via which people can benefit from power, they largely perpetuate

Conclusions 207

domination. Therefore, in order to overcome the preservation of the status quo and continued capitalist exploitation, people cannot put their faith in the mere elaboration of public policies and institutional dialogues. Together we must dismantle the whole structure and that includes the hegemonic discourses, forces and vehicles of economic inequalities, as well as persistent political, cultural and ethnic stratifications. Within local contexts, we must, in short, engage in new forms of being, thinking, living and interrelating that confront the mental and material frameworks that legitimise structural violence. Only with these commitments can we begin to visualise real changes that might assist in the creation of new political economic models.

This book has brokered many contemporary theoretical discussions within a specific location, underlining the concrete embodiment of political problems and economic expansion. By mapping the key trends of the global–regional–local interface of power as they bear on Mezcalenses' lives, it contributes to our understanding of how policies and rhetorics act as mental frames to sustain the social, economic, political and cultural structures. In this operation we observe an adaptation of local practices to global processes, but can also witness an inverse pattern. However, the purpose of this book was not only to detect the relations, practices and working of networks of power transnationally, but also to bring to light how people—entangled in ambiguities and contradictions—are fighting back against these geographies of power. Here transnationalism has surfaced as a force that can either fragment or unite the community, to uphold or disassemble the global structures of power and institutions, their discourses and stratifications that traverse geographic, collective and personal frontiers. In this context, an end to divisions might arise and images of realities and subjectivities are elaborated in all their complexity and sometimes paradoxical continuity. In this case, Mezcala, with its own specificities, reflects a national and regional trend of transformations, aspirations, exclusions and struggles complicated by the performance of neoliberal governance. By the same token, Mezcalenses do not represent a romanticised version of indigenous people claiming autonomy; even if they are elaborating alternatives and producing 'cracks' in the system, they are penetrated by and embedded into the system, reproducing and self-perpetuating some of its excesses. Mezcala is a small example of this complex and modern working of neoliberal governance, but concrete, clear and daily lived through 'democracy', 'urbanisation', 'industrialisation', 'development' and 'multiculturalism'.

Learning from Lived Realities: A Pragmatic and Epistemological Input

Throughout these years I have learned many things from Mezcalenses about the past and present of my region and of the world, especially in regard to colonisation and capitalism through local history, politics, economics, the environment, living conditions, tourism, migration, citizenship, education and ethnicity. What is more, in the course of this research, I have also learned many things regarding research-activism, to deal with many issues regarding time, trust and participation

208 *Conclusions*

and found a way to give the strength needed to the voice of Mezcalenses. Local knowledges have proved extremely useful and valuable in understanding our reality and contributing to the construction of our line of reasoning. In view of that, we must consider that the forms of thinking that emerge in this dialogue can be forces of resistance against the global system, but also in the face of the hegemonic knowledge production. Nevertheless, I am aware that the production of knowledge is political and affects those involved (Blackwell *et al.* 2009); in this sense, in spite of the contributions that participants' voices and views make to this book and the shape it has taken, this research has not been collaborative at all stages and in all ways, and thus I assume all the responsibility for its production. The time constraints and methods of this research project, as presented in the Introduction, have not allowed me to establish a dialogue with the participants in which we might have more fully discussed the results, and, if necessary, made adjustments. Yet, what it does propose is a different way to do research, suggesting how, in our scholarly engagements, we might think of alternatives that subvert the hierarchies, impositions and interpretations that undergird the world system.

Nonetheless, I should stress here that the production of this work was with all my good intentions to support their struggle, and therefore, my commitment persists with the participants and with the community as a whole. In this sense, prior to the finalisation of this book I returned to the community to present the results of this research supported by booklets that I elaborated in Spanish where I explain the objective, methodology and outcomes. I have done this mainly in a meeting of Club Mezcala in LA, and in another meeting with members of Colectivo Mezcala in Mezcala. Although in these meetings not all participants attended, the reactions of those who did were widely positive, and mainly consisted of questions regarding the lives and positions of other groups and expressions of how much they learned. Actually, in Mezcala they proposed that I present the results in the *plaza* so all Mezcalenses could hear and learn the different visions, experiences and projects of each other. Unfortunately, in spite of my persistence and willingness, as *comuneros* must approve this event, up to now this has not been possible as they are still surrounded by problems and their rhythms of life are quite different from those of a researcher coming from outside the community.

On another note, my aim was not only that this research be pragmatically and epistemologically valuable for Mezcalenses, but also for manifold communities navigating these geographies of power. In this sense, this publication is a first step towards sharing Mezcalenses' experiences, knowledges, visions and projects with other researchers involved in similar projects and societies immersed in broader tendencies and junctures of the workings of neoliberal governance. I sincerely believe they can engage with and learn from this dialogue for the reconstruction of their realities and the stimulation of other ways of thinking. However, the reader should consider that, in line with the arguments of this book, the complexity of realities cannot be encompassed and encapsulated within a single research project, and thus there is still much work to do. For

Conclusions 209

instance, although politics and multiple institutions and their relations have been investigated, the analysis of the role of the Catholic Church requires further attention. Additional research should elaborate on the ideological force of religions, how they weave their relationships transnationally and make use of discourses to legitimate their positions within the interfaces of power.

Moreover, some issues, such as the Latino identity and its interplay with other identities, should be explored, together with the force that new generations of migrants are gaining. This analysis would be useful to clearly visualise the impact over and of the communities of origin by future generations of migrants. In addition, considering the contributions of other studies in relation to different kinds of analyses of the contours of power, I believe that an articulation of other analytical frameworks (for example, through a gender lens) could prove useful in grasping the reproduction of power and the character of relations among actors (examining, for instance, elite networks and their symbolic-subjective dimensions). Such approaches might provide a more complex and complete understanding of reality and the functioning of the global system. In this way, I expect that the portrait of neoliberal governance painted here can only be sharpened and complemented by other studies that reflect on the multiple domains in which hegemonic rhetorics and relations of ruling are perpetuated, operating from the local to the global and serving the structures of domination and the functioning of a capitalist world system cast in the image of modernity/coloniality.

References

Alvarez, Sonia E., Evelina Dagnino, and Arturo Escobar. 1998. "Introduction: The Cultural and the Political in Latin American Social Movements". In *Cultures of Politics, Politics of Cultures. Re-visioning Latin American Social Movements*, edited by Sonia E. Alvarez, Evelina Dagnino and Arturo Escobar, 1–29. Boulder, CO: Westview Press.

Blackwell, Maylei, Rosalva Aída Hernández Castillo, Juan Herrera, Morna Macleod, Renya Ramírez, Rachel Sieder, María Teresa Sierra, and Shannon Speed. 2009. "Cruces de fronteras, identidades indígenas, género y justicia en las Américas". *Desacatos* (31): 13–34.

De Angelis, Massimo. 2005. "The Political Economy of Global Neoliberal Governance". *Review (Fernand Braudel Center)* 28 (3): 229–57.

Delgado-Wise, Raúl. 2006. "Migración e imperialismo: la fuerza de trabajo mexicana en el contexto del TLCAN". In *México en transición: globalismo neoliberal, Estado y sociedad civil*, edited by Gerardo Otero, 195–214. Zacatecas, Mexico: H. Cámera de Diputados LIX Legislatura; Simon Fraser University; Universidad Autónoma de Zacatecas; Miguel Ángel Porrúa.

Hernández Castillo, Rosalva Aída, and Victoria J. Furio. 2006. "The Indigenous Movement in Mexico: Between Electoral Politics and Local Resistance". *Latin American Perspectives* 33 (2): 115–31.

Smith, Michael Peter, and Luis Eduardo Guarnizo. 1998. "The Locations of Transnationalism". In *Transnationalism From Below*, edited by Michael Peter Smith and Luis Eduardo Guarnizo, 3–31. New Brunswick, NJ: Transaction Publishers.

Postface

John Holloway

I don't know where you live, dear reader, but why would you be interested in what is happening in the indigenous community of Mezcala in Mexico? At first sight, it looks as if a book like this should be of interest only to the people of the community itself, the author's friends (of course) and specialists in area studies interested in examining from afar communities such as that of Mezcala.

I think my own position would not have been very different some 25 years ago. And then something happened that changed our concepts of time and space. Something that broke otherness, something that broke the backwards-forwards movement of progress. Suddenly what we thought was behind us stood up in front of us, what seemed to be outside us rose up inside us, from the depths of our being.

I am thinking of the Zapatista uprising of the first of January 1994, their great ¡Ya basta!, Enough! Not just as a single event, and not just in one place, but as the coming to the surface of a latency that seethes in all the world. The uprising was and is a revolt of extraordinary creativity, and among its many other achievements it has led to a resignification of studies of the indigenous.

Other-ness is shaken, identity is broken. As Antonio García de León put it in his preface to the first collection of Zapatista communiqués: 'as more and more rebel communiqués were issued, we realised that in reality the revolt came from the depths of ourselves' (1994: 14). The impact of the Zapatista movement has arisen from the realisation that the indigenous of the south-east of Mexico are far more than that. Their anger, their dignity, their hopes, their revolt against a society that denies them, all this touches us because it is not just 'theirs', it is 'ours', it is an anger-dignity-hope that comes from inside us, that is directed against the same society that negates our humanity too.

This awareness spills over from the Zapatista uprising to all studies of indigenous communities in Mexico or elsewhere. These communities are part of the same society as ourselves, that is to say, part of the same social tension, the same social antagonism: they too are attacked by the movement of capital, they too resist. Hence, surely, the subtitle of this book, *Mezcala's Narratives Of Neoliberal Governance*: it does not make sense to speak of the people of Mezcala outside this social context, just as it does not make sense to understand ourselves in abstraction from this context. Third-person discourse reveals itself to be not only misleading but part of the general violence of this society.

Postface 211

The Zapatista uprising also turned time around. It broke progress. Particularly, it broke the link between radical thought and progress. Benjamin had already pointed to the fatal consequences of coupling revolutionary thought with the concept of progress, and the Zapatistas made a practical mockery of any such coupling and, in the process, posited the thinking and making of an anti-progressive and anti-identitarian left as a central challenge. It has become manifestly absurd to think of indigenous organisation and modes of living, whether in Chiapas or Mezcala, as being backward or underdeveloped. More and more, the patterns of community and solidarity in such communities, the strength of their resistance against the depredations of capital and their relation to the natural environment are seen as being pointers towards a possible future for humanity, rather than as a backwardness from which we must help them to escape.

The breaking of identity and the breaking of time are inseparable from the breaking of the pretence of scientific objectivity. There is no third person, no 'object' of research. Or rather, the scientific objectification of the indigenous or any other social group is part of their social objectification, part of the process of turning them (and us) into the objects of social development. It is part of that progress that, guided only by the blind pursuit of profit, is driving us forward towards the possible annihilation of humanity. An honest science—and this is an important theme of this book—must move differently, reject objectification, reject monologue: it must listen, it must dialogue, it must think from below, it must turn science upside down, conscious that the only scientific question that remains to us is how do we get out of here, how do we pull the emergency brake on this train that is hurtling us towards our collective death?

This book is an exploration of some of these (and many other) themes through a detailed account of the community of Mezcala and the ways in which they both reproduce and resist patterns of domination in their community. It is not an analysis of an objective 'them' but a careful thinking of how we understand the world that surrounds us and of which we are part. It is a pleasure for me to write this postface, to be present here in these final pages.

Reference

García de León, Antonio. 1994. "Prólogo". In *Documentos y Comunicados: 1º de enero/8 de agosto de 1994*, edited by EZLN, 11–30. Mexico City: Ediciones Era.

Index

accumulation 11, 67, 122, 157; of capital 66–7, 101; by dispossession 77, 88n15, 141
agency 15, 16, 189, 195, 205; cultural 194
agriculture 1, 18, 58, 59, 60, 63, 66–7, 68–71, 74, 76, 86, 154, 156
Alonso, Ana Maria 6, 146, 169
Alonso, Jorge 1, 21n10, 53n11, 146, 159n7, 160n14, 160n17, 185
alternative(s) 15, 32, 33, 72, 94, 97, 123n2, 129, 137, 148, 150, 152, 158, 206–8; economic inputs 74; meanings 140; plans 18; projects 19, 60; way of life 172
'alternative development' 136
'alternatives to development' 159
American 21n13, 85, 93, 175–7, 181, 182, 197n6; city 143; life 65, 80, 102, 132, 177, 179; Mexican-American 62, 87n4; myths 80; North-American 154; place 132; society 175; values 93, 179, 181; stereotype 181; see also United States, the
'American Dream' 18, 21n13, 85, 93, 94, 100–5, 109, 122, 123n3, 202
anti-immigrant 62, 78; sentiment(s) 79, 85, 101, 181
Asamblea General de Comuneros 12, 14, 21n9, 43, 44–9, 52n1, 133, 136, 154, 159n4, 185
aspirations 16, 18, 67, 74, 101, 104–5, 123n3, 129, 150, 203, 207
authentic 6, 38, 52, 190, 196; authentically 193; authenticity 51, 168, 189–92; inauthentic 20n2
authoritarian 28, 32–3, 37, 44, 48, 50, 151; authoritarianism 28, 29, 32, 37, 50–1
autonomy 11, 19, 28, 73, 138, 139, 141, 146, 148, 152, 156–7, 158, 168, 180, 185, 186, 189, 190, 204–7; autonomous 148, 153,

193, 202 (life 185; paths 158; perspective 152, 155; posture 45; practices 158–9; project(s) 16, 19, 156, 204); autonomously 116, 119, 124n11, 154

backward 32, 75, 129, 147, 150, 170; backwardness 142
Bastos, Santiago 7, 10, 21n11, 29, 41, 45, 49, 54n22, 128, 141–2, 146, 166, 169, 183, 185
barrio(s) 1, 12, 41, 44, 65, 107, 109, 117, 152, 173, 179, 186; see also jueces de barrio
Bauder, Harald 61, 65, 68, 102
belonging 29, 44, 105, 170, 174, 176–7, 182, 191, 205; see also sense of belonging
Bicentenario 54n24, 135, 148, 193
Bienes Comunales 39, 40, 41, 43, 49, 52n1, 99, 159n2
border 1, 18, 62–4, 66, 67, 76, 77–80, 81, 84, 86, 94, 100, 114, 123, 176, 180, 192, 206; (s) 77–8, 145, 153, 166, 172, 174–5, 182, 192, 194, 205–6; control 62, 68, 176; cross-border 93, 113, 179, 182; militarisation 176; security 62; see also transborder
boundaries 105, 106, 113, 179, 205
Bracero Programme 58, 60–2, 64; bracero(s) 61–2, 87n3, 100
bribe(s) 42, 54n22, 98, 133, 137, 141, 144, 148, 159n2

cacique(s) 5, 27–30, 31, 34, 36–7, 40–1, 46, 50, 51, 53n4, 171; *caciquismo* 17, 37, 98, 132, 160n11; *cacicazgo(s)* 34, 36
California 7, 15, 58, 61, 64–5, 83, 107
capital 45, 61, 62, 66, 67, 68, 84, 101, 122, 142, 151, 158, 191; accumulation 66,

Index 213

67, 101, 159n6; ethno- 173; global 82; human 102; mobility 63, 140; social 59, 65, 68, 77, 84, 85, 94, 100, 103, 111, 121, 159n6, 186, 204; symbolic 85; tourist 134; transnational 76, 141; *see also* foreign capital

capitalism 59, 76, 80, 84, 87, 88n12, 129, 138, 153, 154, 190, 207; global 167; neoliberal 68, 78, 138; capitalist 11, 16, 19, 33, 38, 46, 52, 63, 66, 78, 81, 86, 94, 129, 133, 136, 142, 148, 150–1, 152, 156, 194, 202, 207 (relations 66, 86; structure 11, 78, 81); *see also* capitalist world system cast in the image of modernity/coloniality

capitalist world system cast in the image of modernity/coloniality 15–16, 18, 19, 34, 37, 45, 60, 68, 77, 80, 86, 87, 97, 102–3, 118, 121, 130, 140, 148, 151, 155, 157, 158, 160n17, 170, 172, 174–5, 181, 185, 186, 191–2, 195–6, 204–5, 207–9

Cárdenas, Lázaro 28, 38, 41

cargo(s) 7, 20n5, 179, 197n4

Catholicism 197n3, 197n11; Catholic 7, 53n7, 53n10; *see also* Church; priest

change(s) 4, 15, 17, 31, 33, 52, 59, 60–1, 65, 84, 85, 117, 121, 134, 140, 151, 153, 157, 196–6, 204, 207; internal 52; institutional 96–7, 159; political 4, 15, 17, 29, 32, 59; social 4, 12, 15, 182, 194–5, 205

Chavez, Leo R. 65, 79, 101

Church 106, 115, 124n8, 197n3, 209

citizen(s) 29, 44, 49, 53n4, 53n11, 104, 106, 109, 121, 181; participation 32, 37, 50; rights 113; subcitizen(s) 12, 68, 102, 113, 175, 204

citizenship 11, 18, 68, 93–4, 100, 103, 107, 113–14, 123, 176, 177, 181–2, 205; dual 106, 180; informal 102; 'substantive' 107; transnational 110, 113–14, 121, 181–2; 'cultural' 181–2

class 10, 11, 33, 38, 68, 78, 80, 84, 114, 132, 135, 143, 149, 171, 172, 176, 181, 189, 194–5; lower 77, 132; middle 1, 28; popular 28; power 10, 132; social 26, 123n4, 176; struggle 10; upper 76, 132, 143

clientelism 17, 18, 28–9, 32–3, 35, 36, 38, 50, 98–9, 109–10, 121, 132; clientele(s) 10, 27, 28, 32–3, 34, 41, 48, 51, 94, 97–8, 100, 123n4, 135, 202; clientelist practices 29, 38, 71; patron–client relationships 28, 36, 53n2, 109, 132

Club Mezcala 13, 18, 86, 93–4, 105–7, 108–11, 114–20, 121–3, 179, 180, 197n3, 197n6, 204, 206

co-option/optation 31, 33, 43, 85, 106, 112, 122, 133, 141, 148–9, 170, 171, 190, 202, 206; co-opted 42, 45–6, 48–9, 54n20, 137, 145, 190

Coca(s) 5, 9, 166, 185–6, 189, 190, 192–3, 205

Colectivo Mezcala 9, 13, 18, 75, 138, 141, 158, 193, 204–6

collective/collectivities 16, 170, 190, 193, 195; action 156, 179; empowerment 170; goals 144; identity 169, 193–4, 206; labour 154; memory 152, 186; needs 110; objectives 195, 205; organisation 107, 153; participation 159; projects 152

colonialism 5, 10–11, 135, 196; internal 10, 88n13, 189, 191; neo-colonialism 100; colonial 5, 10, 16, 60, 132, 170, 171 (forms of oppression 6, 11, 204; images 171, 192; legacy 159, 195; past 12, 18, 130, 132; relations 66, 77, 86, 202; structures 10, 11, 136); postcolonial 9, 10; *see also* decolonial

colonisation 7, 27, 67, 132, 207; decolonisation 10; recolonisation 76, 86, 128, 203; colonialist 11, 19, 52, 66, 85, 94, 129, 136, 148, 152, 196 (system 121, 130)

Comaroff, John and Jean 168, 172, 190

commodification 6, 132–3, 135, 137, 146, 185, 189, 203

communitarian work 95, 124n10, 193

communal 5, 27, 38, 46, 122, 155, 156, 157, 179, 196, 206; land 7, 38, 45, 116, 142, 159n5, 166; life 75, 154, 174; organisation 98, 122, 138, 206; values 144, 153, 157, 159

community of origin 84, 93, 94, 103, 105, 106, 111, 113, 122, 172–3, 179, 182, 209

comunidades sátelite 101

conflict 13–15, 17, 18, 26, 141, 148, 158–9, 177; family 142; internal 52, 149, 196, 204; land 130, 142; social 11, 191

contamination 63, 67, 71–2, 128

corporations 28, 32, 38, 66; multinational/transnational 10, 61, 66, 72, 132

corporatism 17, 29, 32, 33, 36, 44, 51, 132; corporate networks 10; corporatist 28, 29, 31, 106, 133

214 *Index*

corruption 17, 18, 27, 33, 34–5, 38, 46–7, 50–1, 53n11, 62, 70–1, 97–8, 118, 135–6, 141, 144, 151, 189; corrupt 29, 38, 40, 47, 49, 96–8, 100, 121, 133, 149, 202
counter-hegemonic 44, 145, 158, 188, 190, 193, 194
coyote(s) 62–3, 79
criminalisation 11, 62, 77, 79, 85–6, 101, 144, 151, 167, 176, 203
critical thinking 15, 188
culture 6, 7, 9, 10, 14, 27, 75, 85, 87, 101, 118, 120, 132, 135, 137–8, 139, 147, 152, 157–9, 175, 177–8, 183, 185, 186–7, 190, 191, 203, 205; Mexican 118, 180, 196, 203; *see also* political culture
cultural identity 5, 102, 152, 167, 189
cultural politics 137, 148, 206

De Angelis, Massimo 10, 16, 121–2
De Sousa Santos, Boaventura 11
De Vries, Pieter 30, 118
decolonial 7, 9, 10
dedazo 30, 35, 50
delegado(s) 13, 17, 21n9, 26, 27–30, 34–6, 38, 40, 45, 50–1, 86, 117, 171
Delgado Wise, Raúl 67, 113, 206
democracy 6, 11, 26, 31–4, 41, 51, 87, 149, 158, 195, 202, 206, 207; 'democratisation' 33, 117; simulated democracy 33, 37, 50, 149, 202; democratic 31–4, 50, 152, 158, 194, ('advance' 17, 27, 32, 34, 37; undemocratic 32); 'democratic nationalism' 38
deportation 62, 85, 177, 197n2
deterritorialisation 86, 105, 179
development 4, 12, 16, 18, 33, 45, 66, 85, 87n1, 93, 99, 101, 107, 109–10, 112, 122, 129, 130, 133, 134, 137, 140, 142, 144, 150, 151–2, 153, 154, 157, 160n11, 171, 179, 202, 205, 207; developmentalism 12, 18, 136; discourse of 11, 87, 129, 151, 158, 192, 202–3; plans 130–1, 135, 140, 149; post-development theory 12; projects 108; 'reflexive development' 153; rhetoric of 18, 60, 87, 93–4, 104, 114, 128, 130, 137, 143, 151, 153, 172, 186, 202; social 87; 'sustain' 134, 206; sustainable 134, 136; tourist 130, 133; underdevelopment 76, 131, 191; uneven 131, 143, 150; *see also* 'alternative development'; 'alternatives to development'

dialogue(s) 14, 20, 115, 118, 156, 189, 195, 206–7, 208
diaspora 143, 180, 182, 195; diasporic community 203, 206
Díaz-Polanco, Héctor 142, 191
dignity 157, 160n17, 195, 196, 202, 210; dignification 19, 168, 183, 186, 196, 204
diversity 7, 15, 16, 52, 196, 203
difference(s) 6, 11, 17, 18, 21n8, 27, 50, 68, 74, 78, 86, 107, 115, 135, 140, 142, 148, 170, 174, 176, 182, 183, 185, 191, 194, 195–6, 202, 203, 206; social 5, 76, 78, 84; system of differentiation 194, 205
discontent 15, 28, 38, 71, 97; social 28, 31
discourse(s) 11, 12, 17, 19, 20, 34, 44, 51, 112, 121, 128, 167–8, 194, 196, 203, 204, 207; anti-immigrant 79; capitalist and colonialist 66; Coca' 186, 189, 190; of 'democratic nationalism' 38; of 'development' 11, 87, 94, 129, 143, 151, 158, 172, 174, 192, 203; hegemonic 93, 118, 122, 129, 167, 168, 171–2, 181, 185, 190, 194, 196, 207; modernisation 11; national 6, 187; of *neoindigenismo* and *desarrollismo* 206; official 9, 187; of power 184, 'progress' 11, 18, 135, 139, 149, 158, 192; state 168, 194
discrimination 6–7, 15, 27, 36–7, 50, 52, 62, 66, 83–5, 102, 112, 149, 169–71, 175–7, 184, 186–8, 195–6, 205; self–101, 168, 176
domination 9, 33, 34, 52, 65, 69, 86, 121, 131, 142, 145, 147, 151, 157, 156, 170, 179, 194, 207, 209

Echeverría, Luis 41, 130
economic crisis 15, 66, 75, 80–1, 88n12, 114
education 37, 76, 78, 85, 88n15, 94–7, 99, 101–3, 115, 123n3, 134, 156, 177, 179, 186–7
ejido(s) 38, 45, 53n12, 88n15
El Salto 1, 61, 63, 66, 74–5, 130, 132
election(s) 26, 29–30, 31–2, 34, 37, 38, 40, 41–2, 43–4, 46, 48–50, 52, 54n23, 106, 160n14, 160n15
elite(s) 10, 18, 30, 31, 33–4, 35–7, 47, 48, 49, 53n7, 62, 67, 77, 84, 86, 88n15, 94, 107, 110, 118–19, 128, 130, 132–3, 135, 136, 137, 140, 141, 143, 146, 150, 152, 157–8, 166, 168, 170–1, 184, 191, 194, 196, 203, 205; 'elite democracy' 33; discourses 183; dominion 202; elitist

Index 215

presidium 148; local 12, 15, 41, 50, 52, 98, 132, 133; networks 53n6, 209; plans 129–30, 140, 149, 151, 191, 202
employment 4, 5, 18, 62, 63, 65, 66, 68, 77, 82, 83–4, 96, 101, 104, 114, 142, 153, 154, 157, 202; lack of 58, 59, 62, 74; self- 157; underemployment 76–7; unemployment 59, 69, 77, 81, 86
empowerment 45, 85, 105, 112, 118, 119, 136, 138, 143, 150, 157, 170, 179–80, 181, 190
environment 72–3, 87, 88n15, 121, 132, 150, 207; environmental degradation/ deterioration 63, 71, 87; environmental programme 145
epistemic struggle 14, 20; epistemological input 207–8
Escobar, Arturo 105, 131, 137, 140, 206
ethnicity 11, 68, 78, 84, 114, 123n4, 167, 168, 172, 194–5, 207; ethnic (category 181; claims 156; classification 168; groups 5; hierarchies 9, 66, 135, 183, 196, 204; identification 184; identity 6, 10, 167, 169, 179, 183, 190, 192, 196; pan-ethnic 181; position 176; stratification 80, 171, 181, 207
ethnogenesis 19, 168, 183, 185–6, 189–90
etnofagia 142, 158
exclusion 12, 28, 32, 33, 34, 37, 43, 45, 50, 52, 60, 63, 65, 66, 68, 84–7, 97, 99, 103, 112–14, 116, 120, 121, 139, 144, 149, 157, 160n10, 169, 176, 186–7, 190, 194, 196, 204–5, 206–7
exploitation 60, 66, 68, 76, 77, 86, 88n15, 104, 133, 137, 196, 203, 207

family 15–16, 30, 32, 36–7, 53n10, 59, 86, 99, 101, 104, 107, 117, 174, 193; activity 70; business 74, 97; cacique 36, 50; conflict 142; confrontations 44; connections 138; problems 80; remittances 106; strategy 65, 105; support 82
field(s) 16, 58, 61, 63, 64–5, 69, 71, 74, 75, 78, 80, 82, 83, 87n1, 174
fiesta(s) 20n5, 52n1, 110, 179, 184; *de la Virgen de la Asunción* 117; patron-saint 124n8, 20n6
'First World' 20n7, 68, 87, 93, 101, 122
fishing 1, 18, 58, 59, 68, 71–4, 76, 86, 101, 156; fishermen 20n6, 71–4, 88n11; 'fishing luck' 72; fish shortage 63, 71–3, 87

flexibilisation 66, 76, 88n15; (labour) flexibility 83
folkloric 6, 135, 147; folklorised 192; 'folklorising strategy' 203
foreign capital 130, 132, 151; U.S. capital 84
Foreign Direct Investment (FDI) 63, 75, 76
Fox, Jonathan 106, 110, 113, 120, 175, 182
Fox, Vicente 31, 108–9, 124n6
Fraser, Nancy 195
fraud 29, 33, 44, 46, 48, 50, 71
freedom 77, 93, 144; 'land of freedom' 177
frontier(s) 19, 87, 108, 113, 207; across 103, 114, 174, 175, 205; beyond 181; northern 58, 63, 64, 77

geographies of power 15, 20, 27, 52, 99, 122, 131, 194, 202, 204, 207, 208
gender 11, 21n8, 40, 63, 68, 76, 78, 84, 138, 172, 209
global system 16, 18, 21n18, 68, 80, 86, 174, 175, 204, 208, 209
global–regional–local interface of power 12, 80, 203, 207
'glocal' 4, 174
globalisation 10, 76, 141; neoliberal 4, 6, 10
Gonzalez Casanova, Pablo 10, 191
governance 11, 15, 33, 34, 204; global 11; market 99; *see also* neoliberal governance
government(s) 10, 33, 37, 45–8, 49, 52, 61, 70, 72, 87n3, 95–7, 99, 100, 106, 108, 112, 114–17, 118–19, 122–3, 123n2, 123n5, 124n6, 130–1, 134, 135, 137, 140–1, 145, 146, 148–9, 151–2, 153, 155, 157, 159n5, 160n11, 166–7, 169–70, 180, 187, 189–91, 196, 203, 205; local 26, 32, 72, 108, 132; of 'core' countries 66; Mexican 6, 62, 65, 78, 87n1, 87n4, 88n10, 97, 105–6, 112–14, 122, 124n6, 132, 149, 180; Municipal 46–7, 50, 117, 119, 124n8, 134, 139, 148, 152, 159n3; U.S. 31, 61–2, 68, 114, 122, 123n4, 140; self- 73, 185, 190; national 66, 105; 'traditional government' 45, 52n1
'governmentality' 121
Green Revolution 60, 87n1
Guadalajara 1, 7, 32, 48, 58–9, 60–1, 66, 86, 96, 103, 133, 138, 193
Guarnizo, Luis Eduardo 84, 93, 112, 206
Gutiérrez Aguilar, Raquel 157

216 *Index*

Hale, Charles R. 11, 194
Harvey, David 77, 88n14, 131, 149
health 71, 72, 83, 87, 94–7, 99, 101, 103, 123n4, 134
hegemony 29, 97; U.S. 12; hegemonic (culture 191, 205; instruments 145, 158, 190; knowledge 20, 208; machinery 19; meaning 140; models 16; structures 16, 158, 206; system 170, 182, 190; order 87, 140, 189–90; processes 183; rhetoric(s) 11, 16, 69, 159, 179, 202, 206, 209); *see also* counter-hegemonic; discourse, hegemonic
hierarchy 28, 41; labour 66
hierarchies 6, 9, 11, 18, 33, 76, 84, 88n15, 93, 94, 100, 105, 107, 111, 114, 130, 131, 133, 170, 171, 175, 182, 185, 194, 195, 203, 208; class 149; economic 50, 151, 196, 204; ethnic 66, 183, 196, 204; 'internal hiearchies', 194; past 5; social 6, 18, 37, 50, 68, 121
Hijos Ausentes 7, 20n6, 117, 124n8, 178, 197n5
history 5, 7, 12, 13, 27, 135, 137, 139–41, 144, 145–8, 151–2, 154, 155–6, 158, 159, 183–5, 186, 187, 189–90, 192, 193, 194, 197n9, 203, 204, 206, 207; historical (connection 9; memory 60, 158, 184, 187; processes 7, 17, 33, 35, 86, 114, 182; of resistance 7, 158, 183; of struggle 190; values 135); workshops 140, 156, 186
Holloway, John 38, 88n12, 153, 157, 160n17, 189
home(s) 104, 132, 140, 172, 174; homeland 193
Hometown Association (HTA) 13, 106, 119, 121–2, 180
housing 87, 94, 101, 114, 154; developments 1, 134, 151
human rights 136, 150, 166, 190

identification(s) 9, 167–9, 171, 181, 190, 194, 196, 206; self- 166; ethnic 184
identity 5–7, 9, 10–11, 13, 15, 16, 17, 18, 19, 21n16, 37, 52, 74, 87, 94, 102, 105, 113, 123n1, 129, 137, 140, 144–5, 146, 148–52, 155–6, 158, 159, 167–70, 172, 174, 176, 180–5, 186, 187–9, 190–2, 193–4, 195–6, 197n8, 202–6, 209; anti-189; Coca 192–3; collective 169, 193–4, 206; ethnic 6, 10, 167, 169, 179, 183, 190, 192, 196; indigenous 6, 9, 169, 171, 174–5, 183, 186, 189, 192–3, 196;

Latino 85, 209; multiple 167, 168, 174, 182; national 6, 121, 148, 176, 180, 187; pan-ethnic181; self- 168; subversive 194; transnational 182; *see also* cultural identity; 'politics of identity'
identity politics 19, 167, 195
ideology/ideologies 6, 12, 31–2, 50, 105, 123n1, 170, 171, 194; national 167; ideological 31, 69, 113, 122, 131, 137, 143, 169, 187 (constructions 148; force 128, 209; 'ideological state apparatus' 96; legacy 170; power 10, 142, 180; subjugation 144)
illegality 62, 68, 72, 77; 'good illegals' 177; illegal (actions 47; activities 30; acts 51; border crossing 79; immigration 62, 65, 68, 79, 88n7; migrant 103, 123n3, 177; paths 141; sale of land 40); Illegal Immigration Reform and Immigrant Responsibility Act (IIRIRA) 77; *see also* undocumented
imagined community 179, 203
indio(s) 169–70, 175, 185; 'indio hyper-real' 170; *indio indómito* 189; *indio permitido* 6
indigeneity 19, 168–9, 175, 183–5, 189, 191, 192, 194
indigenous 5–6, 7, 77, 138, 166, 169–70, 175, 183–4, 185, 187–8, 189, 192–4; communities 5, 10, 13, 14, 20n2, 27, 73, 77, 96, 128, 138, 150, 156, 171; cultures 147; groups 166, 187; identification 169; identity 6, 9, 169, 171, 174–5, 183, 186, 189, 192–3, 196; language 166; national struggle 138; non-indigenous 168; pan-indigenous 190; past 9; people(s) 1, 5–6, 7, 9, 14, 38, 88n15, 142, 149, 169–70, 175, 187, 191, 194, 195–6, 203, 207; settlements 94; *see also* indigeneity; *indigenismo*; Indigenous *Knowledges (IK)*; indigenousness; *neoindigenismo*
indigenismo 6, 147, 168, 170; *see also* *neoindigenismo*
indigenousness 19, 168, 189, 192, 196, 204
industrialisation 29, 59, 60, 63, 75, 130, 207; Import Substitution Industrialisation model 87n1; urban-industrial development 4; *Programa de Industrialización Fronteriza (PIF)* 63
industries 37, 59, 60–1, 63, 65, 66, 71, 75–7, 82, 85–6, 88n14; industrial (corridor 63; employment 4; zone 1, 60, 67, 130, 132)

Index   217

inequality 65–6, 68, 78, 81, 86, 121, 130,
143, 149, 157, 160n10, 169, 202–3, 206;
economic, social and cultural 105, 122;
inequalities 60, 76–7, 84, 87, 103, 112,
131, 133, 137, 147, 170, 191 (economic
68, 207; global 194; social 107);
political 29
informality 30, 34, 36, 88n10, 94, 105,
121; informal (channels 18, 94, 97, 190;
citizenship 102; institutions 206;
intermediation 29, 32; jobs 74; modes of
prejudice and discrimination 170;
negotiation 98; networks 53n6, 206;
politics 52, 94, 110–11, 116, 121–2,
130, 151, 157, 191, 202; practices 30,
68, 97, 144, 152; relations 144, 152;
polity 118; sector 63; system 157;
workers 97); informalisation 194; *see
also* informal power
informal power 11, 18, 27, 29, 30, 31–3,
36–7, 49, 50–1, 86, 94, 97, 100, 110,
112, 121, 141, 153, 157, 158, 202; *see
also* informality
Institutional Ethnography (IE) 14
institutions 10, 12, 15, 17, 19, 28–9, 33,
34, 38, 45, 46, 49, 51, 54n24, 66, 69, 78,
84, 97, 99–100, 114, 116, 121, 129, 130,
135–6, 141, 144, 148, 158, 160n10, 170,
186, 191, 196, 202, 206–7, 209;
institutional (arrangements 10, 44;
change 96–7, 159, 195–6; dialogues
207; 'institutional paralysis' 141;
isomorphisms 66; lethargy 151;
network(s) 16, 27, 48, 51, 106, 128,
142; oppression 170; structure(s) 10,
33–4, 49, 66, 121, 130, 135, 156, 196);
institutionalisation 18, 29, 30, 94, 105,
107–8, 134, 136
*Instituto Nacional de Antropología e
Historia (INAH)* 46–7, 134–5
interfaces of power 209; *see also* global–
regional–local interface of power
intermediaries 28, 33, 35, 37–8, 44, 53n4,
65, 69, 98, 106–7, 112, 139, 158, 180;
intermediary role 50; intermediation 29,
32, 98
internal colonialism 10, 88n13, 189, 191
International Financial Institutions (IFIs)
10, 31, 66–7, 97
international relations 31, 78, 119, 176
intersectionality 172, 203
invasor 45–50, 54n21, 54n22, 116, 130,
133, 140–5, 156, 160n14, 191, 203
invasion(s) 5, 130, 137, 160n14, 202

Island of Mezcala 1, 5, 7, 47, 74, 134, 136,
145–6, 148, *149*, 156, 159n2, 166–7,
184, 187, *188*, 189–90; islands 1, 6, 60,
131, 159n5, 160n9

juez de barrio 12, 21n9, 29, 45–6, 52n1,
53n3, 117, 119, 123, 124n10
justice 149; 'distributive justice' 45; social
122, 195

Kinsman, Gary 16, 144
Knight, Alan 37, 53n4, 111, 132, 170
kinship 173–4
knowledge 10, 14, 20, 50, 52, 96, 99, 106,
137, 140, 147, 156, 167, 186, 187, 192;
hegemonic knowledge 20; hegemonic
knowledge production 208; inherited
187; production 11, 14
knowledges 1, 4, 14–15, 17, 121, 152, 159,
183–4, 185–6, 187, 204, 208;
Indigenous Knowledges (IK) 185,
187–8, 197n9; local 15, 16, 19, 20, 129,
145, 156, 158, 204, 208

labour 18, 59, 61–2, 63, 66, 67–8, 76, 77,
80–4, 85, 86, 88n5, 88n15, 94, 102–3,
117, 121, 129, 134, 137, 154, 156, 174,
176, 203, 205; 'affective labour' 180;
cheap 61, 62, 76, 77, 80, 104, 119;
collective 154; dynamics 17, 59, 60, 68,
80, 81; market 61, 65, 68, 76, 81–2, 128;
migration 61, 67–8, 86, 111, 104; new
international division of labour 84;
opportunities 65, 67; *see also* work
Lake Chapala 1, 5, 6, 63, 69, 71–2, 88n10,
132, 135, 141, 154; lake 1, 15, 58, 71–3,
88n11, 128, 141
land 5, 7, 12, 20n2, 38–9, 40–2, 44, 46, 49,
52, 52n1, 53n12, 54n18, 54n19, 58–9,
60, 71, 73, 75, 85, 87, 88n15, 116, 118,
128–30, 131–2, 134–7, 138–40, 141–3,
145–6, 151, 152, 153–4, 158, 159n4,
160n9, 172, 174, 178, 179–80, 184–5,
186, 190, 192–3, 203, 204; communal 7,
38, 45, 116, 142, 159n5, 166;
conservation 51; defend the 52, 139–40,
196; grabbing 135–6; invasions 130;
'land of freedom' 177; market 128, 141;
privatisation 41, 50, 132, 133, 135, 138;
regularisation 132, 145, 153, 160n12;
'vacant land' 205
language 5–6, 83, 85, 101–2, 166, 173–4,
175, 177–8, 185

218 *Index*

Latin America 33, 37; Latin American 6, 15, 17, 113
Latino(s) 83–4, 101, 113, 176, 177, 181–2, 197n1, 209
law 196; agrarian 54; communal 47; customary 26; laws 66, 68, 102, 190 (twisting of 144, 151; manipulation 47, 49); public 30; rule of 49, 53n4
Leff, Enrique 134, 148
legitimacy 68, 138, 167, 190; legitimate (indigenous people 196; owners 20n2, 146, 189; social structures 168)
Levitt, Peggy 94, 197n3
Leyva Solano, Xochitl 14
liberalisation 131–2; *social liberalism* 97; *see also* neoliberal governance; neoliberalism
library 15, 94, 114–21, 139, 153, 197n9, 206
Los Angeles (LA) 4, 13, 35, 58–9, 65, 79, 80, 93, 101, 106, 108, 118, 122, 193, 208
Lopez, Ann Aurelia 60, 71
López y Rivas, Gilberto 141, 186

market(s) 11, 37, 69, 76, 99, 130, 148, 151, 190–1; international 72; labour 61, 65, 68, 76, 80–2, 128; land 128, 141; logic 11, 149; private 142; property 130; values 122
marginalisation 18, 27, 36, 44, 59, 85, 94, 101, 110, 112, 134, 135, 137, 144, 150–1, 154, 176; marginality 94–5
Martínez Moreno, Rocío 7, 21n11, 41, 50, 52, 134, 139, 145, 151, 186
Martínez Novo, Carmen 132, 171, 192
maquiladora(s) 4, 18, 63, 66, 68, 74–6, 81, 88n5, 88n15
Massey, Douglas 104
meaning(s) 10, 19, 26, 103, 129–30, 133, 137, 143, 144, 145–6, 148, 151–2, 155, 157, 159, 183, 17–18, 192, 193–4, 196, 203–4, 206
media 29, 31, 38, 141, 144–5, 174, 189, 193
membership 64, 107, 113, 114, 174, 180, 182–3
memory 137, 147–8, 152, 167, 175, 183, 186, 188; collective 186; historical 60, 158, 184, 187; memories 172
mentalities 80, 122, 159, 171, 176, 182, 196
mestizaje 5–6, 9, 168, 170, 185, 192; *mestizo(s)* 6, 7, 169, 175, 187, 192

Mexican Independence 5, 130, 135
Mexican Revolution 6, 29, 38; post-Revolutionary 27
migration 1, 7, 13, 17, 58–9, 60–5, 67–8, 76, 81, 99, 101, 104–5, 121, 134, 140, 144, 150–1, 168, 178, 192; control 101; illegal 62, 65, 68, 79, 88n7, 123n3; migrants 4, 7, 13, 18, 51, 52, 61–2, 64–8, 77–86, 87n4, 93–4, 101–7, 108–14, 115–20, 121–2, 123n4, 124n6, 124n8, 140, 142–3, 150, 160n12, 172–7, 178–83, 192–5, 197n11, 204–6, 209; Immigration Reform and Control Act (IRCA) 67, 88n8; police 64; policies 77, 79, 85–6, 122, 176; *see also* anti-immigrant; *Programa 3x1*
militarisation 79, *149*; border 176; military (measures 77; presence 141; spectacle 148; *see also* paramilitarisation
mobilisation 35, 52, 114, 117, 123n3, 144, 152, 158, 186; *see also* social movement(s)
'modernisation' 4, 11, 29, 45, 66, 68, 93, 122, 130, 136–7, 145, 150, 170, 178; theory 16; modern (consumption 76; country 6, 149; nation-state 146, 168; society 75; subjects 178, 194; principles 175; working 207); 'modern culture' 101; 'modern life' 16, 104, 129, 151; modernisers' 46; modernity 5, 9, 149–50, 157, 171
multiculturalism 9, 170, 191–2, 203, 207; multicultural (country 149; policies 6; rights 191; society 113); multiculturality 172
Municipio 13, 21n10, 28–30, 34–5, 37, 38, 46–7, 50, 86, 97, 109, 111–12, 116–20, 152, 153, 157, 170–1, 193
Municipal President 30, 31, 32, 34–5, 37, 42, 47, 108, 111, 116–18, 134, 139, 171, 179
myth(s) 7, 18, 68, 80, 94, 104–5, 146, 148, 167, 184, 192; *see also* 'American Dream'

narrative(s) 5, 13–14, 16, 21n16, 137, 167; counter-hegemonic 188; imagined 146; master 11, 170; of modernity 12
nationality 68, 78, 148; national (culture 175, 185; discourse(s) 187, 196; fantasies 146, 150; identity 6, 121, 148, 176, 180, 187; ideology 167; imaginaries 11; project 6, 9, 76, 149, 172, 203); 'national history' 203;

Index 219

nationalism 38, 114; *see also* government, national

nation-state 15, 105, 113, 146, 168, 181–2, 183, 205

nature 133, 151, 156, 184, 203

Nederveen Pieterse, Jan 134, 136

neoindigenismo 9, 168, 170, 191, 203, 206; *see also indigenismo*

neoliberal governance 10–12, 13, 15, 16–20, 26–7, 30, 33–4, 36–8, 43, 45, 46, 47, 49, 50–2, 59, 60, 66, 69, 71, 75–7, 80, 84–6, 88n12, 93–4, 97, 99, 103–4, 105, 106, 109–10, 112, 114, 121–3, 128–9, 131–3, 134, 135, 136–7, 141, 147, 151–2, 153, 156–7, 158–9, 167, 170–2, 176, 178, 179–82, 185, 187, 189, 190–2, 194–6, 202–5, 206–7, 208–9; *see also* neoliberalism

neoliberalism 10, 18, 59, 66, 75–7, 84, 136, 140, 157, 159n7; neoliberal (agenda 137; form 10; logic 154; model 16, 17, 20, 59, 81, 84, 87, 186; multiculturalism 170, 191–2; paradigm 18, 97; policies 12, 31, 52, 67, 68–9, 76–7, 98, 142; practices 132; processes 11, 15; project 12, 93, 142, 149, 189, 191, 194; rationale 144; restructuring 67–8; system 121; values 158); *see also* capitalism, neoliberal; globalisation (neoliberal)

networks 4, 10, 13, 15, 17, 18, 37, 59, 64–5, 67, 80, 84, 86, 93, 103, 106, 119, 121, 129, 157, 174, 181, 189; clientele 98, 100, 123n4; informal 53n6, 206; institutional 12, 16, 27, 51, 128, 142; of power 11, 13, 16, 18–20, 33, 38, 48, 51, 68, 77, 84, 86–7, 105, 117, 118, 128, 130, 133, 137, 168, 184, 194, 196, 206–7; social 64–5, 77, 87; solidarity 130, 137, 141, 145, 148, 152, 155, 158, 159n6, 168, 170, 194, 204–5; support 73, 85, 101, 103–4, 114; translocal 107, 119; transnational 64, 77, 80, 84, 145, 196

Non-Governmental Organisation (NGO) 136

North American Free Trade Agreement (NAFTA) 68

Oportunidades 97, *98*, 119

opportunities 4, 16, 58–9, 65, 80, 81, 85, 86, 96, 99, 101, 103, 120, 144, 160n10, 172, 174, 175–6, 177–8; 'business opportunities' 133; economic 61, 67;

education 96, 99; employment 4, 101; job 79; labour 65, 67

oppression 6, 20n7, 32, 142, 156, 191, 196; colonial forms of 6, 11, 204; system of 59, 80

Ong, Aihwa 113, 181

paisanaje 174; *paisano(s)* 82, 180; *Programa Paisano* 106

Pansters, Wil 37, 168

Paraje Insurgente 154, *155*, 157, 170, 197n9

participation 4, 7, 11, 27, 34, 41, 99, 108, 109, 110, 112, 114, 117, 136, 151, 160n15, 194–5, 197n3, 204; collective 159; citizen 32, 37, 50; democratic 158; migrant 110, 119, 179; political 29, 97, 110, 111, 177, 181–2; popular 121, 153, 205; transnational 181

Partido de la Revolución Democrática (PRD) 32, 34

Partido Revolucionario Institucional (PRI) 26–7, 29–30, 31–2, 34, 36–8, 40, 42, 44–5, 50, 53n10, 97, 98, 117, 119, 150; *priísta* 33, 51

Partido Acción Nacional (PAN) 30–2, 34, 109, 133

patronage 29, 31, 98, 117

paramilitarisation 144; paramilitary 141

Paredes, Vicente 21n11, 133, 189

peasant 15, 20n6, 28–9, 32, 38, 60, 67, 68–71, 77, 88n15, 110; *see also* agriculture

Peña Nieto, Enrique 38, 53n10

place 7, 19, 104, 128, 129, 131, 132, 134, 137, 140, 146–8, 158, 168, 172, *173*, 174, 177, 180, 182–3, 195, 204; of origin 172, 179; 'storied places' 152; *see also* sense of place

planning 97, 130–1, 137; plans (agricultural 38; alternative 18; authorities 148; development 135, 140; elite's 129, 140–1, 151, 191, 202; tourist 6, 130, 134, 149; government 190; of the Mexican state 13; of neoliberal governance 135)

police 47, 141, 160n10; immigration 64

policies 6, 11, 17, 18, 38, 52, 59, 62, 66, 68, 69, 80, 84, 94, 99, 121, 176, 181, 195–6, 207; economic 10; immigration 77, 79, 85–6, 122, 176; multicultural 6; neoliberal 12, 31, 52, 67, 68–9, 76–7, 98, 142; public 207

220 *Index*

political culture 11, 17, 26–8, 32, 34, 36, 38, 43–4, 46, 47, 49, 50–2, 67, 94, 106, 108, 111, 112, 119, 121, 128, 130, 136–7, 141, 143, 151, 170–1, 180, 192, 202, 204, 206

political economy 59–60, 68, 77, 84, 114, 151; political economic (processes 17, 114, 182; models 207)

political party/parties 26–30, 31–2, 34–6, 45–6, 47, 50–1, 97–9, 116–17, 133, 159n7, 160n8; political (actor 144, 151; campaigns 31, 99, 113, 181; figure 12–13, 17, 27, 29, 38, 50, 53n3; force(s) 31, 34, 45, 93; game 34, 94, 108; influence 110, 119; intermediaries 33, 98, 106–7, 158; participation 28–9, 97, 109–11, 177, 180–2; pluralism 32, 50, 86, 117; support 29–30, 108, 110, 124n8, 205); politician(s) 10, 40, 53n6, 99, 108, 110, 113, 135, 159n2, 160n14; *see also* position, political; representation, political

political struggle 140–1, 145; *see also* change, political

political system(s) 27, 30, 38, 51, 118, 160n10, 174, 206; political (exclusion 175–6; organisation 27, 157, 174; *see also* inherited political culture; political structure; power, political

politics 17, 27–8, 29, 31–4, 36–7, 43–5, 50, 85, 105, 107, 108–9, 113–14, 115, 118, 137, 148, 159n7, 174, 194, 203, 207, 209; formal 41, 116, 121; informal 52, 94, 110, 116, 121–2, 130, 151, 157, 191, 202; local 11, 34, 36; of reregulation 99; U.S. 112–13; traditional 32, 138; *see also* cultural politics; identity politics; politics of identity

'politics of identity' 140, 148

Portes, Alejandro 12, 59, 62, 101

positioning 15, 167, 169, 183, 190, 192, 194–5, 196

positionality 169, 183, 196

poverty 49, 59, 69, 71, 84, 86, 128, 136, 154; alleviation programs 97

power 5, 12, 15, 17, 19, 27, 28–9, 30, 31–2, 35, 37–8, 46, 47, 49, 50–1, 53n2, 66–7, 77, 86, 98, 108, 110–11, 112, 114, 115, 116–17, 118, 119, 121, 122, 123, 128, 129, 132, 135, 137, 138, 141, 145, 146, 149, 153, 157, 158n7, 160n10, 169, 170, 179–81, 189, 191, 195–6, 203, 206, 209; anti- 158, 160n17; class 10, 132; discourses of 184; game of 47, 113, 168;

ideological 10, 142, 168, 180; moral 21n9, 130; political 86, 119, 130, 151, 204; purchasing 69, 81; relations of 5, 10–11, 16, 19, 28–9, 32–3, 38, 44, 88n12, 99, 156–7, 167, 169, 176, 182, 183, 185, 186, 206; state 30, 138, 196; *see also* informal power; geographies of power; interface of power; networks of power; structures of power

power-holder/s 28, 32, 35, 157; powers (economic and political powers 130; external 139; local 158; global 158, 189, 204)

prestanombres 133, 141

pride 138, 169, 171, 184, 188, 191; symbol of 146, 193

priest 40, 105, 109, 111, 115, 117, 119, 124n8, 142, 160n11, 178, 179, 197n11; *see also* Catholicism

privatisation 7, 60, 66, 76–7, 131, 133, 138–9, 146

Procuraduría Agraria 46–9, 131

Programa 3x1, 94, 108–9, 111, 117, 119, 121, 123n5

Programa de Certificación de Derechos Ejidales y Titulación de Solares (PROCEDE) 131–2, 135, 138, 141, 145, 150, 159n3

progress 4, 12, 16, 18–19, 45, 75–6, 93–4, 97, 100, 101, 105–6, 107, 111–12, 114, 116, 118, 120–1, 122–3, 128–9, 130–3, 134, 136, 140, 142, 144, 147, 149, 151–2, 153, 158–9, 171, 191, 196, 205; discourse of 11, 18, 135, 139, 149, 158, 192; enemies of 6, 51, 99, 117, 150, 179; ideas of 45, 93, 105, 122, 130, 136, 144, 153–5, 157, 203; lack of 6, 59; rhetoric of 60, 87, 93–4, 104, 128, 137

progressives 46, 111, 122, 171, 202

public consultation 139, 186

public space 107, 140, 144, 182

public work(s) 44, 108, 111–12, 117–18, 120, 137, 143, 151, 152, 160n9

race 11, 68, 78, 84, 114, 143, 167, 172, 176, 182; Critical Race Theory 170; ethnic/racial (classification 9, 168; hierarchies 183; identities 167); racial (stratifications 172, 175, 181; structure 170, 192); racialisation 175; *see also* racism

racism 6, 9, 27, 36, 43, 45, 52, 60, 78–80, 84–7, 103, 114, 168, 170–1, 175, 176,

178, 185, 191, 197n2, 203; racist practices 19, 83, 175; *see also* race
recognition 6, 10, 11, 28, 39, 41, 47, 50, 51, 93, 107, 114, 150, 159n2, 159n5, 160n15, 166–7, 170, 175, 180, 182, 185, 189–90, 195, 197n6, 202; non- 166, 192
relocation 66–7, 77, 80, 86, 114, 128, 203
remittances 104–5, 106, 108, 115, 124n6, 179; economic 105, 122, 143, 180, 203; social 94, 105, 122, 143, 178, 180, 203
representation(s) 19, 38, 51–2, 135–6, 148–9, 175, 178, 191; crisis of 51–2, 204; elite's 191, 203; hegemonic 206; of space 147; state 159, 204; political 53n 11, 196
repression 28, 33, 38, 140, 144, 151, 189, 203
research-activism 14, 207
residency 80–1, 86, 128, 155
resistance 16, 17, 46, 137, 141, 144, 149, 157–8, 185, 188, 206, 208; history of 7, 158, 183
Resolución Presidencial 41, 44, 131, 183
respect 7, 13, 32, 42, 75, 93, 109, 114, 115, 150, 169–70, 177, 178, 191, 195, 202, 205
rights 6, 10, 34, 40, 62, 68, 85, 87n4, 88n14, 88n15, 103, 107, 113, 124n6, 140, 148, 167, 180–3, 170, 175–7, 180–3, 185, 186, 189–90, 194, 197n5, 205; cultural 170; historical 185, 190; human 136, 150, 166, 190; multicultural 191; political 110
rhetoric(s) 5, 11–12, 13, 17–18, 19, 33, 59, 68, 75, 86–7, 93, 122, 130, 168, 192, 207; hegemonic 11, 16, 69, 159, 179, 202, 206, 209; of multiculturalism 52, 172; of 'modernisation' 137; of *mestizaje* 169, 192; *see also* development, rhetoric of; progress, rhetoric of
romanticisation 16, 12, 180, 184, 191, 195, 203, 207
Rosaldo, Renato 170, 181

salaries/wage(s) 60, 62, 66, 67–8, 70, 74–6, 80–1, 83–4, 86, 88n13, 101, 176; 'subsalary' 66
Salinas de Gortari, Carlos 31, 38, 53n10, 68, 131
Sánchez, Rosaura 169
Sassen, Saskia 59, 62–3
Secretaría de Cultura Jalisco (SCJ) 46–7, 134

Secretaría de Desarrollo Social (SEDESOL) 97, 118–19, 123n5
security 65, 101, 140, 154; border 62–3, 80, 114; insecurity 13, 83, 103, 106; (U.S.) security policies 77–80, 86, 88n7, 176; social 123n3
Selee, Andrew 28–9, 32, 53n4, 113
self-definition 189–90
self-determination 152
sense of belonging 64, 182
sense of community 7, 19, 100, 107, 156, 168, 174, 179, 180, 184, 186, 194, 196, 204, 206
sense of place 105, 137, 140, 152, 206
Señorita Jalisco LA 93, 108, 118; *Señorita Mezcala* 118, 193, 197n6
social movement(s) 13, 15, 138, 141, 156, 160n14, 189; theory 16; *see also* Zapatista(s)
social programme(s) 31, 71, 97–8, 119, 123n4
social problems 17, 119, 121
social relations 9, 10, 14, 53n7, 122, 129, 137, 157–9, 160n17, 167, 180, 203–4, 206
solidarity 156–7, 186, 193, 206; networks of 130, 137, 141, 145, 148, 152, 155, 158, 159n6, 168, 170, 194, 204–5; 'solidarity economy' 154
space(s) 5, 7, 10, 11–12, 17, 18, 19, 20, 45, 52, 59, 66, 67, 79, 85, 86, 93, 112, 121, 122, 128–30, 133, 135–6, 137, 143, 144, 146–7, 152, 156, 158–9, 167, 170, 172–3, 175–6, 179, 180, 182–3, 186, 189–91, 193, 195, 203, 205–6; commodification of 146; defence of 137; of dispute 196; of negotiation 108, 123, 137; of political struggle 141; representation of 147; social 5, 189; transnational 62, 137, 203; *see also* public space
Spaniards 27, 166–7, 184
Spanish (language) 173, 177, 193, 208
Spanish Conquest 5; *see also* colonisation; Spaniards
state 6, 7, 9, 18, 27–9, 33, 41, 45, 50, 53n4, 66, 96, 100, 103–4, 106, 108, 113, 114, 116, 121, 130, 137, 136, 141, 146–8, 153, 156, 158, 160n8, 167–8, 176, 186, 189–90, 192, 194, 205; authorities 47; discourses 168, 194; formation 26, 147, 168, 181; government 116, 148; governor 31, 133; institutions 144, 148; level 38, 109, 111, 133, 144; logics 11,

222   *Index*

state *continued*
97, 138, 149; Mexican 6, 11, 13, 107,
121, 166, 170, 180; practices 157, 167,
168, 194; representation 158, 204; *see
also* nation-state; power, state
status 29, 64–5, 67, 84, 141, 178, 105, 110;
legal 68, 84, 101, 113, 123n4, 181;
migratory 76, 84; subordination 172,
195; of subcitizens 175
status quo 65, 85, 134, 168, 179, 192, 207
Stavenhagen, Rodolfo 189
Stephen, Lynn 64, 78, 83, 174, 182
strategies 13, 15, 17, 33, 47, 78, 106, 114,
121, 132, 136, 142–4, 152, 159, 179,
181, 202, 203–4, 205; *etnófaga* 158;
family 65; 'folklorising strategy' 203;
and identity 183, 185, 190–1; of
neoliberal governance 11, 110; survival
16, 58–9, 65, 74, 85, 103, 105, 118, 121,
137, 168, 173, 193, 196
stratification(s) 6, 18–19, 59, 76, 80, 86,
179, 196, 207; class 80, 181, 171; ethnic
80, 171, 172, 175, 181, 207; racial 172,
175, 181; social 77, 105; 'transnational
system of stratification' 181
structure(s) 11, 18–19, 20, 28–9, 32–3, 42,
84, 85, 93, 101, 102, 104, 107, 111, 114,
116, 119, 168, 171–2, 175–6, 180–1,
182, 204, 207; class 33–4, 38; of
domination 34, 65, 86, 157, 209;
political 17, 26, 38, 59, 207; of power
11, 16, 19, 29, 38, 52, 86, 106, 110, 121,
147, 182, 189, 195, 205–7; racial 170,
192; social 5–6, 7, 11, 12, 16, 18, 27, 38,
51, 68, 71, 94, 102–3, 114, 168, 170,
175, 178, 187, 196, 203, 205, 207; *see
also* colonial, structures; institutional,
structure; hegemonic, structures
struggle(s) 1, 5, 7, 14, 15, 16, 19, 31, 73,
103, 117, 137–40, 148, 152, 153–4,
167–8, 170, 184, 185–6, 187–9, 190,
194–6, 204, 206–7, 208; class 10;
political 140, 141, 145; social 46;
transnational 114
subjectivity 14, 101, 173, 181–3, 192, 196;
subjectivities 12, 114, 148, 182, 194,
207
subjugation 194; ideological 144;
subjugated (actors 13–14, 15; position
65)
subordination 12, 28–9, 61, 68, 80, 141,
151, 172, 176, 191, 194; subordinated
(positions 66, 102, 169, 169; subjects
175; status 195)

technocrat(s) 10, 31, 88n6
territory 5, 6–7, 13, 18–19, 20n2, 26,
39–40, 42, 44–5, 47, 50, 51–2, 75,
128–9, 130–1, 135–40, 143–4, 146,
148–9, 151–2, 154–6, 158–9, 159n5,
160n16, 166–7, 168, 172, 174, 180, 182,
183–5, 186, 188, 189, 192, 193, 195,
196, 197n8, 202–4, 205–6;
deterritorialisation 86, 100, 105, 179;
extraterritorialisation 37, 98, 106; new
territoriality 86, 151, 158, 202;
reterritorialisation 105, 179; territories
15, 18–19, 76, 86, 129, 133, 137, 148,
202
Título Virreinal 5, 20n2, 39–40, 166–7,
183, 184
Tijuana 7, 54n23, 58–9, 62–4, 86, 104,
117, 119
tourism 54n24, 87, 124n6, 128–30, 132–6,
137, 139–40, 143–4, 146–8, 150–1, 152,
154–6, 159, 190–1, 207; attraction
134–6; cultural 134–5, 203; residential
4, 18, 131, 134, 141–2, 144, 203;
tourist(s) 74, 143, 151 (industry 1, 130,
133, 191, 202; plans 6, 130, 149);
'tourist bubble' 132; *turismo
comunitario* 130, 153–6, 159
Torres-Mazuera, Gabriela 54n18, 86
traditional authority 13, 27–8, 38, 45,
51–2, 158, 166–7, 171; traditional
(figure 46; government 45, 52n1;
politics 32, 138); 'traditionalists' 46,
111, 122, 171, 202; *see also usos y
costumbres*
tradition(s) 5, 7, 52, 74, 122, 130, 138,
155, 171, 205; traditional 150, 171
(forms 63, 202; life 130, 142, 152;
medicine 73; structure 42); *see also usos
y costumbres*
transborder 117, 129
transnational community 7, 172, 174;
transnational (citizenship 110, 113–14,
121, 181–2; identity 182, 194; living 93,
101, 112; migration 172, 178, 193)
transnationalism 19, 106, 147, 206–7;
transnationalisation 11, 94, 106, 110,
121–2, 168, 196, 203; transnational
space 62, 137, 203; *see also* networks,
transnational

undocumented 62, 64, 68, 79, 83–5, 123n3
union 19, 52, 60, 73, 119, 105, 107, 153,
157, 167, 189, 196, 205–7; 'united front'
195

United States (U.S.), the 7, 12–13, 15, 21n13, 37, 54n22, 59, 60–4, 66–7, 77–9, 80–1, 84–5, 86, 87n1, 94, 100–4, 106, 109–13, 119–20, 122, 123n3, 123n4, 124n6, 141, 151, 173, 175–7, 179–81, 193, 197n3, 206; culture 177; economy 67, 76–7, 79; government 31, 61–2, 66, 68, 87n3, 114, 122, 140; interests 33, 76; politics 112–13; retirees 132, 143; society 84, 101, 113, 174, 177, 181; values 86, 132
urbanisation 59–60, 63, 75, 122, 129, 130, 171, 207; urban-industrial development 4; urban centres 85
usos y costumbres 13, 17, 26, 28, 42, 47, 52, 52n1, 75, 86–7, 122, 139, 172, 179, 183, 187; *see also* traditional authority; traditions

Velasco Ortiz, M. Laura 63, 76, 86, 103
violence 11, 13, 29, 31, 67, 80, 86, 98, 140, 144, 151, 157, 197n2, 202, 210; structural 159, 160n10, 207; violences of the border 176; violent (actions 143, 149, 191; measures 133; scenario 141; strategies 47, 202)
voice(s) 4, 13–14, 16, 21n9, 34, 36, 40, 45, 52, 72, 98, 109, 110, 112, 123, 138, 147, 170–1, 188, 189, 194, 202, 205, 208

vote(s) 30, 32, 40, 42, 44, 45, 48–9, 54n18, 98–9, 124n6, 160n15; buying 46, 48, 54n23; *see also* election(s)

'war on drugs' 78, 140
welfare 98, 111, 121, 196
white standards 177; supremacy 100, 176; whiteness 113; 'whiten' 6, 177; 'whitening' 169
work 34, 58, 60–1, 63–5, 67–8, 70, 74–7, 78, 80–5, 96–7, 99, 104, 140, 141, 153–4, 156; worker(s) 4, 28–9, 58, 61–3, 65–6, 76–7, 81–4, 96–7, 103; *see also* communitarian work; labour
world-system *see* capitalist world system cast in the image of modernity/coloniality

young fighters/supporters 7, 13, 45–7, 75, 99, 115, 130, 138–40, 141, 144, 145, 148, 151, 152, 153–7, 158–9, 160n14, 160n15, 166, 170, 186–7, 194, 197n9, 204, 206; *see also* Colectivo Mezcala
younger generations 74–5, 124n11, 131, 140, 156, 167, 186, 188, 205–6; young (people 51, 74–5, 82, 96, 99, 119, 123n2; migrants 120, 123n3)

Zapatista(s) (EZLN); 13, 15, 138, 159n7, 189
Zibechi, Raúl 16, 157

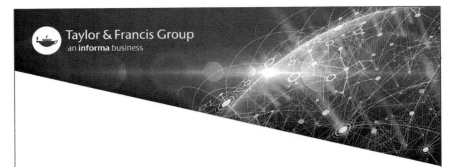